Bedford
Forrest
and His Critter Company

Southern Classics Series

SOUTHERN CLASSICS SERIES

M. E. Bradford, Founding Series Editor

Donald Davidson	The Tennessee, Volume I
Donald Davidson	The Tennessee, Volume II
Caroline Gordon	Green Centuries
Caroline Gordon	None Shall Look Back
Caroline Gordon	Penhally
Caroline Gordon	The Women on the Porch
Johnson Jones Hooper	Adventures of Captain Simon Suggs
Madison Jones	The Innocent
Augustus Baldwin Longstreet	Georgia Scenes
Andrew Nelson Lytle	Bedford Forrest and His Critter Company
Andrew Nelson Lytle	A Name for Evil
Andrew Nelson Lytle	A Wake for the Living
John S. Mosby	The Memoirs of Colonel John S. Mosby
Thomas Nelson Page	In Ole Virginia
William Pratt, Editor	The Fugitive Poets
Elizabeth Madox Roberts	The Great Meadow
Allen Tate	Jefferson Davis: His Rise and Fall
Allen Tate	Stonewall Jackson: The Good Soldier
Robert Penn Warren	John Brown: The Making of a Martyr
Robert Penn Warren	Night Rider
Robert Penn Warren	World Enough and Time
Owen Wister	Lady Baltimore
Stark Young	So Red the Rose

Bedford Forrest

and His Critter Company

ANDREW NELSON LYTLE

with a preface by Walter Sullivan

J. S. Sanders & Company

NASHVILLE

Library of Congress Catalog Card Number:
91-67518

ISBN: 1-879941-09-0

Published in the United States by
J.S.Sanders & Company
P. O. Box 50331
Nashville, Tennessee 37205

J.S.Sanders 1992 Edition
Second printing June 1993
Third printing November 1993
Fourth printing March 1995

Manufactured in the United States of America

TO MY GRANDMOTHER

MOLLY GREAVES NELSON

who has heard on the hard turn-pike
the sudden beat of his horses' hoofs
and the wild yell of his riders.

CONTENTS

ILLUSTRATIONS

PREFACE

We hear little about Nathan Bedford Forrest now. When our attention is directed to the Confederate Army, we are likely to think of Robert E. Lee or Jackson who earned the name "Stonewall" at First Manassas or the dashing J.E.B. Stuart who scouted far behind enemy lines and wore a plume in his hat. We think of Longstreet who may or may not have faltered at Gettysburg and of Pickett who made his famous charge during that same engagement. We are perhaps likely to think of these men because they were officers in the Army of Northern Virginia which won battle after battle during the early years of the Civil War. Forrest served with the Army of Tennessee which was a good army poorly led. Albert Sidney Johnston fought well at Shiloh, but died before he could consolidate his victory. Braxton Bragg, as readers of this book will discover, was a bungler who was continued in command of the Army of Tennessee too long. Joseph Johnston was not left in command long enough, and John B. Hood slept while an entire Union army slipped out of his grasp. Why, then, did Andrew Lytle choose to write of Forrest, a soldier whose victories have been overshadowed by the failures of the Army of Tennessee?

The answers to this question are both simple and complex. The most basic facts of Forrest's life are sufficient to fire any author's imagination. He was a tall, strong, and ruggedly handsome man who, with less than a year of formal schooling, made a million dollars by the time he was forty and turned out to be a military genius when he went to war. Mistreated and betrayed by his commanders and hunted relentlessly by his enemies, he fought numerous battles, usually against superior forces, and never lost until the end, when he had no army left with which to fight. He was wounded four times, had twenty-nine horses shot out from under him, and killed thirty men in hand-to-hand combat. After the war he helped the widows of his fallen soldiers as long as he had means to do so, he tried and failed to build a railroad, and he served as grand wizard of the Ku Klux Klan in an effort to restore white dominated order to the South. Lytle's claim that Lee called him the greatest general in the Confederate army cannot be documented. But Sir Douglas Haig, commander of British Forces in World War I, studied his campaigns carefully, as did Erwin Rommel, the famous "Desert Fox" of World War II. An account of his battles was published in 1930 by Captain Eric William Sheppard, O.B.E., M.C. Employing his cavalry frequently as mounted infantry, Forrest devised basic tactics for the kind of mobile warfare that was fought by tanks and motorized infantry in the Second World War.

Such a life begs to be written, and authors less skillful than Andrew Lytle began to write it almost as soon as the Confederate banners had been furled. John Morton and William Witherspoon, both of whom had served under Forrest, wrote their memoirs. General Thomas Jordan and J. P. Pryor sent their manuscript to Forrest for corrections and brought out their life of him in 1868. Captain J. Harvey Mathes and Dr. John Allen Wyeth composed their biographies near the turn of the century and gathered material from the surviving veterans of Forrest's command. Lytle drew heavily from Wyeth and also talked to some ex-Confederates, but by the late 1920s their ranks had thinned and memories had grown dim. This seems to have been of no great consequence to Lytle. His book has no footnotes and only a scanty bibliography. His biography was going to be as much a work of the imagination as of fact; he was pioneering the form that Shelby Foote was to bring to brilliant fruition in his three-volume history of the Civil War.

Lytle was drawn to Forrest not only for the extraordinary dimensions of his character, but for what he represented in Lytle's vision of the South. In "The Hind Tit," his contribution to *I'll Take My Stand*, the Agrarian manifesto published in 1930, Lytle, using the early demographic studies of the Old South made by Frank Owsley and his own recollections of rural life, celebrated the small landowner, the yeoman farmer, and drew an invidious distinction between him and the cotton snob. Forrest came from the plain people and remained loyal to his roots. He was born in Tennessee, son of a blacksmith who migrated to Mississippi in search of land, which in Lytle's view is the only material possession of enduring value because, though the land is a hard taskmaster, it sets one free. Lytle's ideal farmer, as described in "The Hind Tit," is almost totally self-sufficient, building his house with his own timber, growing his own food, making his own clothes.

This is what Bedford Forrest and his family did. By the time the
father died, their cabin was finished but there were still land to be
cleared and fences to be built, most of which Forrest accomplished. His
brothers plowed; his sisters cared for the cows and the chickens, ran the
spinning wheel, and sewed the clothes; Bedford tanned skins and made
shoes and leggings for his family by firelight. Although his mother was
a strong and strong willed woman who bore many children to two
husbands, Bedford was the youthful patriarch in a society that Lytle
conceived to be essentially patriarchal. Forrest did, or assigned to
others, the basic work that made the land produce; he was therefore
responsible for the survival of his people. As he began successfully to
trade livestock, the fortunes of the family were augmented by his skill.
But this account simplifies what was and remains for Lytle a spiritual
matter.

Life, properly lived, requires that those who live it have a sense of
order rooted in the divine. A principle of Agrarianism is that farmers,
dependent as they are on weather and the seasons, understand better
than any other group that sun and rain are gifts from God. And God
is king, the supreme patriarch who makes all laws and shapes all
fortunes. Neither heaven nor earth, neither the community of saints
nor that of men is organized along lines that are strictly democratic.
Everyone has a place in the scheme of things, and each person
achieves goodness and freedom in his life by working diligently at his
own calling. Lytle thinks that everyone should know this from experience and from observation of the way the world operates. But many
refuse to learn, or they ignore the truth in favor of a program of self
aggrandizement. In 1930 Lytle warned against this by admonishing
small farmers, particularly in the South, to halt what he saw as their
rush toward destruction. The cotton snobs had been brought low by
the Civil War, to be sure, but they had prepared their downfall by
trading their self sufficiency for money. They had violated the land
by making it a producer of wealth. At the time *I'll Take My Stand* was
published, small farmers, no less perverse than any other group of
human beings, were preparing their own ruin by their own pursuit of
riches, thereby emulating the cotton snobs, who by now had gone
broke and moved to the cities. A tragic aspect of this development was
that even should the small farmers succeed in becoming large scale
planters, they would have sacrificed their old life of piety and content-
ment for an uncertain, mundane existence based on abstraction, on
wealth that had no intrinsic value.

Worst of all, in regarding the land not as provider but as capital, the plain people of the South were abandoning the old patriarchal order and affirming the plutocratic system that ruled in the cities of the North. The old mysteries of soil and sky, which were manifestations of the unfathomable Maker of the universe, were forgotten in favor of the mysteries of the futures market, where every day thousands of pork bellies were bought and sold by people who would neither make nor take delivery of the product, many of whom had never seen a pig. A drought in Mississippi might alter the price of cotton in Chicago, but for the traders, the cotton, like the pork bellies, remained an abstraction on which the price would rise and fall mainly according to the manipulations of businessmen. If a market for cow chips had been established, they would as willingly have dealt in them. There was Wall Street, too, where not even lip service was paid to such primary realities as cotton and hogs. Here one could buy shares in companies that made soap and bread and women's underwear, all of which the farmer once made for himself. In such a world it is Jay Gould or his modern counterpart who causes your shares to fall, but these cannot fill the role of patriarch left vacant when the yeoman farmer betrays his ancient system of order that included God. With the loss of the concept of God, all systems of order become relative and start to shift continually. Of most importance, without God the patriarch to serve as example, the sense of the family as a patriarchy is lost. Mutual respect among members of the family deteriorates. Each person begins to elevate his own personal interests above those of the group. Thus, order is destroyed with the failure of discipline. When the family ceases to exist as a patriarchy, the larger social and political patriarchies—community, state, country—that take the family as their foundation are lost as well. Thus begins the plunge into general chaos. So Andrew Lytle argued in 1930 when he was writing his life of Nathan Bedford Forrest.

To put this another way, Lytle was called to write about Forrest because Forrest fit a philosophy that Lytle wanted to propound, but to say this engages a paradox. Shelby Foote, whose accomplishment demands that we respect his judgment, says that a proper writing of history requires the combined talents of historian and novelist and that these are rarely found in a single human frame. Most novelists lack patience to research properly, but they know that facts alone do not constitute truth, that truth is an order that exists within the facts and must be discovered. Historians, Foote maintains, are indefatigable at gathering material, but almost none of them knows how to write. Furthermore, they are not interested in learning. What is worse, they are ideologues who start with a position, a thesis; then they include in their work only the facts that help to prove what they have decided is true in the first place. If what I have said above is accurate, this seems to place Lytle not among the novelists, where he surely belongs, but in the ranks of the historians.

Lytle's two part thesis is that the South would have been better off if it had won the Civil War and that it would have won if the authorities in Richmond had paid more attention to the western theater of operations and furnished the Army of Tennessee with better generals. Except for Forrest, who is the doomed hero, few commanders connected with the Army of Tennessee escape Lytle's scorn. He castigates Albert Sidney Johnston for not taking the offensive in the opening stages of the war, when, Lytle believes, he might have fallen upon a divided Union army and destroyed it. Once battle was joined at Forts Henry and Donelson, Johnston was guilty of poor judgment, but in this campaign there was more than enough culpability to go around. The missed opportunities, the heroic suffering of the soldiers, and the self serving posturing of the commanders strike a theme that was repeated often both in Lytle's biography and in the sad history of the war in the West. Forrest refused to surrender. He told his superiors that he had promised the parents of his soldiers that he would take care of them and he meant to keep his word. Thus he becomes what he will remain for Lytle throughout the biography: the patriarch who is also a general, the father figure who controls and protects those in his care.

Larger figures than Floyd and Pillow and Buckner, who surrendered at Fort Donelson, were needed to serve as foils for Forrest's greatness and to show why, even with Forrest on their side, the Confederacy lost the war. These were easy to find. Chief among them, according to Lytle, was Braxton Bragg, an incompetent and vain commander, jealous of his own prerogatives, a stern and often cruel disciplinarian who wasted the lives of his men by fighting when he should have retreated and retreating when victory was in his grasp. That Bragg was less than a military genius is clearly evident even to amateurs who study his battles. After Chickamauga, his subordinate generals declared their lack of faith in him and asked that he be replaced. But Jefferson Davis, more loyal to his old friendship with Bragg than to the country over which he presided, did not replace him, and Bragg did not resign. Later, when the removal of Bragg could be delayed no longer,

Davis, still more concerned with personal relationships than with public duty, called Bragg to Richmond, where as the president's military adviser, he could continue to work his mischief against the soldiers in the field.

Bragg was not completely without virtue. He drilled and worked troops long and hard when they were in training. The soldiers complained, but they were tough and well disciplined when they broke camp and went into the line. Bragg was well schooled in tactics, and his incompetence and timidity may have been the result not so much of stupidity or cowardice—as Forrest thought and Lytle thinks—as of poor health. He suffered from migraine headaches that came without warning and doubtless rendered him less effective throughout his career than he might otherwise have been. But when all that can be said in his favor has been said, he remains a blunderer. He is, for Lytle, an example of all the mistakes that Confederate commanders had made and were to make in the prosecution of the war, and he was the enemy and betrayer of Nathan Bedford Forrest. He is the antagonist, and when he enters the pages of Lytle's *Forrest*, the structure and tone of the book change: it ceases to be historical study, marshaling evidence to support a premise, and becomes historical narrative with a hero and a villain as distinctly identified as those in any novel. The Confederate bureaucracy with which Forrest must deal, the Union armies that he will oppose, even the generals commanding opposite him are abstractions when compared with the solid presence of Bragg, whose purposes are to elevate himself and to harm Forrest. Ideology is put aside for the sake of drama.

The first hundred pages of Lytle's book, those which I have characterized as historical study, can be understood once Bragg comes on the scene, as preparation for the main story. The early successes of Forrest reach a climax with his capture of Murfreesboro soon after Bragg takes charge of the army. Bragg publicly commends Forrest's boldness and promises him command of all the cavalry in middle Tennessee. But he breaks this promise, places most of the troops that Forrest has recruited and armed under Joe Wheeler, and sends Forrest west to start over again. Once more, after Chickamauga, Bragg gives Forrest's troops to Wheeler, and in a famous scene reported by Dr. J. B. Cowan, who witnessed it, Forrest damned Bragg for his meanness, called him a coward whose orders he would no longer obey, and threatened to kill him if they ever met again. But this was not the end of the struggle between them. Late in the war Forrest proposed a campaign that

embodied the last faint hope for Confederate victory: he would go into
Tennessee, break Sherman's supply lines and relieve the pressure on Joe
Johnston's army north of Atlanta. But Bragg was now in Richmond as
the president's military adviser, and the answer was no. More than a
dozen years later, riding in Forrest's funeral procession, Davis blamed
his misuse of Forrest's talents on his generals. "I was misled by them,"
he said. "I saw it all after it was too late."

According to Lytle, the true hero is in some ways divine. He is god-
like in his fidelity and his courage, in his pursuit of what is right and
honorable. Since he is doomed to operate in a fallen world and is
engaged in combat with the forces of darkness, he can win battles, but
he can never finally win a war. Yet he claims a kind of victory by the
example he sets: by his willingness to endure in the face of great odds,
to suffer the pains of the struggle, and to keep faith with his cause.
According to Lytle, because of Forrest and men like him, the end of the
Civil War did not mean the end of the Old South. The moral and
cultural values for which the Confederate Army had fought lived on in
the lives of the old soldiers and in the inherited memories of their
descendants. The loss came when, for later generations, the memories
grew dim. Perhaps this book, and others like it, can remind us of what
we have forgotten and help to restore in our society some of the virtues
that we seem to have misplaced.

Nashville, Tennessee   WALTER SULLIVAN

INTRODUCTION

This is a young man's book. To have anything more to say about a book you did fifty odd years ago brings you hard up against the matter of time. The young author shows a familiar visage, as enigmatic as the portrait of a great-grandfather "struck" in his youth, gazing into the close air of the parlor. You know you are kin, but *that* youth belongs to the ancestors. Therefore to redo or revise in any real sense would mean to make another book. Fifty years can change more than the use and control of language. The world may go on for a thousand years and, outwardly at least, be always the same. Then something appears out of nowhere, so sudden does it seem, and a shattering takes place; as for example when the stirrup was introduced into Russia by the Sarmations riding out of Siberia. They stopped with the conquest of Russia, but the stirrup did not stop there. The Goths took it into Rome. It ended the stalemate between the mounted archers of Parthia and the Roman legion. It had its long history in Europe. It came to an end as an instrument of military power about a hundred years ago in Alabama.

Everywhere east of the Mississippi the Confederacy lay in ruins. The great Lee had surrendered, and the Army of Tennessee, constant in defeat, workmanlike always, was stopped forever at Goldsboro. But Sherman had reported that "There will never be peace in Tennessee until Forrest is dead." His very name, so long as his troops were intact, made all these larger victories unsure. Reports had it Davis was fleeing Richmond to join him, cross over into the Trans-Mississippi department and there carry on the war with Kirby-Smith. And then the news. Forrest had *surrendered*. The Wizard of the Saddle had dismounted for the last time. He had been whipped in his last fight, the one general who had always won and whose victories were always thrown away by others in higher places. The war was now indeed over. The Republic of the Founding Fathers was no more. A certain ideology used by a sectional group of new men and interests had usurped the name "Union" to undo the political union. The Numerical Majority, as Calhoun called it, had triumphed over the Federal system; and, since numbers never rule, indeed cannot, but are always manipulated by some active minority, such rule is never representative of the whole except in rare moments of pressure or emergency.

History has borne Calhoun out; it has also made his predictions seem too local and domestic. Wise as he was, it was not to be expected of anybody in the eighteeen forties and fifties to foresee so quick an end to Britain's hegemony of the world. The tragic consequences of change, and so Calhoun viewed them, would therefore involve only the internal health of the union and not foreign entanglements. For the United States to be strong enough to intervene in the quarrels of Europe and emerge the dominant power in the West, would have seemed fantasy to those politicians who saw Senator Mason rise in the Senate to deliver the dying Calhoun's last words. And yet ten years later a war was fought and won, the ultimate consequences of which would be just this.

So in a very literal sense the Civil War was the first World War. It not only created a powerful nation of organized resources and potential military might, but the greater world wars took their pattern from the American one, even to the trench system Lee set up at Petersburg. These wars were internecine, all of them; but it was not in this that we find the crucial resemblances. In view of a common Christian culture wars within Europe would of necessity be internecine, but at least at one time there were Truces of God. What this country brought to Europe was unconditional surrender. The actual phrase was used by Roosevelt in the Second World War, but it was not his phrase. Grant had delivered it to the Confederate Command at Fort Donelson in February, 1862. Its implication is total surrender or total destruction, or slavery, or whatever. A strange alternative to be delivered by one

Christian state to another; and yet it had precedent in Sherman's harrying the lands of Mississippi and Georgia, whenever Forrest was out of the way.

The result of these wars has been the self-exhaustion of Europe, the loss of prestige before the world, and another possible shift in power from West to East. We seem to accept this with a fatalism strangely foreign to us. The battle of Lepanto was fought and won by a Christian prince. Since that time Christendom, if we can still call it such, has been free of danger; but there is a strange resemblance between that time and this. The Christian princes were divided among themselves as in our world wars; they were threatened by their own invention, the firearm, which the Turk added to the first use of the disciplined regiment. We have only to remember Spengler's warning as to the folly of teaching the techniques by which the West had overwhelmed the world and wonder. Will the time come when we will pray for another Lepanto? There is no Christian prince today strong enough to take a stand. This country is presumably strong enough at least to risk a defense, but to stand always on the defensive is to prepare for defeat. It was Davis' great failure of policy to which he committed the Confederacy.

So the great change in the world this time is not technological, although there are plenty of new tools. It is obviously spiritual. Yeats' trembling veil is at last rent. The nineteenth century abandoned God officially, and the faith of Christian communicants was absorbed into the powerful western will; and this will set out, openly at last, to know and control not only nature but the universe. In the late stages of any society there is always the aging form and the formlessness of the new *pistis*; but this is no new faith; it is a perversion of faith, the final and open acceptance of Machiavelli's science of politics, the politics whose end is absolute power, whose technique is reason without any theological restraint. This prince will do anything, assume any role, to bring about his ends. Certainly Stanton, Lincoln's Secretary of War, was the most ruthless and greedy of all the Machiavellians. There is strong circumstantial evidence that he had to do with Lincoln's assassination, when the Northern president set in motion a peace which would bring the country back to a status quo.* It took a while for this to dominate Northern policy; but after Grant and Sherman took over the command the entire strategy became Machiavellian; any means justified the end. In the Wilderness campaign and at Cold Harbor, Grant's slaughter of his own soldiers was not merely lack of imagination. It was the sacrifice of the individual, the humane, the personal to the force of abstract mass; for unconditional surrender, that is, absolute power was his end. And yet he was a kindly man. He almost pushed it too far, for excessive loss in an army's manpower comes in time to shatter morale. Forrest had all the energy of the western man, his terrific will; but he was fighting for the traditional element in our society. He was able to use against the enemy his own method. He, too, asked for unconditional surrender, and added or I will put every man to the sword. But he never lost the sense that an army is composed of individuals. Nothing threw him into a temper so much as the useless loss of men. It was his care of man and beast, the thorough inspections of harness and shoes and the possibilities of entry and exit, that turned his fighting force into the most efficient body of horsemen in the South. His soldiers would follow him anywhere and did, because they knew this. He always fed them, and he always brought them out, and usually stronger than they had entered the campaign. For this and other reasons he was the crucial figure in the crucial, the Georgia campaign, and the Northern high command knew it.

Sherman said "War is Hell," and by this he meant total war, openly carried out upon the civil population, with the shrewd understanding that if the source of supply was cut off, the armies would dwindle and perish. Partly due to Forrest he was unable to lay waste sufficient territory to dismantle the army before him, but his subordinates' attitude toward the civil population, as is always the case, brought home to the people of the South the meaning of this un-

---

*Why Was Lincoln Murdered? by Otto Eisenschiml (New York: Little Brown & Co., 1937).

Christian policy. It placed Forrest in the role of avenger, for he never failed to punish the enemy. The outcry in the North when Fort Pillow was so savagely reduced by him comes from the fear that the very forces the new Machiavellians had released could be returned in kind.

A circumstance in my own family bears out how this dangerous power acted in a specific instance. My grandmother as a little girl was playing outside her house with other children. A Union soldier up the street shot into the crowd of children and she was hit in the neck just short of the jugular vein. When she ran into the house to her nurse, the blood was in her shoe and covered an apple she still held in her hand. Nobody ever knew why the man shot into the group of children. He got on his horse and galloped out of town and was never seen again, and was certainly not apprehended by his own officers.

Of course this incident could have happened at any time, in peace or war, and for any number of reasons. The point to be made is the official enemy attitude toward the incident. Though she was obviously bleeding to death, a doctor was forbidden, since her father had not signed the oath of allegiance. A young officer from Kentucky took the responsibility of getting her one; but later a squad of soldiers arrested her father and took him away cursing to make him sign the oath, and later still in the night she watched the soldiers troop by her bed, staring, enormous and dark, as their bayonets scraped the ceiling. This was the image she kept as an old woman. She must have got it from her mother's helplessness before this invasion of privacy at such a time. This was the change that was to come over the world: the helpless made to feel their helplessness. "It is well," General Lee said at the height of his success, as Pelham's small battery was holding up the attack of fifty thousand men at Fredericksburg, "It is well that war is so terrible. Were it not so, we should grow too fond of it."

As the wars grew even more terrible and world-wide, and the results more abstract and inhuman, we began to feel the abyss

below us. We cry for peace, not for a life of peace but from the fear
of annihilation. Yet the Christian dies alone. The fact that millions
may die at the same time is meaningless, for it was Christ's promise
that at world's end each separate person would find his own body
and rise up his complete self. And he would be judged as an individual among a neighborhood of individuals. This was the intrinsic
meaning of Christianity; and it was new, the promise of immortality
for everybody. Before Christ's coming the East looked to some
world cataclysm as we do. They feared utter annihilation, as we do,
for they had no sense of the Christian individual. We have lost,
although not completely, our sense of it. As our high priests, the
scientists, feel they are conquering nature, the mass of individuals
grows more ignorant about it and, therefore, about human nature.
The public does not really comprehend the meaning of a rocket
to the moon. They've already been there in the comic strips. This
public is Calhoun's Numerical Majority with a vengeance. And
the minority of rulers has shrunk to the Supra-individuals or super-
men such as Stalin and Hitler — or Roosevelt and Churchill. They
have become the sources of destiny, if not of salvation, since they
have had to assume, willingly or not, the power and will which was
once God's. Believing only in Machiavellian power, Stalin starved
to death some millions of his countrymen. Henry II put on sack-
cloth and ashes and walked across England merely for his implication in the murder of Becket. But he was a Christian monarch who
believed in damnation.

The world over which Forrest's men rode and fought was closer
to Henry II's than it is to ours. They are centuries apart; yet those
centuries knew the orderly return of the seasons, saw the supernatural in the natural, moved about by foot, by horse and at sea
by the wind. We have put our faith in the machine. This is the
concrete showing of the nature of our change. We view the tech-
nology of its laws as if they were as automatic as nature's. But
the machine is not nature. It is man-conceived but not man-con-
trolled; hence the monstrousness in serving it. The machine was

meant to ease and speed up man's business a little, not change the look of nature. If it keeps up, it will change the nature of man, for we are moving so fast nobody is still long enough to see what is before him. The highways which are supposed to connect communities are becoming the community. In certain states the wilderness is growing again, but this time it is owned by paper corporations. The one image to clarify and define our state of being is the tons of trees growing, to be chewed up, to make paper, to advertise Lydia Pinkham's female tonic. In the beginning was the Word. Is it to end a flux of printed matter offering nostrums at a price?

It may, for we are losing that immediate and substantial sense of our surroundings which remind us of our humanity. Our last frontier is the heavens. Our pioneers are already there, and the world looks no more familiar than it does on a map. In the old wilderness a man was sometimes by himself, but he was never alone. He made a slow progress. To camp on the wilderness trail, compared to our travels, was almost to settle. And he did indeed settle each night; his eyes made the flora and fauna about him a familiar hiding place. He might go astray or become bewildered, but he was never lost. He knew where he was, because he knew who he was and where he wanted to go. And this was always forward. Between stations he would "remove," as he said, further on. His descendent wants to leave the world altogether. What a man hanging to a ball in space will learn remains to be seen. But whatever, he will be the man quite without location.

Location is that other force in our inheritance which balances our need for movement. It is the family which represents it and maintains it. The family does not flourish among abstract ideas. It is substantial, concrete, sensible. There was no Augustinian here separating psyche and physic. Flesh and spirit moved the one in the other, confined by the internal mystic form of belief. It was the basic unity of the Christian community, and hence the state. It carried authority. No matter what talents an individual might have, the family was always greater than he. It was this kind of a community that Forrest surrendered in 1865, but it was not delivered until over a hundred years later. It was the community into which I was born and in which memory called Forrest the great hero.

The hero saves not only by his prowess; he saves by the divinity within himself. Indeed his prowess depends upon this divinity. The hero's most perfect image is, of course, Christ the man-god. There is no hero unless the odds are overwhelmingly against the thing he stands for, or the rescue which takes him upon his quest. They are the powers of darkness; they show in the brutal weight of matter, the seemingly irresistible forces of mass. Since fear and desire make all of us tremble, the first quest of the hero is triumph over himself; and afterwards he follows the quest, a selfless and devoted individual on the way of becoming an archetype. Indeed because he is devoted, he is fearless. We do not know all the circumstance of Forrest's triumph over himself. We know it only in his actions and because of one statement; he bought a one-way ticket to the war; that is, he had committed himself without reservation of goods or person. This is of the very quality of heroism, because it is a triumph over death. It is also the secret of his triumph over great odds. Never thinking of himself, he is free to think of the enemy; and so he finds the weakness which will topple all the weight and mass. There was never a greater half-truth than the statement that God is on the side of the biggest battalions. Moscow and Napoleon's retreat stand for refutation of this.

But in the end the hero always fails. He either dies as Roland dies; or the cause for which he fought is lost; or he wins the fight and the calculators who take over gamble it away, as with Forrest. Never in the world are the powers of darkness finally overcome, for they inhabit matter; nor, without the conflict of the cooperating opposites of light and dark, good and bad, would life as we know it be. What the hero gives us is the image of his devotion and selflessness and the knowledge that he can save us from the powers of darkness — at times. Forrest had shown himself to be the hero who could save absolutely, or so the young man thought who wrote this book.

Monteagle, Tennessee, 1984   ANDREW NELSON LYTLE

PART ONE

THE WILDERNESS ROAD

A general officer ought to know that war is a great drama, in which a thousand physical or moral causes operate more or less powerfully, and which cannot be reduced to mathematical calculations.

JOMINI: *The Art of War.*

BEDFORD FORREST

PART ONE

THE WILDERNESS ROAD

CHAPTER I

A Basket of Chickens

A N hour before sundown two women were riding home along a narrow, stumpy trail. The trail, a bent arrow ripping into the wilderness, pointed its head ominously to the west where the Indians had gone.

As it grew darker, the North Mississippi forest pressed its timbers and the poison of its bottoms about the trail. The horses, as if they sensed this hostility, increased their pace.

Fannie Beck rode ahead. Mariam Forrest, her sister, followed behind. Large, muscular, and heavy-boned, she sat one hundred and eighty pounds in her saddle, holding the bridle with one hand, supporting a basket of chickens with the other. The varmints had wiped her out. Her nearest neighbor, nine miles away, had given her these for a fresh start. She was holding them carefully, for chickens could not be bought in the wilderness. They were a luxury to be raised at the cost of infinite care.

The two sisters said little. Settler women had little to say, but plenty to do, and Mariam Forrest had more than plenty. William, her husband, had died before he could drive his stake well into these parts, before he could provide for a parcel of chillurn whose bellies had to be filled and greased.

It might have been better if they had kept on in Tennessee. William warn't doing so bad blacksmithing, and they did manage to get

3

enough out of the ground to feed and clothe the young-uns. But the Indians had been sent further west by the government, and the Cherokee and Chickasaw country had been opened to settlers. The lard was rich, but somehow Mississippi air didn't smell as fresh as Tennessee air. There's no smell like cedar. But she had more to do than smell air.

She wondered when people would stop hunting new ground and work well what they already had. It was a terrible bother to begin all over again just after you'd got settled down and got to know your neighbors; and special worrisome after the chillurn filled the place. It was good to go out with a man when you were young and had no chillurn, but this going and going. . . . The horse threw back its ears and stopped dead in its tracks.

"Go on there."

The horse obeyed, but kept its ears alert.

Bedford was taking his father's place, and right well, too, for such a young one. He always had had a heap of energy. As a child he could make more noise playing and could yell louder when he was being whipped than any other child in the settlement.

Both horses were shying and trembling.

"What's the matter with these critters?"

"Want to get home, I reckin."

"Must smell a snake in the bushes."

Then it was dark. Night comes suddenly in the wilderness. They were yet a mile from the cabin.

A scream, shrill as a woman's, sent the horses quivering on their haunches. The women knew it was no human voice. A panter, hungry after blood and meat, had got their scent.

The horses broke into a run. The scream came from the forest again and again, each time a little nearer, until the cat could be heard springing his heavy weight in the smashing canes. The chickens made peculiar noises as they jostled about. Mariam Forrest tightened her arm about the basket.

Fannie thought of the creek winding in front of the cabin, of its red, slippery banks. She called to her sister to drop the chickens. Then maybe the panter would let them be.

Mariam's cheekbones were flushed, and there was battle in her eye. She had had her chickens stolen before, but that was in the nighttime when she was asleep.

"I'm not going to let any varmint git *my* chickens," she said.

They had reached the creek. Fannie's horse was sliding down the bank. The children, hearing her shouts, came out of the cabin and stood, wide-eyed, watching the race.

The cat leapt into the road. Mariam's horse was feeling for the bank. The cat crouched and sprang. Whinnying with terror and pain, the horse jumped into the creek, the cat perched on his haunches. With his fore paws he slashed at Mariam's neck and shoulders.

The frenzied plunges of the horse were shaking the cat into the water. He fell off, ripping the clothes from Mariam's back, tearing the flesh from her shoulder. With stubborn self-possession and no sound of pain she pulled the trembling horse up to the other side. Very tenderly Bedford lifted his mother from the saddle, while the blood from her gashes trickled down her back, along her arm, dripping into the chicken basket.

He carried her into the cabin, and they poured turpentine into the wounds and dressed them. As soon as her pain was eased, Bedford reached up and took down from its pegs over the fireplace his father's flintlock.

"Where you goin', Bedford?"

"I'm goin' to kill that beast if he stays on the earth."

"It's dark, son. Wait until daylight and you can see better what you are doin'."

He shook his head. "The trail will be too cold for the dogs to follow then."

She said nothing further. Those gray-slitted eyes so much like her own had set with a stubborn fierceness. In the firelight she had seen his face flush red, and the rangy, adolescent body tighten with anger. She knew him well enough to know that further argument was useless; nothing but the panter's scalp would make him mild again.

Bedford stepped under the low lintel, out into the dark. The dogs forgot their fleas and jumped about him. A sharp word of command, and he crossed the creek. The old hounds got the scent. He called the young ones who, with much zeal, but no discrimination, had hurried away too hastily, and followed the pack into the wilderness.

As she listened to the receding noise, Mariam Forrest, with Calvinistic stoicism, lay on her rough bed and bore the twinging pain. The pack was soon out of hearing, only a very distant yelping rising with strength enough to come back to the cabin. How could that boy keep up, she wondered, they had gone so fast?

He kept up. When the dogs began to outdistance him, he called the oldest, cut a grape vine, tied it about his neck, and followed at a slower pace until late in the night. At times the pack would be entirely out of hearing, but the old hound knew what he was about. He dragged Bedford over cane-brakes, through briar patches, into marshes and bottoms.

After midnight Bedford lost his strength; his face was thorned, and no sound from the hounds. Then a far-away music, the continuous yelps of the pack, told him the panter was treed. He forgot his exhaustion and hurried to the spot. The youngest were leaping up the trunk; the older circled at a safer distance. It was very dark. The trees were tall, and little starlight came through the thick tops; but out on a high branch two luminous spots moved in a fixed arc. He raised his gun; then slowly he lowered it.

His pursuit had been bold, relentless. He suddenly grows cautious; he decides to wait for daylight. A shot now, in the dark, might not be fatal. It would give the panter a chance for his life, not a great one, but a sporting chance. But Bedford was not a sportsman. A sporting code implies that under certain conditions an advantage is refused. It is a tenuous link between a natural and an artificial life, the ultimate refinement of a form which lacks an objective. Pioneers had no use for an empty form. Necessity, not pleasure, sent them on the chase.

So Bedford sprawled his six feet one and a half against a root to wait. The forest around had grown chilly, expectant, very still; the gnats and mosquitoes were letting up as they always do before sun-up. There had not been so many mosquitoes to bother with in the Duck River country, and perhaps as he lay there he felt a homesickness for Tennessee and the easy life of his childhood.

He was a man now, and the head of the family. No panter, nor anything else, should hurt them. In time he would build a finer cabin for his mother, one with a dog-run, a smoke-house in the rear loaded down with lard and meat, and just back from the house cribs full of corn and oats. He would raise more cotton. Maybe he would buy some niggers.

The cold light of the sun brought him to his feet. There before him, clearly now, at full length on a strong branch, lay the panter, snarling, lifting his upper lip to bare his white teeth at the dogs, his claws caught in the bark.

The boy put a fresh primer in the pan of his flintlock, drew a steady bead on its heart . . . The panter took no notice of him . . . and sent a bullet through it. The beast fell to the ground with a thud. Calling off the pack, Bedford cut off its scalp and ears and set out for home. As he plunged through the underbrush there was pride in his heart. He had stalked, shot, and scalped his quarry. Merciless, inexorable, the way of the wilderness was to kill or to be killed.

As merciless, as inexorable, the Mississippi swept by on the western border of the state, eating away the banks before Memphis, before Vicksburg, draining the countryside, the Big Black, the Tombigbee, Tishomingo Creek, the Yallabusha; and, miles to the north, the rivers of Bedford's native state, the Tennessee and the Cumberland, flowed towards its south-moving current.

CHAPTER II

New Ground

A T Southwest Point the Wilderness began. The ferry at the Point
was the last white settlement in East Tennessee, for the Wilderness was Cherokee hunting ground. Stretching east and west and extending miles to the south, it isolated the old Mero District along the
Cumberland from the more settled parts of the state. Half a mile east
of the ferry, on a piece of land at the inflow of the Clinch into the
Tennessee, a log fort reminded the Cherokees of the treaty and warned
them that the Great Road through the Wilderness must be kept open
to travelers.

The Indians, who made no demands of nature other than the use
of the forests for hunting, of its streams for fishing, and of a little
cleared ground where the corn might tassel, could not understand
what mortal danger this highway would bring to their culture. They
thought of it only as a trace permitting the white people to settle their
nations on the old Shawnee hunting grounds. But the white people
were not primarily interested in hunting. They were going west to
clear the land and grow more corn than they could eat. These agrarians
would destroy the forests, and inevitably the nomadic Indians. The
arrow cannot withstand the plow.

In 1806, during Jefferson's second administration, Nathan Forrest
and his family waited to take the ferry. They had come all the way
from Orange County, North Carolina, to settle in the Mero District.
This large section of land centering about the Cumberland River
had been named for Miro, the Spanish Governor of New Orleans, in
the days of territorial politics when Spain controlled the river traffic.

But Tennessee had never been very Latin, and since the Louisiana
Purchase made the Mississippi an American river, the foreign name
was being dropped and people from North Carolina and Virginia were
speaking more and more of going to the Cumberland settlements. And
this is probably what the Forrests called it as they stocked themselves

for the journey. Fodder for the beasts and provisions for the caravan
sufficient to last the whole way had to be carried along.

Nathan had been able to tell when he neared the Wilderness by the
price of corn. It rose from a quarter of a dollar a bushel to a third,
three-quarters, and finally at Kingston to a full dollar. The first fortunes in the new country were laid on the ferryman's toll and the high
rates of hospitality. Where every cabin was an inn, the lone hunter
scalped Indian and immigrant alike.

The Forrests had been on the move for a good many years. They
were a part of that vast restlessness which had spread over Europe after
the breakdown of medieval life, and which, because it could not be
contained entirely by the rigid discipline of nationalism, continued by
overflowing into the Americas. Here, in the newly occupied continent
of North America, the Europeans set about to appease their nostalgia
for feudalism.

But it was a slow business. Nathan Forrest's sire, old Shadrach,
was not among the first to come to terms with nature. He left Virginia in 1740, still a pioneer, to settle in North Carolina. Virginia
land, that is, its best land, was in the hands of the squires and the rich
men who fashioned their ways after the English gentry of the eighteenth century, and not after an earlier day when baron and yeoman
met on freer ground. So Shadrach found North Carolina more to his
liking. There were better chances there to settle on good land. The
farms were small, the slaves few, and the people who owned them
worked alongside them in the fields. North Carolina, though strictly
governed by its squires, was a yeoman state.

Shadrach spent a long life, sixty-six years, in this country of free-
holders. There was a wrestling with the forests and the fields which
informed the North Carolinians of the only natural peerage among
men, a peerage based on a relative possession and enjoyment of nature.
There were rich men and poor men, but the rich men did not at this
time pretend that, because they possessed more of nature's goods than
their fellows, they were better men in the sight of God; or, if they did,
they were soon put in their place, and in no uncertain manner. So long
as the poor man, the man who either from preference or incapacity
lived by hunting and fishing and by working as little of the ground
as possible—so long as he held on to his steading, he was economically,
and therefore in this Republic politically, independent. But economic
and political independence did not mean that all men were equal in
these matters, although there was much open talk that it did. Any

Indian fighter knew that equality and independence were two separate things, especially in social matters. There were certain forms of social life that members of a community enjoyed in common, such as court days, barbecues, and deer or bear hunts; and others of a more private nature, the mingling of individuals for no better reason than that they preferred one another's company. This being a matter of taste, social equality or inequality was entirely irrelevant to any discussion of what part it should bear in the new Republic.

The fresh influx of Scotch Irish and the purchase of Louisiana upset the first stages of the hardening Colonial cultures and sent the European-Americans, still pioneering, to the Mississippi Valley. Here there was more and better land, and Jefferson had said that the pursuit of happiness was possible only where every man owned the fields he worked. Then, and then only, was he beholden to no other, for he could house, clothe, feed, and warm his family by his labors. This self-reliance was not possible where men hired out to factory masters, for at that moment their living became dependent upon the will of another. The natural corollary to economic dependence was the falling-apart of the Republic, and because Hamilton and the Federalists tried to destroy the rights of the states and make the central government the tool of the rich men, Jefferson and all good Republicans drove them out of office.

For the same reason Jefferson was suspicious of the New England factories and urged the citizens of the new Republic to settle on the land. So Nathan, that he might be one of these free citizens, had set out for Tennessee. Old Shadrach, thinking of the days of his youth, and wanting, perhaps, to live them over again, now in 1806 a wizened, leathery old man, decided to go with him.

They had at last reached the Great Road and were waiting their turn at the ferry. This passage through the Cherokee lands was the last stretch they would have to make; but of all that had gone before, it would be the most difficult and the most dangerous, although the Wilderness was not the place of dread it had been during the Indian wars. But there was about the decision to pass through it a finality which did not permit a turning back.

This, in itself, was enough to think about; but there were other things. In dry weather travelers had been known to perish of thirst, while others more resolute had barely saved their lives by the tedious process of shaking dew into shells before the sun could suck it up. Careless immigrants, failing to tie their horses close to camp, had lost them to Indians and had been left afterwards to wander and starve in the forest, or to fall by an arrow. The peril and hardships of the frontier fort-settlements had all become a part of the Great Road's tradition, and warned the Forrests to be careful as they tried the road.

It ran first level, then hilly, passing through a fine chestnut woods as far as Little Cane and Big Cane Creeks. On the other side of Big Cane the ground sank low and swampy. Wagons and carts went down to the axle in bad weather, and the struggling horses plunged deep into the mire. Relief from this came with the Barrens, an unproductive land growing scrubby bushes and thin grass, with now and then a tree. Here the road ran fine and dry.

Twelve miles from the Clinch the Cumberland Mountains rose out of their foothills, steep and more difficult than they appeared at first. On one of the range's summits ran Mammy's Creek, a clear mountain stream, banked by tall spruce and white pine trees. From their tops the Cumberland parrots squawked at the travelers. And miles beyond, the way was littered with loose stone slabs, and wise riders dismounted to protect their critters. The wagon teams were constantly slipping and falling, and only the slow patience of the slobbering oxen and the slow talk of their drivers brought the caravans to Spencer's Hill, a byword for catastrophe. Spencer was one of the first settlers in the Cumberland country who rode alone and unharmed through the Wilderness during the wars, until on one trip, here on this slope between the rocks, he was tracked and killed by a Cherokee brave.

When the Forrests climbed to the top of this fatal spot, they found it bald and covered with stumps, and the farther side littered with logs. Previous travelers had felled all the trees to use them as brakes for their carts and wagons, which otherwise would have run over the oxen lumbering down an almost perpendicular descent.

About half-way through, the beautiful Crab Orchard Valley spread before the eye of the footsore and weary. Then to Daddy's Creek, Obey's River, and three miles farther, Drowning Creek—all the difficulties unique to these barriers the Forrests surmounted until finally they came to the last mountain of the Cumberland range. At this place there was a parting of the ways. The road to the left wound toward Caney Fork; the one to the right, to Fort Blount. The latter way the Forrests took, breaking their journey in Sumner County across the Cumberland River near the town of Gallatin. Here Shadrach died, before he had been there long enough to decide whether he had found the good country or not.

For when he and Nathan struggled west behind their oxen, passing or being passed by hog-drovers and cattle-drovers, lone horsemen, and men with their wives seated behind them, other oxcarts or wagons, some few on foot, small bodies of slaves for the increasing demand of the Southern markets, peddlers from New England, and a few high-swung carriages of revolutionary officers, lunged by them on the way. These officers, riding beside their freight, carried in their pockets the symbols of state sovereignty in the form of large grants of land for services in the Continental Lines. Behind them followed their few slaves, wagons and stock, the family pictures, household furniture . . . a microcosm of the Eastern plantocracy, ready to bring the form of the old life to the Mississippi Valley.

To Shadrach this was the squires again, getting ahead and gobbling up the best land. It is likely he continued in his belief, until worn out with his years and his journeys he was laid to rest near the limestone and beneath the cedars of Sumner County.

But the carriages put no fear into Nathan's heart. There were hearty greetings passed, a hail of comrades, of different degree, perhaps, but comrades who understood the rights of man, who had stood back to back through a long war to maintain these rights, and were now going west to perpetuate them.

After his father's death, Nathan tarried a year or so in Sumner; then moved on and settled down in Bedford County, in the Duck River country. The forest had oak, hickory, gum, walnut and chestnut trees, all good indications of rich soil; and on the hills there were cedars for fences. Near the banks of the streams the cane grew tall and rank. This was food for the stock during the winter. Nathan cleared some ground and set out a fruit nursery. Perhaps it didn't quite suit, but the chillurn came so fast he'd have to stop and blow a spell. Worn-out women and increasing families stopped many a good man before he was ready.

His oldest son, William, learned to be a blacksmith. In 1820 he married Mariam Beck, a woman of Scotch Irish ancestry whose family had moved in from South Carolina and settled near Caney Springs.

The year of their marriage was a year which set all people who loved the Union to thinking. It was the year of the Missouri Compromise, the gentlemen's agreement between the slave-holding and other states that this institution should be allowed to flourish only below the Mason and Dixon Line. The Federalists, as a party, had been thrown from power in 1808 because the Jeffersonian idea of government appealed to most of the people all over the Union. They had failed in their efforts to take New England out of the partnership during the War of 1812, even with the help of the British Governor in Canada who sent his agent, John Henry, to Boston in 1809 for this purpose. He saw that it was impossible to sever the Union at the moment, and it was said among specific circles that it was he who suggested to the Federalists that they get up some sectional question on which the prejudices and passions of the people could be permanently divided. The sectional question at which he hinted was slavery.

It had now grown very rapidly. "This momentous question," wrote Jefferson, who had retired to Monticello to prepare for the grave, "like a fire bell in the night, awakened and filled me with terror." He considered it the death knell of the Union, for "the question is a mere party trick. The leaders of Federalism, defeated in their schemes of obtaining power by rallying partisans to the principles of monarchism —a principle of personal, not of local division—have changed their tack, and thrown out another barrel to the whale. They are taking advantage of the virtuous feelings of the people to effect a division of parties by a geographical line; they expect that this will insure them, on local principles, the majority they could never obtain on principles of Federalism. "

A year later Mariam gave birth to twins. Even at this early date this remarkable woman showed herself willing to do more than her share. The girl was called Fannie and the boy Nathan for his grandfather and, in evidence of the strong local political attachments of the time, Bedford for the county in which he was born.

There is little known about Bedford's childhood years. The story is told by a friend how once when he and several children were out blackberry hunting, a rattlesnake coiled suddenly among the briars. All the children dropped their baskets and ran away—all except Bedford. He grabbed a solid stick and moved warily towards the rattler. Presently, when he came out of the thicket, he brought the snake hanging over the stick, its head beaten into a pulp and its shiny belly swinging lifeless down to the rattles at the end of the tail.

Another time, while he and one of Mr. McLaren's young-uns were watering the stock at the creek, his playmate's Barlow knife slipped into the water. In those days a Barlow was the most precious possession in the settlement. The two boys were overcome with the catastrophe, Mr. McLaren's young-un so completely that he could do nothing but cry. Bedford tried to comfort him; and he promised to get his knife back for him. Riding to the bank, he stripped to the skin and waded out near the spot where it had fallen in. He went under and remained in the water as long as he could hold his breath, grabbing about the gravelly bottom. After coming to the top many times with handfuls of sand and pebbles, he finally came up with the Barlow.

On the way to the creek lived a neighbor with two ferocious dogs. It had been a custom with the boys to rock these dogs; then race by on the back of their critters. One day Bedford's animal balked and threw him headlong among them. As he flew through the air in their direction, he expected to be torn to shreds the moment he hit the ground, but instead, as he jumped to his feet, he was amazed to find that the dogs had tucked their tails beneath their legs to make for the safety of their master's yard. Bedford never forgot this incident, nor its lesson: how his enemies who actually had him at their mercy, were startled into flight because they did not receive the usual rocks and sticks, but the unexpected, sudden, and enormous pellet of a boy.

When the time came for him to be sent to school, William and Mariam put him under Colonel John Laws, at the log academy. Years later Bedford met his old master before the works of Corinth, riding in the company of other Confederate officers. Bedford hailed him cordially and asked Colonel Laws if he knew him. When he made an honest reply, Bedford said, "You ought to know me. You've whipped me often enough. I am Bedford Forrest." After they had parted company, his old teacher turned to his companions and said, "Bedford had plenty of sense, but would not apply himself. He thought more of wrestling than his books. He was an athlete."

Bedford's grandmother had borne Old Nathan eight children, five boys and three girls. Of the boys all were traders but one, and he was a tailor. One day Bedford was in his uncle's shop, sitting quietly on the cutting table. Four or five young bucks were lounging and drinking in the shop, and as the moments passed, they grew happier and more frolicsome. Seeing the quiet gray-eyed boy watching them very solemnly, they decided to have a little fun with him. They offered him drinks and, when he refused, began to taunt and jeer. A large-framed man, named Adams, was the leader of the crowd. For a while Bedford made no reply, but as Adams grew vicious, he told him in his quiet way to go off and let him alone. He had done him no harm and didn't want to be plagued. In the meantime, he had picked up his uncle's shears and worked them apart. Mistaking Bedford's reserve for cowardice, Adams made a lunge in his direction. With the quick, easy motions of an animal Bedford jumped to his feet, holding in each hand a part of the shears. Without a word, but with a look that made Adams sober, he charged the drunks. They fled in dismay and tumbled out of the shop. The word got around next day that if the boy's uncle and several men had not caught and held him, some of the drunks would have been badly hurt.

He could not have been more than fourteen years old when this happened, because about that time his father, William, pulled up his stakes and was again on the move through the Wilderness. It looked for a while as if with William the wandering of the Forrests had come to an end. Upstanding, sober, and courageous, he had attained a position of respect in the settlement, and his influence was felt in its affairs. But like all the Forrests he was restless, and he was not yet willing to make his truce with nature.

When he had toughened into middle manhood, Tennessee had changed mightily. The large planters had torn down their log houses, or were covering them over with clap-boards. They were raising mansions of brick and cedar, with outhouses and broad lawns. A little town, Chapel Hill, had grown up near the Forrest's steading. When Nathan settled down with his family, the great planter and small farmer dressed alike. Both wore leather pantaloons, hunting shirts, and leggings as they all lived in one-crib cabins or dog-runs. But the dress and manners of the rich were changing with their changed dwellings. And as their lands pushed back the edge of the forest, the slaves increased considerably. In Bedford County alone they were one-fourth of the population as early as 1818, but William did not own any slaves; and it was becoming the common desire of the Southwest to own slaves.

The invention of the cotton gin had changed the whole tenor of its development. The Cherokee Nation was forced to sell the Wilderness and go beyond the Mississippi. West Tennessee proper (Middle Tennessee was first called West) was purchased by Andrew Jackson and Isaac Shelby, United States Commissioners, from the Chickasaws, October 19, 1818. All of these lands were being cleared by slaves and by smaller settlers so that the universal plant, cotton, might grow.

The two forces, planter and pioneer, the European and the American, which had passed each other on the Great Road in Nathan's time, had merged under the common influence of cotton and brought about the change William felt. The one was static, historical, cultural; the other dynamic, revolutionary, imperial. Compelled to mingle, each had offset the other. The planter's inertia magnetized the pioneer's energy into his circle. This gradual absorption of the pioneer brought sufficient motion with him, until from the give and take of the two opposite forces there was coming about a metamorphosis of each into a particular way of life, to be called Southern.

For a while after 1800 Tennessee was able to grow from a thousand to fifteen hundred pounds of seed cotton to the acre, but both the Volunteer state and Kentucky were soon discovered to be too far north for the culture of this plant. The frost killed it before the boll could open. These states then became furnishing states to the Lower South, furnishing not only corn, pork, and whiskey, but a pattern—an incomplete one certainly—which the Black Belt might use to fashion its communities after. They were the oldest slave states in the West; but, because of the plantation system and its influence on the newer arrivals, they had done their pioneering very rapidly.

But apparently William, lacking the good fortune which made men planters, was not satisfied with his position in Tennessee's hardening culture; so in 1834, two years after South Carolina's threat of Nullification, he settled down on Tippah County land, not far from the village of Salem. The third generation had forgotten Jefferson's advice that only so much, not too much, land was necessary for a free life. Pioneering was becoming perverted from its purpose, as desire for better land became a habit. The means was fast becoming the end. The West had set itself to accumulate land, not that it might live freely, but that it might grow cotton and be wealthy.

An agrarian economy was basing its culture on the pay of an industrial economy, which by its nature is hostile to it. This is full of peril, but it does not of necessity mean corruption, for a farmer might still take the pay of Industry and not be dependent upon it. The chief, and probably the greatest, peril is the difficulty of establishing a religion, for men with their minds on power are distracted from building their culture around the altar of a God, and only such a culture can thrive. Bishop Asbury wrote prophetically in his journal as early as 1797 that "with so many objects to take their attention, with good health and good air to enjoy, and when I reflect that not one in a hundred came here to get religion, but rather to get plenty of good land, I think it will be well if some or many do not eventually lose their souls."

William, before he was able to do more than build another cabin and clear a little ground, died still a nomad and left his wife, Mariam, a widow.

CHAPTER III

The End of the Road

THE widow had now only Bedford, a sixteen-year-old boy, to play a man's part and support his six brothers, three sisters, and a fatherless baby. This was hard on the boy and harder on the widow-woman, but they both had iron constitutions and an iron courage. Under Mariam's eye Bedford did more than support her. His axe rang surer, the fence rails stood squarer, and the new ground grubbed cleaner than ever before. He began to branch out and trade a little. Gradually a few border luxuries were seen about the cabin, as his industry and thrift made themselves felt.

But this did not come until about 1840. In the meantime, the hard work in the fields was matched by that of the household. Mariam was a firm mother. There was little time for foolishness. When she spoke, her children minded her. The wool and cotton must be spun into yarn, and the yarn into cloth for shirts and dresses. The meat must be killed at the right time, salted down, and put away in the smoke-house; and the fat rendered into lard. There was corn to be sent to the mill, candles to be made from tallow, ash-hoppers to be filled for soap-making, and fruit to dry.

So hard were they pushed that Bedford often sat down at candle light and fashioned shoes and buckskin leggings for his younger brothers. He was always very proud of this. Barely turned a man, with no experience in family matters, to take from the new ground and forests their victuals and with his own hands to make their shoes, gave him a sense of achievement he was never to feel again.

Always there were the swamps to fight, and he and the rest of the kin were struck with the fever. Two of his brothers died, and his three sisters, including the one twin-born with himself. It looked for a long time as if he would follow her; but, finally, after a prolonged

adolescence, he got back on his feet again. He was now twenty years
old.

The country-side had by this time begun to fill up. No longer did
Mariam and her sister Fannie, have to travel nine miles to visit a neighbor. They had one living near by who had an ox, large, unyoked, and
of a roving nature. Somehow the Forrest corn looked greener and
juicier than the crops on his master's land; so he threw down the
fences and began to root and destroy the Forrest crops. Bedford protested, but his neighbor paid him no mind. It was no fault of his if
their fences were too weak for his cow.[1] If the widow-woman didn't
want her corn tromped, let her boy build stouter fences.

Bedford's reply was that if he caught the ox in his fields again, he
would shoot him. The neighbor answered with a sterner threat. In a
few days the beast was found again on the wrong side of the line.
Bedford made good his threat after sending word to the owner. He
reloaded quickly, for he heard him running through the thickets.
Scarcely had Bedford rammed in his shot when the neighbor mounted
the line fence, rifle in hand. Just as he was straddling the top rail, Bedford lifted his piece to his shoulder, drew a steady bead, and fired. The
man tumbled to his side of the line, jumped to his feet and ran towards
his cabin without taking time to look to the rear. Apparently it was
simpler for an ox to go through a fence than for a man to climb over.

His neighbor lost an ox because he thought Bedford was bluffing.
Others fooled by his bluffs were to come to greater grief.

In February, 1841, a small company of volunteers marched out of
Holly Springs to assist Texas in her struggle for independence. Bedford, almost twenty-one years old, marched off with them. His hard
work and shrewd trading had so improved the family's fortune that
he was able to leave his mother in the hands of his younger brothers.
He went off with a light heart, no longer confined by home-making.

When the volunteers reached New Orleans, a serious mismanagement of the funds disrupted the company. Many, possibly, were already
tired of the journey and homesick when they reached the Southern me-
tropolis; and it is likely that their inability to hire a boat to Galveston
was secretly a great relief. New Orleans must have seemed to these
boys from the farms and towns of the interior a more exciting place
than far-away Texas.

Bedford was not one of those who lingered in New Orleans. He
had set out to fight for Texan independence; so on to Texas he went.

[1] Oxen were familiarly referred to as cows.

A few of his nature, or inspired by his zeal, followed after him. It was no self-conscious moral snobbery that led him on to Galveston. It was merely his nature and training to remove all obstacles in the way of his purpose.

When this remnant of the company reached its destination, the men found Texas had no need of them; so those who had the money returned the long way home. Others settled down where they were, and Bedford split enough rails at fifty cents a hundred to pay his way back to Tippah County. If he had started out with any illusions about the romance of war, this military venture must have taken them completely away, for there is little evidence that they ever again returned.

In four and a half months he was home again, bringing back no military glory but the seeds of disease; and he was disabled by an illness which lingered into the autumn of that year. Lying in bed for such a time, he was able to reflect upon his journey to Texas. Going to and from New Orleans, his settler's eye had scanned the rich bottom lands bordering the Mississippi River. At great distances the most enterprising planters had large plantations cleared away, with gangs of slaves under their drivers moving about the fields, among the tree stumps and loose new ground, the sweating mules and blasphemous drivers wrestling with stubborn roots and briars; and penetrating to the steamboat, the sharp nasal voice of the long-stooping overseer could be heard—"Step along there. Don't kill that mule. Step along . . ." More often, when the boat neared the hill country of Northern Mississippi, it passed smaller holdings and rough cabins; but it was not always possible to tell about cabins, for many of the great planters were too busy clearing new ground to put up more than a dog-run or two for their families. Bedford did not miss the significance of the sights which moved before his eye, for he never looked idly.

When he got well again, he began trading horses with an uncle. Their venture was successful in a small way, for the Forrest family, if they knew anything, knew horse flesh.

He then returned to his mother's, where he remained until the autumn of 1842. One day during the rainy season, as he was returning home with an ox wagon, he found the creeks overrunning their banks. The rise of fresh water creeks in this part of the country was very rapid, too rapid for the slow-pacing oxen; so, as he was crossing the stream in front of the home place the wheels stuck fast in its middle. He cracked his whip and spoke to the cows, but the wheels did not budge. One of his brothers saw his trouble and ran for Mariam. She arrived and found the animals confused by her son's profanity and his cracking whip. She ordered him to calm himself and to let the cows rest. He replied that the water was rising too fast.

He jumped from the wagon and got a cross-beam. Mariam took the whip. Bedford pushed the beam under a rear wheel, and Mariam cracked the whip. But still the wagon held fast to the sinking bottom. She called out that the water was getting over his new boots. He told her he could get another pair. Presently Bedford threw down his beam and strode through the rising current towards the team. He leaned over and bit an inch of flesh out of one of the oxen's ears. The animal lunged forward, and the wagon was pulled safely to the opposite bank.

"Now, mother, all we have to do is to put some turpentine on that ear and sit down and eat Dinah's biscuits."

On day, he wondered what it was like to be drunk. He had noticed that it made some men fight and others cry. Being a pretty rough fighter, he decided not to get drunk in public; so he took his jug to the woods. There, if he was a mind to fight, he told some friends later, he knew he couldn't hurt the tree trunks. He never knew what happened; but when his senses returned, he was sick with a fever that turned into a bad case of pneumonia. He promised Old Marster that, if he would spare his life, he would never take another drink. Old Marster heard his prayer, and Bedford kept his promise.

About this time his uncle Jonathan, living at that time in Hernando, Mississippi, about twenty-five miles south of Memphis, offered his nephew an interest in his mercantile concern. Bedford saw his chance and took it.

Old Jonathan had gone security on the bond of one Martin Jones, the guardian of some orphan children. This involved the old man in a quarrel with the planter, William Matlock. Matters presently reached that point where it was no longer manly to use words. The difference must be cleared up or forgotten. It was very difficult to forget a grievance in a frontier country, and only one way to clear it up.

So, on March 10, 1845, William Matlock, sustained by two brothers and his overseer, decided to bring the matter to a head.

The road from Memphis rose on to the square of Hernando. The court house, according to the plan of Southern county seats, squats in a broad park in the center of the square. Around it, wagon teams and horses are hitched to the fence rails separating the court house lawn from the four thoroughfares that lie between the hall of justice and the store houses on each of the four sides. One of these houses belonged to old Jonathan Forrest.

This spring day, purely by accident, young Bedford happened to be in town. William Matlock, Jefferson Matlock, James Matlock, and the overseer Bean, with the slow precision of men who must not be hurried, sank their boots in the wet clay, already furrowed and dug up by the wheels and hoofs from over the county. Each boot, lifted and set down nearer Jonathan's store, was marked with a fresh, red smear. There was no sound other than eight continuous sucks, as the eight heels advanced nearer.

Before they had gone half the distance across the square, everybody knew what was bound to happen. Business was suspended. Trades were dropped as the traders sought convenient covers, but not so convenient as to hide the view. They knew that four men could not be afraid of one old man.

Somebody ran to the back of the store and told Jonathan. He got up with an old man's jerk and spat into the ash-box beneath the stove; then reached in the drawer and moved to the front of the building, out onto the square. Bedford had appeared from nowhere in particular and was talking. He was telling the Matlocks that the quarrel was none of his, but that four men against one was not fair, and that he was not going to stand by and see his uncle assaulted in any such manner. If there was to be a fight, it would be a fair one, not four against one. His voice was gentle, so gentle that one might wonder why it was not muffled by the stone-like movements of his jaw.

Jefferson Matlock made a quick draw and shot at Bedford. He missed. Old Jonathan took a forward step and fell on the square, his thin blood filling a well made by a horse's hoof. All four now turned on Bedford, but two were not swift enough. Jonathan's nephew emptied the two barrels of his pocket pistol, and two Matlocks dropped in the mud. Only the third Matlock and Bean were left to send hot lead to snip his clothes and burn his flesh. One of the balls struck him, but not hard enough to take him off his feet.

Empty-handed, Bedford now faced the two remaining assailants. There was no time to reload; so he waited, unflurried, looking about for some suitable weapon to continue the fight. The Matlocks saw him standing there, confident, with no sign of fear, as certain as fate; and their shots flew wild. A murmur of admiration rose from the scattered bystanders. One of them freed himself from the general hypnosis and ran forward with a Barlow knife.

Bedford took it in his left hand and charged his enemies. Their nerve had already been badly shaken; and for a boy of twenty-five to hold them, armed with pistols, in such contempt, disturbed it further. Before they could rally from such an unexpected attack, he had slashed and disabled the third Matlock. Bean did not wait his turn. He remembered the affair was no concern of his and faced his feet in the opposite direction.

Bedford's courage had so aroused the sympathy of the people of Hernando that the three men he had disabled, despite their wounds, were arrested and held without bail, to be tried for murder. Bedford was also arrested, but immediately released on the grounds of self-defense. It was only after much time, harsh confinement, and great expense that the Matlocks eventually got free.

Shortly after this, as Bedford was riding down the road one April Sunday, he met a wagon stalled in a bad mud hole. It was carrying the widow Montgomery and her daughter, Mary, to church. These were the kinswomen of the Richard Montgomery who was killed at the storming of Quebec. So far their driver had not been able to budge the wagon. Nearby, two men lolled on their horses, interested spectators in the struggle with the North Mississippi clay.

Bedford rode forward and asked if he might assist them. When his services were accepted, he hitched his horse, waded back to the wagon and carried the ladies to dry ground. Then, putting his shoulder to the wheel, he and the driver were able to get it onto firmer ground. Turning upon the horsemen, he told them they were ungallant and unfit to be in the presence of ladies, that if they didn't ride away immediately, he would give them the worst whipping of their lives. The gentlemen did not tarry—perhaps they had heard of the fight on the square—but turning the heads of their horses in the opposite direction, they rode silently away.

Mrs. Montgomery and her daughter thanked him profusely. Bedford then introduced himself and asked to call, for whatever his shortcomings, to let slip an opportunity was not among them; and he had held Miss Mary in his arms.

He made his appearance the very next day and found, to his amazement, the same men waiting in the parlor. He ordered them out a second time, and a second time they obeyed.

When Miss Mary walked into the parlor, Bedford told her she should put herself in his hands, for certainly such men would never be able to protect a woman through life. She seemed not to take this unkindly, and after a short courtship, they were married in September of that year.

He moved his wife into a weather-boarded dog-run not far from the center of the town. Having taken on added responsibility, he worked extra hard to make a fortune. He extended his trading to slaves. He ran a stage line on the plank road between Hernando and Memphis. He set up a brick yard, for he was shrewd enough to see that the prospering planters were no longer willing to live in their pioneer dwellings. The culture had begun to harden in Mississippi as it had hardened in Tennessee, only at a more rapid pace. This last-named venture got him into trouble. In 1849 he made a large contract to build an academy; and an agent, who had the power to draw on him at a Memphis bank, drew out the money for his own purposes. This breach of trust wiped out practically everything he had accumulated up to that time.

In the face of this misfortune he redoubled his energy, with such good luck that he was able to move to Memphis three years later with a fresh stake. He became a broker in real estate; and taking his brothers in as partners, set up a slave mart. After he had worked the local business, he would take caravans of horses and slaves into West Tennessee and as far north as Kentucky. His speculations were bold, but they were generally successful, because they were based on sound judgment and resolute execution.

Shortly after he had changed his residence to Memphis, he was forced to make a speedy trip to Galveston. In his haste to return to Tennessee he risked passage on the steamboat *Farmer,* a leaky tub captained by one of the most reckless men on the rivers. He jumped aboard just as the gangplank was being pulled in. That night, after he had gone to sleep, he was aroused by the angry voices of gamblers in an adjoining saloon. He had ridden across country that day and was very tired. Not to be able to sleep annoyed him, but when pistols were cocked over the gambling table, his temper got away from him. Half-clad, he threw open the door and stalked into their midst, imperious, dishevelled, an angry flush on his face. He spoke to the gamblers peremptorily as if he meant to be obeyed; and what promised to be a general mêlée was soon quelled. He left the Saloon and went out on deck to be cooled by the fresh river air. He was startled to find the chimney stacks red hot as far up as the cabins, which were kept from burning by a constant line of servants throwing water on the timbers. At the same time all kinds of the most combustible material was being thrown into the furnaces to increase the speed and keep ahead of a rival boat.

He appeared at once before the captain and protested, but the captain was drunk with liquor and the race. He replied that he was a hundred yards ahead of his rival, was only six miles out from the landing, and that he would preserve that distance or "blow the old tub with every soul on board to hell!"

Bedford walked to the extreme after part and waited for the crisis. He did not have long to wait. Near the shallow waters of Rockfish bar the boilers blew into the sky. The old tub and sixty souls, including the captain, were blown to hell.

Memphis in those days was a river town. Today it is a city with a water front, but no longer do steamboats tie up at its landings. In the fifties it was the queen of river towns, receiving from the Mississippi whatever it chose to wash onto its levee. It was reckless; it drank fine whiskey; men shot at each other and fell off the sidewalks into the dusty streets. It was the trade center for the interior, and its floating population was large. Bands of robbers, adventurers, desperadoes of all sorts, often in the guise of honest men, sauntered through its saloons, and lay in wait on the waterfront or in dark places.

The more law-abiding element had been worked up over numerous such affairs, particularly since the courts and the city government had shown themselves too frail to cope with the growing spirit of border violence. Their resentment came to a head one fine June day in 1857.

Joe Able and his son, John, stood out in the citizens' minds as the most objectionable gamblers and rowdies in the town. The father killed a man in a public saloon and had to clear out to escape arrest. He left his wife and daughter in the care of John. A man named Everson was called to account by young Able for insulting his mother. They were seated on the sidewalk in front of the Worsham House, discussing the matter. Presently the boy was seen to rise excitedly and strike Everson in the face with his pistol. The jar set it off and sent a bullet plowing through his skull, killing him instantly. Able walked to the jail house and surrendered.

The news soon spread, and a large body of men gathered in front of the Worsham House, smelling the bloody sidewalk and talking angrily. Pouring in from the various streets, the crowd soon grew to large proportions; and leaders were beginning to show themselves to make articulate the sullen swell of their resentment. Bedford Forrest had been attracted to the spot, along with the mayor and other prominent citizens. They took counsel together, and Bedford appeared on the balcony above the Worsham piazza. He soon got the attention of the mob and told them it was no matter for them personally to settle. He advised them to deliberate, at any rate to wait for the morrow. He told them a meeting had been called by the mayor in the Exchange Building to discuss the increasing lawlessness and to take steps to put it down. This had the intended effect. The clamor for immediate vengeance subsided, and the people returned to their homes.

The next day the Exchange overflowed into the streets. The intervening night had done nothing to calm the spirit of violence. A sullen restlessness could be felt by the mayor and his officials on the platform. Bedford Forrest was among those presiding. Scarcely had the meeting effected its organization when a carpenter, Vergison, called out, "Let's hang him and git it done with."

The mob broke the doors down getting out, and the mayor and his leading citizens were left in the empty hall, pondering what to do. They had been defied by massed anarchy, and they were afraid. They debated plans of rescue, but did nothing. Into these debates slid a fever, caught from the mob itself, which at that moment was taking the keys away from the sheriff. Still they debated, not one of them daring to do what clearly was his duty, to go save the city's prisoner, or lacking the strength to do that, to admit incompetence and hang with him.

One citizen living in Memphis at the time reported that the mayor turned to Bedford and said, "Forrest, go save him"; and that Bedford asked, "Do you tell me it is my duty as a citizen to rescue that boy?" The mayor told him it was, and when asked why it wasn't the mayor's duty as well, this gentleman admitted that it was, but that fear had got the better of duty.

The report came back to the Exchange that the mob had been delayed by the improper adjustment of the rope, and Bedford quickly left the building and the buzz of frightened argument behind. When he reached the navy yard, a place then considered excellent for breaking necks, the rope had been satisfactorily adjusted and thrown over young Able's head. Mrs. Able and her daughter were there on the rope walk beside him, begging mercy of the three thousand hungry, implacable faces spread backward from the river. The boy, pale and slender as a girl, not yet of age, faced his executioners defiantly. His head thrown back a little melodramatically, he argued without a tremor in his voice that he had just provocation for his action, that

this would be made evident if he had fair trial, and that all he asked
was the right to this trial. But his voice was drowned by a chorus of,
"hang him, hang him."

His fearless composure in the face of death and the greater moral
pressure of mass action dispelled any hesitancy that Bedford might
have had to act. He pushed through the mob to the assistance of one
of his own kind. Jumping to the rope walk, he slashed the rope, shook
his enormous shoulders like an animal, and jumped back into the
crowd with John Able.

The three thousand were so taken by surprise that, for a moment,
they did nothing; but as the raveled edges of the rope hung there
futilely, like a piece of twine, their eyes were filled with blood. They
recovered from a mass paralysis in a single leap of rage that sent them
churning and twisting aimlessly, the unity of their action broken
by the impudent courage and contempt of one man. They clawed
and fought one another. Their leaders were drowned for the moment
by the terrific weight of so much plunging energy. It swept away the
few friends who had gathered about Bedford, striding where he could
and pushing where he had to, gripping young Able with one hand
and a vicious-looking knife with the other.

He drew himself and his charge between two stacks of lumber
promptly enough to be saved from the crushing throng which actually
swept over them. A few of the leaders held to the lumber and stabbed
at him from above and from the sides. Up to this moment his movements had been swift, calm, and well-ordered. But this direct attack
changed him in an instant. He stepped back, his nostrils quivered, his
eyes lit up, and his face flushed like a plate of bronze; and before they
knew why, those who had cornered him at the lumber stacks were
fleeing in every direction. This rage of battle had come on Bedford
back in his uncle's tailoring shop in Chapel Hill. It always struck
him at a certain moment in every fight.

Moving at the right moment, he reached the jail house and locked
Able in his cell. But the mob had not yet been mastered. It had only
been thwarted; so it was not long before it had surrounded the building, threatening, more resolved and more vicious than ever. And to
find the door shut, the door that once before had opened so readily
to its demands, was an added irritant. The leaders called out that if
it were not opened, they'd bust it open; and they wouldn't be long
about it. At the height of their threats, it swung on its hinges and
quickly slammed to with a very definite, a very final, bang. Alone,

without any possible support, Bedford Forrest was left between it and the three thousand men he had robbed of their victim.

He walked forward and was speaking. In each hand he held very steadily a six shooter, and the handle of his knife stuck out of a belt where all might see it. Without braggadocio, but very earnestly, he called out in a clear, firm voice, "If you come by ones, or by tens, or by hundreds, I'll kill any man who tries to get in this jail."

He sounded and he looked as if he meant what he said; and as he stood there prepared to execute his ultimatum, not a man moved. He had cowed the leaders by his tactics and broken the unity of the mass by his strategy. He had challenged them in small units, not as a whole. The moment this happened each individual began to consider whether the prisoner was worth facing those guns in his hands and that knife in his belt. With the morale of the leaders broken, there was no one to reanimate the mass feeling; so gradually three thousand individuals surrendered to their master. They did him homage by quickly dissolving into the side streets.

The next day, about the streets, in the slave mart, over saloon bars, dinner tables, on the levee, the name Forrest could be heard, a refrain which returned at a regular beat to every conversation.

At the next election he was chosen an alderman. Into the doubtful ethics of the council he brought an invigorating honesty, sound judgment, and a care for the Public Thing. But he had very little political ambition; so, after serving his one-year term, he resigned in 1859.

He closed out many of his business enterprises in Memphis, gave up speculation in slaves and took those on hand to his large holdings in Coahoma County and became a cotton planter on a large scale. This same year a small group of men, led by a horse-trader with homicidal cravings and a message from God, crossed into Virginia to be the rallying point for a revolt of slaves that never came. The country's nerves immediately went to pieces, and all thoughtful men suddenly realized the gravity of its condition.

But this was not the reason Bedford gave up the business. It was honorable in the Southern feudalism to own slaves, but very dishonorable to traffic in them. This prejudice against slave dealers has many remote causes, but one very definite cause. The close personal association between slave and master, particularly between slave and mistress, caused the planters tacitly to ignore the economics of his condition out of respect for him as a person. The slave understood his relationship, that he owned the master as much as the master owned him.

It was facetiously said in Virginia when men maintained worn-out plantations at no profit purely to feed and clothe their slaves that the trees would have posters advertising for runaway masters. Because the slave dealers looked on the negro only in terms of trade, Southerners considered them as debased.

Bedford, being a Southern man, mitigated the usual evils of the bargaining as much as he could. He never separated a family, and he always did his best to find and buy the husband and wife, when either one was missing. He treated his slaves so well that he was burdened with appeals from them to be bought. When a purchase was made, he turned him over to his body servant, Jerry, with orders to wash and dress him in clean garments from head to foot. But even with this fine treatment, so much bad odor hung to the profession that he finally decided to abandon it and take those negroes he had on hand and set up as a planter. The slaves had influenced this decision by coming to him in a body with some such proposal.

He did so well with cotton that he raised a thousand bales in 1861 at a profit of thirty thousand dollars. The wandering of the Forrests had at last come to an end. Bedford had established himself as one of the rich men of a feudal culture, fast becoming static. The Wilderness had been reduced to a planting and farming country, and the Great Road, which for half a century had stretched continually southward, was now come to its end. But before Bedford and the people like him could settle down and begin to live on the land, they would have to fight a more strenuous enemy than the Wilderness.

CHAPTER IV

The Irrepressible Conflict

"THIS Union is a lie! The American Union is an imposture—a covenant with death and an agreement with hell. I am for its overthrow! Up with the flag of disunion!"

These are the words of William Lloyd Garrison, the father of the abolition societies, who publicly, on the fourth day of July, inaugurated his movement by giving the Constitution of the United States to the flames.

So long as Garrison's disciples attempted purely political action on the question of abolition, they received a pitiably small hearing from the great body of the American people. Garrison was burned in effigy all over the Northern states, and his radical followers bent on the destruction of the Union were informed very realistically with tar and feathers that the Union must stick together. This was in the days when Calhoun spoke for the South, Webster for the North, and Henry Clay for the West.

The abolitionists, by themselves, might have gone on for some time without effecting their ends; but unfortunately for the Union, after the dissolution of the Whig Party, the old Federalist-Hamiltonian element looked around for new allies. It was now more important than ever that it destroy the rights of the states and form a powerful central government, for so long as the states remained autonomous, industrial capital was effectively controlled. Calhoun had whipped them out on the tariff and Andrew Jackson on the Federal bank. The cotton states were, therefore, able to sell their staple as free men bartering with other free men. But this new class of Hamiltonian-Industrialists growing up, particularly in Pennsylvania, was not willing to make a fair profit on their machines; and so long as the Southern states remained powerful and uncontrolled, they had to be content with such an arrangement.

If the South could be broken politically, it could be forced into a position of economic serfdom, depending on those who would control this strongly centralized government. The Black Republican party was formed towards this end. William H. Seward, one-time Governor of New York, was its inspiration. He saw that the abolitionists had, by their thirty-year education of the popular mind, created a general antagonism in the North against the South and, over large areas, a great hatred; and he determined to use this to gain power for himself and his industrial supporters.

Since the Constitution recognized property in slaves, Mr. Seward made his first attack on this compact, but not as the abolitionists had attacked it. They did not dispute the constitutional guarantees; but, admitting them, advised the disruption of the compact. Mr. Seward was more subtle. He began to institute a policy which would destroy the Union in fact but keep it in name and physical appearance. "You answer that the Constitution," he says, "recognizes property in slaves. It would be sufficient, then, to reply that the constitutional recognition must be void, because it is repugnant to the law of nature and of nations." For a people to abrogate their articles of agreement in favor of the law of nature and of nations was for them to place their destiny in the hands of the party in power, which would interpret this very general law in the light of its interests. It was this kind of argument which frightened old Calhoun and caused him to urge secession, which was thereupon soberly considered at the Nashville Convention of 1850. The Southern states did not heed his warning, for their strong emotional attachment to the Union clouded the force of Calhoun's logic. He could not teach them that the purpose of the Union was to sustain their independence, and that this was now possible only in a Southern Union, since the commercial and industrial states had upset the balance of power in their favor.

Calhoun saw that as time went on there would be less and less that was common between the two sections, and that any union to be actual must be a union of common interests, or a union of interests of equal power. This was no longer so. There was, as Mr. Seward announced, "an irrepressible conflict" between the two sections. He pretended that the conflict was a moral matter of slavery, but this was for strategic reasons. Nobody knew better than he that it was the conflict between a people living almost entirely on the land and a people loyal to a commercial and fast-growing industrialism which demanded that the duty of the citizen must be not life, liberty, and the pursuit of happiness but a willing consumption of the produce of Northern manufacture.

The new party he created in 1854 made loud protestations of devotion to "free speech, free press, and free men." It pretended to more and better republicanism than the Democrats, for it desired to apply republicanism to negroes. Hence the name Black Republican, for it bore no more resemblance to genuine republicanism than an old Federalist did to a Jeffersonian Democrat. The abolitionists thought its program did not go far enough, but one of them, Wendell Phillips, saw how cunning were its tactics. "It is the first crack in the iceberg," he said. "It is the first sectional party ever organized in this country. It is pledged against the South."

So the two factions, the abolitionists and the disciples of Hamiltonian monarchism, set about to revolutionize the government. Their failure to elect Frémont and Dayton in 1856 pointed out the most serious obstacle to their success: the border states of Kentucky, Missouri, Illinois, Indiana, Ohio, and Tennessee. These states were predominantly agrarian and had been settled chiefly by Southern people. In the past they had been bound to the South through such ties and by the Mississippi River. Being "furnishing" states for the Cotton Kingdom, most of their commercial interests were with Southern merchants. This was rapidly changing, however, for by 1860 the railroads which connected the Northeast and the Northwest had diverted much of the trade from the Mississippi River to the eastern markets. But as it always takes some time for such a change to impress itself on the large body of people, the borderland as a whole sympathized with the Southern traditions; and for this reason it would require the greatest political genius to make them into willing Black Republican tools.

The task was difficult, but Lawyer Lincoln showed them the way. The only point of friction between the Lower South and the borderland north of the Ohio River was over the right of new territories to determine whether or not slavery should be introduced without their consent. The Missouri Compromise had been a gentlemen's agreement in which the South agreed not to use its right north of the Mason and Dixon Line. It was a sacrifice on her part for the sake of peace. But now, with the territory gained in the Mexican war to be divided, the issue was re-opened. Douglas, running for the senate on the Democratic ticket, ignored this difference of opinion between the two sections. Lincoln, with political ambitions, in the famous series of debates through Illinois, drove him into a corner and forced him to admit the right of new states to determine whether they would be slave or free. This "right" was unconstitutional as it would prohibit Southerners from carrying their property into all parts of the Union. Douglas's reply alienated the Southern wing of the Democratic Party from supporting his candidacy for the presidency in 1860 and in this way split the party.

So Lincoln was chosen by the Black Republicans as the only man who could disguise the sectional basis of the party and carry the border states north of the Ohio. The campaign speeches of the party became all things to all men. In the Southern counties of Illinois, Indiana, and Ohio their speakers dwelt on the preservation of the Union; in the northern parts of these states, particularly those counties made up from New England stock, they waved the bloody abolition shirt.

The *Helper Book,* which had been published a year before, and a hundred thousand copies of which had been circulated by subscription of the leading Black Republican members of Congress, was the chief campaign document of the Lincoln canvass in all parts of the Union which had come under the influence of the abolitionists. It threatened the people of the South with death and destruction.

"Against slaveholders as a body we wage an exterminating war. We contend that slaveholders are more criminal than common murderers. The negroes, nine cases out of ten, would be delighted at the opportunity to cut their masters' throats.

"Smallpox is a nuisance; strychnine is a nuisance; mad dogs are a nuisance; slavery is a nuisance; and so are slaveholders; it is our business, nay it is our imperative duty, to abate nuisances; we propose, therefore, with the exception of strychnine, to exterminate this catalog from beginning to end." After reading the book, it was clear to the South what were the intentions of this sectional party.

Four men were running for the presidency: Douglas, representing the Northern Democrats; Breckinridge, the Southern wing of the party; Bell, for the Know-Nothings, a party which ignored the issues at stake in an appeal for all men to stand by the Union; and Lincoln for the Black Republicans, although he did not at this time understand the consequences of his alliance.

Lincoln carried every Northern state except New Jersey; but although he received a majority of the electoral votes, he did not receive a majority from all the people. He was nearly a million and a half in the minority. His party was in power, but it did not have the confidence of the borderland; and without this, it could not take action against the South.

From the returns in these states along the Ohio, two things stand out. The first is the slight change which took place in the former party alignments. This indicates that the issue of Union or disunion was not popularly regarded as the chief issue of the campaign. For example, the slave-holding counties of Kentucky voted for Bell, not Breckinridge. This candidate got his largest support in the mountainous regions where slavery was negligible. The second is the conservative attitude of the voters. In nearly every part of the Borderland they expressed their preferences for Bell and Douglas, as they stood for the policy of compromise and conciliation. There is little evidence to show that these states generally thought of the election as the final political contest between the sections.

The confusion was due to the very poor political leadership in the South. Its chief hope for success lay in gaining the sympathy of the Border country, either to assure its peaceful departure from the Union or to persuade the border to withdraw with it. The South needed a Calhoun to clarify the issues and point out that the agrarian tradition, South and west, was in danger.

South Carolina, trained in this stateman's logic, withdrew so soon as the returns had been counted and it could assemble a convention to act. In January, 1861, five other states, Mississippi, Alabama, Florida, Georgia, and Louisiana, followed South Carolina. Tennessee, Virginia, Kentucky, and Missouri hesitated; and it now became the policy of the two governments to influence their action.

The Democrats and the border slave state of Kentucky did their best to patch up the matter, and the Provisional Confederacy at Montgomery, controlled by such moderates as its president and vice-president, showed themselves willing to listen to compromise. Senator Crittenden, from Kentucky, had already come forward with his proposition, the extension of the Missouri Compromise to the Pacific Ocean; but it was voted down by the Black Republicans. Douglas then introduced a plan of his own, and this was also voted down. He turned towards the opposition and said:

"If you of the Republican side are not willing to accept this, nor the proposition of the Senator from Kentucky, Mr. Crittenden, pray tell us what you are willing to do? I address the inquiry to the Republicans alone, for the reason that in the Committee of Thirteen, a few days ago, every member from the South, including those from the cotton states—Toombs and Davis—expressed their readiness to accept the proposition of my venerable friend from Kentucky, as a final settlement of the controversy, if tendered and sustained by the Republican members. Hence the sole responsibility of our disagreement, and the only difficulty in the way of an amicable adjustment, is with the Republican Party."

When all the measures for peace had failed, this senator pointed towards that part of the chamber where the Black Republicans had their seats and called out with vigor, "You want war."

And apparently they did, but they could not have it as matters stood, for at the time of Lincoln's inauguration, there was only a slight sentiment in the border states in favor of coercion as a means of preserving the Union.

The blundering at Charleston played into Lincoln's hands. One of Beauregard's lieutenants took upon himself the responsibility of firing on Fort Sumter when a fleet with provisions anchored off Charleston harbor. The Republicans used the cry that the flag had been fired upon to stampede the country, particularly those states which were doubtful, into war. Lincoln called for 75,000 volunteers to enforce the law of nature and of nations, which had become at this moment the purpose of his party.

This forced North Carolina, Virginia, Tennessee, Arkansas, and Texas into secession. Kentucky and Missouri determined to remain neutral.

Governor Harris of Tennessee realized that no state could remain neutral, and so managed to ally his state with the Lower South, although the Union sentiment was almost as strong in Tennessee as it was in Kentucky.

When Jefferson Davis called for 32,000 volunteers to protect the new Confederacy, many times this number answered the call. Bedford's mother was living at this time several miles out of Memphis on the Raleigh road. She had married a Mr. Luxton after her husband's death, and Bedford had several half brothers and sisters. One of these, Joseph, an eighteen-year-old boy, had been clerking in Memphis and enjoying the independence of a bachelor's life. He had enlisted in a town company and came out to see his mother before marching off to camp. He was dressed in a neat gray uniform, decorated with much gold lace and other fancy trappings.

People accused Mariam Forrest Luxton of being set in her ways, but this accusation made no impression on her habits and beliefs. The strongest of these was that her children should obey her and that no meal was so good as that which was made from corn grown on her own land and shelled under her personal supervision. As her son went to bed that night, she told him, "Joseph, I want you to get up early in the morning and go to mill with that sack of corn." She seemed not to consider that her son was a soldier now and living away from her roof.

At breakfast next morning—breakfast was by candle-light in Mariam's household—the gold-laced warrior's seat was empty. The old lady said to the servant waiting on the table, "Tell Mr. Joseph to come to breakfast right away," and added as the boy went off on his errand, "I am not going to put up with any city airs on this place." She then occupied herself with pouring the coffee and attending to the service of the meal. The servant presently returned with a message from her son that "he did not intend to go to mill; she might as well send one of the niggers with the corn."

When this message was delivered, she was just in the act of pouring out a cup of coffee. For a moment she seemed dumfounded at this impertinence, but not for long. She set the half-filled cup and the pot on the table and asked to be excused, directing that the breakfast proceed as she would return in a few minutes. She marched out into the yard, broke off three or four long peach-tree switches, and went directly upstairs, pulled her eighteen-year-old warrior out of bed and gave him such a thrashing that it brought back childhood memories. She made him put on an old suit of farm clothes and, accompanying him to the gate, lifted the two bushel sack of corn and slung it on the horse's back and waited in the yard until Joseph was on his way to the mill.

She came back into the dining-room, her eyes flashing and her face red from anger, to take her seat at the head of the table. "Soldier or no soldier, my children will mind me as long as I live."

Her oldest would never have questioned her discipline. It was said that when he was a lieutenant-general he was as docile in her presence as a child.

But there was another sort of recruit who came in from the country to answer Davis's call; and if he rode, it was on the back of a mule. The last of the Yeomanry, too, went to war. He brought with him no fine candies, but a jug of molasses, a sack of corn, and his father's musket which, if outmoded, could knock a hole in a man. One more friendly and generous than the rest drove his best cow into camp.

These young men were without medieval visions. They were going out to fight because they had heard the Yankees were coming down to tromp their fields and tear up their barns. They were the plain people, the freest people in the South, whom the cotton snobs referred to as the "pore white trash." And they were going away, leaving their steadings to their women-folks, to defend their particular way of life, although they would not have spoken of it in such flat terms. These men made up the largest body of people in the South. There were some four millions of them living in the hill country, on the borders of the plantations, and in the newly settled states like Arkansas and Missouri. The only difference between them and the cotton snobs was that of a generation or two, and the difference that the rich snobs were ashamed of their pioneer ancestry and they were not. Davis and his advisers made one great mistake that overshadowed all the other errors of policy: they chose to rest the foundations of the Confederacy on cotton and not on the plain people.

Bedford Forrest had risen from obscurity, like the majority of Southern leaders, like Davis himself; but there was no cotton snobbery in his make-up. He showed that his stock was strong enough to stand the responsibility of large properties. Instead of using his influence to get a commission, he enlisted as a private in White's Tennessee Mounted Rifles. This was in June, 1861.

A few days after his enlistment, certain citizens of Memphis made a trip to Nashville and convinced Governor Harris and General Polk, the bishop who had laid aside his vestments for the sword, that the ranks was no place for Forrest. The result of their trip was the commission of Lieutenant-Colonel, and the authority to raise a battalion of mounted rangers.

He began its organization at once. He scattered his agents through Mississippi, North Alabama, Middle and West Tennessee. Bedford himself set out for Kentucky. This state's neutral position made it a recruiting ground for both governments. Bedford realized that it was not only an excellent place to secure equipment, but that every man he brought out of the state would weaken by so much the enemy's armies.

On July 20, he bought out of his own purse 500 Colt's navy pistols, 100 saddles, and other equipment. But after he had made the purchases, he found it would be a serious matter to get them out. He

N. B. Forrest—Before the War

was a suspect, and he had overheard the Hon. J. J. Crittenden say he ought to be arrested. Fortunately, word was brought him at Louisville that a company was being organized for his regiment in Meade County. He went there and found the Boone Rangers, some ninety strong, under Captain Frank Overton.

Returning, he and two friends were able, from time to time, to carry the pistols under their linen dusters to a livery stable, whence they were subsequently taken to a Mr. Garrison's farm as so many bags of potatoes. The saddles were ordered to a tannery three miles out as so much leather. Here a detachment of Overton's troops appeared after dusk with wagons and hastily moved the freight southward, taking up the pistols as they marched toward the mouth of Salt River.

Lieutenant-Colonel Forrest, so soon as his orders were given, mounted his horse and rode leisurely in the opposite direction. On the outskirts of Louisville he quickly changed his course, circled the town and joined the cavalcade by picking up the tracks the wagons had made.

Pushing on toward Brandenburg, he found the Boone Rangers ready to take the field. So he left the same day, marching for Clarksville, Tennessee, by way of Bowling Green. The rumor soon reached him that two companies of Home Guards were waiting at Munfordsville to contest his march.

Following the Boone Rangers were many fathers and kin who wanted to stay by as long as possible. Bedford lined these up with the Rangers, under the Confederate flag, as a train passed by for Munfordsville. So imposing was the array that the passengers, when they arrived at the town, reported a regiment advancing. When the "regiment" arrived, the main force of the Home Guards had dispersed.

He arrived without mishap in Memphis the first of August, and in six or eight weeks he had raised eight companies, 650 rank and file. Parson D. C. Kelly persuaded the Alabama companies to join his command. A shrewd observer, he noticed that he could always get his requisitions through the various departments ahead of every other officer except Colonel Forrest. The success of a fighting unit is largely due to getting the right thing done at the right time. Kelly had the judgment to recognize this virtue in Forrest.

When the battalion was transferred to the Confederacy, Bedford was elected the colonel, Kelly the major, and by the last of October it reported ready for duty. It was ordered to Colonel Heiman, who was throwing up earthworks at Dover, Tennessee.

In the meantime, the Confederacy had won a great military victory in the East and had lost a great political battle in the West. They were Bull Run, and the loss of Kentucky to the Lincolnites, as the Republican government was called at this time in the Southwest. Of the two events, the loss of Kentucky outweighed the moral advantages of the military victory at Manassas. Lincoln himself had said that to lose Kentucky was almost to lose all; and he played a masterly game of politics to hold this state in line. Davis was like a child in his hands. Kentucky wanted to remain in the Union and keep its slaves too. Lincoln told them it was not a war against slaveholders, but a war to preserve the Union. This was exactly what Kentucky wanted to hear, and when Lincoln removed Frémont in Missouri because he declared his determination to free all slaves in that state, the doubtful Kentuckians were convinced. Davis played into Lincoln's hands when he allowed Polk on September 3 to occupy Columbus to raise fortifications guarding the mouth of the Mississippi River. The Borderland, generally, was driven further into the enemy's camps by the action of the Lower South in closing the Mississippi River to the Northwest in an attempt to coerce this section onto their side. This proved very bad tactics. It frightened the Borderland and threw their sympathies, which were all with the South, the other way. It showed them a very good reason why the Union ought to be preserved. It seemed the only arrangement by which they could command an outlet to world markets.

There was now left the Confederates only one card to play: they must conquer Kentucky by arms. This would make their extreme northern boundary on the Ohio River, which was deep and broad and easily defended. It would allow them close contact with southern Indiana, Illinois, and Ohio, which were still sympathetic and only needed some such manifestation of the Confederacy's strength to come over. As it was, Illinois and Indiana together sent ten thousand men into Southern armies. It would separate Missouri from the East and bring that state definitely on their side. The Lincoln general, Lyon, a dyed-in-the-wool abolitionist, had already prepared the ground by his violent action against slaveholders and all those who wanted to remain neutral.

On September 10, the good friend of President Davis, General Albert Sidney Johnston, was placed in command of the Confederate forces in the West, with the exception of the Gulf Coast.

On the fifteenth, Johnston assumed immediate charge of operations.

It remained to be seen whether or not he would play the only card that might make the Ohio River the Confederate line of defense.

Without losing any time, he took the offensive. On the seventeenth, Buckner with five thousand men was thrown into Bowling Green. Hardee was called from northwestern Arkansas. Johnston kept his four thousand men moving about in such a manner as to leave the impression that a large force was about to invade Kentucky.

The Northwest was thrown into a panic, and justifiably so, for Major Anderson, who surrendered Fort Sumter, had been made a general and put in charge of the Department of Ohio. Under his orders were three able lieutenants, Nelson, Sherman, and Thomas, and between ten thousand and twelve thousand recruits, disorganized and widely scattered.

Johnston could, at this time, have concentrated twenty thousand as raw recruits for an offensive. At no other time of the war were the Lincoln fortunes so at the mercy of the South. Over the five hundred mile front there was in Virginia an army of one hundred thousand in a theatre of war one hundred miles wide; in Missouri, sixty thousand disseminated over as great a front; in Kentucky the twelve thousand unorganized tenderfoots along, but not protecting, three hundred miles. This presented the dangerous and clumsy military situation of a heavy right and left, and a skirmish line for a center.

But the information at Johnston's headquarters was grossly inaccurate. This general believed as fact the exaggerated rumors of the strength of the Northern forces from their newspapers. Instead of marching to the Ohio River, he took up a line running through Columbus on the left, Bowling Green, the center, the Cumberland Gap on the right. He believed he was doing a very bold thing in going this far into Kentucky, for he was thinking, at this time, of his own supposed weakness, not of the enemy's.

So the Confederates lost this singular opportunity, one which, if it had been only partially successful, would have delayed indefinitely the invasion of the Southwest and entirely changed the face of the military situation. Even as late as November 10, Sherman said: "If Johnston chooses, he could march into Louisville any day."

When Colonel Forrest reported to Colonel Heiman at Fort Donelson, Johnston had settled down to strengthening his line. On October 8, Sherman, relieving General Anderson, was called to the command of the Department of the Cumberland.

Hopkinsville fell to the Confederates and Forrest, who had been operating his cavalry against gunboats, was ordered to report there to General Tilghman. This point had now become the outpost of the main body at Bowling Green.

Nothing startling happened to Colonel Forrest and his men. He made several reconnaissances in force, captured a richly laden transport, and hardened his men by long marches in severe weather, in the course of which these raw recruits, unaccustomed to such exposure and many of them weakened by camp diseases, suffered greatly. He lessened complaint, however, by sharing their hardships with them.

On these forays his green soldiers learned one very certain thing, that it was his single will, impervious to argument, appeal, or threat, which was ever to be the governing impulse in their movements. Everything necessary to supply their wants, to make them comfortable, he was quick to do. But he would not change his plans—not to please them, at least. The command grumbled, but when the work was achieved, it took pride in the achievement. The sooner soldiers learn they have a commander who intends to command, the sooner are they able to get down to the serious business of fighting.

It was customary to place the corn in piles in the center of the camp, and after reveille for each trooper to shuck so many ears for his mount. One morning Forrest found that a certain horse had slipped his halter and was having a fine time crunching away in one of the piles. The boy who owned him was brought up and dressed down for his carelessness. He protested that his horse was smarter than any other horse in the camp, and that no halter would hold him. The colonel then gave him minute directions about tying it. The boy retired from his superior's presence with a promise to obey the instructions and with an ill-concealed pity for his colonel's failure to appreciate the intelligence of his critter.

The following day the boy was again ordered to appear before the commander. He was threatened with arrest for disobeying his orders. "I done like you said, Colonel; but they ain't no halter that kin hold that critter of mine." Forrest told him that he himself would tie up the horse that night, and that he wanted the young trooper to stand by and learn how it was done.

The next morning the halter the colonel had fixed hung empty from its pole, and the critter was found, as usual, crunching away in the pile of corn. The boy tried not to hurt his superior's feelings, but there it was. There warn't no man could keep him from slipping his

halter if he took a notion to do it. Forrest took his defeat gracefully.
He examined the critter carefully and said that any horse that smart
was due to have more corn than the rest.

In these idle days of drill, dress parades, and guard mounts, a
Yankee detachment crossed the Ohio and abducted some Kentuckians
sympathetic to the Confederacy. While a squad was out hunting for
the murderer of the battalion's surgeon, it met ten Baptist preachers
on their way home from Illinois where the yearly association had been
held. They were noted Unionists, and camp life had grown dull; so
the boys thought they would have a little fun. They brought them in
and delivered them into the hands of the colonel. Forrest saw at once
how useful they would be in forcing the return of the gentlemen who
had been carried across the Ohio. He lined up the parsons and spoke
to them in language they recognized at once as the vocabulary they
had been wont to ascribe to the Lower Regions. Keeping eight as
hostages, he set two at liberty with the threat that if the abducted
Kentuckians were not returned within twenty-four hours, he "would
hang the remainder all on one pole." The two brethren left his headquarters with the smell of sulphur in their nostrils.

Harassed by the gruesome picture of eight three-hundred-gallon
Baptists hanging altogether on one Secession pole, the parsons be-
stirred themselves as they never had done in the service of the Lord,
and at the appointed time appeared with the kidnapped.

.   .   .   .

Some time in October, Lincoln's Secretary of War, on his way
back to Washington from Missouri, stopped at the Galt House in
Louisville, and there held a conference with General Sherman. It
was a hot day, and he lay upon his bed in calm repose, waving the
flies and heat away with a palm leaf fan. He had come out to satisfy
his generals in most of their reasonable demands and make a general
tour of inspection. Frémont, from whom Price was about to take
Missouri, had been replaced by Halleck, the methodical. Halleck
would not embarrass the government by issuing proclamations freeing
the slaves, and he had got Missouri well under control. The Secretary
felt very well pleased with his tour of inspection. It is true he had not
intended to stop over in Kentucky until Sherman had asked for a
conference, for his journey had been very fatiguing, and there were
matters to be looked to in Washington. But it was just as well he had,
however, because he could give some attention to the President's

favorite project of removing the Confederates from loyal East Tennessee. Turning very pleasantly to his eccentric-looking general, who had been earnestly outlining a plan of campaign to his superior, he said:

"Well, how many men will you need to conquer the Southwest?"

"Two hundred thousand to make the invasion, and fifty thousand to hold Kentucky."

The Secretary dropped his fan and sat squarely up in bed, like a Jack-in-the-Box.

"Two hundred thousand," he shouted; and he looked at Sherman as a man would look when he found that by accident he was locked in the same room with a lunatic.

The Secretary hastened back to Washington, and shortly after Sherman received an order relieving him of his command. The press openly informed the public that General Sherman's arduous military duties had affected his mind, and that he was temporarily relieved from duty that he might find some much-needed rest. This incident is important in one particular. It showed the state of mind of the Lincoln policy, that the war was important in the East, not in the West. The government which first realized that the war would be decided ultimately on western battlefields would have a decided advantage.

On November 15, Don Carlos Buell assumed command of the Department of the Ohio. This general was a soldier who understood his theatre of war. An army sets out to defeat an enemy that politicians may make their own terms. The best way to defeat an enemy is to rout its armies.

Buell tried to make his authorities see this, but Mr. Lincoln wanted to divert all of his forces to relieve the "sufferings" of the East Tennesseans. Buell knew the quickest way to this end was not to invade East Tennessee, but to crush Johnston. He submitted his plans to McClellan in a personal letter. They were comprehensive and called for a large force. It was already seen that Sherman's estimate was not so far wrong.

In West Tennessee, near the Kentucky border, the Cumberland and Tennessee Rivers, after passing through the state at right angles, come within ten miles of each other and then run parallel through southwestern Kentucky until they flow into the Ohio, the Cumberland above, the Tennessee at, Paducah. Where they begin to run parallel, two forts had been thrown up by the Confederates, Fort

Henry on the Tennessee, Fort Donelson on the Cumberland. Their strategic importance was vital. They constituted the most vulnerable part of the three-hundred-mile Confederate line.

Buell proposed that a heavy column move up these waterways while another moved on Nashville, east of Bowling Green. At the same time direct from Lebanon, by way of Somerset, an expedition against East Tennessee (this as a bribe to Lincoln's fears).

McClellan, who if given the world could conquer the world, dismissed Buell's letter from his mind. Like his chief, he too was thinking of East Tennessee. He was thinking how easy it would be for the Confederate authorities to hurl large masses of the Butternuts through this section to the detriment of his flank. Buell next wrote to Halleck in Missouri and was rewarded with a great silence.

This divided opinion in the enemy ranks continued to make life very dull for Forrest's battalion. Towards the close of December, however, he did run across a considerable body of Lincoln cavalry near the village of Sacramento. His scouts reported them numbering five hundred or more. The official report sets them down at 168.

The enemy was in a strong position, a grove of trees on either side of the roadway. With his few at hand, Forrest galloped forward, at his side a Kentucky belle who had ridden into camp to give him information, infusing as he gallantly recorded "nerve into my arm and . . . knightly chivalry in my heart." Bedford, it is seen, was to this extent affected by the romantic conception of gold-laced war.

This was his first real fight. He threw out a skirmish line to hold their attention until his scattered troopers might catch up. Quickly scanning the situation, he gave out his battle order. Kelly was to circle and strike the right flank, Starnes the left and rear. He listened with impatience for the noise which would tell him the movements had been completed. Presently, he saw Kelly swing around and Starnes reach a threatening position. He drew his saber, strained his eye for the first evidence of confusion in the enemy ranks. He sensed it; then, rising in his stirrups, ordered the charge. It was little better than a horse race. His men kept no sort of formation. Their greatest effort was to keep up with the leader, who, standing in his stirrups, pointing his saber at a thrust, looked like no ordinary man.

The enemy broke and fled over the icy mud of the December road. Bedford, far ahead of his own men, ran into a squadron whose officers had succeeded in rallying. He was soon fighting for his life. A quick, driving thrust, and the bluecoat, Captain Bacon, fell from his mount.

The Confederate captain Meriwether was close behind his commander. No Kentuckian could ever afford to let a Mississippian outride him in his own state. He rode hard, mighty hard, to meet a bullet in his brain. Next, Bedford and a Captain Davis collided. Davis' shoulder was knocked out of joint, and he quickly surrendered. Other horses, going too fast to stop, fell over those fallen in the road, until a pile of men and horses stopped all further pursuit.

Riding away with the prisoners of war, all the wounded being left in the care of kindly people, the Yankees first being paroled, Forrest's command felt very pleased with itself and its colonel. Their immediate superior was pleased. General Albert Johnston was pleased. He sent a very complimentary note to Forrest, commending his accurate report of the affair.

As they rode into camp, Major Kelly also felt satisfied with the day's work; but his pleasure was mixed with concern for the future. He had chosen a commander who was a magnificent fighter, but one too reckless with his person and his forces to live long enough to be of value to the cause. His disregard for ordinary tactics, even if he lived, would make his career, in all probability, a brief one. He wondered, perhaps, as they drew up to dismount, if he had done well to advise the Alabama contingent to throw in its lot with Colonel Forrest's.

PART TWO

DONELSON—A TRAGEDY OF ERRORS

PART TWO

DONELSON—A TRAGEDY OF ERRORS

CHAPTER V

Gray Lines Cross a River

IN November, at Belmont, across the river from the fortifications of Columbus, lay a camp of Confederates. Grant, nibbling the waterways, went there to capture it, but was driven away by Polk's subordinates. For the rest of the year all was calm along the western front, but it was an ominous calm for Albert Sidney Johnston. It indicated enemy preparations for an advance. The opening of 1862 broke into this with the noise of troops converging.

On January 10, Colonel Forrest, reconnoitering the strength, position, and intention of the Federals on Green River, satisfied himself that their activities foretold an early forward movement. He so reported to his immediate superior, General Clark, burned the bridges on Pond River, a small but deep tributary to the Green, and retreated to Hopkinsville.

Buell's plan of campaign was taking form in Halleck's mind. With two armies at Cairo and Paducah, under Grant and C. F. Smith respectively, he was perilously close to the Cumberland and Tennessee; and Buell was always a threat to Bowling Green.

On the nineteenth, at Fishing Creek, Zollicoffer was killed and his army cut to pieces by Thomas, one of Buell's lieutenants. The remnants, under Crittenden, retreated or, better, drifted southward. The Confederate right was no more.

There was now no doubt in General Johnston's mind that what he feared was about to come to pass. On the twenty-second he wrote: "To suppose, with the facilities of movement by water which the well-filled rivers of the Ohio, Cumberland and the Tennessee give

47

for active operations, that they will suspend them in Tennessee and
Kentucky during the winter months is a delusion. All the resources
of the Confederacy are now needed for the defense of Tennessee."
Among the resources of any government is the bold strategy of its
generals, bold enough to cover such defects as numerical inferiority,
a lack of discipline, or poor supplies.

The merits of this particular resource did not occur to Johnston,
as they did to another Confederate general in like circumstances,
General Lee during the Seven Days. The Western commander made
an effort to meet the situation. He ordered Buckner with eight thousand
men to cover the line before Green River back to Clarksville, a line
which protected his river forts from Buell. Orders, at the same time,
were dispatched to General Tilghman to strengthen Forts Henry and
Donelson. Major Gilmer, chief engineer to the Western armies, hurried to the spot to inspect the positions and make any changes he saw fit.

While this officer was going about his business, Halleck was making plans for the invasion. A movement was to be undertaken by land
and water against Fort Henry with U. S. Grant as its leader. Commander Foote, the pious, was to steam his ironclads up the Tennessee
and reduce the water batteries while the infantry under Grant invested
the rifle pits. With the garrison thus surrounded and taken in reverse by
the gunboats, it was expected to surrender or try to cut its way through
the investing lines. After Fort Henry was disposed of, the same tactics
were to be directed against Donelson.

On February 2, all was ready. The men aboard the transports, Foote,
on his flagship, squared himself on the poop. He looked once at his
ironclads, swept the river with his eye, glanced at the sky (none too
promising), then gave the signal. Foote's gravity was not this time
self-righteous. The river was at flood-tide, while the engines were none
too strong to meet the dangerous push of the water; and, just below the
surface in unknown parts of the river, the treacherous torpedoes rode
at their moorings, waiting to deliver sudden death to the unfortunate.

There was an expectant moment; then the wheels turned over—
the invasion was under way. Out of the black stacks heavy smoke rolled
in the damp air above the water to blow darkly southward, prophetic
of disaster.

The same day General Beauregard stepped into a train at Centre-
ville, Virginia, bound for the West. He had been ordered to report
to Johnston and take charge of the army at Columbus. It was thought
the popularity of the victor at Bull Run might bring more men to

the standard and in other ways assist the cause. After the complete route of Zollicoffer's force on the right of the western line, some uneasiness about the judgment of the general commanding manifested itself at Richmond. Beauregard would bring with him not only the weight of his name, but a sound military knowledge.

On the fourth, the fleet of gunboats anchored six miles below, or north of, Fort Henry. On the fifth the flag officer inspected the crew in their quarters and offered up a prayer for success; and on the same day Beauregard stepped down from the railway coach at Bowling Green.

Johnston welcomed him with cordiality. He at once explained the emergency his department must face: Halleck and 125,000 men (Grant had only 15,000 men). The disaster at Fishing Creek, Colonel Forrest's report of preparations for an advance in the Green River vicinity, and the massing of troops at Cairo and Paducah, all pointed out that the inevitable invasion had at last got under way.

To meet this, Johnston told the newly arrived general, he had scattered over his long front 45,000 recruits, mostly indifferently armed and disciplined: at Columbus, 17,000; at Forts Henry and Donelson, 5,500; on the Clarksville line, 8,000; and at Bowling Green 14,000. With the most strenuous efforts, against the apathy of the people and the wasting of disease, he was able to distribute only this many fighters. The prospects that glory might cover these arms seemed so slim to Beauregard, and the actual situation so different from the representations made to him, that he seriously considered returning to Virginia.

However, the next day, February 6, found him inspecting the works at Bowling Green. While the generals were so occupied, news reached them of Grant's aggressive presence on the Tennessee. There could be no longer any doubt about the Federal intentions. Johnston's hand had been forced.

From guarding a long frontier with tenuous bodies of troops he must prepare to face the armies of the enemy.

By using the interior, or shorter, lines of communication it was possible to concentrate the greater part of his scattered bodies and put an army in the field to meet separately those moving against him, even supposing them to be as large as he had figured. The thought of Halleck's 125,000 would not then be so depressing; for, subtracting from this number what the Lincoln general must keep in Missouri, and granting the different routes of invasion to split further the remainder the Confederates would have a single army equal to, or almost equal to, each of the different invading bodies. They might, even, in some instances be more numerous. This disposition of his troops would present the fascinating possibility of defeating Halleck and Buell in detail.

It was plain to see where the first blow must fall. Beauregard, therefore, urged the immediate evacuation of a position so salient as Bowling Green and a swift concentration at Henry and Donelson. It would mean the loss of some territory, but a loss which was unavoidable, since Bowling Green, without an army in the field, would fall of its own weight by a turning movement. In addition to the unreckoned advantage of concentration, the movement, while greatly shortening the Confederate line of defense, would put a river between Johnston and Buell.

Johnston temporized. Such a concentration, he told Beauregard, if he failed to repulse Grant, would open the way for a complete destruction of his army between the combined forces of this general and Buell; and it would hazard the loss of military supplies he had collected at such advanced posts as Bowling Green and Clarksville.

A general, certainly, must consider the eventuality of defeat; but why he should attempt to predict the outcome of a pitched battle (a thing Napoleon said no man could do) in favor of the enemy, was not clear to Beauregard. Particularly was it not clear how the two enemy generals could effect a junction, or cut off his retreat. Buell's movements must necessarily be slow. The roads this time of year were atrocious. And he faced the great difficulty of crossing a formidable river without pontoons, in the face of opposition, and in mid-winter, while Johnston, having use of the railroads and the side wheelers, could meet Grant and, whatever the outcome, could keep his face to Buell before this general was over the river.

But, when his army was in grave danger, to give as an excuse for not concentrating its scattered wings that some of his supplies would be placed in great hazard filled the bold Creole with forebodings most melancholy. It disclosed the fact that his superior had, to face the fact of an invasion, no definite plan of defense.

On February 6, Fort Henry fell after an hour's bombardment. It fell while the generals at Bowling Green debated. The flames leaped high above the river, and in their consuming heat the great chance to concentrate the Confederate forces east and west of the Tennessee went literally up in smoke. Had the Confederate headquarters desired to reconsider and accept Beauregard's advice, it was now too late. The enemy had relieved it of the effort of a decision by severing all easy connection between Columbus and the rest of the department. Its garrison under Polk was not only cut off; it was threatened with annihilation. And Nashville, the base in the West, if Donelson succumbed as quickly as Henry, must fall. With this a fact, Middle Tennessee and Kentucky would be lost to the enemy and, if Buell were vigilant, the army at Bowling Green would be cut off from retreat and cut to pieces. There was every reason to believe that Donelson would be no more effective for defensive purposes than Henry. It was only twelve miles away. In all probability Grant was then marching against it. The Confederates had to act, and at once, if anything was to be saved from the wreckage.

Such thoughts chased each other through Johnston's mind. He called another meeting of the general officers in Beauregard's quarters, where that commander had been confined by a throat infection, to consider what was to be done, or rather what line of retreat to pursue. There were two routes: the army could withdraw over the railway bridge at Clarksville, or at Nashville. Clarksville was nearer to Bowling Green.

Beauregard advised Clarksville, not to retreat, but to concentrate what was left against Grant, retaining east of the Cumberland just enough men to deceive Buell and impede his progress. His view was discredited. "The slight resistance at Fort Henry," writes Johnston, "indicates that the best open earthworks are not reliable to meet successfully a vigorous attack of ironclad gunboats, and although now supported by a considerable force, I think the gunboats of the enemy will probably take Fort Donelson without the necessity of employing their land force in co-operation." This misfortune would mean the loss of the Cumberland River and a further division of Johnston's forces, and the sickening prospect of their detailed annihilation, the reversal, therefore, of the hopes of Beauregard's policy.

In the emergency, Johnston finally decided to collect, if he could, his scattered armies at Nashville; and, if a further retrograde movement was necessary, then to withdraw through Stevenson, Alabama, and reunite somewhere along the Memphis and Charleston railroad with the West Tennessee brigades whose safe withdrawal he turned over to Beauregard. His quickest route, even if he refused the offensive, was across the bridge at Clarksville. He ordered the retirement by both routes.

The army at Bowling Green under Hardee was ordered to retire east of the river; those forces under Buckner and Floyd from Hopkins-

ville and Russellville to pass over the Clarksville bridge. He thus divided
his forces further in the retreat, leaving seventeen thousand to retreat
before Grant, fourteen thousand before Buell. At this time there was
no expectation in his mind to deliver battle in the vicinity of Donelson.
He hoped only that the troops already south of the river under Floyd,
and those which would cross, might hold the fort until Hardee could
safely effect his withdrawal to Nashville.

February 7 passed and no reports were received of Donelson's fall;
the eighth, the ninth, the tenth, the eleventh . . . all passed without
any notice of Grant's activity. He was still lingering from caution, or
indifference to his danger, at Fort Henry. Foote's flotilla had not been
seen. Fort Donelson from its bluffs still guarded the passage towards
Nashville, ready to collect what toll it might from unwelcome
traffic. If the fall of Henry was the beginning of a well-directed invasion under Halleck, the delays in the Northern camps, their lack of
co-operation between their different wings, pointed to some hitch in
the campaign. Victory is often the result of the quick uses of such errors.
But the delay and seeming lack of co-operation among the Lincoln
generals were more serious than any hitch in a campaign could ever
be. Fishing Creek and the thrust at Henry were not parts of a general
plan of campaign. They were separate actions by individual department commanders. The determined, unified campaign into Confederate territory existed only in the Confederate generals' minds.

The thrust at Henry had been made not from military, but personal,
reasons. Halleck was ambitious. He wanted the supreme command in
the West. He attempted through McClellan to secure this prize; but
McClellan, a friend of Buell, and for other reasons, refused the request. Halleck, not to be denied, determined to force his government's
hand. Grant's unsupported presence with fifteen thousand men at
Henry, in the midst of forty-five thousand, was the first step towards
this end.

The danger to which Grant was subjected would force Buell to
send troops to his help, thereby placing them under Halleck's orders.
And any offensive Buell might undertake in Central Kentucky would
have the appearance of assisting the primary offensive on the rivers.
To minimize his colleague's chances for glory, Halleck asked Buell to
make a diversion against Bowling Green. Buell replied with some asper-
ity that the time for diversions was gone.

Buell, however, was not able to come to Grant's assistance or even
to make an effective diversion against Bowling Green. He had for some

time set before his superiors, and before Halleck, this very movement as their true line of operations; and when he thought the suggestion had been dropped, he suddenly found that Halleck, without consultation, had set it in motion, and when his brigades were scattered in the mud of Eastern Kentucky preparatory to an invasion of East Tennessee. Halleck had taken Buell as much by surprise as he had the Confederates. The fortune of war, very subtly, to suit the gentility of his character, was offering alluring opportunities to Albert Sidney Johnston.

But Johnston made no change in his marching orders, orders which had been given with the expectation that Donelson would quickly fall. He seemed to have forgotten that he meant, "if any fault in his movements is committed, or his lines become exposed when his force is developed, to attack him as opportunity offers." So imbued was he with his friend Davis's passive-defensive policy, and his feudal defense of territory as such, that Johnston's mind froze with one intention, a quick and expeditious retreat, causing him to throw away the advantages of his interior lines and to misinterpret the enemy's delay. Up to and through the eleventh of February, Johnston regarded this delay as a stroke of luck making probable Hardee's safe withdrawal from Bowling Green. It was a stroke of luck, but he was to find that Good Fortune expects not appreciation but complete enjoyment of her gifts.

The orders to march were received with pleasure by the rank and file, although there was some uneasiness among them after the fall of Henry. It had been so sudden, and they had not been informed of the real causes. Those who had joined for quick and continued action welcomed the possibility of a fight, even if they had to march to the rear to get it. Drills and guard mounts were obnoxious to these spirits, and many of them had not had time to learn the regulation commands. So, more often than not, such orders as "Men, tangle into fours. By turn around! Git," mingled in the early dawn in loud, familiar tones with the sharper West-Point commands.

On the evacuation of Hopkinsville, Colonel Forrest brought up the rear as far as Clarksville, where he was detached and told to report to General Pillow. This officer ordered him to Dover. He arrived Sunday, the ninth, on the east bank. The next day he drew up his regiment to be ferried over the river.

He inspected them sharply before they boarded the ferry; then, as they moved off, his keen eye traveled down the squadrons, covering man and mount with a swift, comprehensive glance. The riders were not dressed for parade. Both man and beast were splotched with the mud of the Kentucky and Tennessee roads, but Bedford was not interested in appearances after a forced march. He was looking to see who had been hard on his mount, whose critter had cast a shoe, had corked itself; if any were limping; if any trooper had carelessly let his horse's back get rubbed.

The men, as they passed, knew what he was doing. They had become accustomed to these quick, accurate inspections. Around the camp fires, as a topic of gossip when horseflesh did not hold sway, some extraordinary discovery of neglect by him was always in place. And the delinquent knew to his sorrow what it meant not to pass. So, when he checked them up the first time, they often grumbled, but they obeyed, out of respect and from fear.

An officer usually controls his men in four ways: through fear, through respect, through love, or by his position. The last named is adequate for the garrison, but unreliable on the field. Fear alone is negative control and treacherous. Love and leniency too often go hand in hand producing sporadic results, while a soldier will, out of respect for the officer as a man, fight well so long as there is no unusual emergency. But to fear and respect the commander's military capacity at the same time brings the happiest results. An officer who possesses the hearts of his men by these two qualities holds his ranks in the palm of his hand. Bedford Forrest was such an officer.

As he sat there on his charger, his immense shoulders making the shanks of his stallion look puny, his head, imperiously turned, his face, stubborn and bold, no trooper thought of disobedience. They all knew, that is, all but the foolhardy, that his iron arms and mighty shoulders could handle any man in the regiment. After sixty-five long and turbulent years those of his soldiers who are left, when they speak of him, and that is often, always describe the mightiness of those shoulders as an ancient speaks of the pride and strength of his youth.

Consequently, Bedford's regiment was unusually disciplined. There was no stamp of automatic reaction about his young men, and most of them were young men, which a formal discipline leaves as its mark. They had a free, open look about them, an easy way of sitting their mounts, their bodies following the pace of the horse without effort, their muscular repose like a replete wildcat's stretch in the sunlight. About a few there was a fierce independence, the hard, unrelaxed stare of the zealot; but most were careless, indifferent of their dress, of their speech, of their officers, careless of all save their mounts and their colonel, seeming to regard life indifferently, giving it the same attention they would give a hoe-cake, relishing it when the meal is mixed with boiling water, eating it when slapped together. There is an art about this careless informality which an idle observer might confuse with disorder, not able to see that it is evidence of that highly precious, infrequent discipline which never fails in misfortune, the voluntary surrender of the will, judgment, and responsibility for life to another. It is the nearest approach men ever go in deifying one of their kind. The basis of this, like that of religion, is fear; but a fear which is forgotten and called love when the fruits of victory soften its pains and labors.

But the pains of labor were more in the trooper's mind at this point. Bedford Forrest was only a cavalry colonel, with some reputation; still untried, without a formal military education, crossing a river to take part in his first major engagement. His was one of the bodies of troops hastening to sustain the reputation of fire-eating Pillow, Kentucky Buckner, and the political-minded Floyd.

During the passage, he could examine the west bank and see Dover as it straggled about its rough hilltop. A little to the northwest another hill rose up, Dover's cemetery on top of it, and still farther down the river a ridge stretched along its bank, rising a hundred feet above the water. About the Cemetery Hill the Confederates had placed their supplies, while upon the ridge the fortifications of Donelson had been raised.

Just at the fort the river flows west, then turns abruptly north, bringing all traffic within easy range of the guns; and since the passage was narrow, the upper and water batteries had to be silenced before the river could be opened to strangers. On the crest and running down the slope facing the Cemetery Hill earthworks had been thrown up, and positions selected for artillery. Abbatis of felled trees and sharp-pointed saplings strengthened its defenses from this side, but Major Gilmer discovered on his arrival that this part of the works was commanded by the Cemetery Hill, which in turn was commanded by an uneven set of ridges, one-half to three-fourths of a mile away and spreading around the fort, the base of supplies, and Dover. So he and General Pillow took upon themselves the responsibility of laying out rifle-pits along this high ground.

This action of theirs changed the whole nature of the defense, for the works they ordered were to be three miles in extent, beginning in Hickman's Creek on the right and going to the south of Dover. They turned Donelson into an armed camp, requiring an army, not a garrison, to defend it. When Henry had fallen, only one-third of these works was up, and in spite of the unique vigor of Pillow's nature they were still incomplete when the cavalry colonel and his troopers reached the vicinity.

While he was drawing fodder for the horses, Forrest was ordered to make a reconnaissance towards Henry. He did so and reported to his superior that, from the preparations going on in the Northern camp, he expected Grant to make an early forward movement.

The movement would have to be made over two roads, one twelve and the other fourteen miles long. The northern, or Fort Henry road, reached the vicinity of the battlefield near a Mrs. Crisp's house, opposite the Confederate right. Here it bent like a crescent to follow the rifle-pits and then connected with the other, the Wynn's Ferry road, which ran directly east and west between the forts on the southern side. Bisecting this road was another, going from Dover to Charlotte and from there to Nashville, while hugging the river, and at the moment covered with backwater, was still another leading to the Cumberland Iron Works and hence eventually to Nashville. Upon these last-named wagon-roads depended the Confederate connection with Albert Sidney Johnston.

Floyd had been put in charge of operations in this theatre of war, and he was, at the moment, organizing a force at the Iron Works to act against the flank of the enemy. Pillow was there conferring with him and the fort was in command of Buckner when Grant, on the twelfth, began to advance. He moved forward in two columns. One column under C. F. Smith, a West Point superintendent and one-time professor to his superior, took the upper road; McClernand, the lower, with his own division and a brigade of Smith's. Together they numbered almost 15,000. A small reserve had been left at Henry under Lew Wallace, and additional reënforcements (10,000 of Buell's men) were expected under escort of Foote's flotilla.

The two columns moved with facility. The weather was mild for February, more like fall than winter; and there had been for ten miles not the slightest opposition. So it was with some degree of surprise that the Northern advance came very suddenly to a halt, two miles in front of the objective.

Acting Brigadier-General Forrest lay across the line of march with all the cavalry in the fort, about 1,300 strong. He had been sent forward in observation, and it was almost by accident that the Federals had any opposition. On the approach of the enemy he quickly dismounted his men and took up an oblique position sweeping the road. It was this which caused such a sudden halt. For several hours the Confederates, keeping up a steady fusilade from behind trees, rocks, and depressions in the soil, hung about the bluecoats with the angry sting of honey-bees at the approach of a robber. By swift, hard blows and sudden withdrawals he drove their cavalry back upon a body of infantry, checked a flank movement and so harassed the advance that Grant's entire army was held in check and hesitation for several hours. Colonel Forrest kept at this until Buckner ordered him back into the entrenchments. Grant, without further opposition, began to spread his infantry and artillery around the Confederates.

This continued throughout the afternoon of the twelfth until day-dawn of the thirteenth. McClernand found it would attenuate his lines too much to surround completely the Confederate left; so Grant ordered Wallace up from Henry and directed McClernand, until reën-forcements arrived, to occupy the enemy, but not to bring on a general engagement. Grant had in mind not only those battalions Wallace would bring, but those moving by water as well.

On the thirteenth, Floyd abandoned his plan and arrived at Donelson with a small brigade. This brought all the Confederate forces in this theatre of war within the bag around Dover. It only remained to be seen whether Grant could draw the cords. This he expected to do. Flag-officer Foote was bringing the iron-clads to reduce the water batteries. His infantry was to their front.

There was grave uneasiness in the butternut ranks. It was not openly admitted, but the Southerners felt in their hearts that the gunboats were invincible. In spite of the concern felt so generally they worked away on their rifle-pits, determined to fight it out. Buckner command-ed the right, Pillow the left, and Colonel Heiman the center of the line. The center was a hill, cut off from the right and the left by the low ground around Indian Creek. This stream divided about this hill, meeting in the valley behind it to flow west into the Cumberland. This time of year it was swollen, making communication between the left and right difficult.

As McClernand drew closer, the Confederate batteries delivered such severe punishment, particularly Maney's which stood out in the open in front of Heiman's line, that he decided to take the hill. Turning against it a heavy cannonade between eleven and twelve o'clock, he launched an attack with four regiments. On the face of it, this was a foolhardy thing to do, to throw without support a single brigade against breastworks which could be reënforced from the whole Confederate army. But the Northwestern volunteers advanced with enthusiasm to their work, ignoring with a beginners' optimism the ominous mien of Maney's, Grave's, and Drake's guns, a direct line of fire doubly crossed. McClernand's left advanced along a ridge obstructed with abatis, the right up an open hill, at the top of which stood Maney's battery, the common target.

His gunners, in relief against the sky, fell in quick succession, but like the dragon's teeth two rose up where one fell down. Maney himself was hit, standing out there in the open, rolling his iron balls among the moving pins. Still on they came, until for a brief moment it seemed their self-confidence might sweep them over the guns. Then suddenly, the long line of yellow breastworks, full of Heiman's tall men, turned into flame. The bluecoats staggered, braced up, and for fifteen minutes shot blindly at the yellow piles of gravelly dirt before they broke back down the hill. At the foot they rallied about their flags to move up once more, but the concentration of death in so small a place was too great for them. Badly shattered and full of lead, they fell back permanently, while the smoke from burning leaves and burnt powder covered their withdrawal.

The first blood to the Confederates. This handsome repulse stiffened their morale. They did not know that it had been against orders. The same day, the thirteenth, the gunboat *Conestoga* steamed within range of the water batteries and opened a cannonade. After throwing one hundred and fifty shot among the ravines she withdrew discomfited, a hundred and twenty-eight pound bolt in her engine room.

The weather changed in the afternoon. It snowed; the snow turned into sleet, and a sharp wind, blowing from the north, drove through the butternut cloth with a vengeance. To make matters worse, the enemy boats arrived during the night, and the transports began to unload fresh levies which would be put in motion next day to take their places between Smith and McClernand. They had only two or three miles to march.

The Confederates, with such thoughts on their minds, shivered and dug away on their entrenchments. Bedford and General Bushrod R. Johnson took off their coats and worked with the men. There was no comfort to be had anywhere that miserable night. Even those who were fortunate enough to reach a fire found that its virtues turned to ashes when they tried to enjoy them. Their rears scorched while the front part of their clothing stiffened with ice. Nor was there any escaping the dilemma. To change position meant only to thaw what had been frozen and to freeze what had been scorched.

The dawn of the fourteenth was welcomed only because it brought the night to a close, for the weather remained as cold as ever. Floyd met with his general officers and determined, in view of the reënforcements, but particularly because of the gunboats, to reopen the way to

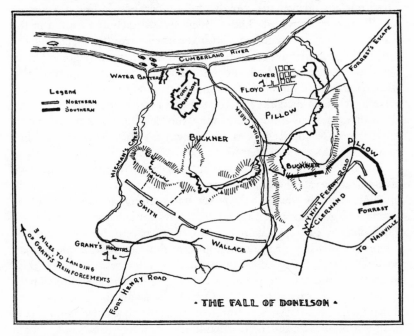

· THE FALL OF DONELSON ·

Nashville by a sally on the enemy's right. The sally was planned for the afternoon.

Why he put the attack off is not clear. All morning the Confederates lay idle in their works while the divided wings of Grant's army slowly and steadily drew together. Time was precious. Every minute Floyd delayed, he allowed the enemy to strengthen, lessening continuously his chances to escape, for he seems not to have thought he might defeat the enemy in battle. His army, although his fears denied it, was as large as one wing, larger than the other. The opportunity to smite them separately, before they could effect a junction, dangled before him. The thirteenth had been lost. On that day the minds of the Confederate generals remained in a state of suspended animation, and whatever opportunities they had for a counter stroke were wasted. But the fourteenth was open, either to crush or to escape from the enemy. Rarely does opportunity knock twice, and knock so vehemently, at the same door. Floyd hardened his heart to these knocks and waited, fascinated at the approach of the odds piling up against him.

Then, about three o'clock, the fleet of gunboats, four ironclad and two wooden, steamed up the Cumberland towards the water batteries. The ironclads opened fire, slowly and deliberately at first, then more rapidly as they advanced. The wooden vessels anchored a mile in the rear and began throwing shot into the ravines and hills behind the fort. With the first report, whatever activity there was going on in Donelson ceased, and the hilltops in view of the water rapidly filled with spectators, some anxious, some fearful, some merely interested, some looking on as if they were at the last great cock fight . . . but all with eyes fixed immovably upon the developing attack. Colonel Forrest took Major Kelly and rode down a small ravine where they could get a close and protected view.

For an hour the outcome hung in the balance. There were only two of the Confederate guns which were damaging at long range. One of these accidentally got spiked. When its booming no longer split the ears of the gunners, a feeling of depression settled down upon them. Their chances of victory were reduced fifty per cent, for at the present range the small artillery, eleven pieces, did no more damage than pop guns. And, Foote, when he made the discovery, became reckless. With the regularity of a pendulum swinging only in one direction, as if they would drive into the western bank itself, the gunboats bore down upon the fort. At three hundred yards they backed water, quickly swung around, two on the east bank and two on the west. Anchored at this distance, they turned loose their broadsides on the batteries.

The fate of the garrison, now, seemed definitely sealed. The heavy projectiles hurtled through the air tearing great gaps and fissures in the parapets, burying, almost, the guns under the débris. The fury and the noise cracked over the Cumberland, constricting its surface, leaping over its banks to reverberate around the ridges and down the ravines. At the height of this, Bedford turned to Major Kelly and shouted, "Parson, for God's sake, pray, for nothing but God Almighty can save that fort."

But the gunners no longer felt the need of supernatural power. On the contrary, a feeling of elation ran through their hearts at this close range work. For the first time their lighter cannon had become effective. Foote, with a valor born of overconfidence, had stuck his neck out. The gunner-boys proceeded in a very direct way to chop it off.

A solid shot plunged through the pilot-house of the flagship and carried away the wheel. The *St. Louis,* out of control, drifted with the current. Its pilot was dead, the one on the *Louisville* wounded. A 128-pound shell struck the anchor of the *Carondolet,* smashed it to bits, then jumped over the vessel with a part of the smoke-stack.

Then, as luck would have it, a shot got stuck in the *Columbiad,* the big gun. There was a moment of dismay, but only a moment. For ten good men and true stepped over the parapet, and in air so thick with lead as to imperil the passage of a bird, cut a young tree down, rammed the shot home, washed the bore out with water, and took their positions back on the platform.

"Now, boys," said the gunner, "see me take a chimney." The *Carondolet's* flag-staff and its chimney dropped far into the current. This seemed definitely to turn the tide of battle. Harder and faster fell the battery shot, stripping side-armor, cutting boat-davits, breaking wheels, smashing rudders, until one by one Flag-Officer Foote saw his boats twirl aimlessly in the river.

Floyd, at his headquarters, was startled by a great noise, the shouts of triumph rolling back from the river. It was no ordinary cry of triumph. There was about it the sound of a mighty Thanksgiving, shattering as its echoes rose and fell the specter of the invincible gun-boats. They were found to be vulnerable, made of the material of this world, and therefore open to destruction.

The repulse of the river fleet having been successfully achieved, it only remained for Floyd to follow it up with his sally which had been arranged for four o'clock. It was now half after the hour. This meant that the afternoon was going rapidly towards night. Floyd conferred with Pillow. It was too late to attack, he thought. Floyd postponed it until morning.

The spirit of the Confederate soldiers that afternoon was at its height. It could have swept all before it. The men would retain their self-confidence next morning, but that spontaneous feeling of invincibility would be lost forever. If every man had been in position ready to act as soon as the river contest had been settled, Floyd might have loosed its vehemence upon the enemy; but, now, before this could be done, the early winter night would set its darkness down.

That evening, another council was held, the brigade and regimental officers attending. As an impetus to the meeting Floyd had received a telegram from Albert Johnston, admonishing him to save the army even if he must lose the fort. This was like dropping the baby in the fire; then calling on it to crawl out without getting itself burned.

But the commanding brigadier had little time to speculate on the telegram. He was explaining the order of battle. Pillow was to make the assault on the right of the Northern line and retake the road which led to Nashville. Buckner, as soon as Pillow's attack was well developed, was to strike their center and assist in the attack on his left. Colonel Head, with 450 men, was to march into Buckner's abandoned rifle-pits and hold them while the attack was going on. If it proved successful, Buckner could act as rear guard and protect the withdrawal. Colonel Forrest with all the cavalry was to keep to the extreme left and protect the line from being flanked in that direction, as well as to assist in the general attack. The officers were dismissed to lead their troops into position. The weather, heretofore so bitter, did not seem so unbearable that night as on the nights before.

CHAPTER VI

The Blue Racer Circles, and the Rattler Coils, in the Tennessee Bottoms

WITH the first light of day, after the mists had lifted from woods and river, the frozen dampness shone fitfully upon the backs of 20,000 bluecoats tightening their lines about Donelson and Dover. Besides these, on board the transports and on the march, 7,000 more were within easy call. So at last, on the fifteenth, Grant had completed his investment of the place.

This done, at an early hour he left the field to confer with Foote. The repulse of his gunboats had considerably changed Grant's plans. There were, necessarily, re-adjustments to be made. Taught by McClernand's rash movement against Heiman that an overzealous subordinate may disastrously upset plans, he made it clear to his division commanders that they were not to leave their positions without specific orders. This, if any part of the army were attacked in its general's absence, prohibited the other parts from going to its assistance. It seems a strange order, but it was an early characteristic of Grant's that once he had made up his mind about an opponent, he was slow to change it; and stranger still, he apparently expected his enemy to conform to these opinions. And this time he had made up his mind that Floyd would remain on the defensive-passive and stay behind his works.

But the Confederates, their butternut clothes diamond-backed with fresh mud, had been concentrating all night in front of Oglesby's brigade of McClernand's division. Their subdued preparations, their certain movements, whirred ominously. As Grant rode off, they were collecting their venom to strike.

If a buzzard, floating upon the acrid odors of powder and stale sweat, had looked beneath him that morning, he would have seen a mighty blue-black racer, its tails in the swamps of Hickman's Creek, its head on high ground south of Dover, its body gliding among the slopes and bottoms between, waiting to squeeze the breath from its

natural enemy, a rattler, coiled around Dover, and swaying dangerously with its poison.

At five o'clock, the skirmish line shook its rattle of musketry, and
a little after the Confederates struck. They drove through the underbrush and thickets with difficulty, in a line like a wedge, flattening out
against the enemy as its point struck simultaneously McArthur's left
and Oglesby's right.

The fight at once became close and bloody. The Southerners, in
their fall-colored clothes, rushed in to make their shotguns and squirrel
rifles count. They met a stubborn resistance. It took almost two hours
for Pillow's division to become completely engaged. The Northwest-
erners met them at every point, holding to the ridges as if they belonged to them by undisputed inheritance. The Confederates, however,
were not deceived. They knew a squatter when they saw one, and
they knew better what would happen if he were not driven from
the land.

Pillow and Johnson now launched a general attack. They moved
through the woods like "cats;" they "skulked," as Oglesby reported
"behind every hiding place, and sought refuge in the oak leaves, between which and their uniforms there was so strong a resemblance
our men were continually deceived by them." They also dropped behind stumps, counted out their double B shots and two drams of powder, leveled their long smooth-bore barrels, drew beads on patches of
blue appearing through the smoke in the fir underbrush, and let go.
The long smooth bores carried the double B shot like a slug and tore
large holes in an enemy's flesh, or broke and scattered against some
young sapling. Many a hunter who could bring a squirrel out of the
highest tree found it was a different matter when a squirrel also had a
rifle. Holding to the trees like chipmunks, they moved forward slowly
but regularly until sharp orders brought them to a halt. The lines were
quickly and roughly dressed. Then men waited, grim-lipped, for the
charge they had been told to expect; and the icy leaves cracked and
broke beneath thousands of heels digging in the ground. A moment of·
nervous silence; then the unhesitating, the explicit, bugle, and with a
sudden sweep, as if the ground had jumped up, Pillow's men went
forward.

In the meanwhile, Colonel Forrest had been traveling the extreme
left of the line. The country over which he was moving was almost
impossible for cavalry—the Federals made no attempt to use theirs—
but his orders had been clear. Suddenly, after a slow and trying pro-

gress, he discovered he had turned McClernand's right and was well
in his rear. Rising slightly in his saddle, he peered through the vines
and branches. There was exultation in his eyes, gray like two balls of
shattered steel, so alert, so savagely clear, for he was where he had
set out to be, where he could do the most damage. To the front the
sound of the rebel yell rolled over the ridges. He turned swiftly and
gave an order.

As McArthur and Oglesby braced themselves for Pillow's on-
slaught, the rebel yell filled the country-side, echoing even from
the ravines to the rear, except that hoof-beats and wilder shouts mingled
there, too realistic, as McArthur found to his undoing, to be echoes.

Forrest, rising in his stirrups with his might, holding his sword
poised for its work, tore out of the woods like some terrific apparition,
his men and their excited critters, almost gone to pieces from dodging
saplings and brush, hard after him. About the same time Pillow and
Bushrod Johnson struck from the front. The shock was too great.
McArthur could not withstand the weight of both attacks. He withdrew, intact but overpowered, to his left and rear, uncovering as he
went by Oglesby's right. Oglesby, in turn, to keep from being turned,
withdrew, and so on down the line.

The Federals rallied on a second line and held fast. After some
time, their fire extended towards their extreme right, indicating a
design to turn the Confederate left by a counter. They were at one end
of an open field. Colonel Forrest was at the other. He ordered a charge,
but it failed. The ground was too miry for the weight of cavalry, but
he so manœuvred to their front and right that they hesitated and
were checked, for General Johnson was given time to come up with
sufficient infantry to meet the counter. He fell against it and knocked
it to pieces. It was a most opportune moment, for the Federals were
almost out of ammunition. Repeated calls had been sent for reënforcements, but Grant's officers had strict orders to remain in position. All
they could do was refer the couriers to Grant, and he was to the rear
and some miles away.

By 9:30 the enemy's right was in full retreat. Oglesby, the most
stubborn of McClernand's lieutenants, ceased to have any formation.
He had left upon the field 836 dead and wounded to tell how valiantly
the Illinoisans had fought. His men, as they fled, held up their empty
cartridge boxes to tell why they must go away. This was one, but not
the only, reason. The long hunter's rifles were a better reason.

Lew Wallace, commanding the center, like the fine officer he was, decided in the emergency to disobey Grant's orders. He sent Cruft's brigade to reënforce the dissolving right. As it came upon the field, the 25th Kentucky (Federal) in its eagerness to fight began firing on the regiments it had been sent to support. This was the straw that broke the back of McClernand's resistance.

There was panic in the air. Forrest, the son of the wilderness, whose life had been one long lesson in detecting such moments, knew the crisis had been reached. An advance all along the line would not only open the way to Nashville. It would curl the enemy's lines into the swamps of Hickman's Creek. He galloped to Bushrod R. Johnson and pleaded with him to give the necessary orders. General Johnson refused. The enemy, he thought, after so obstinate a stand, would not of their own accord withdraw so rapidly. They were drawing the Confederates into ambush. Certainly he would advance, but cautiously. Forrest looked desperately for Pillow, but he was not on this part of the field. He was gone to find out why Buckner had not come out of his works.

Thwarted and unable to influence the battle at the decisive moment, and ordered to look out for the left flank, he galloped forward. Seeing a battery about to leave its position, he swooped down and took its six fine guns, its horses, and a number of prisoners. He then followed up the retreat and found a body of troops, the last hope of stemming the gray tide, at right angles to their general line of battle, strongly fixed in a deep road cut. Into this covert he went, never glancing behind to see if his men followed. He had no need for this. Their only worry was that he would keep too far ahead, these men who rode with Forrest. The critters who from fatigue or from wounds lingered shamelessly behind sorely tried the patience of their riders. Into their ears fell the strangest mixture of blasphemous endearment and abuse, fit, the chargers must have thought, only for a mule. Before the Confederate hoofs could beat upon them, this last resistance melted into the general retreat.

The Confederate right had now done its share of the work. What was left of McClernand's division was reforming behind the two fresh brigades of Lew Wallace, brigades which should have been occupied by Buckner. But while the left was sweeping everything before it only a heavy artillery duel took place between the centers. Believing he would have to bear the brunt of the retreat, Buckner had attempted to keep his men as fresh as possible. It seemed not to have occurred to him that without his assistance there might be no withdrawal.

Finally, after a delay of several hours, Pillow ordered him from his works. The attack had been delayed too long, however, to expect that Grant's divisions might be rolled into the swamps of Hickman's Creek —his broken right had already recovered from its momentary panic and was re-forming behind Wallace—but there was still a chance to withdraw in safety towards Nashville. This chance depended on Buckner's possessing that part of the Wynn's Ferry road to his front.

There was one very serious obstacle to Buckner's advance, a section of artillery which the Confederate gunners had been unable to dislodge. Pillow looked hastily about: "They must be silenced. Forrest must do it."

At the end of a ravine sloped a hill; on top of this hill were the damaging guns, formidably planted at the head and sweeping the approaches, and it was up this avenue the sally had to be made.

At the moment Bedford was galloping towards the center. Pillow rode out to meet him. They conferred together, the general and his cavalry colonel, the one pointing his nervous finger towards the battery, the other rising slightly in his stirrups to scan better the hill-top and its long flashes of steel in the woods behind.

It seemed almost a desperate venture. Bedford hesitated a moment, while from his charger's wounds, measuring time's awful finality, the blood dropped regularly to the ground. In the front and to the right, Buckner's men under Brown, moving over ground bristling with abatis and snow-clad undergrowth and broken by ravines, had been subjected to a terrible exposure in their piece-meal assault on Wallace. For a moment they were thrown into critical confusion. The possession of the Wynn's Ferry road meant departure. Forrest said suddenly, "I can try."

Immediately turning off, he drew a part of his command up in an open space for the work ahead, in column of squadrons. To his rear Colonel Roger Henson and his Kentucky orphans lay idle. Cavalry might take the guns, it could not hold them against infantry support; so Bedford asked for the Kentucky colonel's co-operation.

The order to charge was given, with instructions for the first and second companies to deploy to the right and left as they advanced. Hanson followed as eagerly, withholding the fire of his men. The smoke of battle hung to the ravine like an ugly fog, and the hail of lead rattled the vines and undergrowth, until it fell, melting little holes in the frozen ground. A man would drop, but the ranks closed up upon his empty place. A horse would stumble and plunge forward into the snow, roll on his back and kick his legs convulsively for a while. The rider, jumping out of the saddle, would pull up his pants and move forward on foot, keeping his eye skint for the first emptied saddle.

They reached a narrow clearing. Bedford half-rising in his stirrups —the men knew what this meant—swung high his blade towards the enemy and charged the hill. Immediately from the hoofs of his men's horses clods of frozen turf filled the air. The Kentucky regiment, still holding its fire, followed the gallant Hanson at quick time. The entire hill-top broke into flame, and from the gray infantry lines fifty men dropped before its heat. But on they moved, these thoroughbreds from the Blue Grass and the Pennyroyal, to break the crimson ribbon that would end the race. Up to fifty yards they went without moving their guns from right shoulder. There they were stopped by Hanson's voice, and there they began to pour a destructive fire into the battery's support.

In the meantime Forrest's riders had fallen upon the battery. About it a hand-to-hand struggle ensued for some minutes. The gunners stood their ground and fought manfully, so manfully that they fell in piles about their guns. At one spot the feet of the artillery horses splashed in the blood of the slain and the wounded, until black from the weather it froze along the surface of the snow. Bedford reached the position on foot, for his charger, bleeding from seven wounds, lay on the hill-side where he was stopped. Bedford's overcoat had fifteen bullet marks on it and through it. He was truly a son of the gods. Only so close, not too close, would they allow death to approach him.

The position was gained and held. Hanson had seen to that. What seemed impossible had been accomplished. Graves's battery was ordered up to secure it. Brown's brigade had recovered and driven the enemy from two positions in succession with no great loss of men. The Confederates were now masters of this part of the Wynn's Ferry road. Pillow had driven their right a mile, and his men were masters of that part of the field. The plan advanced by Buckner in council, despite certain blunders, the worst of which had been made by this general himself, had been carried out to the letter. The way to Nashville was open. The order to march, not the enemy, stood between Floyd's forces and a reunion with Albert Sidney Johnston. But that order was destined never to be given.

At a little past two o'clock in the afternoon Pillow ordered his own and Buckner's brigades back to the rifle pits.

CHAPTER VII

Capitulation . . . to a Picket Fence

IN the dead of night, between one and two o'clock, when man's physical resistance is supposed to be at its lowest, Colonel Forrest was aroused from a heavy sleep and told to report to General Pillow's quarters at Dover.

As he left camp, he passed Johnson's and Heiman's men huddled together to keep from freezing. They had been massed for a second sally, a second attempt to reach Nashville, which was to take place at daylight, provided the enemy had not reinvested.

He arrived at Mr. Rice's house and was sent up to Pillow's room. For a moment he hesitated in the doorway, his immense shoulders blocking the entrance and casting on the wall opposite a shadow, grotesque, admonishing. Before him, gathered about a table and its usual decanter, were the three generals who held in their hands the fate of Tennessee and possibly that of their cause. Three is a mystic number, and there was a suggestion of magic, of black magic almost, acting upon that council of officers at that hour of the morning.

He stepped in and saluted. He was told at once that a set of scouts had returned with the information that the enemy was reinvesting. He said he did not believe it. He had been over that part of the field late in the evening gathering up arms and removing the wounded, and he had seen no sign of hostile forces. As late as nine o'clock that night men of his command had passed over the ground and had reported no return of the enemy. Since the fighting had ceased at two o'clock, it seemed reasonable to believe that Grant, if he had intended to reinvest, would have done so much earlier. And furthermore, he did not credit the report because the Yankee right was badly handled and in no condition to resume its position.

He was ordered to send out two scouts to verify his statements.

They returned in an hour and reported that they had seen no enemy, but that his campfires of Friday were ablaze.

Floyd and Buckner ignored the fact that the scouts did not go close enough to the fires to verify the impression that they had been made by a reinvesting army. They put together the fact of the fires with the information received from other scouts, the appearance of long, heavy lines of what seemed armed men, and decided that the avenues of escape were closed. Colonel Forrest surmised that these were not new, but old, campfires which the wind, being very high, had fanned into flame and which the wounded had fed to keep from freezing. He suspected this to be the case because very few of Grant's wounded had been collected up to the time he had inspected the field. The Confederate relief parties had carried some Northern men to these very fires, had wrapped them and left them there.

But his conclusion was not credited. To Floyd and Buckner capitulation seemed inevitable.

Pillow urged that the attempt be made anyway to cut their way out, or to make another fight and hold the position one more day until the boats which had left with the wounded could return and ferry the command to Clarksville.

To this Buckner answered: "I cannot hold my position half an hour after the attack." In the afternoon Smith had driven Head back and made a lodgment in the works before Buckner could return to his position.

"Why so, sir? Why so, general?" asked Pillow in a nervous, sharp voice.

"Because I can bring into action not over four thousand men, and they demoralized by long and uninterrupted exposure and fighting, while the enemy can bring any number of fresh troops to the attack."

"I differ with you. I think you can hold your lines. I thin'k you can, sir."

"I know my position, and I know that the lines cannot be held with my troops in their present condition."

"Then," suddenly replied Pillow, "we must cut our way out."

Buckner said that if he attempted this he would be seen by the enemy, be followed and cut to pieces.

Bedford Forrest then spoke up eagerly and assured Buckner that he might withdraw his men under cover of the cavalry.

Buckner answered as if he had not heard him, and it is doubtful if he had, for by this time his heart had hardened to Pillow. The attempt to withdraw would mean the sacrifice of three-fourths of the entire army, and it was not right to sacrifice three-fourths to save one-fourth.

Floyd, who rarely spoke at this conference, except to intone with the tragic notes of an Aeschylean chorus, assented that it would be wrong to sacrifice three-fourths to save one-fourth. One of the strange things about the defense of Donelson is that none of the accounts speaks of the commander as taking any active part on the actual field of battle. It is very difficult to visualize him as being in any way connected with Donelson.

Then Bedford, in a desperate attempt to save the situation, agreed to cut his way through any part of the enemy's line the generals might designate, and then lead the army out through that gap. For good measure, he again promised that the enemy cavalry would not harass their flanks or rear.

To this Floyd and Buckner's reaction was a vague allusion to artillery that would be brought to bear upon them.

With this Bedford, little given to argument, turned contemptuously and stalked angrily out into the night to cool his temper and settle his bile. He hesitated at the door and said loud enough to be heard, "There is more fight left in these men than you think."

But if he had thundered when he spoke, he would have made no impression on the council. The fatal combination of certain qualities of character belonging to Floyd, Pillow, and Buckner was now forcing the climax to this tragedy of errors being enacted around Donelson. For the first, but not the last, time these butternut soldiers were to see their victories vanish at the hands of their commanders.

Albert Sidney Johnston had made the first of a long series of blunders when he failed to concentrate immediately south of the river, and a second almost as serious. He should have gone to Donelson himself, and taken charge, and let Hardee manage the retreat from Bowling Green, particularly since Donelson was threatened in fact and Bowling Green only potentially. There is this to be said for Johnston, however: he had received a correct estimate of Grant's strength, and he sent sufficient troops to meet him. But here it is hard to follow his reasoning. Unless he changed his mind as to Grant's strength, why did he fear to meet him in a pitched battle? At any rate, after dividing his army, he did well to place that part of it not under his direct supervision under one general. But if his decision was sound, his choice of general was disastrous.

Floyd, under certain circumstances, was a capable officer. He had had a minor success in the West Virginia campaign; but here he was singularly unfitted for his position. His military knowledge was limited, for it had been chiefly acquired while he was Secretary of War under Buchanan; and he was unfitted by nature to use the talents of his lieutenants. He was impetuous and extremely sympathetic, possessing that flexible quality of mind so valuable to a certain class of politicians which allowed him to accept a foreign set of ideas as his own. There was a strong antagonism of character and feeling between Pillow and Buckner, and the influence of each swayed Floyd. At times he became Pillow's mouthpiece, at times, Buckner's. To this it is possible to trace much of the accumulation of errors, blunders, and wasted opportunity which culminated in the final disaster.

Floyd's original plan of campaign was a good one. Buckner concurred with him that it was the best. It was, in brief, to retain a heavy garrison at Fort Donelson under Pillow while all the rest of the troops were concentrated at Cumberland City to act upon Grant's flank as he approached to attack. Under this arrangement, so long as the flanking body of Confederates remained undefeated, the enemy could not besiege the fort. If it were defeated, it held the railroad to Nashville and could retreat by this means. Pursuit would be difficult on account of the rough and broken country, and at the expense of leaving the rear open to attack by Pillow. At the worst it meant the sacrifice of Pillow, rather than the whole army, to Johnston's safe withdrawal to Nashville.

But Pillow was not the sort of general to be an Isaac to Floyd's Abraham, and he had a Mexican War reputation which was not to be taken lightly. When Buckner was despatched by Floyd to Dover on the eleventh to bring out his own brigade to Cumberland City, Pillow refused to let it go. He wired Albert Johnston; then went in person to Floyd to explain his disobedience. Johnston wired Floyd Pillow's despatch and, as was proper, refused to interfere at such a distance. Then Pillow came down upon Cumberland City like a whirlwind and swept Floyd off his feet.

Floyd had been under Buckner's influence for several months. That meant that he weighed military chances by positions, the number of regiments, and not by the more intangible resources of an army. Buckner overestimated the strength of the enemy, but he was sound in thinking no good would come of locking up the army within the fort. This was Pillow's idea. He was a fire-eater, possessed tremendous energy, the respect of his troops and his superiors; but his enthusiasms were likely to be unstable. And he had an inordinate amount of histrionic ability which would not permit him to accept a post of such great danger with so little chance for a flourish.

But at the time, he honestly felt that if all the troops were concentrated at Donelson, victory was certain. And in the light of after events, there is much to be said for his position, provided he had been the senior brigadier. He could have aroused the enthusiasm of the soldiers, and this is a tremendous advantage among green troops, as no other general on the ground could have done. But he was not the senior brigadier.

Floyd was never convinced by Pillow, but he allowed him to argue, and while they argued Grant moved around Donelson without any obstruction. It then became too late to withdraw Buckner. The only thing left to do was to accede to Pillow's request and move the rest of the troops, too few in themselves to be a flanking army, into the fortifications.

Floyd's mistake was to argue with his lieutenant. Jackson would have put him under arrest, but Floyd did not believe strongly enough in his own plan. He never believed in anything strongly enough, if we are to judge from his actions here, to act with unequivocal decision, and Buckner was away at Dover and could not be on hand to reenforce his beliefs with argument. So the senior brigadier entered the arena at Donelson with the feeling in his heart, if not on his lips, "He who enters here leaves all hope behind."

He had been silent when he should have asserted himself; he was now to order when he should have remained silent. Having given up his own plan for Pillow's, he should have supported Pillow's throughout. Instead of this, he gave his right ear to Buckner, his left to Pillow, until his mind became the battlefield for their ideas, resulting in the loss of the army and victory for Grant.

He reached the fort with his brigade just before McClernand completely invested the feeble rifle-pits. Buckner at once pointed out to him what a trap he had allowed himself to fall into. (It was not the trap he thought it was. Buckner's conclusion was drawn from the erroneous impression that 50,000 troops were with Grant and that the river fleet was invincible.) He was horrified and jumped at Buckner's plan for the relief with a naïveté which caused Buckner great concern, such concern that he remembered it throughout his long life of battles, military and political. This was the plan to break the enemy's right.

It was to take place the thirteenth. Pillow delayed it; the gunboat battle further delayed it, and afterwards it was in reality too late. The vacillation between the two generals was now thoroughly under way. Pillow took all the tools away from Buckner's men to strengthen his part of the line. This did not make their relationship more cordial.

In the council held the night of February 14, Floyd was still alarmed. The repulse given to the gunboats did not relieve his mind a whit. He expected them to return in greater strength; so he was still anxious to reëstablish land communication with Nashville. He gave what he thought were minute orders for the army's extrication. He even established a rallying point beyond the lines in case the assault was successful, but he made no detailed preparations about the withdrawal, such as the number of rations that should be prepared; whether blankets or knapsacks should be taken; what should be the order of march for the different commands; who should take the advance, who the rear. Such necessary instructions were left ungiven, although Buckner proposed that his men cover the retreat. This was forgotten next day. The truth of the matter seems to be that the commanding general did not expect the sally to be successful. He had entered Donelson with the feeling that his army was a sacrifice to Johnston's safe withdrawal to Nashville; and the army's valor, its victories, all facts, never changed his abstract conception of the situation.

Pillow agreed to the plan, not because escape was its purpose, but because he saw an opportunity for an offensive which he hoped to turn into a Confederate victory. So when the battle opened, the two wings went in with different purposes: the left under Pillow hoped to roll McClernand, Wallace, and Smith into the swamps of Hickman's Creek and leave them buried in its mud; the right under Buckner expected only to open the road to Charlotte and Nashville. Pillow came within a hair's-breadth of winning a complete victory. Buckner spoiled his chances by remaining behind, "to save his men" who would bear the brunt of the retreat. As it happened, Buckner, when he did send part of his command to the attack, opened the Wynn's Ferry Road and drove Wallace's men beyond it.

Just as he was congratulating himself on the success of the movement, he received the order from Pillow to retire to his former position. This order has never been explained, and Pillow's reasons for it can never be exactly known, for he carried them with him to the grave. The only plausible one seems to be that he expected next day to complete the partial victory of the fifteenth. But in any case he had no authority to order the troops off the field. That belonged to Floyd.

Floyd, when he saw what was taking place, ordered a halt. But after consulting with Pillow he withdrew his order and allowed the movement to complete itself. In extenuation of Floyd it has been advanced that Smith's feint on his right required additional troops to hold that part of the line. But in case of the withdrawal Buckner had counted on his abandoned works being taken. He had agreed to cover the retreat, but he could not cover what was not going to take place; so he rushed his regiments to Head's assistance and returned to the entrenchments resolved that the game was over and that Pillow was to blame.

At this last, final, and fateful council Floyd allied himself definitely to Buckner, because for once Buckner agreed with his only permanent belief, that it had been preordained that the army was lost the moment it entered the works around Dover.

Buckner, when he said it was impossible to hold his line any longer, probably meant that with Pillow's meddling and Floyd's impotence the sacrifice would be useless. Pillow's sharp, peremptory language had already destroyed all chance for persuasion. He was, therefore, in no condition to listen reasonably to Forrest when he explained why he thought the enemy had not reinvested. Floyd had never been in any such condition as on that cold, dispiriting morning.

There was still one other chance of escape. Forrest's scouts reported that the river road, although flooded, was open. Here the medical director, thinking of civilians and not of soldiers, stepped in and said that all the men would die of pneumonia if they attempted to wade out in their present condition and in such weather. Floyd could not hear of this.

Since the majority of the council was bent on surrender, it only remained to put it into effect. There was, for the moment, a pause. It was broken by the voice of the senior brigadier. He announced that for reasons peculiar to himself, it would be impossible for him to surrender to the Yankees; and he asked if he turned his command over to his inferiors, might he leave with the Virginia troops. Then General Pillow spoke up and said that there were no two men in the Confederacy the Yankees had rather have than Floyd and himself, and would it be proper for him to retire with the general commanding? Buckner replied that the two senior generals might depart if they left before negotiations were opened with the enemy.

Colonel Forrest reëntered the room at about this stage of the session and listened silently to the one-time Secretary of War, to the professional general, to the Mexican War veteran and law-partner of President Polk as they sacrificed a victorious army. This was his first disillusionment about that class of Southern leader he was to term loosely, "West P'inter."

"I turn over the command," said Floyd.

"I pass it," chirped Pillow.

"I accept it," intoned Buckner.

Pillow was to waste a great deal of paper explaining those three simple words, for since he had chafed so under another's control, it seems strange that such a fire-eater would forego the opportunity to take charge and fulfill directly his conception of what the operations should be. The hour and the situation was analogous to that other in the High Priest's kitchen, but unlike that other situation there was no rooster to crow three times and remind this Peter of his duty. The Yankee army had eaten them all.

He, apparently, was affected by the weakening around him and by the reports of heavy reënforcements; but the more likely cause of his failure to rise to the occasion was the lack of a thoroughly conceived plan of campaign. Pillow could handle an assault admirably and snatch a victory from the chances a pitched battle might offer, but the present task required more self-control than he possessed and a different sort of imagination. He therefore preferred, as Buckner acidly remarked, the comforts of his own feather bed to the hard planks of a prison camp.

As the negotiations came to a close, Colonel Forrest strode forward and asked if they were going to surrender the army. Buckner replied that they were. He told them he had not come out to surrender. That he had promised the parents of his boys to look after them. That he did not intend to see them die that winter in prison camps in the North. That he would not surrender if they would follow him out. That, in fact, he was going out if only one man followed.

Pillow reports that he gave him permission to leave, and that he and Floyd considered going with him. If this was true, their impatience did not allow them to wait. Pillow rode out, and Floyd left with his Virginia troops on a boat bringing corn and ammunition to the fort.

In an hour's time, through the black morning before sun-up, a long line of troopers, a company of artillery, and foot stragglers, some 1,500 in number, moved southward along the icy roads—a sullen protest against the decision of the generals. Colonel Forrest and his younger brother, Jeffry, rode at the head, straining their ears to hear any hostile noise to the front. The column moved slowly, for the trooper could see scarcely farther than his horse's head.

The word to halt went down the line. A subaltern and three men who had been sent forward to reconnoitre rode up. They reported that the enemy in line of battle was moving across their path. This was identical with the reports of Floyd's set of scouts. Bedford called for a volunteer to verify this finding, but no horseman rode from the ranks.

The colonel's hesitation was brief. He called Kelly, turned over the command with peremptory orders, that if he himself did not return, to carry the men out the best way he could, but to carry them out. In the meantime he was to continue upon the route they had determined upon.

With this understood he called Jeffry, and the two brothers disappeared in the darkness. When they reached the position where the enemy was reported waiting to dispute their march, the woods were gray with the first morning light. They were on that portion of the field which had seen the most stubborn fighting. As it grew brighter, the carnage of battle appeared gradually from the dark. The faces of the dead looked gray as wood ashes lying on the white ground, drawn and tightened in an agony so intense that its silence seemed to fix time onto eternity. As if the cold winter air had suddenly frozen them in action, staring eyes, gaping mouths, curiously contracted legs writhed in a mighty effort to break apart the irresistible bond which was holding them fixed forever in a sort of abstract animation. One clutched the branch of an overhanging tree and hung half-suspended. Another with compressed mouth, a hole in his head, his hands fiercely tight about his musket, pushed against its butt, plunging the bayonet up to its hilt in the ground. One other sat against a tree and, with mouth and eyes wide open, looked up squarely at the sky, as if he were strangely amazed at the sudden approach of day.

The brothers rode on about their business. Listening intently and scanning the dim horizon, they neither saw nor heard the troops which had been reported. But presently they pulled up their bridles and their shivering horses came to a stop. They saw among the mists rolling up from the earth what looked very much like long lines of men standing on parade but they stood too silently, too fixedly, to be men. Bedford and Jeffry, stealthily and alert, moved closer. After some minutes they reined in their horses and looked in wonderment, for before their close scrutiny the Yankee battle array had resolved itself into a long, stolid line of picket fencing.

The hasty inspection of the scouts had mistaken it for fresh divisions of the reinvesting force. When the information was carried to the generals at Dover, the fate of the Confederates was sealed.

To make sure of this hypothesis, the two men rode three-quarters of a mile up the ridge until they came upon the camp-fires of the enemy with their wounded clustered about them. Bedford questioned these men and was told that only a few scattering parties from both sides had been among them that night, that they had rebuilt the fires to keep from freezing, and that kindly farmers of the vicinity had gone about with lanterns to allay, as much as possible, the suffering.

Having assured himself that Buckner was surrendering on false information, and it now being too late to do anything about it, Bedford hurried back to his men. He met them where the water overflowed the Cumberland City road. Lined with ice, the water looked formidable. The colonel again called for a volunteer to test the depth and, when none readily responded, he rode quickly in, splashing through to the other bank, he sank no deeper than his saddle skirts. The command was soon splashing after him, while Kelly remained with a rear guard until all had crossed.

The way was now clearly open, with no pursuit in sight; so the column proceeded towards Cumberland City at a slow pace. Both men and mounts were greatly exhausted after four days of hard work and steady battle, with little rest and little food. The butternut cloth was stiff from the weather, and the men often dismounted to keep from freezing. But in the face of all this physical exhaustion, the troopers were beginning to feel in their commander a confidence which neither time nor event could shake. A soldier is eager and willing to follow a leader in the tightest places only so long as he believes that leader can get him out again.

As the mixed column rode away from the ill-fated scene, a bugle sounded off, subdued but clear in tone, from the parapets of Donelson. It was opening negotiations for capitulation, the surrender of the fort and 10,271 prisoners of war. Colonel Forrest turned his head to listen, and the melancholy notes died off. The bugle which had sounded the charge the day before had announced the capitulation not to the strategy of Grant, but to a long, stolid line of picket fencing.

PART THREE

FORREST OR BRAGG

PART THREE

FORREST OR BRAGG

CHAPTER VIII

A Birthday Party

ON July 9, 1862, Colonel Forrest crossed the Tennessee River at Chattanooga, going west. He had under his orders Terry's Texas Rangers, Wharton commanding, and Colonel Lawton's Second Georgia regiment, all told about one thousand men and what was as important, mounted on the best blood Georgia and the plains of Texas could furnish.

He had crossed an obscure colonel; he would return a general. In four days his name would be on the lips of the Southwest, while a report of his exploits would be read before the troops of an army. But as he turned his horse northwestward, this lay behind the spurs of the Cumberland Mountains which rose up, admonishing, to his front.

Five months of hard, bitter days had passed since he rode out from Dover that Sunday morning to move slowly for Nashville. Darker hours than those, probably, never would obscure the hopes of the Confederacy. But all the disappointment, demoralization, and terror which swept through the Southwest and through the army at that time disturbed Colonel Forrest very little. In the face of it he grew calmer and increasingly efficient. His troopers acted with the regularity of veterans. When the usual regimental reports announced daily so many "absent and unaccounted for," volunteers actually increased the strength of his regiment.

Although General Johnston was notified before morning light, the news of Donelson's fall did not reach the people of Nashville until later in the day. A victory had been announced in the capital, but the details were vague and unsatisfactory; and so, when the sun rose increasingly higher and the verification had not been made, the nervous excitement became almost unbearable. A prominent Catholic family had prepared a dinner for Beauregard and his staff, who were expected in the city on official business. As the mistress left the house for the cathedral, the table sagged under the weight of heavy linen, plate, and candelabra. The bishop was going to preach and then return with her to bless the board. But as he rose up among his flock that Sunday, he knew that Beauregard must find sterner entertainment for himself and staff. The bishop had just heard the news, that the ox was in the ditch at Donelson. He discarded his sermon and tried to prepare his communicants for the calamity. As he spoke, a lone person entered, walked down the aisle, and delivered a note to Beauregard's hostess. It read: "Come home at once."

The lady rose hastily and left the cathedral. The others as they watched the long black sweep of her dress, understanding unconsciously what her departure meant, fled into the streets. In a few minutes the city was shaken by panic. People ran about aimlessly. They threw pitchers out of second-story windows and feather beds after them. An officer walked up and down in his tracks, cursing and stumbling over his sword. The civil government vanished. The Jews barred their shops. The president of a railroad, also a quartermaster in the army, loaded his property on a train and steamed away south, leaving the supplies to their fate. Mobs collected and began breaking down the doors of the government warehouses and plundering what might mean the life of the remaining part of the army. Floyd was put in charge of the city and ordered to bring off these supplies. He failed utterly to cope with the situation and marched away to Murfreesboro on the rumor of Grant's approach.

The command over Nashville then devolved upon Colonel Forrest. In a few hours he had restored the capital to order. He rode into the mob, beat his pistol over the leader's head, brought out the fire engine and turned ice cold water—it was February—on the rest, put guards over the warehouses, telegraphed for rolling stock, restored the mayor and council to authority, commandeered every vehicle in the city and began at once removing the supplies out of danger. After working steadily three days and nights, he had emptied most of the warehouses and withdrew twenty-four hours after Buell's advance had occupied Edgefield on the other side of the river, and then only at the mayor's request.

This general gloom lifted somewhat when Halleck's timid, uninspired policy allowed Albert Johnston to withdraw and concentrate his scattered garrisons into an army which he threw against the Northern right under Grant at Shiloh. The green recruits and mismanagement by Johnston's corps commanders delayed the attack a whole day. This delay and the complications resulting in Johnston's death on the field robbed the Confederates of complete victory, for it gave Buell ample time to reënforce Grant towards the end of the first day.

The cavalry had taken no very prominent part in this battle, but Colonel Forrest dressed a detachment in blue overcoats and sent them reconnoitering that night among the enemy. He discovered Buell's arrival and reported it to a superior, adding entirely gratuitously that the Confederates ought to make a night attack or quit the field. This was a very important piece of information, because Beauregard had called off pursuit that evening on the assumption that Buell was at Columbia, Tennessee. Forrest was told to report to the general commanding, but his headquarters were not to be found; and when he reported to Hardee that he had been unable to find Beauregard, the cavalry colonel was ordered back to his command and Hardee seemed not to understand the significance of the find.

In consequence the battle was resumed next day, and Beauregard, having succeeded to the command, was forced on the defensive and finally to withdraw from the field. But he withdrew in good order, and if the Army of the Mississippi had not completely accomplished its purpose, it had crushed the right wing and fought the left wing of Halleck's forces to a standstill.

For there was no pursuit. After several days Sherman with a considerable body of infantry and a regiment of cavalry set out towards Corinth. Forrest had been left with the rear under Breckinridge. He was at the time on the Monterey road with a squadron 150 strong when, coming towards him, he saw this enemy advancing in three lines of battle. Captain John Morgan and others opportunely came along, increasing his strength by 200 more. The position, a ridge, was advantageous; so Forrest gave the orders to hold it until his regiment could be brought up.

The Yankee cavalry was thrown into temporary confusion as it crossed a stream. The shrill bugle on the hill sounded out the charge, and before the enemy knew quite what had happened, Forrest's men had struck and scattered them. As the blue horse broke, it ran over the first line of its infantry, which now in the general disorder offered slight resistance. The whole advance was thrown back upon the main body in demoralized segments. The slaughter was supposed to have been considerable, many of the mounts being transfixed by their comrades' bayonets, while as many as seventy were reported captured.

Colonel Forrest suddenly discovered that nothing but blue uniforms were about him. He had ridden far ahead of his own men into the Yankee reserves. The Confederates, very wisely, had stopped short of the main body and were now retreating with their prisoners, completely unaware of the danger to their commander.

"Knock that man off his horse! Stick him! Kill him! Kill the God-damned rebel!" Hundreds of rifles, at such commands, levelled upon the general target. A ball struck his horse. One struck him. It entered above the hip bone, penetrated to the spine, and ranging around, lodged in his left side. His right leg hung uselessly in the saddle, numbed by the shock. By any scientific computation of averages, Bedford Forrest should have been killed. But failing this, the simple numerical weight, hundreds against one, would have paralyzed most men into submission. But numbers, as such, left unmoved the individual who had taken a boy away from the Memphis mob of three thousand.

He turned simultaneously with the first volley, cleared the road with his revolver, and his charger sprang in great leaps towards the ridge. He reached his own people, still seated.

Turning the command over to the next in rank, he went to a field hospital nearby. The surgeon, unable to locate the ball, advised him to go to the rear as rapidly as possible. Taking his Adjutant, Captain Strange, Bedford set out at once for Corinth. On the way the wound grew so painful he was forced to dismount and take passage in a buggy, but the rough, jolting road made the pain far worse; so he remounted his horse. Late in the night they reached their destination. The horse died soon after. When the colonel was furloughed, it seemed likely he would soon follow.

If Bedford had been forced to give up his life at this point, it would have been well spent. His sudden, vigorous attack had evidently convinced Sherman and, through him, Grant that immediate pursuit would be inadvisable. Disgusted with their behavior, but somewhat puzzled himself, Sherman ordered his regiments back to camp.

This was the first and last time he and Forrest would meet directly on the field; but from now on, in the great game of strategy about to be played for possession of the Southwest, the fortunes of the two would be increasingly intermingled, and Sherman would be increasingly puzzled, until he would say rather desperately in 1864, "I've got to get Forrest if it takes ten thousand lives and breaks the treasury."

The rank and file of the Southern army found its morale greatly restored by Shiloh. They had seen the enemy in large numbers break and run before their onslaughts, and victory snatched away only by a piece of fortuitous circumstance. This rearguard action of Colonel Forrest's, as its report spread through the army, was added proof to strengthen the growing belief in ultimate victory. It denied that God always places himself on the side of the biggest battalions, an axiom which had so far chilled the initiative of the general officers. So when Halleck recovered sufficiently to move against Corinth by slow advances with the Army of the Tennessee, the Army of the Ohio, and the Army of the Mississippi, the Confederates felt confident of as decisive a victory as had been won by them on the first day around Pittsburgh Landing.

Some discontent arising in Forrest's regiment, he returned before he was completely recovered from his wound. Halleck was creeping around the heavily fortified town, and all were looking for the great battle which might settle the matter. On May 21, he wrote to a friend in Memphis:

D. C. Trader

Sir your note of 21 ins is to hand. I did not fully understand the contints and ask for information—the amount you ask for—is it for a publick contribution or is it for my dues due the log [lodge] I wish you to give me the amt due the log from me as you did not state it in your notice or the amount asked for. I had a small brush with the enemy on yesterday I succeeded in gaining their rear and got into their entrenchments 8 miles from hamburg and 5 miles behind farmington and Burned a portion of their camp at that place they were not looking for me—I taken them by surprise

I captured the Rev. Dr. Warine from Ilanois and one fine sorel stud. their army is at this time in front of our entrinchments. I look for a fite soon and a big one when it comes off. cant you come up and take a hand. this fite will do to hand down to your childrens children. I feel confident of our success

Yours respct

N. B. Forrest

But the big fight Bedford was looking for did not come. Beauregard decided the risk was too great. He had something under 50,-000 men—and this was all he could hope to get—to confront Halleck's 125,000 (not imaginary this time). With such odds it would be easy for the Northern general to bottle him up in Corinth, and Beauregard was too good an officer not to realize the significance of this. Instead, he withdrew to Tupelo, fifty miles farther south.

Tupelo, Mississippi, had many advantages over Corinth. The climate was better, and the water purer. The health of the army picked up at once. But its chief advantage was that it allowed Beauregard time . . . time in which the enemy might blunder. He had studied Halleck's character, and it was developing that Halleck's objective was not Beauregard, but Southern territory. To hold this territory he would be compelled to spread out his soldiers over it. The initiative, in such a case, would change sides; and the South would see the wisdom of keeping the army intact. The price Beauregard had to pay was temporarily to lower the good morale of his men. This refusal to do battle was forcing upon them the conviction that they could not successfully meet such great odds.

To add to the despondency and the perilous condition of the cause at this time, the river forts had fallen one by one until traffic was open from St. Louis to Vicksburg on the north and from New Orleans to Port Hudson on the south. A bare two hundred miles connected those states west of the river with the rest of the Confederacy.

When the Southern star was hanging to the horizon, uncertain whether it would fall or rise, Halleck stepped in, according to schedule, and again served the cause. Instead of following and forcing the Army of the Mississippi to battle, he set about securing Kentucky and Tennessee, apparently not realizing that the only permanent way to secure those states was to destroy the army in the field.

Buell (Halleck's politics were successful; he had been given supreme command in the West) was sent with the Army of the Ohio, about 30,000 men, to reduce East Tennessee. Other divisions were sent west of the Mississippi, and Grant was condemned to inactivity by his orders, which were to keep two divisions ready as reënforcements for Buell. Ths meant that he had actually tied up all his forces in the campaign, although no more than one-third was put in the field. After making these dispositions, he went away to Washington to serve as military adviser to Lincoln. His call to Washington was a great blow to the Confederacy in the West, but there was consolation in the thought that he might serve the cause as well there as here.

In the midst of these developments Colonel Forrest returned finally to duty. He had been forced to undergo an operation for the extraction of the ball, and this had taken and kept him away from his command for several more weeks. While he was on furlough, he made a speech at a rally in Memphis and told the audience: "I've got no self-respect for a young man who won't join the colors." Now, after his return, he found that he was being recognized as a man with military talent. He was at once despatched with a picked staff to Chattanooga to reduce the cavalry in Middle Tennessee and North Alabama to order. Colonel Saunders, an Alabama gentleman of age and influence, had come to Beauregard with this request. It was thought the cavalry in those parts, provided they were put under better control, might be of great use to the cause.

Beauregard and his subordinates were now busy with the consideration of the best way to turn back the tide of disaster. An advance into West Tennessee would not afford protection to Alabama and Georgia. Governor Brown was already shouting at Richmond through the mails that Georgia must not be left unprotected. An advance into Middle Tennessee by crossing the river at Florence, Decatur, or any neighboring point would have the disadvantage of placing the Confederates between the armies of Grant and Buell under circumstances enabling these two commanders to throw their forces simultaneously upon them, while they could not, in that event, depend upon any material aid from Kirby-Smith, the Confederate general in East Tennessee.

There was one other line for an offensive. A rapid march through Alabama, by way of Mobile, to Chattanooga would save that city and with it the communications between the East and the West; it would protect Georgia, prepare the way for an invasion of Middle Tennessee or Kentucky, and without the disadvantage of any force lying between the Army of the Mississippi and Kirby-Smith.

While these various plans were under consideration, Beauregard left the army. He had not been well for some time. He was sick on the field of Shiloh, and ever since an affection of the throat had sapped vitality which his duties as chief of an army could not well afford to lose. His physician had finally become so insistent about a furlough for recuperation that he acquiesced. He had piloted the army through the dark days (excluding Shiloh, where he blundered badly after Johnston's death), and now when the tide was beginning to turn, he must turn the wheel over to another.

He called Bragg to his place on June 27, expecting that Bragg should serve until he was well enough to return to duty. In taking this action he offended President Davis by notifying him after it had become an accomplished fact. Davis reprimanded Beauregard by making Bragg's appointment permanent. And hence, so simple a thing as a cold, the one which had confined Beauregard to his quarters at Bowling Green, was to play a rôle of unknown, but immense, importance in the destinies of the Confederacy.

For it had placed Braxton Bragg in command of its most important army, and Braxton Bragg was not the officer to command that army. As its head, he was thrust upon the scene in the rôle of Ægisthus. The magnificent Lee and the invincible Jackson were to wage such war in Virginia that history would come to ignore the importance of western battles. But it was there that the war must be won and lost, for the heart of the Confederacy lay in the lower South, between the mountains and the Mississippi River. To lose Tennessee permanently was to lose the cause, since Tennessee was the strategic center of the whole defense.

Four men, Davis, Bragg, Joseph E. Johnston, and Forrest, were to be the principals upon this theatre of war; but not until Bragg cast his shadow across the stage did the drama about to be played assume definitely its tragic form. He was the shadow, the element, that complicated the plot. All the strength of the other three, instead of gathering to fall in unison upon the enemy, became lost in the toils which gathered upon his entrance.

But at the time Bragg seemed to many to be the man of the hour. He had distinguished himself at Shiloh. After Johnston's death he took command of the right and gave it a head. And he still seemed to be the man of action, for the day he took command, he sent a division to Chattanooga to protect it against Buell's advance.

Buell, now that Halleck was no longer present to interfere, was rapidly approaching that city. He had taken Nashville as his base and was putting the Nashville and Chattanooga road into shape to haul his supplies. Halleck had first ordered him to use the Memphis and Charleston, but as this road lay between country occupied by both armies, it was easily broken. The road leading out of Nashville, through country held only by Northerners, did not have this disadvantage.

Bragg, profiting, as was only proper, by the staff discussions prior to his promotion, the insistence of Governor Harris of Tennessee, and the correspondence with Kirby-Smith, had about decided to move the rest of his army to Chattanooga with the hope of retaking the state. But while he was wavering between the different plans, Buell was taking the offensive out of his hands.

He was almost at the gates of the key city, the gate between East and West. In the beginning of June he had two divisions at Battle

Creek, a small stream running into the Tennessee within a few miles of Chattanooga. The road was repaired as far as Decherd, and an entire division was working on it between this depot and Stevenson. In North Alabama the rest of his army was concentrating, waiting for the order to move up.

An army is not moved with the speed of an individual, and so even if Bragg was accurately informed of the danger at Chattanooga, all the odds were that the city would fall, unless Buell might be delayed in some way.

There was now left only one very effective way: break his line of communications. Colonel Forrest was crossing a river to try this way. With 1,000 troopers he intended to delay the march of an army of 30,000.

It seemed very foolhardy. He must place himself a hundred and fifty miles from base, with the Cumberland Mountains between, and a brigade that had plenty of courage but no particular confidence in itself or its commander; in fact, quarrels over priority of rank had pretty badly shattered its morale. It was not without cause that one officer of rank complained that the expedition was rash, inconsiderate, and likely to lead to disaster.

But if Colonel Forrest had any qualms, he kept them to himself. Riding at the head of the column, holding his legs out from the saddle, he held his eyes fast to the mountains to his front as if he would absorb them and see what lay beyond. Suddenly he turned his head, gave a terse order, and galloped forward. The brigade followed after, the amber dust of the dry clay road rising up from their short lopes to settle silently, almost surreptitiously, in the fence corners and nearby fields as they passed on obscured in its heavy clouds, prophetic of a more acrid dust to be met on the journey.

Pushing steadily forward, the command passed through a valley, a steep spur, another valley, and then mounted slowly the last considerable spur of the Cumberlands. By July 10 Forrest had reached its crest at Altamont.

While his troopers were sleeping hard in the cool mountain air, another raider, John Morgan, who had gone on a raid of his own in his native Kentucky, was half a mile from Horse Cave on the Louisville and Nashville road, squatting down in the mud and rain to feel the pulse of the state. His operator, George Elsworth, had tapped the wires at this point, and for two hours had been draining them of important news. At 11 P.M., having learned all he wanted to know, Mor-

gan decided to close for the night. In spite of the weather and the hour
he was full of devilment; so, as a finishing flourish, he dictated the following ironically humorous document:

Nashville, Tenn. July 10th, 1862.

Henry Dent, Provost-Marshal, Louisville, Ky.

General Forrest, commanding brigade, attacked Murfreesborough, rout-
ing our forces, and is now moving on Nashville. Morgan is reported to
be between Scottsville and Gallatin, and will act in concert with Forrest,
it is believed. Inform general commanding.

Stanley Mathews,
Provost-Marshal

It has always been singularly unprofitable to examine into the
sources of prophecy; nevertheless, while Morgan stood in a Kentucky
thunderstorm listening in over the enemy's wires, Forrest, several
hundred miles away on the crest of the Cumberlands, after exhausting
Governor Harris and Andrew Ewing of valuable information, was
coming to the conclusion that Murfreesboro, rather than any other
point on the line, should be the end of his march.

Rising early next morning, the command soon passed through
Beersheba Springs, the half-way stop between Nashville and Chattanooga, and before the war a resort for the aristocracy of the Lower
South who fled every summer to the mountains to escape yellow
fever. It was not typically Southern in that it represented only the
great. The log hotel, built by slave labor, grew from the ground around
a court, two rooms deep, the front room for the lady, the room in the
rear for the body servant. To these double apartments there was only
one entrance, the front one. With all the idle black bucks loose about
the place, the maid-servants were just as well off without back doors.
As the squadrons filed in, Mrs. Armfield, the wife of the founder, had
several sacks of coffee opened and the haversack of each orderly filled
for his mess.

Late that day, the eleventh, they arrived at Rock Martins, a stone
house between Sparta and McMinnville. Here Colonel Morrison's three
hundred Partisan Rangers from Kingston and several companies of
Tennesseans and Kentuckians under Major Baxter Smith arrived and
increased his strength to 1,400. The men and horses rested until the
twelfth, when other scouts returned with a full report of their findings.

Forrest held a council of war—his first—and made his decision. He
would strike Murfreesboro.

Drawing up the command on the road, Colonel Forrest rode out
and took post front and center. He told his men what he intended to
do, and he called on them to sustain him in the attack. If the command had been tried, this would not have been necessary. But these
men were not veterans. They were little better than recruits. But recruits filled with enthusiasm are equal to veterans, and on very hazardous duty even better, for their judgment never questions their enthusiasms. Colonel Forrest knew this and he was making the best
of it. Then tomorrow, he told them, was his birthday—he would be
forty-one—and he would like to celebrate it in a becoming manner,
particularly since he would have occasion to so near his birthplace.
The riders promised to contribute what they could to the jollification.

With this promise in his ears, he put the command, in the early
afternoon, in motion for the last jump, forty-six miles before day-dawn
and a battle afterwards. They passed through McMinnville and, traveling over a plateau of foothills, descended into Woodbury, the seat of
Cannon County, at eleven o'clock that night. Woodbury was nineteen
miles from their destination.

As they rode down upon the square, they found the women of the
town moving about like a swarm of mad hornets. That afternoon the
provost-marshal of Murfreesboro, Captain Oliver Cromwell Rounds,
had come and taken away all their men and boys and locked them
up in his jail-house. The gray horsemen looked like the Avenging
Sword of the Lord to these women. They got busy and filled both man
and mount with all the food and drink they could carry, while into
the troopers' ears they poured the tales of their woe. On top of this,
they heightened the villainies of the Yankee soldiery by telling of
six Confederates who were to be hanged at dawn, who were, "to put it
into the rich language of a Northern correspondent, about to expiate
their crimes on the gallows."

This was all that was needed to drive away fatigue and instill into
flagging spirits zeal for battle. After feeding and resting two hours,
the command left Woodbury with a mission. Colonel Forrest had
promised the women that their menfolks would be back by sundown
next day.

Greatly animated, the brigade rode steadily forward. Only nineteen rolling miles were left them to travel. Five miles out from Murfreesboro the order to "dismount, fix-saddles, and tighten girts" went

down the line. The men knew what this meant. Even the horses sensed what lay ahead. Sleep, fatigue, sore backs . . . all were forgotten in the alert, nervous expectancy. After this had been done, the march was resumed cautiously, Colonel Forrest riding at the head of the column that he might see and not be seen, that he might surprise and not be surprised. His scouts were his most intelligent men; but, remembering Fort Donelson, he never afterwards relied entirely upon any eyes but his own to find the one flaw in the enemy's position that would be his undoing.

As they drew near the edge of town, phantom horsemen rode out of the cool mist into the head of the column. They were scouts with news that a picket of only fifteen lay just ahead, as yet unaware of an enemy's near presence. This picket must be gathered in, if the attack would be a surprise. Colonel Wharton with a picked detachment was sent forward on this duty. Circling the main turnpike on a hidden byway, he got in behind it and advanced as if he were Northern cavalry from the town. Not expecting an enemy to come from that direction, the picket was captured without the firing of a gun.

There was nothing now to warn the enemy sleeping in their tents. The garrison, the Ninth Michigan, the Third Minnesota, a Kentucky battery of four guns, and a squadron of the Seventh Pennsylvania Cavalry, about 1,500 of all arms, were peculiarly helpless in case of surprise. There had been a quarrel between Colonel Lester of the Third Minnesota and Colonel Duffield of the Ninth Michigan. This quarrel had sifted down to the rank and file until some of the Minnesotans and Michiganders had had a civil war all their own on the square and streets of the town.

To prevent a recurrence of this the two commands were encamped two miles apart. Colonel Duffield was on the Liberty Pike, half a mile east of the town, and with him was the Seventh Pennsylvania Cavalry, somewhat detached in Colonel Maney's lawn. Lester, with the Third Minnesota and the battery, occupied the east bank of Stones River, just off the Nashville Pike. One company guarded the jail and square and the quarters of General Crittenden, who had just arrived to take command and restore the tone of the brigade. He was not, however, to take charge until the morrow. In the meantime, he was sleeping in the tavern on the square, dreaming perhaps of the blessings of the peacemaker and the peacemaker's rewards.

Not until this moment, when he had as certain a knowledge of the situation as he could get, did acting Brigadier-General Forrest complete the plan of attack; but then it was suddenly done. He became at once a mass of animation. Sharply, authoritatively, he gave his lieutenants their orders. They were full and explicit, without an *if* or a *but*. He ordered his force divided to strike simultaneously the camp in town and the buildings, to hold in check the body on the river and its artillery until Colonel Duffield had been overcome. This meant that his brigade must be divided into three parts. The order, under the conditions that the brigade had not acted before as a unit, was a hazardous one. A prudent officer would not have attempted such a gamble.

The citizens of Murfreesboro had gone to bed Saturday night with heavy hearts. The morning light would bring the execution of six of their people, and their houses were filled with the kin of one hundred and fifty more whose exact fate was unknown. Nothing they felt, but an act of God, could save their town from this extremity of oppression.

James Paul, a spy, and Captain Richardson, who, escaping from prison, had accidentally fallen into his company and was captured with him, were among the condemned.

"Just about daylight on the morning of the thirteenth I was aroused from sleep by my companion Paul, who had caught me by the arm and was shaking me, saying, 'Listen! Listen!' I started up, hearing a strange noise like the roar of an approaching storm. We both leaped to our feet and stood upon an empty box, which had been given us in lieu of a chair, and looked out through the small grating of our prison window. The roar grew louder and came nearer, and in a very few seconds we were sure we could discern the clatter of horses' feet upon the hard turnpike. In a moment more there could be no doubt as to the riders of these horses, for on the morning air there came to our ears with heartfelt welcome the famous rebel yell. . . . Almost before we could speak the advance guard . . . came into sight and rushed by us on the street, some halting in front of the jail.

"Within the prison yard one company of Federal troops had been stationed, and, seeing they were about to be surrounded by the Confederates and that our rescue was sure, several of these soldiers in wicked mood rushed into the passageway in front of our cell and attempted to shoot us before they ran from the building. We only saved ourselves by crouching in the corner of the cell by the door, a position upon which they could not bring their guns to bear. Before leaving the jail one of the Federal guards struck a match, and, lighting a bundle of papers, shoved this beneath the flooring of the hallway where the planks were loose. . . . The jailer had fled with the keys. . . . The metal doors were heavy, and it was not until some of our men came in with a heavy iron bar that the grating was bent back sufficiently at the lower corner to permit us to be dragged through. At this moment Forrest dashed up and enquired of the officer in charge if he had rescued the prisoners. He said they were safe, but added that the jail had been set on fire in order to burn them up, and the guard had taken refuge in the courthouse. 'Never mind,' he said, 'We'll get them.'

"I shall never forget the appearance of General Forrest on that occasion; his eyes were flashing as if on fire, his face was deeply flushed. . . ."

It was Lawton's Georgians who took the jail, the depot, the telegraph operator, large stores; and it was Morrison's Georgians, with four companies of the Rangers, who surrounded the courthouse. This done, immediately squads of the Texans scrambled into the tavern and houses to bring out the provost-marshal and any other officers who might have spent the evening in the city on official or unofficial business.

In an hour's time the details returned with Crittenden and other valuable prizes, but the prize sought by all, Captain Oliver Cromwell Rounds, had successfully eluded every searching party. A matron of the town, seeing this dilemma, suggested that the provost-marshal might be found in a very respectable mansion not twenty paces from the square. She intimated, entirely gratuitously, that while Captain Rounds portrayed the cruel nature of his illustrious namesake, he had not been so studious, nor so zealous, in the study of the high moral character of the Puritan leader. This gratuitous information was all by way of saying that chivalry should not restrain the gray gentlemen from entering, even, the sleeping chamber of the young lady of the house.

And there they found the captain, tucked away safely between two feather beds. They jerked him out, marched him forth, as unceremoniously attired as he was, and mounted him upon a horse. The detail, accompanied by the captain, then galloped through the main street of the town with their flags, the tails of the captain's night shirt giving gently to the breeze.

But there was little time for such foolishness.

While this was going on about the square, Wharton's Texans had charged on the trot into a line of platoons and struck the Ninth Michigan as they were tumbling out of their beds. Right over the tent ropes into the camp they charged, shooting right and left and yelling as if they were on a big round-up. Unfortunately, through some misunderstanding, four of the companies had followed Georgia into town. This reduced the weight of the attack and allowed the Yankee officers to rally their infantry and make a handsome stand behind wagons and other cover hastily got together. From this barricade they poured a galling fire into the Rangers. It became so severe that Wharton, himself painfully wounded, gradually retired before it. Without informing his superior of his plight, he withdrew with the prisoners four miles on the Woodbury pike. This action of Wharton's was very indiscreet—there was a rumor afterwards of court-martial—for it left the rear of the Georgians unprotected.

Among the prisoners were the Seventh Pennsylvania Cavalry. They had been surrounded just as they were mounting their horses to go to Duffield's assistance. Major Baxter Smith, with a battalion of Tennesseans and Kentuckians, assisted in this affair. He then swung, according to orders, out upon the Lebanon and Nashville pikes to cut off all retreat in those directions.

Lawton had already thrown the rest of his regiment between Lester and the town, but since Lester had the artillery, it was a very doubtful matter how much longer he could be kept on ice.

This was of great importance, for so far, in spite of the surprise, nothing of a decisive nature had blessed the Confederate arms. Wharton had been repulsed. The final outcome at the courthouse was uncertain. It was well built and well defended. The garrison, for several hours, had withstood every attack against it. With artillery the matter would have been simple, but the Confederates had none.

After several abortive efforts to storm the brick structure, Forrest took personal charge of the operations. He drew up two storming parties, one on the east side and one on the west side. In front of these he placed a line of men in single file. He gave to each leader an axe and instructions. They were very simple: the axe must be kept in the air until it reached and battered in the doors. And in this relay fashion the building was carried, although even after the entry a fire had to be built to smoke the enemy down from the second story. These Michiganders were stubborn, brave men.

The prisoners were brought together, and Captain Richardson

asked to walk down the line with the acting general. "They tell me these men treated you inhumanly while in jail. Point them out to me." Richardson replied that he wanted to call attention only to one man, the one who had tried to fire the jail.

A few hours later, as the lists of the privates were being called, this man did not answer to his name. It was repeated in a louder tone, and still there was no answer. "Pass on," Forrest commanded; "It's all right." There was a momentary silence, and the numbering continued.

One part of the plan had succeeded. He now moved on to the second, the reduction of the Third Minnesota. Lester had marched it several hundred yards from its camp and formed a line of battle in front of Lawton. They were skirmishing at long range. Lester had left a hundred men at the camp, on the river, and these were posted strongly behind wagons and ledges of limestone rock.

Leaving Lawton in front, Forrest circled to the rear with six companies of Tennesseans and Kentuckians and drew up his men for a charge. It was made with vigor, but the fire from the wagons was too much. The horsemen retreated in disorder. The companies restored their formation, and Forrest rode to the front. He said distinctly and clearly, "Major Smith, lead the charge." Smith tied his reins to the saddle, and with sword in one hand and pistol in the other galloped at the wagons, but the Confederates were thrown back a second time. Forrest was furious. Six companies had failed to reduce two. For the third time he drew them up into the proper formation. He then made them a little talk. It was a talk they never forgot. As he sat there on his charger, his head thrown up, they were led to understand that there was one thing he could not tolerate: leaving the field in the face of the enemy. This time they followed him over the wagons, and the position was carried. A negro camp-follower emptied his gun at the colonel. Without interrupting the business at hand, Forrest turned, fired, and the man fell over the wagon wheels.

The Georgians heard the firing and mistook it for a rear attack on the main body. They charged Lester from the front and rode over and through his men, but the Northern colonel quickly re-formed his broken lines on an elevated ridge, and waited.

This was the crisis of the day. A false move and the Confederate brigade might have to recross the Tennessee in sections. It was evident to all that the position would be hard to carry. The men, knowing their commander, or thinking they knew him, were about to brace

From "Battles and Leaders of the Civil War." Courtesy of the Century Company

The Cavalry in Bragg's Invasion of Kentucky

themselves for another charge. But there was to be no more charging. Bedford Forrest promptly changed his plan of operations with the resource that was to leave him so often unmatched on the field of battle. He had decided that a successful charge would not be commensurate with the losses it was bound to entail, for he had just learned of Wharton's repulse and departure.

Leaving enough men to keep Lester in place, he burned the camp and sent off the prisoners and the captured property; despatched a staff officer after Wharton's squadron; then moved rapidly back to Murfreesboro.

It was now one o'clock; and, although something had been accomplished, many of the Confederate officers had concluded it was time to break up the meeting and go home. Some, even, went up to the commander and tried to persuade him that this was the thing to do. They told him the garrisons from Nashville, Shelbyville, and Lebanon might arrive any minute and cut him off from retreat.

It had almost become ingrained in the Confederates in the West that a partial victory was all that could he hoped for. But Forrest's mind did not work that way. He knew it was whole hog or none. At Shiloh and Donelson he was only a subordinate, but now the last word was his; he was commanding. The same individual that had sat under the tree until day-dawn to remove the last possible chance of the panther's escape answered abruptly, "I did not come here to make half a job of it; I mean to have them all."

He hastened to spread his men around the Ninth Michigan. Major Smith was dismounted as skirmishers. As soon as he opened a brisk fire around the barricade, the second Georgia took its position on the enemy's left and prepared for a foot charge. These operations were done quickly, confidently, and with a great show of prowess.

When the skirmishing was at its height and the bugle alone kept the Georgians in their place, and not before, a flag of truce carried the following into the barricade:

Murfreesboro, July 13, 1862.

Colonel:—I must demand an unconditional surrender of your forces as prisoners of war, or I will have every man put to the sword. You are aware of the overpowering force I have at my command, and this demand is made to prevent the further effusion of blood. I am, Colonel, very respectfully, your obedient servant,

N. B. Forrest,
Brigadier-General of Cavalry, C. S. A.

To Colonel Duffield.

Most feints fail because they bear all the earmarks of feints. If Forrest intended this for a feint, he successfully disguised its nature, for it looked like business to Duffield. "An unconditional surrender or I will have every man put to the sword" was not the phrasing of chivalry. Chivalry had come to mean to the Yankee authorities a pleasant suing for terms. This was straight, plain, unequivocal language, a new kind of Confederate talk, and talked by a man who somehow left the impression that he meant what he said. This impression was strengthened, perhaps, by Duffield's conscience. His men had been hard and strict on the people of the countryside. Captain Rounds had been a terror. Duffield possibly felt that Forrest's troopers were itching for the slightest excuse to put every man "to the sword." At any rate, he didn't expect aid from Lester. (The messenger he had sent to that officer had been arrested.) Both he and his second in command, Park-hurst, had been wounded, he grievously so. All remaining doubts, if he had any, were dispelled as Lieutenant Colonel Walker galloped into view with the squadron of Texans who had retired with Wharton. This was good evidence of an overpowering force. So without further parley, and much to the surprise of the Confederate officers, Duffield surrendered.

This was "half the job." To have them all meant to capture the body on the river. This promised to be a more formidable undertaking. The Minnesotans had not been handled as badly as the Michigan troops, and they had a battery of four guns. Forrest lost no time, for he knew its value. While he was receiving the prisoners at one end of the town, Captain Strange, his adjutant, was galloping towards the other end with the same ultimatum.

Lester asked to confer with Duffield. Permission was readily granted. Forrest knew that it was unlikely that Duffield would advise against a course which he himself had adopted, and he had already tried to persuade Duffield to surrender Lester. And then he had another reason for agreeing so readily to the conference. As Lester was escorted to and from the Maney house where Duffield lay wounded, Forrest marched and counter-marched his troopers behind the Carney and the Lytle Woods until they were twice seen. This had a profound effect on Colonel Lester.

He asked for an hour's time to come to some decision. He was told he might have thirty minutes. In an hour reënforcements might take the decision from his hands. So Lester called together his company officers and together they read the little note. Although it was painfully explicit, its sentiment was the kind to appeal most effectively to abolitionist officers. If they must surrender, it offered them a very noble, a very humane reason for their action. They would prevent the further effusion of blood, some of which would be their own. As they pondered upon how many gallons it would be, they voted unanimously upon its preservation. It was said afterwards that their men were not so anxious to be saved as their officers were to have them saved; but this was afterwards, and the men had not read the little note.

By three o'clock the last of the troops that had been in occupation of Murfreesboro were in Confederate hands. By six o'clock the prisoners were numbered, and the head of the squadrons was leaving town. Major Smith remained behind to destroy the railroad and a bridge at Christiana.

They encamped that night at Readyville, half-way to Woodbury. On their way, all along the road they had met in buggies, wagons, and on foot the men of Woodbury going home to their women. Enough had already reached the town to make good the promise that they would be home by sundown next day.

From Readyville Forrest sent scouting parties in every direction to learn what effect his raid had had, and particularly to discover the strength and direction of all hostile movements, for he was by no means safe, encumbered as he was with almost as many prisoners as he had soldiers. This fact impressed itself on his attention very forcibly when he found, that after detailing the guards, he did not have enough men left to drive his captured wagons and artillery.

This had all the appearances of an embarrassing dilemma, but Bedford Forrest knew no shame. He only knew that he did not intend to lose any of his spoils. In looking about for some way out of the predicament, he cast his eyes upon the source of his trouble, the prisoners. Separating them from their officers, he rode out among them. He frankly explained the cause of his embarrassment and promised that if enough of them would volunteer to serve as his drivers, he would parole the entire lot at McMinnville and let them go home.

Crittenden, the staff, and the regimental officers stood apart in curious bewilderment. Their wonder was entirely natural, for it is not usual for captives to be so interested in the words of their captor. At the end of his speaking a lusty Yankee voice sang out, "Three cheers for General Forrest." Then the rocky banks of the east branch of Stones River did a unique thing—they echoed over the broken country the shouts of Northern soldiers for a Confederate colonel.

As these reverberations subsided, Crittenden and his brother officers looked very forlorn and lonely, and they must have felt a deep humiliation. They had already given up to this man Forrest everything honorable warfare should expect of them: their posts, their commands, themselves; and now they were losing the respect and admiration of their own men. They were learning that for those who came to make war on his country Bedford Forrest was asking that the last bitter drop be drunk, that the dregs be crunched and swallowed.

In this fashion, with the fraternity of a common admiration, the gray and the blue moved off and went into camp at McMinnville. According to his promise, Forrest paroled the file. While they, with two days' rations in their sacks, were scattering in the direction of the Ohio, the rank was moving under escort towards Knoxville to be delivered along with the spoils into the hands of Kirby-Smith. This done, the jaded Confederates and their critters were allowed to feed and rest.

The rest was well earned. Since leaving Chattanooga, the riders had covered nearly two hundred miles, in which they had crossed the difficult Cumberlands and made a forced march of forty-six miles, half of this distance being over the Barrens between McMinnville and Woodbury. And as if this were not enough, when the limit of endurance had about been reached, their commander had called upon them for an all-day battle and twelve other miles afterwards.

Forrest had shown himself to be hard and unrelenting. His men complained, but they obeyed; and after they had captured between eleven and twelve hundred of the enemy, a brigadier-general, staff and field officers, a battery of four pieces, forty wagons, three hundred mules, one hundred and fifty horses, and full equipment for every man in the command, they forgot they had ever cussed him for a hard-driving man.

Besides this very concrete evidence of success, there had been an immense destruction of property: the depot, the telegraph, $200,000 worth of supplies. There was also a sufficient amount carried off to bring the enemy's loss up to $500,000. Included in this reckoning were 150,000 rations intended for Buell's army. The Army of the Ohio was put at once on half rations.

By tearing up the Nashville and Chattanooga railroad and keeping it broken for two weeks, Forrest had prevented the offensive against

Chattanooga and made it possible for Bragg to take the initiative away from Buell in the Kentucky Campaign. He had done this under the nose of 30,000 men, within the immediate presence of twelve regiments scattered along the line, and when they had been warned of his probable intentions. And he had done it with a command which had had confidence neither in itself nor in him.

It was the first decisive victory Confederate arms had achieved in Tennessee; and coming at a time when repeated reverses had made the Southwest despondent, it had an enormous moral effect, both on the population and on the army.

To the Confederates with their small armies (needlessly small—their size was due to Davis's departmental system) Forrest showed a way to equalize the superior numbers of the enemy. If he could mislead the enemy into thinking that they were outnumbered, it was actually not necessary to have a strength as great as theirs. Superior numbers, weightier artillery, and more efficient equipment do not in themselves assure victory. That Forrest understood and practiced this, and under such adverse circumstances, set him apart as the first officer in the West to offer the hope of a vigorous, imaginative policy.

Also, together with Morgan's raid into Kentucky, the descent upon Murfreesboro sustained the growing opinion that the South had a ready-made cavalry which could neutralize or delay the greater masses of the enemy. This was to be of inestimable value to the Confederacy, particularly in the Western theatre. In Virginia the Army of the Potomac was close to its base, either by rail or water, and raids upon its lines of communication could not so seriously embarrass its movements. But here in the West the problem was different. The distances were very great; and consequently the ultimate success of the invading armies was not only dependent upon the maintenance of these very long lines, but it was actually possible that they might be cut off and starved into capitulation.

Forrest, falling upon Buell's line and breaking it with so much apparent ease, advertised this as the weakest spot in the enemy's offense. It was particularly weak, because the North had no cavalry to speak of, and it took Lincoln and Halleck a long time to understand the necessity for that arm of the service, and a still longer time to produce it. In the meantime, "The cavalry operations (Confederate)," reported Fry, Buell's provost-marshal general, "controlled all the subsequent operations of the Army of the Ohio. . . ."

The prospects for the Confederacy were now indeed bright. With an invincible cavalry to put the enemy into strategic corners it was only left to the infantry to drive them to the wall. We will see how well Bragg was to take advantage of his opportunity.

Among Forrest's own followers a transformation had taken place. He had taken them into the venture as several bodies of men lacking the feeling that they were the part of the whole; he brought them out a unified brigade, possessing a spirit and a capacity for the execution of delicate operations. This was because he had brought them victory, not victory at any cost, but at the smallest possible cost of their lives. He had a second time made the most powerful appeal to a soldier's confidence. And the ruses by which he had forced Duffield and Lester into capitulation were of a kind to appeal particularly to soldiers who had been farmers. This marching and counter-marching before Lester bore a very strong resemblance to certain mule-swapping tricks generally familiar.

To the people of Middle Tennessee, who had submitted to the most humiliating indignities with little hope of relief, he became overnight their particular ideal of what a soldier should be. They could not understand strategic gains, but they could understand his kind of fighting. It was as plain and as heartening as sow-belly and corn bread. The women now felt that they had a defender. They began to threaten tyrannical officers like Captain Rounds with "Forrest will get you for this," or "I'll tell Old Forrest on you." They soon learned that he was a bogeyman they all believed in.

It is told in Murfreesboro that after the surrender and while Forrest was waiting impatiently to withdraw with his booty and his prisoners, a stately, gentle-featured lady stepped out of her residence on the square and walked towards the town's deliverer. As she swept her skirt along the red brick walk, she held in one of her thin white hands a small lace handkerchief and, in the other, a silver spoon.

"General Forrest," she asked, "will you back your horse for me?"

Bedford lifted his hat, and, with his heavy black hair falling down his shoulders, bowed; then pulled on the reins.

Leaning over, she scooped up a spoon of dust from the ground where the horse had been pawing and poured it carefully into the folds of the handkerchief. Without any more words she bowed very low and turned back towards her house, bearing away with her the silver spoon and the little piece of bulging lace.

CHAPTER IX

Separating Grant from his Base

"THAT was a gallant, brilliant operation of Forrest's and has given us one of the most obnoxious of the enemy's leaders. Such successful efforts deserve immediate reward, and I will cheerfully meet with you in recommending Colonel Forrest. This affair, added to his gallantry at Shiloh, where he was severely wounded, *marks him as a valuable soldier.*"

This appeared in a letter from Bragg to Kirby-Smith. In another to Beauregard which asked for a criticism of the proposed campaign in Middle Tennessee and Kentucky is the following: "Crittenden is quite a prize, and the whole affair in proportion to numbers *more brilliant* then the grand battles where *strategy* seems to have been the staple production of both sides."

This admiration is illuminating in light of the future relationship between the two generals. When their service together began with such frank admiration on the part of the commanding officer, it is puzzling to witness how quickly they became estranged. It is puzzling until, on closer inspection, the seed of trouble is found in the very spontaneity of Bragg's admiration. His reaction to the fall of Murfreesboro is not the critical interest of a professional soldier: he shows no curiosity, apparently, as to the tactics of Forrest's assault. His enthusiasm is very like that of a layman's, that is, it is emotional. He had contrasted the raid with strategy, but a realistic soldier knows that every operation, whether it succeeds or fails, is strategic; so, really he meant to contrast good strategy with bad; but good strategy bears a very peculiar connotation to Bragg. It is good when it fits in with his plans, and only then is it good, no matter how successful it might be. As Forrest had no interest in Bragg's career except in so far as it was identified with the cause, it becomes plain that when two such men ever cross, there will never be peace between them.

But at the moment Bragg was very friendly. Forrest had shown he was the very person to prepare for his advance. Bragg sent him fuller directions by Governor Harris. To prevent the concentration of Buell's army, Forrest was ordered to keep broken the Nashville and Chattanooga and the Tennessee and Alabama roads. Bragg, himself, promised to attend to the Memphis and Charleston. It was hoped that this activity in Buell's rear would divert attention from the movements at Tupelo and leave a false impression in the enemy's mind concerning the Confederate offensive.

On July 18, 1862, after a four days' rest, before he had received these instructions, Forrest anticipated the contents. He swooped down on Lebanon, but the garrison heard he was coming and made for Nashville. He halted in Lebanon just long enough for the citizens to victual his riders. A friend to the enemy who tried to skip away to Nashville was caught and then let ostentatiously through the lines. Forrest told him it was no loss: he would pick him up again in a few days. This had the desired effect on the commandant at the capital. It made him stay within his works.

He shifted over to the Hermitage, Andrew Jackson's home. Bedford thought Old Hickory's shrine might inspire his young men to further deeds. A crowd was already assembled to celebrate the battle of Bull Run, and there were many young ladies to squire through the garden walks. While his riders were so innocently occupied, the Yankee general Nelson stirred up the dust on the Murfreesboro pike looking for the picnickers. Forrest sounded to mount and galloped away just in time to get in his rear.

Circling Nashville, he gathered in pickets, destroyed bridges, twisted iron track into loops, and sent a message in to Miller to come out and fight. When this gentleman declined the bout, he moved to Antioch depot, captured it, destroyed its supplies, and burned a lot of wood stored up for the engines.

"Our guards are gathered up by the enemy as easily as he would herd cattle," Buell complained to Miller.

Nelson reached Murfreesboro and learned that he had been going in the wrong direction. He counter-marched over the hot, dry road, first sending ahead cavalry with instructions to pitch into Forrest. This body of horse actually overtook the raiders, but it did not pitch in. Its commander thought it best to wait for the arrival of Nelson's infantry for "advice." When Nelson marched up several hours later and discovered his subordinate had let Forrest slip away, he swore and fumed and shook the sweat from the heavy folds of his immense body.

In the meantime, Forrest had quietly hidden his riders on the Chicken Pike, well secluded behind the hills but close enough to the main turnpike for sound to carry. The moment his sharp ears failed to hear the hoarse, dusty commands, the steady tramp of the Northern column, he slipped out of his hiding place and was soon in a swinging gallop in the opposite direction.

Sookey Smith, a Northern general posted at Tullahoma, wired Buell: "One of my scouting parties last night captured a morning report of a rebel force encamped near McMinnville; it is addressed to Forrest, Chapel Hill, which you will perceive lies between Shelbyville and Franklin. The rebel has not had time to advise him of its capture. Cannot we capture him there or at Shelbyville, where I think his army is?"

Buell replied to his instructing lieutenant, "Forrest is now between Nashville and Murfreesboro." And to inform him how little he understood the difficulties of the race, he added laconically, "Destroyed 3 bridges 9 miles from Nashville yesterday."

Hard on the trail of this came the following telegram from Colonel Fry: "Have 100,000 rations sent by rail tomorrow from Murfreesboro to Stevenson. Show this order to General Nelson. *Be cautious in this."*

General Nelson had assured Buell that "Mr. Forrest shall have no rest." But as it was turning out, Mr. Nelson was getting no rest. He had marched and counter-marched between Murfreesboro and Nashville three times, only to find that he was always going in the wrong direction, for no matter which way he went, Forrest inevitably was heard from in the other direction. This became so confusing that Nelson decided that "with infantry in this hot weather it is a hopeless task to chase Forrest's command mounted on race horses."

"Destroy him if you can," flashed back the order. But Forrest was not to be caught. Six miles out, he circled Murfreesboro and, near Manchester, captured fifteen men and killed three others on his return to base. The next day he bivouacked at McMinnville and remained there in observation until August 10.

On this date he turned over his command to Lieutenant-Colonel Hood and rode alone to Knoxville on business. While he was away, an enemy column of 3,000 infantry and 800 cavalry moved upon McMinnville. Hood fell back to Sparta and notified Forrest. He rejoined his brigade there in four days, after a two hundred mile ride over the Cumberlands.

There was constant skirmishing after his return, as Buell was moving up to meet Bragg's advance. So far Bragg had successfully deceived his opponent. He had moved his army to Chattanooga and now was crossing it over the river and massing. His lieutenant Forrest had done so well that Bragg promised him he should have the whole of the cavalry when it got in from Mississippi.

But about this time, a slight rift passed between them. Bragg sent an order to him to leave a mere corps of observation where he was and retire with his main body into the Sequatchie Valley, "to prevent their incursions and try and cut off as much as possible their communications from out lines."

Forrest decided that the best way to prevent this was to act on their lines, and he notified Bragg to this effect. Without waiting for a reply, he shifted his base to Smithville, then to Woodbury, and so in Buell's rear.

The order had been put in the form of a question, leaving, so Forrest thought, a choice of action. He decided not to return, or in other words he set his judgment against his commander's. Bragg replied through a member of his staff—his other communication had been personal—"I am directed by the general commanding to say that as soon as you accomplish the present object in view you will return and *act according to the instructions you have previously received*."*

This was a rebuke, not a very severe one; but it was meant to convey to the cavalry general that his duty was to obey the suggestions as well as the orders of the commanding general. To disobey a direct order was insubordination; to ignore an implied order was a criticism of the army's chief. Bragg was very jealous of his military judgment; so when all the cavalry had been brought up, General Forrest did not command it. Wheeler, an officer who had been trained at West Point, was placed over the right, Forrest over the left.

He was not long at Woodbury. He crossed the country and struck the road near Manchester. Then moving along its branch towards McMinnville, he destroyed the track and all the bridges in the effort to delay further Buell's concentration.

His scouts met him near McMinnville and reported that the Northern cavalry had been strongly reënforced. There were two

* Italics mine.

divisions of infantry in the town. In the face of such numbers he decided to take post in the mountain pass at Altamont and wait there for Bragg's army.

But in spite of his activity the Army of the Ohio had moved rapidly. When he reached the cove at the foot of the Cumberlands, his scouts brought him the alarming information that Altamont was in the possession of General McCook. On top of this, others came in and reported that enemy columns were moving in his direction from Manchester, Winchester, and McMinnville. All of these roads converged into one which twisted through the cove and up the mountain to Altamont. He had for once outplayed his hand. So well had the toils been set that a telegraphic despatch was sent to Buell announcing the capture of Forrest and 800 men.

But the announcement was a little premature. Forrest, it is true, was as good as captured; but actually he had not been. Throwing men out on all the roads to keep him accurately informed, he rode to the end of the cove and up the Nickajack Trace to the top of the mountain. He rode out onto a point from which he could see in all directions. The day was clear, and the sun had an hour or more before it would drop behind the long line of hills around Beech Grove. He could see for five miles, and as he sat his restless charger so near the brink of the cliff (the road from McMinnville was hidden by a spur) he watched two long, thin clouds of dust roll gradually towards the position of his brigade in the wooded cove. As he studied the surrounding country, the thin, wavering roads running so narrowly through the miles of woodland and scattered clearings, and the two puny columns marching along them, he made his plans of escape. A scout returned from Altamont and announced that McCook was also on the march. The situation was critical.

Looking at the sun once more, he began the rocky descent to his men. When he reached the base of the mountain, his plan was perfected. He had remembered seeing a dry creek bed whose banks were high enough to conceal a man and his horse. He quickly formed his squadrons into column of fours and moved off into the woods. An order for silence went down the line; they had reached the overhanging banks of the creek. A place of easy entrance was reconnoitered, and the command dismounted. Presently dark shadows settled in the trees; a few birds flew noiselessly away; the shadows crept slowly up the trunks; then in one jump covered the entire cove and the creek with the cool dark of mountain dusk. The foothills from Woodbury to Shelbyville had swallowed the sun. Six hundred yards away the enemy was forming a line of battle.

When it was good and dark, the horses of Forrest's command, their heads held up to keep them from stumbling, were passing quietly around the Northern line, hidden by the night and the overhanging banks of the dry creek bed. Next morning, as the Northerners picked their way cautiously forward, Forrest's riders had swung back in the road and were galloping towards McMinnville, some fifteen miles away. Seven miles out, he ran into a body of infantry and cavalry drawn up to intercept his flight. He put the command into a gallop and swept around them, every man yelling at the top of his lungs. This unexpected manœuvre paralyzed the enemy. They got themselves together in time to fire a few parting shots as the gray riders disappeared to the west.

Forrest made his way to Sparta, where he had heard Bragg was moving his army. When the officer who had reported the capture of Forrest and 800 men was called to turn over his booty, he had only a few mules and one spring wagon and some mighty big words: "Forrest was whipped by Colonel Grove's men near Woodbury, Thursday. Friday he attacked the stockade on the McMinnville road and was whipped again and returned up Hickory Creek. He started yesterday for Bragg's camp by Altamont. Was met by McCook's advance and again whipped. He then returned toward Woodbury again but was pursued by one of Wood's regiments, overtaken and attacked at the crossing of the road from Manchester to Smithville and the road from here to Murfreesboro and again badly whipped and dispersed."

He is "whipped" four days in succession, and then when he escapes from the worst trap ever set to catch him with the loss of a few mules and one spring wagon, he is "badly whipped and dispersed." Even the phlegmatic Thomas, who composed this dispatch, should have seen the humor of it.

Forrest reported to headquarters at Sparta. His independent service in Middle Tennessee was now at an end. While Stuart in Virginia had been riding around McClellan's array of divisions, Forrest in Tennessee could not be amused with so simple a game. He had established himself in Buell's rear, near his secondary base, and from there he rode not only around the Army of the Ohio but through it as well and, some were willing to swear, under it. The quartermaster general at Washington from Murfreesboro on had to make added allowances for Forrest's men in the requisitions for this army; and from the supplies they took they must have appeared many-bodied, and, from the rations they drew, big-bellied.

When Bragg and Forrest met near Sparta, the hopes of the Confederacy were soaring. Kirby-Smith, in East Tennessee, had acted with decision. The Yankee general Morgan held Cumberland Gap with a considerable force, but moving by other roads, Kirby-Smith got on his line of communications and forced him to abandon the gap; then turning without delay, Kirby-Smith began his invasion of Kentucky.

On August 30, he met at Richmond a hastily raised force under General Nelson and defeated it with heavy loss to the enemy. On September 2, he reached Lexington and established his headquarters there, sending out detachments to threaten Louisville and Cincinnati.

On the fifth, Bragg made his headquarters at Sparta. Up to this point the mountains had screened his movements. Buell had not ventured very far to meet him, for fear of uncovering Nashville. He had given up all hope of invading East Tennessee when John Morgan on August 12 blew up the tunnel and railway bridge at Gallatin. As Nashville was only a secondary base, Louisville being the primary base, his communications had a second time been at the mercy of the Confederate cavalry.

At Sparta, Bragg had a choice of two routes. He could move northwest into Kentucky, or west into Middle Tennessee. He decided to go towards the Blue Grass country. The tables were now completely turned, and there appeared to the Confederates the dazzling possibility of recovering for the cause both Tennessee and Kentucky; it was open for Bragg to do with artillery what Davis had not done with politics.

The four Alabama companies of Forrest's old regiment were added to his brigade, and his assignment on the left was made. It was his duty to delay Buell's march, for it had now become a race for Kentucky. The same day that Bragg made his headquarters at Sparta, Buell concentrated at Murfreesboro, and that same day Forrest was pushing hard on his rear. He had been allowed to keep his "pets," the four guns taken from Lester, and he pushed them so close to Buell's flanks that this general often had to form line of battle to save his trains. Every time he formed in line, he was delayed by that much in his race for Kentucky.

On September 14, the Army of the Ohio had reached Bowling

Green, but the day before Bragg had pushed into Glasgow, thirty miles to the east. On the fourteenth he attacked Munfordville, and on the seventeenth its garrison of 4,000 men surrendered. Forrest had made this possible by pinning the garrison in the town when it made an effort to withdraw.

It was clear to all that Bragg had definitely outmanœuvred Buell. He lay directly across Buell's line of communications with an army of veterans, fired with their successful march and anxious for battle. Kirby-Smith was within one hundred miles and could support him with men and supplies, although help from that quarter was always contingent rather than certain since neither general was under the command of the other. Davis had allowed the invasion to be undertaken without a head. He had written Bragg on August 15 that Kirby-Smith was one of the Confederacy's ablest and purest officers, and that, therefore, he felt confident of their cordial co-operation. Granting these virtues to that officer, they are not likely to bring victory. The abler the general the less likely he is to co-operate and the more will he insist on his own conception of campaign. Nevertheless, his union with Bragg seemed a likelihood at the time, and if Bragg had insisted strongly enough, he very likely would have gotten it. He would have gotten it if he had delivered battle, at the same time notifying Kirby-Smith of his intention and the necessity of his presence for victory.

The South expected it; it almost went mad with hope, while the whole Northwest, that part of it which was abolition, was in an uproar. But when Buell moved up, Bragg wavered. His mind did a St. Vitus dance: it burned with a fever of battle one hour, and shook with a rigor of uncertainty the next, until the rigor shook whatever resolution he had to stand and fight. Against the advice of his ablest lieutenants and the manifest expectations of the rank and file of the army he turned aside and allowed Buell to proceed on his way, to reach Louisville where he could draw from the Northwest both men and supplies.

All saw the great opportunity Bragg had thrown away, Forrest among them; but, unlike the others, he did not conceal his opinions. He spoke them freely, openly, and profanely. (His exhausted horse had fallen and rolled over him. Any such injury always brought out feelings of injustice.) He had ridden hard, had fought almost daily, for the last two months; he had thinned his ranks and had jaded his men and their mounts all for a purpose, the defeat of the enemy. Now after this pain, labors, and loss, when the trial of a pitched battle would justify the strain to which he had put himself and his command, Bragg threw it all away.

This was one thing he was never able to abide, the useless sacrifice of his men. Whenever one of them went down in battle, there had to be a definite result for payment. It had to be as near certain as the expectation of man is able to require. To him they were not numbers in squads but personalities, and his treatment and demands were patriarchal. The professional concept of sacrificing so many to gain a hypothetical point was anathema to him; and when, as in this instance, one over him in authority so used his power, he raged with all the fierce release of the Wilderness. At such moments he was dangerous to friend and foe alike. It was said that at such times no one got within striking distance. Even his staff, as intimate as they were bound to be, kept safely away. When he was at the height of a rage, Major Strange would say, "We will have to send for ole miss before we can straighten out his kinks." This was what he called his wife. At such times she and his mother were the only people who could manage him. His mother would walk up and put her hands on his shoulders and call his name. She could always pacify him that way.

Bragg expected loyalty to himself; Forrest gave loyalty only to the cause. Things travel fast in the army, and gossip moves by quick, subterranean channels; so that if Bragg cared to listen, and he was to acquire the habit of going out of his way to listen to criticisms of himself, Forrest's statements no doubt came to his ears. At this time he may have paid no attention to them . . . public opinion had not yet overwhelmingly repudiated his leadership . . . but at any rate, Forrest was relieved from command of his brigade the day Buell reached Louisville, September 25, and ordered back to Middle Tennessee. He was told to take charge of that section, raise six regiments, and harass Nashville, Clarksville, and the enemy's communications. He was promised command over all he brought into the service.

Bragg had expected that Van Dorn and Price, the two commanders left in Mississippi, would move against Rosecrans and Sherman the same time he entered Kentucky, sweep them out of the way, take Nashville, and then join him on the Ohio. Combined they had enough troops to hope for success, but there as in Kentucky there was only co-operation. Price received Bragg's order, but Van Dorn's order, dated September 25, did not reach that officer until November 2, over

a month late; and so, left without positive orders, after much correspondence, these officers lost their golden opportunity and allowed themselves to be repulsed by Rosecrans at Corinth.

It may have been Bragg's intention that Forrest should prepare
the way for their arrival before the fortifications of Nashville. This
seems logical, but to Forrest it was very chagrining, for his return to
Middle Tennessee made him little more than a recruiting officer. He
was separated from a brigade which he had equipped and armed from
the enemy; which knew his ways and was willing to follow him to
hell and back. And now he was being shelved as a recruiting officer.
The fighting was in Kentucky, not Middle Tennessee.

But wherever the enemy and Forrest got together, there was bound
to be a fight. With his staff and the four Alabama companies for
escort he turned to the rear, and in five days was in Murfreesboro,
165 miles distant. A better man to rally Tennesseans around the
standard could not have been found, and here he recruited his most
famous brigade: The Fourth (Starnes's), The Eighth (Dibrell's), The
Ninth (Biffle's). Besides these regiments there were some ten companies unregimented, making altogether 3,500 mounted men.

Bragg had promised him command in Middle Tennessee, but no
sooner had Forrest organized these forces he had raised than Breckinridge appeared on the scene with Hanson's infantry and orders to
supersede the recruiting officer. These things happen frequently in
war, and Forrest obeyed like a West Pointer and moved his headquarters to La Vergne.

Nashville was still in the hands of the enemy. It had been Forrest's
intention to capture it as soon as he could get his troops into some
kind of condition. He appreciated the moral and political advantages
that would accrue to the cause, and then he was always restless when
the enemy was idle. No matter what their strength, he could not leave
them. "We'll just give them a dare anyway," he would say. If he
found them too strong to cope with, he would move off; but usually
his dares were not so harmless as they might sound.

So when Breckinridge entered his district, he made the proposition
that they reduce the capital together. Breckinridge, one of the few
political generals who was also a good soldier, agreed.

All the plans were made, and the assault was set for November 6.
The troops were distributed in column on the Franklin, Charlotte,
Nolansville, and Murfreesboro pikes. Forrest with one thousand
cavalry, closely supported by Hanson, moved forward on the Murfrees-

boro pike in the dark and before light carried the rifle pits at the Asylum, six miles out.

Hanson being eager to put his men in action, the attack was ordered at once. It was now day-dawn, and the men eagerly prepared to retake the capital of their state. Just before the orders to move up were given, Breckinridge, receiving express orders from Bragg, called it off. Hanson counter-marched to La Vergne, and Forrest let out his pent-up energy on a feint against the city.

Shortly afterwards Bragg entered Middle Tennessee. His Kentucky campaign had gone wrong at every point, and it was all due to the initial error of letting Buell get to his base without a pitched battle. The two armies later blundered into each other at Perryville and fought bloodily and indecisively. When Bragg's veterans shook the dust of Kentucky from their feet, they shook it off forever. Their general had frittered away a glorious opportunity; and the press, the people, his generals, and his army heaped upon his head all sorts of abuse. He was called the man with the "iron heart, the iron hand, and the wooden head."

He had hoped to conciliate the people of Kentucky by giving orders that nothing was to be taken from the countryside without pay- ment. When a farmer reported that two soldiers had climbed a fence and stolen a few apples, Bragg ordered them court-martialed and had one shot. This severe action, all out of proportion to the offense, had the opposite effect. The farmer was aghast and the community horrified.

Dr. Yandell of Hardee's staff writes the following to a Mrs. Cannon in Columbus, Mississippi:

" . . . By General Bragg's fulsome and bombastic proclamations, so rapidly followed by his hasty retreat, the Confederate army was made ridiculous in the eyes of the world, and for all this, we have nothing to show. Kirby-Smith accomplished something . . . Bragg, nothing. The latter receives his richly deserved reward in the universal distrust and detestation of his army for him, and in the loss of the respect and confidence of his generals. I cannot utter my private opinions or sentiments only; I speak the universal opinion of the army." And later on he recurs to it:

"I went with that noble army, attached to the noble Hardee's staff, filled with pride and hope, success seemed certain. No thought of failure ever clouded my mind. We had able generals under Bragg, and the best army that ever bled in a sacred cause; perfect in discipline

. . . tried and proved in courage, and filled with an unconquerable enthusiasm, prepared to fight against any odds . . . to make any sacrifices, *determined* to conquer. But alas Bragg lost us all. Headstrong and heartless, disregarding the wise opinions of Hardee and Buckner and others, he rushed on to failure; and by his miserable mismanagement had soon to rush back again to the place from which he started to prevent utter annihilation."

By the last of November the army was safely posted around Murfreesboro. Wheeler had been promoted to Chief of Cavalry. Early in December, Forrest was ordered to Columbia to prepare his new brigade of 1800 men for a raid into West Tennessee. The purpose was to break Grant's lines of communication.

After this treatment Forrest had lost all faith in his commander. Bragg had not fulfilled one single promise he had made him, and now he was ordering him into West Tennessee with a fresh, untried brigade, badly armed and badly equipped. He protested to Bragg that to cross the river and throw his small command in the midst of a superior enemy was unjust. Bragg promised the arms would be delivered at Columbia, but as the days and the preparations went on, none arrived.

In the midst of these preparations a young, slim boy, fair-complexioned and under age, presented himself to General Forrest with an order from Bragg making him his chief of artillery.

Forrest looked at him sharply and said with curt finality, "I have a fine battery of six guns under Captain Freeman, and I don't propose to be interfered with by Bragg."

The boy, Lieutenant John Morton, was confused. He had not known of the friction existing between the two officers. He only knew that Bragg had had nothing to do directly with the order transferring him to Forrest's brigade. It was his own great desire to serve under the raider, a desire he had had ever since Forrest's escape from Donelson, and the friendly aid of Bragg's Chief of Artillery had made it possible.

"I don't want to interfere with Captain Freeman," he replied. "I am acquainted with him and nearly all his men. But I want to go with you. I know it won't be long before you capture some guns for me."

Forrest looked more closely at him; then turning away, he said abruptly, "Well, come to see me in the morning, and I will see what I can do for you."

Lieutenant Morton saluted and withdrew from his quarters. The moment he had left, Forrest turned violently towards Captain Anderson—"I'd like to know," he said, "why in hell Bragg sent that tallow-faced boy here to take charge of my artillery? I'll not stand it. Captain Freeman shan't be interfered with!"

This was the unpropitious meeting of the hero and hero-worshipper, between Forrest and the tallow-faced boy who was later in Mississippi to become his chief of artillery and eventually the pride of his general. Nothing but the boy's persistence made it possible. (He had the distinction of recognizing as early as Donelson the possibilities of the unknown colonel.) Next morning Forrest sent him to Wheeler to endorse his transference—Wheeler was as far as La Vergne—and only after he had ridden there and back did the General reluctantly agree to use him. He and his ten men were allowed to go along with the wagons with the uncertain promise that if any guns were captured, he might form a battery. Captain Freeman, it will be observed, was not dispossessed.

While Forrest's preparations went forward, Grant was pushing hard against the defenses of Vicksburg. Sherman organized at Memphis an expedition to go to the mouth of the Yazoo River and strike at the defenses from the rear, at Walnut Hill. He commanded 32,000 men. There were, at the moment, only 6,000 in Vicksburg. Sherman's success would depend largely upon Grant's ability to hold the main Confederate army under Van Dorn, 28,000 strong, along the line of the Yallabusha.

Although Sherman's movement was supposed to be a secret, Pemberton, the Department commander, informed himself of its progress through spies. It became apparent that Grant was the weak point in the campaign, that his retreat would release a sufficient number of men to reënforce Vicksburg and meet Sherman's assaults.

The Confederates thoroughly understood the value of their cavalry now. It, and it alone, could save Vicksburg. Bragg proposed to cut the communications in West Tennessee while Van Dorn took the cavalry of his army and destroyed the immediate depot at Holly Springs. The successful outcome of these two raids would throw Grant back on the Memphis and Charleston railroad and force Sherman to operate alone.

But as Forrest delayed his preparations, Grant advanced. Bragg grew impatient and on December 19 ordered Forrest to move at once. He replied in writing, calling Bragg's attention to his ineffective armament and to the promise to furnish the brigade with better equipment. There were, besides other handicaps, only ten rounds of caps for the shotguns and many flintless muskets. Bragg, instead of explaining the urgent necessity, replied curtly to march without delay.

Forrest was now convinced that Bragg intended him and his command as a sacrifice to his dislike. He was ordered to cross a river three-quarters of a mile in width, without any means of ferriage, in mid-winter, and while gunboats were constantly patrolling its surface. Once across he had to elude or defeat a force many times his number, and he had to do this with a freshly organized brigade, badly armed, and for these arms only ten rounds of caps. It looked very much like a forlorn hope to so careful an officer as Forrest. And it might have been but for his private conviction as to the real reasons for the raid.

It is unlikely that Bragg expected Forrest to be a sacrifice to Pemberton's safety. It is still more unlikely that he expected to rid himself of his subordinate. It is more probable that he expected his lieutenant to repeat Murfreesboro in West Tennessee, and there to draw the arms and supplies he would not, or could not himself, furnish. He, on his side, very likely was annoyed at Forrest's delays. He was annoyed because he could not understand them, for in spite of the efficient way Forrest had delayed Buell in his race to Kentucky, and in spite of the way he had cut off the retreat of the garrison at Munfordville, Bragg had convinced himself that Forrest was only a partisan raider, and that he could not operate with the army. He might make picturesque and successful dashes on the enemy's lines of communications, but he lacked a West Point education and therefore he could not understand the ways of strategy. Bragg no longer remembered his hankering for more of Forrest's brilliance and for less of the kind of strategy the western armies had suffered from and were to continue to suffer from. The reason is obvious: Bragg, himself, was using this kind of strategy and worse tactics, and he was getting the same kind of results, drawn battles followed by retreat. There is just the vaguest suggestion of animus in this communication to Davis, November 24, 1862. ". . . 5,000 more I send, under Forrest and Morgan, on partisan service, for which and *which alone* their commanders are peculiarly and especially suited."

Forrest was never the partisan that Morgan was. It was one of the wastes of the Confederacy that he was used for this service and not set earlier to more valuable operations. His very brilliance obscured more valuable talents. This brilliance had confused Bragg. It was to confuse Davis and others. It was the result, not of dash, but of a thorough knowledge of the military situation and of a carefully planned movement, elastic enough to meet any exigency of battle. By finding and placing the enemy at a disadvantage, Forrest always had the odds on his side, and his generalship was so careful that he preferred never to act until the odds had turned in his favor. His protest now came from his belief that the enemy, not he, had the greatest advantage.

This is the instinct of a great commander, an instinct that Bragg lacked. Because Forrest showed contempt for numbers, for which he had too great a respect, Bragg regarded him as reckless, daring, and loving a gesture, for all these qualities were considered to make up the partisan. Forrest was daring, but never reckless; and he never made a gesture in his life. He had a contempt for numbers, because numbers in themselves are unimportant. The character of the commander is the important matter. By understanding that and playing upon it, Forrest always was able to throw his mass upon the segments of the enemy; or, if the enemy massed, he would manœuvre until the enemy became scattered or had fallen into a false position; then strike like the wind and destroy him before he had recovered from the surprise of the attack. It is a fundamental criticism of the two generals that he, without a military education, should have grasped this, the Napoleonic method of war, while Bragg, a professional, who had had the opportunity to study the actual campaigns, did not.

So, the next day, December 11, put entirely on his own responsibility, Bedford Forrest against his will set out from Columbia. His command had grown to some 2,000, and Napier with another 400 would join him west of the river. Now that the expedition was definitely under way, he put every ounce of his strength to make it a success. Carpenters had preceded the march to make two ferry boats, and days ahead scouts had scattered throughout the country to locate the enemy's position, determine his strength, report as to the roads, bridges, and to transact special business for the brigade.

Many days before he set out, the Northerners got wind of the raid, but they never learned just where he was going. The day he left Columbia, Rosecrans (he had replaced Buell) wired Grant at Oxford, Mississippi: "Tell the authorities to look out for Forrest."

This message was relayed to Dodge at Corinth; to Sullivan at Jackson, Tennessee; to Davies at Columbus, Kentucky; who in turn sent the message on down to their various subordinates. The officers at Forts Henry and Donelson were warned, and the garrisons in Kentucky.

While the enemy was looking for him somewhere in general but nowhere in particular, he was crossing quietly at Clifton on the two flatboats his carpenters had made. Each boat carried twenty-five men and horses at a load. The process was slow and tedious and done in a blinding rain. They were poled upstream half a mile, close into the bank, then floated down and across. This was the way the early settlers and traders had crossed the river where the shoals broke into the Natchez Trace. This was repeated on the return trip. The rain was a great advantage; it covered the movement. As a guard against gunboats, sentinels lined the shore in both directions to relay the news of a patrol's approach. In this way, working day and night, the crossing was finished by the fifteenth. That night the brigade encamped eight miles west of the river.

Forrest was now in enemy country, entirely severed from his base and any support. To the north lay Kentucky and a chain of Yankee forts and garrisons; to the south, Grant's army; to the east and behind him, the Tennessee River; to the west, the Mississippi. Hemmed in in this fashion, defeat meant destruction. To add to the difficulties, most of the ammunition caps got wet in crossing. Nevertheless, the next day the brigade marched eighteen miles in the direction of Lexington. It went into camp in time to allow the men to dry their clothes.

The Mobile and Ohio railroad runs like a spine through the western part of the state as far as Jackson. Here it diverges, one branch going to Grand Junction, the other to Corinth. North of Jackson, at Humboldt, a separate road connects Memphis with the Northwest. These roads were the Confederate objectives. To destroy them the Yankees had to be thrown on the defensive, but this required a great deal of cunning, since the various garrisons several times outnumbered Forrest's 2,000. But the first day across the river he managed it.

He had not forgotten the ruse he had used with so much success at Murfreesboro. At night long lines of camp-fires were built, camp-fires indicating a large body of men. He dismounted his riders and marched them as infantry, beat upon kettle-drums, rode details back and forth across bridges all night within the hearing of Sullivan's scouts. Certain notorious enemy sympathizers were captured and placed where they could see this display of force; then accidentally allowed to escape.

Sullivan, in whose hands the railroads were placed, wired Grant on the fifteenth: "Forrest is crossing the Tennessee at Clifton. A large force of cavalry is crossing above. Bragg's army is reported by scouts to be moving this way, through Waynesborough." Again on the seventeenth, "Couriers report several thousand rebel cavalry with

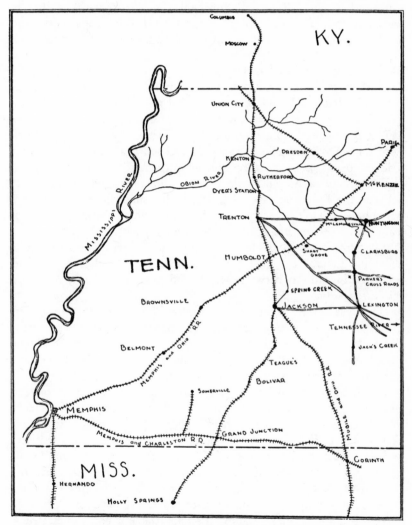

battery seven miles from this side of Clifton near McCorkle's, estimated ten thousand." Forrest's slow marches were not entirely devoted to drying his men's clothes.

A citizen reached the camp with 50,000 shotgun and pistol caps.

This was taken as a good omen. The men did not know that their commander had sent forward agents to procure them. The next day they pushed towards Lexington, skirmishing briskly. On the eighteenth Colonel Robert G. Ingersoll, the atheist, with an Illinois regiment and Hawkins's West Tennessee Cavalry and a section of artillery, 800 in all, fell back across a stream before the advance of "Bragg's army."

The same day Sullivan wired Grant, "Captain O'Hara who went out at daylight yesterday, reports the enemy are crossing the Tennessee River at Wright's Island *in considerable force.** At noon yesterday 3,000 infantry, 800 cavalry, and 6 pieces of artillery had crossed and *were still crossing."* * Later in the day he wired again—"My preparations for defense are good. I can hold Jackson against all their forces if it numbers 10,000, and meet and whip them if they are 5,000." He fails to say what he would do if they were only 2,000. Grant read between the lines and saw what was in his subordinate's mind and wired back, "Don't fail to get up a force and attack the enemy. *Never wait to have them attack you."* * Sullivan replied, "A rumor is here that Ingersoll's cavalry has been whipped and dispersed; know nothing about it." Later, "The enemy have attacked my cavalry. They have been fighting all day between Mifflin and Lexington. *I will hold this post till the last."* *

This was exactly what Forrest wanted him to do, stay cooped up in Jackson and not interfere with the destruction of the railroads. But Sullivan played further into his hands. He called in the outlying garrisons or reduced them greatly, so that only the feeblest protection was left to interfere with the raider's objective.

While Sullivan was busy at this work, Forrest was moving rapidly against Ingersoll, who had drawn up on the opposite side of a creek, to a strong position in a stretch of woods six miles from Lexington. When Captain Freeman wheeled up to the bridge to cross his artillery, he found the floor planks removed. Quickly, details from Starnes's regiment took down a snake-rail fence and relaid the flooring. The guns rolled over, the caissons after them, well protected by Starnes. Biffle and Dibrell moved by a right-hand road under the eye of this chief and, with Captain Gurley leading the four Alabama companies, struck Ingersoll's left and broke it; then swung around and shattered his right under Hawkins. This left one regiment, the 11th Illinois, and a section of artillery to bear the brunt of the next attack.

* Italics mine.

This proved a more formidable job. The artillery was well handled and well protected. Lieutenant Morton had been doing all he could with two borrowed guns to silence it, and he had failed. Forrest now devised new tactics. Supporting his artillery with Starnes and Dibrell, he put up a furious show of battle in the center, while Captain Anderson of his staff made a circuit with Gurley and 250 men to the enemy's rear. So well did Starnes and Dibrell play their parts that Anderson was within 150 yards before the 11th Illinois became aware of its peril.

Then the rebel yell penetrated the steady explosions of powder and Gurley rode down upon the battery. Just as he reached its position, one man was blown in two; but he had pierced the center, silenced the guns; and Starnes and Dibrell did the rest. Colonel Ingersoll, Major Kerr, 150 officers and men, 300 small-arms, mostly Sharpe's carbines, a full supply of ammunition, and 70 horses which were badly needed and immediately put in the service of the batteries, fell into the Confederates' hands.

Colonel Starnes pursued that portion which had escaped, picked up stragglers, and gathered in many valuable arms along the way. There was no further opposition, and the brigade reached the vicinity of Jackson the afternoon of the eighteenth.

It is reported that Ingersoll made a very frank admission to his captor. "I thought I was a soldier, but you surrounded and captured me before I knew what it was all about. I'm not a soldier, and I'm not going to try to be." He got out of the service and played no further part in the war.

This quick and effective dispersal of 800 men supported the General's bluff, but his work was yet to be done; and all his perils lay ahead. Grant wired McPherson this same day, "There will be no further advance of our forces until further directions. The enemy under Forrest have crossed the Tennessee below Clifton and are now near to Jackson. Communication is cut off, so that I cannot hear from there . . . I have reënforced Sullivan to the full extent of the capacity of the road to carry troops, partly from Columbus, partly from Corinth, one brigade from here (Oxford) and by concentrating of the forces of the District of Jackson. Lowe is also moving from Heiman." If all these various bodies converged at the right time, Forrest was lost. But he knew that there are always one or more weak points in every military net. Before sundown of the eighteenth he had put his hands on the first one—General Sullivan. All of Grant's reënforcements were directed to this general. Forrest had sized him up, and he knew that if he blundered with a few troops, he would blunder with many.

Forrest began at once making a great show of assault against Jackson. The pickets were quickly driven in and demonstrations made on all sides; then at eight o'clock that night Dibrell and Major Cox were detached, each with 100 men, to strike the roads. Cox seized the nearest station on the Mobile and Ohio south of Jackson, its guard of 75, their arms and ammunition. He destroyed the track and cut the wires. Dibrell charged the stockade at Carroll Station, eight miles north of Jackson, at two o'clock in the morning, captured 101 prisoners, 100 rifles, and a great quantity of ammunition, stores, tents, and supplies. He fired a volley into a passing train, tore up the track behind it, burned the stockade, and within thirty-six hours had rejoined the brigade. Biffle, at the same time, operated against the road leading towards Bolivar. He took an outpost of 50 men, tore up track and culverts, and returned to the command.

To confine Sullivan within the walls of Jackson until his three detachments had returned, Forrest kept up next morning the fierce show of assault he had begun the previous evening. He threw forward a determined line of skirmishers, flanked by mounted men, brought Freeman forward and directed a cross-fire against Englemann, whom Sullivan had sent on the business of feeling out his enemy.

This officer fell gradually back into the town. He reported naïvely, "The cavalry both on my right and left flanks, weary from hardships to which they had been exposed for the two preceding days, and now under fire from the enemy's battery, fell back one mile toward Jackson, *without having first obtained any orders from me to that effect.*"

Between four and five o'clock, sundown this time of the year, Forrest withdrew cautiously to Spring Creek. He left Colonel Russell's Fourth Alabama behind as skirmishers and a guard for his rear. Later that evening Russell followed the main body of the command and came up with it before day. The brigade was now all together again, with some 500 prisoners, a train enlarged to 25 wagons, the artillery by a section, and most of the men well armed and munitioned.

The first move in the raid was over, and it had been a complete success. The next was now in order.

At Spring Creek he divided up to move north. Dibrell was ordered to destroy the bridge over Forked Deer Creek and the stockade there; Starnes to reduce Humboldt; Biffle to get in rear of Trenton while Forrest with Cox's battalion, his body guard, and Freeman's artillery attacked it from the front. Russell was to hold Spring Creek and cover the rear.

The first hitch came with Dibrell. He failed to take the stockade. It was too strongly fortified, and the ground was too miry for Morton's guns. He fired into a trainload of troops going towards Jackson and, after watching them tumble out of the cars into the woods, moved north to rejoin the brigade. But if Dibrell had failed, Starnes carried out his orders to the letter. Humboldt fell into his hands about one P.M., the twentieth, after a short skirmish, and with it 100 prisoners, four caissons with their horses, 500 stands of arms, 300,000 rounds of small-arm ammunition, a large supply of artillery harness, and other stores not mentioned. Most of this was destroyed for lack of transportation, and Starnes proceeded north to rejoin the command.

In the meantime, Forrest moved against Trenton. He found the garrison strongly barricaded in the depot, reënforced with eight hundred bales of cotton and large hogsheads of tobacco. As an added protection, the nearby buildings were topped with sharpshooters. Charging into the town, he met such a severe fire from these places that he was forced to withdraw to the outskirts of the town. He threw out a line of sharpshooters to occupy the enemy on the buildings; then brought forward Freeman's guns. The Northerners were without artillery; so they surrendered after the third round had been thrown into their citadel.

As Colonel Fry stepped forward to give up his sword, he remarked sadly that it had been in his family for forty years. The General took it, handled it a few moments, and returned it. "Take back your sword, Colonel, as it is a family relic; but I hope, sir, the next time you wear it, it will not be against your own people."

Two of the enemy made the attempt to burn the depot, but Forrest and Captain Strange saw the smoke and ran to the building. They caught the men as they were coming out of the door. Pistols were rammed in their bellies and they were ordered back into the depot to put out the fire.

Trenton was a very rich prize: over 250 prisoners, 300 negroes, 13 wagons and ambulances, 7 caissons, 20,000 rounds of artillery and 400,-000 rounds of small-arm ammunition. Forrest loaded the trains with all he could and destroyed the rest. The booty included a great many horses and mules, but they were all unfit for service and so were returned to the citizens.

When Sullivan discovered on the evening of the nineteenth that

Forrest had withdrawn from around Jackson, he took a strong force
and felt his way in the direction of Spring Creek. He could not be sure
that Forrest's sudden withdrawal after so vigorous an investment was
not a ruse to trick him away from the town; then swoop down from
some other direction and take it. His latest report had set his enemy
down at 20,000 in West Tennessee and others still crossing the river.
The prisoners he took, all instructed directly or indirectly in their
parts, confirmed this illusion. He had already wired Grant that "Forrest has six or seven colonels, but can get no estimate of his force.
Cheatham's brigade is on this side and Napier's also." So when he
made contact with Russell, he left behind him in Jackson 2,000 men
to hold that place. In other words, he took just enough men to make a
reconnaissance in force.

The next morning Colonel Russell, his long auburn beard bristling
in the weather, his gray frock coat buttoned up to the chin under his
overcoat (this was one of his eccentricities for, hot weather or cold
weather, he never unbottoned his collar), rode among his companies.
Half of them he dismounted; the rest he divided between the flanks.
The "infantry" fired a volley, the cavalry charged. Sullivan's men became panic-stricken and fell back across the creek and burned the
bridge after them. Russell's aggressive tactics confirmed in Sullivan's
mind his beliefs and he made no further attempt to recross the stream;
so, undisturbed, the Confederate rear remained in position all day and
that night at eight o'clock wheeled about and rode towards Trenton.

It will be remembered that the other part of the Confederate plan
to frustrate the offensive against Vicksburg was the destruction of
Grant's immediate stores at Holly Springs. About the time Forrest
withdrew from before Jackson, Van Dorn left his army with 3,500
cavalry, galloped to the enemy's rear, surprised Holly Springs, captured its garrison of 1,500, and completely demolished the stores.
On the twentieth he returned to his army. Forrest's raid to the north
had diverted attention from him, and now the attempt to recapture
him before he could return to his lines was to prove of great help
to Forrest. It lessened by a great deal the concentration against him
and *retained* Grant's cavalry in Mississippi at a time when it might
have been used very effectively by Sullivan.

Forrest's prisoners had grown so in numbers that they had become
considerably embarrassing. While Van Dorn was retracing his steps
to his army, Forrest was busy assembling them in squads and placing
guards at intervals. In a very loud tone he sent courier after courier

to different "generals" to bring up their "commands." The couriers took the hint, galloped off, supplied themselves with fresh equipment at the depot, and returned to gallop off with other orders. In the dusk numerous fires were built, and detachments were formed to parade before them and behind them. The reserves had begun to arrive. Later in the evening Dibrell and Starnes came up, and Napier with 430 new troopers. Early next morning, the twenty-first, Colonel Russell brought up the rear. By this time the illusion of a great force had been established.

It was very necessary that the prisoners should be impressed with this illusion, for to the north, at Columbus, General Davies and his 5,000 men must remain behind their works as Sullivan had done at Jackson. What the prisoners, who were about to be parolled, and passed through his hands, had to say to Davis might mean success or failure; it might even mean the life or death of the brigade. This was certainly the crucial point in the raid, for the trestle-work, standing high in the Obion bottoms, had not yet been touched.

The prisoners, altogether about 1,300, were quickly parolled. Hawkins and the other West Tennesseans were sent to their homes. The others, 900 in number were put in charge of Colonel Collins and set under way for Columbus. Captain Anderson took all the bonds and oaths of allegiance which had been extorted from the citizens of the country, piled them in the courthouse yard, and set them on fire. Soon after, Forrest, with his escort, the artillery, and the wagon train, pulled out of Trenton in the direction of Union City. Starnes and Biffle were ordered to remain behind and rest; then to follow after. This time Colonel Dibrell covered the rear.

The brigade, now fully armed and equipped, well supplied with provisions, blankets, and ammunition, and much stronger than when it first entered West Tennessee, was in good condition and fine spirits.

Sweeping northward, Forrest struck in turn Rutherford Station, Kenton, Union City, and Moscow, Kentucky. All these places fell into his hands with their small garrisons and a few supplies. Moscow was the extreme limit of his movement, and dangerously near Columbus.

But Davies, although he outnumbered Forrest two to one, did not think of risking battle. He had heard the rumor that Bragg was on this side of the river. When Grant sent him orders to attack Forrest, he appealed to Halleck at Washington that it would endanger the supplies left in his care and was sustained in his appeal. Now, as the depots along the railroad fell one by one, he became certain that Columbus would be next. "I shall hold Columbus," he wired Halleck.

This officer proved an ideal commander-in-chief to Davies. He ordered Curtis at St. Louis to reënforce Columbus immediately, and to Cairo the wires flashed the order: "Send to Columbus all your available forces." Again on the twenty-second Davies reassurred Halleck, "Think Columbus will be attacked, but am ready for any force they can bring." He then proceeded to load the thirteen million dollars worth of stores on boats in the river to show how ready he was. On the twenty-third he informed Halleck, "I have had no communication with any place south of Trenton which was captured, from which I think all is safe below that point." The very next day he wired in a frenzy, "I am informed General Cheatham has crossed the Tennessee with 40,000 men and is marching north. I cannot hold Columbus against that force. The information had reached me before that he had crossed, but I did not credit it till now." Forrest had played his part around the campfires at Trenton extremely well.

Davies speeded up the loading of the boats, dug more trenches, and ordered the commander at Island No. 10 to spike his guns and destroy his ammunition. The garrison chief at Memphis assured him that such action was unnecessary, and Davies felt greatly aggrieved at his comrade's lack of sympathy. Only he could understand the great danger to the supplies and he was well pleased with the way he "kept Forrest . . . for several days under the impression that I was going to give him battle outside, by movements of trains and circulating reports." He should have known a fox is not caught with a fox's tricks.

While Davies was "saving" his supplies, Forrest, like the devil in Montgomery County, was riding up and down the railroad lines and completely demolishing the tracks. On the twenty-fourth and the twenty-fifth Starnes with five hundred axes captured at Trenton, fell upon the trestle-work in the Obion bottoms. As the chips flew into the slime and water, the trussles, as the boys called them, some as high as fifteen feet, tumbled and broke in the back-waters. At this time of year, in the overflown condition of the bottoms, it was well-nigh impossible to replace the trestle, and certainly not in time to assist Grant in his present campaign. While Starnes was busy on this part of the road, others were razing the culverts and firing the track, until for long distances the rails could be heard buckling and twisting.

While this was going on, Forrest's scouts came in and reported that 10,000 men were advancing northward to cut off his retreat. This information did not take him from his work, the complete destruction of the road. This was done by the twenty-fourth, and on Christmas day he ordered most of his regiments to go into camp. It was the first real day of rest they had had since leaving Columbia two weeks ago. It is true they had stopped along the route long enough to let the horses blow a spell, but no more than that. There had been little or no relaxation. The weather was cold and rainy, the roads atrocious, the work and riding as much as horse and rider could stand, and not a day had passed without a skirmish, or an investment. Captain Anderson, in reviewing all the many hard marches and pitched battles, remembers this as the most painful of all.

Now the boys lie or stroll about the camps, chewing and smoking, drinking the good coffee they have captured, telling over their deeds, looking for lost buddies, and lazying before the big fires. Some have jabbed their ramrods into hunks of dough, made up on the backs of their oilcloth coats, and are holding them before the fire to cook. Others have mixed cornmeal, a pinch of salt, and a little water, wrapped corn shucks about it and are burying it in the hot coals and ashes. A squad is guffawing over the tale of an old woman who complained that "Mr. Forrest and his hoss critters formed a streak of fight in my back yard, tore down my fence, and plumb ruint my ash-hopper." Somebody else, having nothing better to do, cackles like a hen. One of the critters says "shoo . . ." Other hens cackle, and others shoo. This grows until the camp sounds like a poultry yard stirred up over a mink or a weasel.

General Forrest is in high spirits. If he is thinking about those 10,000 men crossing his line of retreat, nobody knows it. He goes from company to company, talks with the officers, singles out those of his riders who have done themselves proud in action, praises them, jokes with them, and they joke back. He lets them know he sees everything they do. When taps sounds out that night, the riders lie down well pleased with themselves and their General. He had given them one whole day of rest, just long enough for their spirits to swell with enthusiasm and self-confidence; not long enough for the reaction of inertia to set in, for tomorrow Forrest's brigade, not Bragg's army, must turn its critters' noses southeast and make for the river.

Many a rider has been able to reach his objective, but not so many have been able to get back to their bases intact, and the General knew that Sullivan, besides the usual military demands, had now his honor to think about. General Haynie had already repaired the culverts as far as Trenton and was pushing hard for Union City. Forrest had one great consolation. If Sullivan had blundered in one way, he might blunder in another.

To avoid Haynie, he swung twenty-six miles to the southeast, destroyed a bridge on the Paducah branch, and bivouacked at Dresden the night of the twenty-sixth. He waited here until all his scouts came in with information exact enough to act upon.

Haynie learned next day that Forrest was at Dresden and recalled the advance to Trenton. He informed Sullivan, who was still at Jackson, of Forrest's new position and also of his *intentions*. He would leave Dresden, surmised General Haynie, and make a run for the Tennessee River, to cross probably at Reynoldsburg, a landing a little to the northeast of Huntington. Haynie then prepared to move directly on Dresden; but, learning that one bridge was down on this road, he suggested to Sullivan that if they should move on the Huntington road, they could fall on Forrest's flank as he fled towards the river. Sullivan arrived at Trenton in the night and ordered this movement to get under way. Colonel Dunham with a brigade, 1,800 strong, left Trenton at eleven P.M. At dawn on the twenty-eighth Colonel Fuller and 2,000 men followed Dunham on the way to Huntington. Sullivan and Haynie moved with this last body.

They now had him on the run. To the north, at Fort Heiman, Lowe was waiting to intercept his retreat in that direction. Gunboats had been up as far as Clifton destroying ferries. Every bridge south of the highroad from Paris to Jackson had been destroyed, and the crossings were now held in force. He might sweep south between Reynoldsburg and Huntington, since cavalry can travel faster than infantry, but he would escape Sullivan only to run into Dodge, who was moving against him from Corinth with several heavy infantry brigades, some cavalry, and artillery. In that case, he stood the chance of being crushed between Dodge, the lower, and Sullivan, the upper millstone.

A tighter cordon than this has never been drawn about any command. But it had one flaw: it had been planned on the assumption, not the knowledge, that Forrest was in flight to cross the river. On the morning of the twenty-seventh, Forrest left Dresden, but he went southeast, not east. That night he bivouacked at McKenzie, about half-way between Dresden and Huntington.

So that night he lay closer to Fuller and Dunham, but above them, with 2,000 men—Dibrell had been detached to watch the flank near Trenton—a heavy wagon train, and eight guns. He lay above

SEPARATING GRANT FROM HIS BASE 129

them and above a sluggish fork of the Obion whose slow current stirred the bottoms and hid the suck of its dark sink-holes. On the other side, while Forrest's riders were sleeping, Colonel Dunham set out in the clammy dark, marching east.

Half-way between Huntington and Trenton was a little town called McLemoresville. Half-way between McLemoresville and Huntington stood an old double-bridge, so rotten that Sullivan's men did not take the trouble to destroy it. Its causeways, leading up to it a quarter of a mile on either side, were bogs of mire, over which no human beings could pass, or so thought Sullivan's men. By sundown on the twenty-eighth Forrest drew up before it with all his command, excepting Dibrell and Cox.

The same evening Sullivan and Haynie struck camp at Shady Grove, ten miles from Trenton, and a few miles to the west of Mc-Lemoresville. Colonel Dunham with the other brigade bivouacked some miles to the east of McLemoresville. Between them, unsafe even for a pedestrian, the double-bridges, foreboding and gloomy, leaned in the swamp timber. Night came suddenly, and a drizzle, part rain, part mist, settled down upon the damp slime of its decayed flooring.

Forrest rode up before it, the drizzle falling from his broad-brimmed hat to settle in his beard. He made a quick inspection; then ordered the men to dismount. In the dark, under torch-light, and at times candle-light, ten men from each regiment were soon cutting timber-forks to strengthen the bridges and repair the trestles. The General dismounted, and with an axe, led his pioneers with his sharp, accurate strokes. In an hour's time the structure was reënforced sufficiently to let some cavalry pass over.

But it was a comparatively simple matter for horsemen. When it came to the heavily laden trains, that was another matter. Exhausted from their forced rides, a sleepless night, the men were in no humor to risk the still shaky bridge in the dark, and in the rain. The feat looked to them as it had appeared to Sullivan's men, impossible.

Old Bedford, seeing the hesitancy, mounted the driver's seat of one of his headquarters wagons, pulled tight on the lines, and spoke to the mules. There was the clatter of their slipping feet; then the harness tightened and the wagon rumbled with hollow noises over the bridge's floor, and in a few minutes it had safely crossed the stream.

After this example, there was no further hesitancy. A wagon of ammunition moved up, but the driver's eye was not so good. He was upset in the muddy water. Another followed, and it too was upset. The situation began to look desperate again. The officers, as well as the men, were growing discouraged. Forrest grew hard and stern, and vicious-tempered. He turned loose upon the evening air choice explosions of profanity. Those who objected from now on kept their objections to themselves and waded out into the stream. After much hard, tedious work and after painful exposure, the wagons were upturned and drawn up on the other side.

Five hundred men and their officers were now ordered up. Into the holes and gullies of the causeway sacks of flour and coffee, as precious as it was to the sow-belly boys, were thrown. These five hundred were quickly divided into lots of twenty men each, each lot moving with a wagon. There were no more spills. By three o'clock on the morning of the twenty-ninth the wagon train was across the Obion.

It now came the artillery's turn. By this time the causeway was so cut up as to be impracticable, but that high, shrill voice penetrated the dark with an order to detail this time fifty men to each gun. The horses bogged, the men cursed, whips cracked, and the details splashed waist-deep in the mud and icy water, keeping their shoulders against the wheels, pulling or kicking the horses. The General stood by, and his voice was a whip to those who lagged; and the strange, uncertain shadows from the torches made harder his jaw and the determined lines of his face. In three hours the artillery was to the south of the Obion and ready for action.

There was a very good reason why these guns must be made ready for action. He now lay between Fuller and Dunham, like a fox between two packs of hounds, not at bay, but in ambush, with full knowledge of their movements while they were in complete ignorance of his. Yet at any moment they might discover his hiding place—their patrols were scouring the woods—strike and drive him into the river.

But no patrol stumbled on the rotten-bridge crossing, and at daylight Sullivan broke camp and marched through McLemoresville for Huntington to get on Forrest's flank as he ran for the Tennessee River.

A few hours later, after Sullivan's rear had passed through the village, the Confederate advance, stiff with mud and work, slipped out of the bottoms and rode in.

Fuller and Dunham reached Huntington the afternoon and the evening of the twenty-ninth, and there they congratulated themselves on their manœuvre. Sullivan, in the pride of his innocence, wired Grant, "I reached Huntington before the rebels knew I had left

Trenton. I have Forrest in a tight place . . . My troops are moving on him in three directions, and I hope for success."

It is true that he had the Forrest who was fleeing to cross the river at Reynoldsburg in a tight place, with troops concentrating from three directions to trap him; it is also true that this Forrest did not know he had left Trenton; but then this Forrest existed only in Sullivan's imagination. The real one was at Flake's store sixteen miles from Lexington, and in the Northern rear.

And here he was, with the situation completely in his hands, deftly drawing the enemy into the very toils they had set for him. When he was at McKenzie, with the detailed reports of his scouts before him, he had divined their plans. To know the enemy's plans is to avoid them. To Forrest it was to use them. He immediately sent Major Cox to get on the Paris-Huntington pike and travel in the direction of Huntington until he met the enemy. Cox was then to fight them and break towards the Tennessee River. This would strengthen the enemy's belief in their assumptions and give him time to make plans for reaching his next objective.

This was the destruction of the stores at Bethel Station, a depot thirty-six miles south of Jackson. It was now the only large depository of supplies for Grant's army. Grant considered it so important that he wired Sullivan that the road south of Jackson must be protected "peradventure."

It was now in Forrest's power to disgrace Sullivan utterly. He had so placed himself that there was no possible way for him to keep Forrest from destroying the stores at Bethel Station if he chose to destroy them. Forrest knew this, but he also knew that such a bold march in the present condition of the brigade would tire his men, break down his horses, and give Sullivan time to unite with Dodge. There would be little chance of breaking through this union and the river too. So he made his plans, first, to destroy Sullivan.

But since Sullivan had concentrated, he obviously could not attack him at Huntington. He must separate his brigades and defeat them in detail on the thirty-first, fall on Bethel Station the second of January; then, his work entirely done, and no obstructions in his rear, he could recross the river and return to his base. So confident was he that he could lure the enemy brigades apart and defeat them that he sent one company forward to cut wires and bridges and prepare forage twelve miles south of Jackson.

All day of the thirtieth he lay perfectly still, resting his riders and their critters. Then early that evening he sent his brother Bill and his independent company, "The Forty Thieves" as the boys called them, to attract Dunham's attention.

Seven miles below Clarksburg lived a Mr. Parker. In front of his house two roads crossed, the one from Clarksburg with the one from McLemoresville, making the apex of a triangle. Captain Bill had been ordered to throw out bait and draw off Dunham towards this apex.

He was entirely successful. Dunham made a forced march to cut off the raider's "retreat." He had the judgment, however, to call on Sullivan for immediate reënforcement. But Sullivan was in no condition to act immediately—Forrest had counted on this. He was so certain he had trapped the raider that to find him not trapped but loose and in his rear demanded of his cautious mind too sudden an adjustment to the changed conditions for him to act quickly. While he was deciding whether this might not be a clever ruse to throw him off the scent, Forrest expected to destroy Dunham.

While his superior was making up his mind what action to take, Dunham moved forward with commendable rapidity and threw himself across "Forrest's line of retreat" at the Cross Roads. The ruse had been a perfect success. The Confederates lay between the two Northern brigades. Sending back four companies on the Clarksburg road to watch Sullivan and delay his advance if he should decide to join his lieutenant, Forrest opened battle with Dunham.

The numbers were about the same on each side. (Dibrell was still detached). But this made little difference, as Forrest intended to whip Dunham with his artillery and keep his cavalry fresh for Sullivan. In this he had very great odds, eight to three, and greater odds, even, in the efficiency of his artillerists. He placed the first gun himself, one from Freeman's battery and commanded by Lieutenant Nat Baxter.

"Very early on the morning of December thirty-first . . . General Forrest rode up to our battery, and ordered me to hitch up my gun and come with him. Having gone about a half-mile in the direction of Parker's Cross-Roads, he ordered some cavalry that accompanied us to throw the fences down, and here we turned into a field with the piece. General Forrest dismounted and went ahead to the crest of a hill and selected a position for my gun. To my great surprise, as I reached the top of the hill I saw the Federals in heavy line of battle not more than four hundred yards away. With the exception of two or three hundred cavalry immediately behind my gun, and one or two hundred dismounted men, who were about one hundred yards in front, behind logs and trees and in fence corners skirmishing with the enemy, there were no other Confederate soldiers in sight. He told me to open immediately upon them, which I had no sooner done than three pieces of artillery from the Union side responded in lively fashion. I succeeded in dismounting one of the guns, to the great satisfaction of General Forrest, who remained with me all through the duel, and was with my piece at frequent intervals throughout the day."

In half an hour the artillery—Morton in the center, a section of Freeman's battery on either flank—had driven the Northerners to the cover of a ridge. The Confederate line, in the same battle order, advanced against the ridge and, after a severe struggle, took and held it.

Dunham made a well-directed charge to regain it, but his men could not face the combined musketry and accurate discharges of grape and cannister. He fell back, after an hour, to the protection of sixty acres of timber-land, enclosed with a snake fence and surrounded with open fields.

As he was falling back, Forrest advanced several guns to a position that would enfilade his line; then sent Colonel Russell with the Fourth Alabama to his left and rear, and Starnes to the right. With these dispositions made, he began slowly and carefully, so that he might save as much as possible the lives of his men, to close in upon Dunham.

This officer, seeing the Confederates had weakened their front, ordered a charge. It was gallantly made, but it again broke down before the rapid and efficient discharges from the Confederate guns, guns loaded with two charges of cannister to one charge of powder. As the blue line fell back, Russell struck its rear and captured the wagon train drawn up in a hollow behind the woods. Starnes moved on the other flank, and the enemy staggered before his charge, but rallied as it fell back. At this time, Forrest ordered the firing redoubled along his front. The balls struck the cedar fence, scattering the rails and driving the splinters through the men lying behind it. In a few minutes the Thirty-Ninth Iowa Infantry, the left of the Northern line, broke and re-formed in a cornfield at the edge of the woods.

Forrest put his mount into a gallop to his left where Napier and his men crouched in the sandy rises. He told them they must break the enemy's right. Colonel Napier rode out among his men and ordered the charge, the last one he was ever to order, and his men dashed hard upon their yells. It was an extravagant charge, Napier and many of his bold riders never returned; but it drove Dunham's right back towards the woods so hurriedly that it abandoned the guns. They could not be dislodged from this second position, however, and Napier's thinned line returned to its former position.

It had served its purpose, if at a great cost: Dunham, without artillery, without his wagons, and surrounded on three sides, was in a desperate condition. Handkerchiefs and shirt-tails went up from different parts of the woods lot.

Forrest ordered the firing to cease and sent forward an orderly to receive the surrender, "to save the further effusion of blood." Old Bedford liked this phrase. It had a nice, full sound, and at the same time, it always got results. It was one of the few technical, military terms he ever took the trouble to learn. It was as near chivalry as he ever got in his dealings with the enemy, and at that the chivalry was always spoiled with the plain, salty phrase, "or I will put every man to the sword."

And it was upon this last-named phrase that Colonel Dunham lingered. His untenable position and the morale of portions of his men told him it was only a question of time, or rather a question of how much time. If he could make it enough, Sullivan might arrive.

In his playing for time, he agreed to let the Confederates proceed on their way. But Forrest wasn't going anywhere. Before he could make Dunham understand just this, from Parker's house, now in the Confederate rear, the sound of sharp-biting musketry interrupted the deliberations.

The General turned sharply and listened. In a moment Colonel Carroll, of his staff, dashed up and shouted excitedly, "General, a heavy line of infantry is in our rear. We're between two lines of battle. What'll we do?"

"Charge both ways!" came the quick, unruffled reply.

He galloped towards the cross roads and found Sullivan, the genius for "tardiness," as he was called by one of his subordinates, had this time not been late. He had surprised Forrest's rear and, at the moment, was among the horse-holders. This meant that the Confederate center was between two bodies of infantry and perilously near to disaster.

While the General was taking in the situation, a Northern officer and a number of privates were upon him and shouting, "halt and surrender." He reined in his horse, said that he had already surrendered some time since and was at that moment on his way to bring up the rest of his command to surrender in form.

With that he swung his charger to the rear and galloped away to rejoin his men; and, before the enemy's two bodies could act together he was slipping between their flanks. Dunham made no effort to cut him off, but he had a very good reason for his inactivity. When Starnes and Russell heard the firing from the Cross-Roads, they sensed what had happened and vigorously charged his flanks.

But Fuller moved forward at a double-quick and captured five wagon-loads of ammunition and two ambulances which drove up at this moment from their place of security; he recaptured the guns Dunham had lost and two others whose horses he had disabled. The horses of three hundred of Napier's and Cox's commands had already fallen into his hands, and this many men were surrounded and captured. Fuller then quickly threw a section of artillery into position and sent a rapid fire into the remaining Confederates who were following their leader off the field. The fire had a very demoralizing effect, especially on Dibrell's regiment. He had arrived from Trenton a few hours earlier, where he had captured and paroled one hundred fifty cavalry, and his men were worn from their forced march.

Forrest took fifty of these and his escort, turned back, and rode down upon the Northern guns. He dispersed their gunners and threw the infantry support into confusion. His blow was swift and hard, and unexpected, like the charge against Sherman at Shiloh; and it gave Fuller a sufficient check to let the Confederate center withdraw without further exposure. As Forrest left, he took off two caissons whose horses had become frightened by the charge and had dashed into his escort.

He got his entire command well in hand in Dunham's rear and set out for Lexington with his train which, minus the five wagons of ammunition, was intact. He reached that town by six o'clock and went into camp. At two o'clock the next morning, he saddled up and moved off in the direction of the Tennessee River.

The young, tallow-faced Morton and Forrest were riding side by side as they were quitting the field. The General was deep in thought, trying to unravel the surprise. He had given McLemore explicit orders to prevent just such a contingency, and McLemore had not been heard from. It looked as if the earth had opened and swallowed him, for certainly it seemed improbable that Sullivan had captured every man in the four companies.

The true condition was one which Forrest could not, at the moment, understand. McLemore's failure to inform him of Sullivan's and Haynie's progress was his own fault. As it turned out, his written instruc-

tions to McLemore were very vague, so vague that McLemore inter-
preted the order to mean merely a reconnaissance; and so he moved,
not in front, but on the flank of Haynie, Fuller, and Sullivan and
returned in time to be a spectator of what he should have prevented.
He escaped before he could become involved in the surprise. Even
with this blunder, if Colonel Fuller had not disobeyed Sullivan, who
had ordered him to halt until he arrived with the rear from Huntington, an order which would have made a delay of an hour and a half,
just time enough for Forrest to have forced Dunham into capitulation,
Forrest would have been in position to decide the issue with Sullivan's
other brigade.

These thoughts were interrupted by a minie ball whizzing by
Morton's face. He saw the General drop his head.

"General, are you hurt?"

Forrest raised his head, took off his hat and saw the big hole in
its brim:

"No, but didn't it come damn close to me?"

Sullivan wired Grant enthusiastically that he had crushed Forrest
and that he needed a good cavalry regiment to go through the country
and pick up the remnants. Sullivan wired this pleasant news and received the expected compliment from Grant; but he didn't believe his
big words, for twenty-four hours after the "wiping out" he was still
in line of battle at Parker's Cross-Roads waiting for a counter attack
on his flank.

Forrest was then ten miles out from Lexington, paroling what
prisoners he had carried off and attending to his wounded. He had
already put the train in motion for the river and had sent ahead a
small detachment to raise the sunken ferries and put them in condition
for the passage. There was no thought of Bethel Station now. The
miscarriage at Parker's house had saved what was left of Grant's
supplies.

As he drew near Clifton, he found "the good cavalry regiment"
across his path. Without stopping to reconnoitre, he threw Dibrell
against its center, broke it, and then scattered the leftward fragment
with Starnes's regiment, and the right one with Biffle.

There was no further difficulty at the crossing, but, expecting a
hurried pursuit, he rushed his men as rapidly as possible. The guns
were first taken over and unlimbered on the opposite bank in case
gun-boats might try to interfere. The wagons were next driven onto

the ferries. There was no time to transfer the critters in this way. After piling their saddles and bridles on the ferries, they were led to the bank and pushed into the water. Once in, they swam after the leader. A detail in a skiff held his bridle and brought the whole lot safely to the other side. There were as many as 1000 critters in the water at one time. The troopers were carried over last, although many did not wait for the flatboats. Some took fence rails and made them into rafts, others discovered skiffs, and a few of the hardiest swam the six hundred yards to the other bank.

One regiment was left in position until the last as a guard for this movement, and with it Forrest placed a section of artillery under Lieutenant Edwin Douglas. His orders to Douglas were to fortify as best he could with logs, rails, and anything he found at hand and, if attacked, to fight to the last so that the main body might escape.

Douglas soon threw his guns into position and, according to the artillery manual, unlimbered and withdrew the horses obliquely to the rear and out of range. The General stood by while this manœuver was being executed. He saw the rapid swing of the horses, and, mistaking it for a cowardly runaway on the part of the drivers, galloped up to the man on the led horse and struck him over the shoulders with the flat of his sabre.

"Turn those horses around and git back where you belong, or, by God, I'll kill you!"

"Gineral, I'm moving in accordance with tactics."

"No you are not. I know how to fight, and you can't run away with the ammunition chest."

A few days later Lieutenant Douglas took a book of tactics to Forrest's tent and explained why it was necessary to move the horses out of range. He offered to give an exhibition drill so that he might better understand the reasons for the manœuver. The invitation was "accepted, and he became greatly interested. In less than a week he had mastered the manual and became an expert among experts in placing a battery and in the use of guns." He called in the soldier whom he had wronged and made a prompt apology.

The crossing began at noon on January 1, and was completed by eight o'clock that evening; the rear then followed, and scattering detachments crossed several days later at different points on the river.

Sullivan arrived on the second and third to find the bird had flown. By lingering at the cross-roads he had lost the last chance he would ever get to destroy Forrest. Dodge, as soon as he learned of his cavalry's defeat, called off the pursuit from Purdy. Only Sullivan sent his men stumbling in the miry, rocky road and blinding rain to make sure that the raider was out of his territory. One regiment reported fifty barefooted men, and another had twenty to desert. They all were torn and bruised and exhausted and disgusted with the march, for they all knew that the march was unnecessary. Their officers were indignant and made known their indignation in their reports. They saw no use in pursuing him when there was positive information that he had already escaped. But then, Sullivan did not *know* this to be the truth. For all he knew this might be just another one of the wizard's tricks.

After this Forrest began to seem a wizard of the saddle to his enemy. Murfreesboro had given him a reputation, but from now on his name in the West, like Stonewall Jackson's in the East, was more and more to become synonymous with victory. Not being a professional soldier, he did not know how to push himself with the Confederate Government as, for example, Jackson had done. He was too busy with the immediate problem on hand to be thinking of his rewards, or of the effect of his actions on the military or on the President.

The fruits of this campaign were very great. He had killed, captured, and wounded fifteen hundred officers and men, and among the officers four colonels of regiments. He had captured five pieces of artillery, three of which were afterwards retaken, eleven caissons, and thirty-eight wagons and teams.

When he entered West Tennessee, more than half of his men were lacking in serviceable arms. When they withdrew, they were well armed and equipped with blankets, saddles, and bridles. Although he had lost some five hundred killed, captured and wounded, he took out with him more men than he had carried in, and he took them out soldiers. For the second time he had accomplished a very delicate operation with raw recruits.

He had made only one serious blunder, and when this promised the complete destruction of his brigade, he was not surprised by a surprise. He had coolly and intelligently extricated his alarmed and scattered troopers from the trap, and in such a way that the Northern general did not risk a pursuit until pursuit was too late.

This one slip had made his campaign incomplete according to his expectations, but the primary objective had been reached. Grant was forced to retreat to Corinth and Grand Junction and leave the Confederate army along the Yallabusha free to go to Vicksburg's defense. Sherman, unaware of Grant's withdrawal, threw his infantry against

Walnut Hill without success. He lost over two thousand killed and wounded and finally withdrew. The garrison at Vicksburg had lost something under two hundred men. Van Dorn shared the honors with Forrest in this.

But it was Forrest alone who determined Grant to abandon the railroad as his chief line of supply and shift to the Mississippi River. It was the first great move in the game of strategy which was being played for the possession of the Southwest. If the rivers could be closed before the North could develop sufficient cavalry to defend the railroads, Northern armies could not maintain themselves in Southern territory. This was the particular military lesson which Forrest's West Tennessee Campaign had shown. It remained to be seen whether those in authority would turn this lesson to account.

Among the captured stores at Trenton was a regulation officer's blade. The General took it, tested it, and ran his finger along its dull edge, for like all officers' swords it was sharp only a short distance from the point. He took it over to a grindstone, and there with an orderly he ground it to a razor's edge. Someone who had been in the regular army protested that this was contrary to all military precedent.

"War means fighting, and fighting means killing," replied the General.

The grindstone turned over.

CHAPTER X

A Bluff and a Streight

WHILE Forrest was fighting the battle of Parker's Cross-Roads, Bragg and Rosecrans met along Stones River at Murfreesboro. On the first day the Confederates had the advantage, breaking and driving the enemy's right four miles. But the Northerners rallied. The pivot of their broken line held firm under Thomas before delayed and piecemeal attacks. And then on the first day of the new year, 1863, the two armies lay opposite each other without fighting.

When it became evident on January 2 that Rosecrans was not going to withdraw, Bragg ordered Breckinridge to take his division and drive the enemy from a hill on the extreme right of the Confederate lines. The attack was set for four o'clock in the afternoon, just time enough for the hill to be carried before night could fall. Breckinridge's orders were, then, to entrench.

The attack failed—from too much success. The orders had been merely to take the hill. The brigadiers could not restrain their men, and they rushed over the hill and beyond to be slaughtered by fifty guns massed upon a rise on the west bank of the river. By ten o'clock that evening the news that two thousand Confederates had fallen in the charge, cast a gloom over the Army of Tennessee. The night of the third Bragg evacuated Murfreesboro and fell back upon Tullahoma.

But in spite of this withdrawal the Northern offensive in the Southwest had miscarried. Grant's campaign against Vicksburg was a complete failure, and Rosecrans's possession of the field was a doubtful victory. His generals had advised a retreat on the first. He had had the courage to hold fast, but he did not have the strength to follow Bragg. Wheeler had circled his rear and destroyed most of his trains at La Vergne. This, in itself, not counting the prostration of his men, would make him content with a barren field and a county town. The state capital remained in his hands, but the Army of Tennessee, occupying a stronger position, was intact. This meant that the ultimate fate of Middle Tennessee had not yet been decided.

The new Confederate line ran behind a long, broken ridge, eighteen miles Southeast of Murfreesboro and extending from Shelbyville on the left to Wartrace on the right. Each flank was protected by strong cavalry guards at McMinnville and Columbia. Forrest, after reporting from West Tennessee, was placed in command at Columbia.

Bragg was pleased with the results of his raid, but there is little reason to believe his opinion of Forrest had changed, or that Forrest distrusted his commanding general any the less. Wheeler, a West Pointer, who had rendered efficient, but not brilliant, services was made Chief of Cavalry and promoted to the rank of Major-General. Forrest, once his superior and the savior of Vicksburg, remained a brigadier. He did not show any resentment at the time; but late in January, when he came directly under Wheeler's orders, his real feelings about Bragg came out with vehemence.

Wheeler was sent to obstruct river traffic on the Cumberland. After he had gone ahead with Wharton's brigade and some regiments from Forrest's command, Bragg sent for Forrest and ordered him to follow after and command his own men. After two days' hard riding he reached the expedition.

He found it shaking in the bitter cold weather, fifteen miles from Dover. The enemy, getting wind of the movement, had held up their boats; so Wheeler, rather than return empty-handed, had made up his mind to reduce Fort Donelson and its garrison of eight hundred men. The first thing Forrest did was to inspect his regiments. He discovered they had been moved without sufficient ammunition, cooking utensils, or rations. He went at once to General Wheeler with this information, and at the same time he asked about the condition in the entire command. A general inspection was ordered, an inspection which should have been made before the expedition left its base; and it was found that Wharton had only twenty rounds of small-arm ammunition and fifty for his two guns, Forrest fifteen rounds of small-arm and forty-five each for his four guns.

The reckless partisan whom Bragg had thought unfit for regular service then made a strong protest to the Chief of Cavalry. The capture of the fort would not be worth the losses it was bound to entail. Even if the works were carried, they could not be held against the gunboats; and in view of the state of the command there was more than the possibility of disaster, for, if the first assault failed, it would be without ammunition, entirely without subsistence, a hundred miles from base and depots of supplies, and faced with the probability of being cut off. The report had already come in that General Jeff C. Davis had set out from Franklin with this purpose in view. Wheeler over-ruled his objection, and the command was put in motion for Donel-son.

On the morning set for the engagement Forrest called aside two of his aides, Captain Anderson and Dr. Ben Wood.

"I have a special request to make of you in regard to the proposed attack on Fort Donelson. I have protested against the move, but my protest has been disregarded, and I intend to do my whole duty, and I want my men to do the same. I have spoken to none but you on this subject, and I don't want anyone to know of the objections I have made. But I have this request to make: If I am killed in this fight, you will see that justice is done me by officially stating that I protested against the attack, and that I'm not willing to be held responsible for any disaster that may result."

His premonition of disaster was so strong—the first Donelson was still green in his memory—that it made him the cause of the miscarriage of the battle order, a simultaneous rush from both sides. Before the bugle sounded, he saw a body of the enemy running towards the river. Mistaking this for retreat, he made an independent charge on horse-back. His charger was killed; and the men, seeing their general go down, withdrew. The next attack was made on foot as Wheeler had planned, but it also failed with great loss. A second horse was shot from under him, and he was badly shaken up in the fall.

The Confederate loss was severe: a fourth of Forrest's men had been killed, wounded, and captured; in Wharton's brigade the killed and wounded numbered sixty. The command bivouacked that night four miles away, hungry, dispirited, and half-frozen. The three gen-erals, Wheeler, Forrest, and Wharton, lay before a log fire in a house by the side of the road. Captain Anderson was left with the rear-guard to cover the withdrawal, attend to the wounded, and bring off a captured caisson.

"It was late," writes this officer, "when I reached headquarters at Yellow Furnace. Arriving there, I asked for General Forrest. The Gen-eral, recognizing my voice, came to the door, and as I was too near frozen to dismount, he came out and helped me down and into the house. Without any ceremony he went to the only bed in the room, jerked the covering from two officers who were occupying it, and brusquely ordered them to get out. My boots were pulled off, I was rolled up in blankets and put in the vacated bed. General Wharton was sitting on the side of the fireplace opposite General Wheeler, who was dictating his report to one of his staff. Forrest had resumed his place, lying down on his chair and his feet well on the hearth. General Wharton said: 'When the signal was given, my men moved forward, but were met with such a severe fire that, with the exception of the Fourth Georgia and Malone's battalion, they gave way. As we fell back I noticed the garrison from our side of the fort rush across to the other side to take part against General Forrest's attack, and, as his command caught the fire of the entire garrison, he must have suffered severely.' Forrest interrupted him, saying in an excited and angry tone:

"'I have no fault to find with my men. In both charges they did their duty as they have always done.'

"'General Forrest, my report does ample justice to yourself and to your men,' answered Wheeler.

"'General Wheeler, I advised against this attack, and said all a subordinate officer should have said against it, and nothing you can now say or do will bring back my brave men lying dead or wounded and freezing around that fort tonight. I mean no disrespect to you. You know my feelings of personal friendship for you. You can have my sword if you demand it, *but there is one thing I do want you to put in that report to General Bragg.** Tell him that I will be in my coffin before I will fight again under your command.'

"'Forrest,' Wheeler replied quietly and with great feeling, 'I cannot take your sabre, and I regret exceedingly your determination. As the commanding officer I take all the blame and responsibility for this failure.'"

And never again, while these two officers were serving in the same army, did Forrest fight under his command. Wheeler, of course, made no mention of this outburst in his report. Forrest's violent defiance was not, as he said, a personal matter, although he undoubtedly resented Wheeler's promotion. Nor was it entirely a protest against Wheeler's neglect of duty and his bad judgment. It was his way of protesting against the Davis war policy in the West, and having a concrete mind, he fixed his opposition upon Bragg, the concrete evidence of this policy, rather than upon the more abstract control which made Bragg possible.

* Italics mine.

Nor was he by any means alone in his defiance. The buddies of those Kentuckians who had thrown away their lives so extravagantly on the third day at Stones River, a move which was made necessary by Bragg's indecision on the second day, were, for a while, almost in a state of mutiny. It had gone the rounds that Bragg had sneeringly doubted their valor. They had already stood a good deal of his nonsense, but they felt it was asking too much, even for the sake of the cause, to have such an insult added to so great an injury. They began packing their sacks to go home. Breckinridge made every appeal his political training had taught him to dissuade them, but without any great success. Finally, only after he had promised that when the war was over he would give Bragg the lie direct, did they decide to remain.

The discontent was so general that Bragg felt the necessity of calling together a council of his officers for a vote of confidence. Davis's sense of reality had not at this time become impaired, and he saw that the mere act of calling the council was sufficient evidence of his incapacity. He therefore ordered General Joseph E. Johnston, the department commander, to take over personally the direction of the Army of Tennessee. Johnston found Bragg at the sick bed of his wife, and his delicate sense of honor did not permit him to break the news at such a time; and later, after Bragg's return to the army, he still refused to relieve him, giving as his excuse that this general's conduct at Murfreesboro had been energetic and skillful, and that he saw no reason to remove him.

The responsibility for Bragg's continuance in command seemed to rest with Johnston, and yet the fact remains that Bragg had called on his subordinates to pass upon his capacity. If Johnston refused to understand the significance of this, Davis did not refuse; and the fact that Johnston could find no reason to remove him does not absolve Davis of his responsibility. The final choice of an army's head belonged to him, not to Johnston.

If for no other reason, politically the action would have been wise, for the people had lost all confidence in Bragg as a general. At Tullahoma he met one of the plain people, clothed in the butternut of the sturdy, who, after intelligently answering all of the general's questions about certain roads, was asked by him if he belonged to Bragg's army.

"Bragg's army?" he replied. "He's got none. He shot half of them in Kentucky, and the other half got killed at Murfreesboro."

While all this was taking place at headquarters, it was well for the Confederacy that Rosecrans lay idle at Murfreesboro. For months that winter and in the early spring the two armies faced each other, with the monotony of winter quarters broken only by cavalry operations around Columbia.

Van Dorn had come up from the Mississippi in February with most of Pemberton's cavalry and assumed command in that quarter. His corps numbered five brigades, about six thousand effective riders and twelve guns—Generals Forrest, Armstrong, Casby, Martin, and Colonel Whitfield.

In the meanwhile Forrest, now a part of a large army, began to see the necessity of the drill-master's routine. Armstrong had to show him what to do at dress parade. He listened closely and carried himself without error. The parades pleased him so much that he ordered his own brigade to perform twice a week. Besides these reviews, picketing and foraging, nothing took place until the first week in March.

Van Dorn, at Thompson's Station, outnumbering the Northerners two to one, captured Colonel Coburn and 1,700 of his men after a very stubborn resistance. General Forrest, by a flank movement, forced their battery from the field; and then, moving on their rear, cut off the infantry's retreat. When Coburn charged to break through and escape, Forrest met him half-way. He never, if he could help it, stood to receive a charge; he always "charged too." He knew it took twice as much resolution to wait for a charging line; so by charging too his men subtly shifted the moral advantages from the enemy to themselves. A famous mount, Roderick, was killed under him here. He leaped to his feet and led the line on foot. Most of the 1,700, along with Colonel Coburn, surrendered to him directly.

Towards the end of the month, acting alone with Armstrong's and Starnes's brigades, after a swift and well-planned march, he fell upon Colonel Bloodgood at Brentwood and captured the entire garrison of 521 men. A stockade, garrisoned by 275 and protecting a bridge over the Harpeth, next caught his attention.

After he had disposed his troops for an assault, he turned to Anderson: "Captain, take in a flag of truce and tell them I have them completely surrounded, and if they don't surrender I'll blow hell out of them in five minutes and won't take one of them alive if I have to sacrifice my men in storming their stockade."

Captain Anderson looked all through his pockets for the little white handkerchief he had used at Brentwood, but it was nowhere to be found. He then suddenly remembered that it had been lost on a like mission to that post. The situation had suddenly grown embarrassing. It was the only white handkerchief in the command. Forrest looked at the bulging form of his favorite aide:

"Strip off your shirt, sir."

And this article, although technically long past the stage for such service, announced to Captain Bassett his fate. His 275 men, eleven wagons, three ambulances, and the stockade's supplies were quickly delivered into the Confederate's hands.

The expedition had done the Northerners much damage; and, as Brentwood lay between Franklin and Nashville, two of Rosecrans's strongest garrisons, it had been much more hazardous than the affair at Thompson's Station. Forrest brought out three ambulances, nine six-horse wagons, two two-horse wagons, sixty extra mules and six horses besides 796 prisoners, although General Green Clay Smith almost recaptured the booty. This was done with a very small loss: one officer and three privates killed; three officers and thirteen privates wounded; and thirty-nine captured and missing.

Bragg complimented the generals before the army, and the tone of his congratulations showed a change of heart towards Forrest. But the press and the people gave the entire credit to the "General and his hoss critters." Van Dorn was damned with faint praise as the official head, while some went so far as to infer that he had failed to make the most of his opportunities. There is no better evidence of Forrest's spreading reputation, than the public reaction to both of these expeditions.

Van Dorn read the papers, overheard the talk of the army; and, as he read and listened, he grew very angry. He called Forrest to his quarters and dressed him down for failing to turn in all the arms he had captured. Forrest answered that he had ordered the property turned over to the quartermaster; but that it seemed fair, since his men had done the work, that they should have the best equipment for themselves. The argument grew heated—it was obvious that the equipment was an excuse to broach the real matter—and Van Dorn was not long in coming to the point.

"I am informed," he said, "that several articles published in the *Chattanooga Rebel,* in which the honors at Thompson's Station and Brentwood were claimed for yourself, were written by one of your staff."

There was a moment of ominous silence. From the muscles of Forrest's powerful body, rage suddenly gathered into his eyes; its violence fell upon the immaculate jealousy of Van Dorn.

"I know nothing of the articles you refer to, and I demand from you your authority for this assertion. I'll hold him responsible and make him eat his words, or run my sabre through him." There was a pause; then, "And I say to you as well that I'll hold you personally responsible if you don't produce the author."

There was no braver man in the army than Van Dorn, and for a moment it seemed that the Vicksburg defenders might destroy each other, since Van Dorn obviously could not produce from the gossip of his staff or his own suspicions the author. A shred of reason returned, and Van Dorn turned to Major Williams:

"Major, do you know the author of those publications?"

"I do not. And I think, General, that you have done General Forrest an injustice to suppose the articles originated at his headquarters."

Van Dorn turned again to Forrest—"I do not assert, nor do I believe, that General Forrest inspired those articles, or had any knowledge of them."

Forrest drew his hand across his forehead as if in a daze and spoke: "General Van Dorn and I have enough to do fighting the enemies of our country without fighting each other."

With these words and a few others the two generals parted, never to meet again. The only other chance they had to see each other was during a reconnaissance in force which Van Dorn made in the direction of Franklin on April 10, and Van Dorn chose to ride with Jackson's division on the Columbia-Franklin turnpike. He left Forrest to himself on the Lewisburg pike.

His two brigades, Armstrong's and his own under Starnes, marched two miles apart, while Freeman's battery was divided between them. Two of his guns moved with Armstrong, and four with Starnes. Forrest rode at the head of the column with Armstrong.

To meet this advance, Gordon Granger, the Northern general at Franklin, had posted Stanley's division of cavalry four miles from Franklin on the Murfreesboro road, with orders to remain on the north side of the Harpeth and guard the crossings at Hughes's Mill. Having sent his other divisions of cavalry on a wild-goose chase to the rear, he dispatched two regiments of infantry and a section of artillery to reënforce Stanley, who was then to cross the Harpeth and take Forrest in reverse.

But Stanley was a very impatient man. He anticipated his superior's orders and crossed the river without the reënforcements. Thinking that Armstrong's brigade was Forrest's entire force on the ground, he was circling to get in its rear when his advance blundered into Starnes.

Starnes had been incautious enough to march without flankers; so both he and Stanley were taken by surprise. Captain Freeman was the first to become aware of the enemy's presence. He quickly threw his guns into position, but not quickly enough. The Fourth Regulars charged down and took the guns, Freeman and thirty-six men. Several caissons dashed to the rear into Biffle's advance and momentarily threw it into confusion. Starnes moved with this regiment. He lost no time, but dismounted its companies and made a counterattack.

At the front, from the the fort which commanded town and river, Gordon Granger opened a heavy fire upon Armstrong spreading around it. Armstrong suddenly relaxed the vigor of his attack, but not because of the fort's artillery. Two couriers, galloping at break-neck speed, dashed up and in the presence of the troops yelled at the top of their voices:

"General Forrest, General Stanley has cut in behind you, has attacked Starnes's brigade, has captured the rear-guard battery, and is right in Armstrong's rear!"

Their excited voices scattered panic in the air; but sharply and confidently that high shrill voice spread among the men like cannister from one of Freeman's guns.

"You say he is in Armstrong's rear, do you? Damn him, that's just where I've been trying to git him all day. I'll be in his rear directly . . . Face your line of battle about, Armstrong. Push your skirmishers forward. Crowd 'em both ways. I'm a-goin' to Starnes. You'll hear from me in about five minutes."

And away he went with his escort. Soon after loud yells, rebel yells, traveled back to give confidence to Armstrong, but not to his men. They had not been allowed to lose confidence. This was not the first time they had faced about and "charged both ways." That fearful rumor which strikes terror to so many hearts, "enemy in the rear," brought only a wink from the hoss critters. It was just another of Old Bedford's tricks. To this day, those few of Armstrong's men who are left still believe it was a trap he had set for the Yankees, for Starnes with his usual skill recaptured the battery and drove the enemy back across the Harpeth. But Forrest was as near frightened as it was possible for him to be in battle, and Armstrong told General Dabney Maury he thought they were all gone up.

When Starnes retook the battery, he failed to retake its commander. One of the Fourth Regulars drove him along on foot with the threat to shoot if he relaxed his speed. Captain Freeman was a large, fleshy man; and when his steps flagged, his captor put a bullet through him. When Forrest was galloping to the rear with the escort, he saw Freeman's large form heaped in a pile. He drew in his reins, dismounted, and knelt by his side. He took his warm, limp hand and held it a while. Forrest's voice was so broken that he could say no more than, "Brave man; none braver."

"The next day," writes the Rev. W. H. Whitsett, "was Sunday, and I officiated at Freeman's funeral. General Forrest stood by the side of the grave, his tall form bent and swayed by his grief. It was a sight to remember always, the sternest soldier of the army bathed in tears and trembling like an aspen leaf with his pain."

Forrest's men never forgot such scenes. They were almost patriarchal. They told the men that Forrest watched over and knew the character of his men. It assured them that he would not take any needless chances with their lives. It somehow maintained the feeling that the South was one big clan, fighting that the small man, as well as the powerful, might live as he pleased. This strong personal attachment for his men was in sharp contrast to Bragg who thought his army could be controlled by the cold pronouncements of army regulations.

.   .   .   .

The highly successful expeditions of the Confederate cavalry about Columbia and Franklin were continually robbing Rosecrans of the fruits of his doubtful victory at Stones River. Van Dorn's vigilance had kept the foraging parties close to his lines, and he was forced to feed his army from a base two hundred and twenty miles away. He could not even get long fodder for his horses, and he could not have it shipped in sufficient quantities to keep them in a healthy condition.

Ever since Buell's removal he had made strenuous efforts to find a remedy for this unhappy state in the increased strength of his cavalry. He irritated his government by daily appeals for more and better horses until Halleck complained of the "enormous expense to the Government of your telegrams, as much or perhaps more than that of all the other generals in the field."

But this did not stop the wires. He complained of bad treatment. This annoyed the authorities who were making a genuine effort to supply his needs. They shipped him enormous boatloads, but most of them were too young or they were otherwise unserviceable. He returned 9,000 to be recruited, and still his cry went up that the enemy had five to his one. The proportion was far less. On May 10, 1863, Rosecrans reported to Meigs, the Quartermaster General at Washington, his effective total to be 6,350. Ten days later the Confederate returns placed their numbers at 13,971, about two to one.

This belief of General Rosecrans, that if he just had enough horses his troubles would be over, was to get him in trouble. He should have taken a hint from Gordon Granger's answer to his query after the last reconnaissance. "You do not seem to understand," said Granger, "why it is so difficult to surprise and crush Van Dorn. In the first place, he keeps every road and lane and hilltop for miles picketed; the country people are his friends and are always ready to give information."

This was an excellent excuse, and a better reason; but Rosecrans was getting tired of excuses, for excuses, no matter how good, did not do away with the Confederate cavalry; and so long as it protected Bragg's flanks, he felt he could not move out against the Army of Tennessee.

So when Colonel Abel D. Streight made his proposition, Rosecrans was in a fitting mood to listen. It was very daring. Streight proposed no less than the destruction of the Confederate lines of communications in North Georgia and all the manufactories of ammunition and guns and other supplies in those parts that made it possible for the Confederacy to carry on the war.

His railroad communications gone, Bragg must leave the rich lands of Middle Tennessee and retreat to the mountains of East Tennessee, if no greater calamity befell him. There, Chief of Staff Garfield informed his commander, Bragg must split his army into small detachments to feed, laying it open to piecemeal destruction. Or, if he fell back to Atlanta, he must surrender the stronghold of Chattanooga, the gateway to Richmond, into Northern hands; and no Northern hands itched more for it than did Rosecrans's. Besides relieving loyal East Tennessee of Confederate control, it would for all practical purposes sever the East from the West and deprive the Confederates of the advantages of their interior lines of communication.

Such an operation was not unknown to the annals of the war—breaking communications had become an art to the Confederate cavalry—but to the Yankees the idea that the game could be played by them was novel and thrilling.

After a great deal of discussion at headquarters and a lengthy correspondence with Dodge at Corinth, the details were decided upon. Streight with a brigade of mounted infantry would leave Nashville, travel down the Cumberland and up the Tennessee rivers, and effect a junction with the forces of Dodge at East Port, Alabama. From East Port Dodge was to advance and menace Tuscumbia. Streight, moving in his rear to throw the Confederates off the scent, at the proper moment was to break away and dash for the mountains and his true objective. He was warned not to take part in the attack against Tuscumbia unless Dodge's safety demanded it.

On April 10, the same day Forrest set out against Franklin, General Garfield ordered Colonel Streight to embark at once on the steamers at the landing. His brigade, about two thousand in all—his own regiment, 51st Indiana; 73rd Indiana, Colonel Hathaway, an officer of superior talent; the 3rd Ohio, Colonel Orris Lawson; 18th Illinois, Lieutenant-Colonel Andrew Rodgers; and two companies of Middle Tennessee cavalry, raised in North Alabama—boarded eight steamers which delivered them at Palmyra on the eleventh.

Here the steamers moved under guard to Fort Henry, while the men marched overland. It had been decided, due to the mountainous country through which Streight had to pass, to mount his command on mules. The supposed advantages were the mule's sure footing and his ability to stand great hardships on less forage than horses.

At Palmyra, as soon as it was light next morning, all hands were set to work to catch and saddle the animals. "I then for the first time discovered," reported Colonel Streight, "that the mules were nothing but poor, wild, and unbroken colts, many of them but two years old, and that a large number of them had the horse's distemper (another thing Rosecrans did not consider—mules frequently catch a "train cold"); some forty or fifty of the lot were too near dead to travel, and had to be left at the landing; ten or twelve died before we started, and such of them as could be rode at all were so wild and unmanageable that it took us all that day and a part of the next to catch and break them. . . ."

He replaced these losses by impressing 150 horses and mules from the countryside, and on April 15 reached Fort Henry. The steamers were delayed taking on rations, but they arrived the same day under escort of two gunboats and Ellet's Marine brigade. The expedition steamed away on the seventeenth and arrived at East Port the nineteenth, one week behind time.

General Dodge, in the meantime, had been advancing steadily from Corinth. The day Streight reached East Port he had driven the Confederates under Roddy across Bear Creek, a stream near and parallel to the Mississippi-Alabama boundary line. But thirteen miles beyond the creek they struck him such a heavy counterblow, capturing two guns, twenty-two artillerists, and a company of mounted men, that he fell back to the creek to wait for Streight's arrival.

Dodge retook one of his guns, but his sharp repulse set him to thinking. As early as April 13, he reported to his superior at Memphis that the Confederates expected Rosecrans to make a movement by way of the Tennessee River and had concentrated six thousand men and eleven guns at Tuscumbia to meet it. His check at Cane Creek supported this belief. He immediately wired Hurlburt to reënforce him with Fuller's brigade of two thousand men. Its arrival brought his entire command up to 7,500 of all arms, exclusive of Streight and the Marine brigade. He now felt able to go forward again. Roddy, with never more than a single regiment, hung upon his flanks.

Streight, as soon as he arrived at East Port, hurried off to confer with Dodge. He left the disembarking to his second-in-command, and by midnight this officer had put ashore and corraled 1,250 mules.

As soon as they felt solid earth beneath their feet again, they threw up their heads and honked long and loud. There never was such a noise. It carried for miles around, and it reached some of Roddy's men. They knew at once whom those mules were calling for, and they set out for Streight's encampment.

When they reached the spot, they found them bunched together and quieted down. Silently and swiftly the boys slipped among them and, like "starters" at a camp meeting when the congregation is slow to get happy, commenced to shout and kick.

Streight returned to find that 400 of his best animals had stampeded. This was on Sunday, the twentieth. Monday and Tuesday were spent in running them down, but only 200 were ever recovered. This was a severe blow to Streight. The success of his movement depended on getting a good start of any pursuing body, and the stampede, besides the loss of time and the mounts at East Port, would delay him further before Tuscumbia in the effort to replace them. So it was not until the twenty-second that Dodge moved forward with Streight trailing in his rear.

The twenty-third he pushed Roddy across Little Bear. That same day at Columbia, some one hundred miles away, General Forrest received orders from Bragg to take his brigade and move swiftly to Roddy's relief.

He detached at once the 11th Tennessee, 600 strong, and ordered its Colonel, Edmondson, to cross the Tennessee River at Bainbridge and report to Roddy. He then set about making a thorough preparation for the work before him, and about three o'clock in the morning of the twenty-fourth he rode out of Columbia in the direction of Tuscumbia. By forced marches he had managed to reach Brown's Ferry, near Courtland, on the twenty-seventh. Here his scouts reported that Tuscumbia had fallen on the twenty-fifth and that Edmondson had joined Roddy four miles east of the town in time to assist in the skirmishing around Town Creek. They gave the enemy's strength with fair accuracy: Dodge, 10,000; Streight, 2,500. Dodge's objective seemed to be the north bank of the river.

Acting on this information, Forrest sent Dibrell with two regiments and one gun to get in Dodge's rear at Florence. He then pushed on to the ferry with the rest of the brigade. Leaving Captain Anderson to attend to the ferriage, he rode ahead with his staff and established his headquarters between Courtland and Town Creek at Colonel Saunders's country house. Later that evening Roddy rode up, and they consulted together about the next day's operations.

Dodge had managed to push Roddy across Town Creek on the twenty-seventh, but he was unable to follow. In the night and next morning heavy rains on Sand Mountain, the source of the creek, swelled the stream ten feet. At dawn, the twenty-eighth, Forrest arrived and arranged his battle line. North of the railway bridge he concealed Edmondson's regiment with rigid orders not to fire unless the enemy attempted to seize the bridge and cross over. Next, resting the right of the line on the Tuscumbia turnpike, he posted Starnes's and Biffle's regiments out of range of the artillery; extending to the left, Roddy guarded the Shallow Ford.

Standing by Captain Morton, he watched a gunner level his piece on Dodge's headquarters across the stream. Just as the sun moved through the pines on top of Sand Mountain, a single shot crashed through the building to announce that Nathan Bedford Forrest had arrived on the scene.

He had arrived on the scene, but not *the* scene, for Colonel Streight had cut loose from Dodge on the twenty-sixth and was moving steadily and unpursued towards Sand Mountain. Dodge had so far done his part: he had detained the Confederates in his theatre of war. And he now replied to the challenge with eighteen guns. For five hours an artillery duel took place between Dodge's batteries and the inferior guns with Forrest.

But Streight had made poor use of his two days' start. When on the twenty-fifth Dodge informed him that there was no doubt but that Forrest had crossed the Tennessee and was in the vicinity of Town Creek, both officers decided that Streight had tarried long enough at Tuscumbia, although he had not yet succeeded in mounting all of his command. Dodge dismounted some of his own men and unhitched the teams from his trains in an effort to supply the deficiency, but when the Mule Brigade set out in the dark of midnight twenty-fifth, 150 men had no mounts and 150 more walked beside mounts who were barely able to carry their saddles.

Streight moved in a blinding rain, a pitch-black night, and on a muddy road. He had hoped to reach Moulton, forty miles away, by the next evening; but the weather conditions and his continuous search for stock forced him to bivouack at Mount Hope, some miles short of his goal. On the night of the twenty-seventh, Dodge sent Streight word that he had driven the enemy, and that he should push on.

Dodge's information was slightly misleading. He had promised Streight that he would drive the enemy as far as Courtland, and he had pushed him only across Town Creek. He had also promised that if Forrest turned toward Moulton, he would pursue.

Meanwhile, early on the twenty-eighth, the artillery duel continued. In the midst of it one of Roddy's best scouts reported the presence of hostile cavalry on the road to Moulton. With no apparent reaction to this information, "as if he had no flank to be turned," Forrest gave all his attention to his batteries. A few hours later another scout returned and informed his commander that the hostile cavalry had reached Mount Hope, thirty miles southeast of Tuscumbia, but only sixteen miles directly south of Courtland. The information indicated a flank attack against Decatur.

Forrest became a mass of action. He gave orders to fall back on Courtland, sent a courier to Dibrell to attack Dodge's outposts and threaten his rear. He called Morton and sent him flying to Decatur with a section of artillery and escort with orders to fortify that town. He threw Roddy and Edmondson between Dodge and Streight. Leaving a section of artillery, Baxter's battalion, and Hannon's regiment in line to make a show of defense, he hurried on to Courtland, where Biffle and Starnes, Ferrel's six guns, and a section of Morton's battery were hastily prepared for pursuit.

Three days' rations were cooked; shelled corn to last the horses two days was issued; and caissons and guns were double-teamed with the best horses. Forrest personally selected the harness. Farriers were put to tightening the shoes and shoeing the barefooted. His company commanders were ordered to tell each man that "no matter what else got wet he must keep his cartridge box dry."

At 1 o'clock A.M., the morning of the twenty-ninth, Forrest was ready to set out. In the dark and in the cold drizzle of an April rain the head of the column, facing south, moved out of Courtland. An hour earlier, Colonel Streight, with Dodge's assurances to give him hope, had left Moulton and struck for the mountains. By nightfall he reached Day's Gap, a narrow defile through which the rough road wound.

Forrest did not reach Moulton until noon. All night and all morning he had ridden, halting at 8 o'clock to feed and rest for an hour; then back into the saddle. At Moulton he learned the nature of the force and the direction of its course—southwest. That meant one of two things: either a raid on the Georgia railroads, or a flank attack on his supposed position at Courtland. The most careful officer in the Confederate armies had not decided when he reached Moulton which course Streight would follow.

Georgia was far from base, across a barren, uninhabited mountain plateau, and by far the most hazardous alternative. The flank attack seemed more likely, for if Streight could get in the Confederate rear at Decatur while Dodge held Forrest's attention along Town Creek, the Confederates could be crushed and thrown into the river. Forrest had made this identical movement too often not to know its effectiveness; and, as strategically it was the most natural thing for Dodge to do, he made his dispositions to meet it. The threat of a Georgia raid might be a clever device to throw him off the scent, draw him south, and leave his rear open; or it might not be.

Dividing his force—he had lingered at Moulton just long enough to cool the backs of his horses and to feed—he sent Roddy to the southeast to develop the enemy's intentions, the other to the northeast. He moved with the second. As his headquarters were always placed where he expected the serious fighting to be done, it seems apparent that up to noon of the twenty-ninth he did not expect it on the plateau of Sand Mountain.

Forrest had not, at this time, learned of Dodge's retreat. His lieutenant, Dibrell, had carried out his orders so intelligently, spreading the rumor of Van Dorn's arrival and supporting it by raising flatboats, building others, seizing the crossings, that Dodge decided to let as few hours as possible rest between him and his base at Corinth. He forgot in his haste that he had promised to send his cavalry after any body of Confederate cavalry that might interfere with Streight's journey to Georgia. He did not, however, forget to fire the countryside.

As the two Confederate columns diverged at Moulton, sunlight broke through the heavy sky just as the General swung into his saddle. In answer to that familiar command, "Move up, men," the riders squatted on the backs of their mounts, tightened their stomachs and hurled quivering on the air the rebel yell. This was the same sunlight Streight's raiders took to be a "good omen."

The rest of that day and all Wednesday night Forrest closed up on Streight at Day's Gap, where this officer had gone into camp in high spirits. He had at last mounted all his command by stumbling upon rich booty south of Moulton. There most of the refugees from Dodge's advance had fled with their slaves, stock and wagons, cattle and sheep, and an abundance of poultry. This seemed to the colonel a just reward for the bold. Well mounted, well started, now in a country of Union sentiment, and *unpursued,* nothing stood in his way. The mules alone caused him concern. From the beginning they had given him no end of trouble. Morning, noon, and night they kept the entire countryside informed of their presence; and their stubbornness when urged forward, the difficulty in stopping them when in full flight, and their general intractable nature was wearing down the patience of their riders. Nor did the infantry's chaffed and burning crotches tend to ease the dilemma. Unfortunately, nobody told Rosecrans, as he gravely deliberated upon a choice of animals, that a mule is primarily a draft animal and only as such endures hardship. When ridden, and especially out of a walk, he breaks down very easily. Due to this oversight, the Mule Brigade left Tuscumbia with relationships between the men and their mounts severely strained.

But Colonel Streight, with a good start in his favor, felt that he could make the mules hold out. He laid his plans to go directly to Gadsden, and there divide his force: one part would attend to the Georgia railroads; the other destroy the Etowah bridge. But just a few hours before reveille aroused the Northern camp to push on to this business, the General and his hoss critters lay down at Danville, four miles away.

But Captain Bill Forrest and his Forty Thieves did not lie down that night. They rode to the outskirts of the camp, captured a vidette of ten men; then crawled within sight of the camp-fires at the foot of the gorge. They reported their findings and, before day-dawn, lay down to sleep. After a short while the most ungodly noises, echoing and re-echoing, came out of the gorge. They sat up and looked at one another wonderingly. They gave up all idea of sleep and broke into loud guffaws. Hundreds of mules, with continuous and anxious brays, were calling for their breakfast.

Forrest's men were already in the saddle, swinging down upon the gorge, and he was with them. He had shifted his headquarters over to Roddy's command. He had directed Biffle to take the best mounted of his own and McLemore's men, seize and hold a gap to the north, and wait for further orders. Streight's intentions were still undeveloped, but Forrest meant they should be disclosed before the day was out. He would press him from the front, and Biffle would head him off to the north. He had run the fox into a hollow log, and his dogs were barking at each end.

But Streight was a wily fox, one of the most skillful and stubborn officers in Lincoln's service. He was well under way before daylight, and by sun-up the wagons and the head of his brigade had reached the crest of Sand Mountain. It was a mile from the foot to the top, and his men were strung out along the whole distance. The rear guard, under Captain Smith, still loitered over the breakfast kettles, stragglers lazied in the sand; and now and then a negro's laugh, rich and spontaneous, rose above the sizzle of the pots. A few men were throwing saddles on their mules, carelessly, as if they were saddling up for church.

Then, suddenly, from nowhere, a shell from one of Ferrel's guns dropped and exploded among the pans. The rebel yell burst from the woods, and behind it the surge of the charge, and before Streight's rear could take in what had happened, into the camp swept the hungry Confederates. But the steaming kettles were too great a temptation. They broke the charge and gave Smith time to rally his men in the gorge.

Streight stood the surprise like the veteran he was. He sent word back to his rear, now his front, to hold until he could form a line of battle. This he did with great speed and skill about three miles from the top of the mountain. He dismounted, sent the mules and wagons out of range, and took possession of a ridge which bent around to the rear. He rested his right on a precipitous ravine; his left on a marshy run; then with his skirmishers he drew a circle around the whole to avoid against surprise and to prevent skulking. Concealed

near the Old Corn Road, which split his center, two mountain howitzers swept the approach.

Scarcely had his arrangements been made when Captain Smith
and his men came galloping towards the ridge. Hard on his heels
Captain Bill's critters kicked the sand from the road. The lines opened;
Smith raced in; the line swung to; a volley rattled; Captain Bill's
horse leaped in the air to meet it, and the captain fell off in the road,
his thigh bone shattered. Behind him lay several of his scouts.

Forrest rode up soon after the advance had been checked. He
promptly scanned the enemy's position. When his men arrived from
the rear, he was ready to align them. Edmondson was the first to
trot up along the Old Corn Road. Forrest gave him orders to dismount;
then threw him into line across the road, parallel to Streight's ridge.
To his left, mounted, he placed the escort, that body of youths who
"are ever ready to undertake what their chief so often looked to them
to do—the fighting of a full regiment." Roddy with his own regiment
and Julian's battalion rode and took position on the right.

There were scarcely a thousand Confederates on top of Sand Mountain when the order, "Move forward," rustled down the front.
Edmondson's advance was steady and resolute; the escort charged
Streight's right flank; but Roddy's men were too eager. They advanced
far too rapidly and exposed themselves to the fire of the entire works.
For a moment they were thrown into confusion. Streight quickly
massed and charged. Roddy's alignment was completely broken and
he was thrown back with a loss of forty out of three hundred and
fifty. Edmondson's flank was now hanging in air; so he and the escort
withdrew in good order, but so rapidly that they left two guns, whose
horses had been killed, to fall into the enemy's hands.

Forrest rallied the command and attempted to retake the position
and the guns, but particularly the guns. He failed and was driven
back to a ridge three hundred yards to the rear. From this position
Streight was repulsed with no great loss on either side; and as he fell
back to his original line, Forrest regained possession of the ridge to
his immediate front.

This firm and rough treatment he had received at the hands of
Streight stirred the General's bile. But when he failed to retake his
pet guns, two of the four he had taken at Murfreesboro in '62, he
flew into one of those rages which were the marvel of his commands.
They were so fierce and intense they ceased to have any personal
quality. They became almost abstract. His men never crossed him at

such a time, for he was far more dangerous than any enemy could possibly be.

He dashed up and down the broken line, beating with the flat of his sabre every straggler who looked longingly to the rear. He told every man to hitch his horse to a sapling—one man in four was usually detached as horse-holder—that if they did not get back his guns, they'd have no more use for their critters. He told them he aimed to get back his guns if every man died in the attempt. He told them many more interesting things which they would experience; and as he told them, his lips flashed like a tinder box. It was said long afterwards that whereas he undoubtedly took the Lord's name, he never took it in vain.

One of his staff, Captain Pointer, rode up to Captain Anderson through the sulphurous air. He unwrapped a small bundle of ham and bread—"Captain," he said, "we had better eat this now, I reckon, for from the way the old man is preparing to get his guns back it might spile before we get another chance at it."

Starnes and Biffle had, in the meantime, been ordered up. They arrived about three P.M., and a new alignment was made. Starnes was deployed on the right, Edmondson on the left, Biffle and Roddy in the center. The escort and Captain Bill's scouts formed a small reserve. At the word of command, they all moved forward—to find the bird had flown. Streight, leaving a thin line of skirmishers behind, had been gone an hour.

He had captured forty prisoners, "representing seven different regiments," from whom he "learned, in the meantime, that the enemy were in heavy force, fully three times our number, with twelve pieces of artillery, under General Forrest in person; consequently I was fearful that they were making an effort to get around us and attack in the rear of our position."

What Colonel Streight feared had come true. He had not been able to elude General Forrest. It is said that he told his men that the most deadly and relentless man in the whole Confederate army was now on their trail. He certainly showed he understood the character of the man he must deceive and that he had made a study of his tactics.

He had thoroughly matured his plan of action. The country between Day's Gap and Blountsville, about forty miles, is mostly uninhabited. Having learned from his prisoners that Forrest had made a forced march of two nights and a day, he naturally expected that his men were far from fresh. By fighting and running he hoped to force them to lay over in the mountains a day or so to recuperate while he, having descended into the valley of plenty around Blountsville, would find fresh mounts and plenty of supplies.

The plan, as a plan, was well conceived. No section of the South was better suited to this kind of warfare. Its deep, sandy ravines, narrow, treacherous streams, and piney ridges made it a very simple matter to form ambuscades, but a very difficult matter to detect them. Besides such advantages, Captain Smith's companies knew every ridge on the mountain and could furnish any number of expert guides.

But this plan had one serious weakness: it did not reckon with the frailty of fatigue in the presence of Forrest's will; nor did Streight consider well enough that Forrest had been brought up in the Wilderness.

When Forrest discovered that the enemy had withdrawn from his front, he divided his force into three parts. He was far away from telegraphic communication, and he had gone too fast for scouts to overtake him (this meant he still had not heard of Dodge's retreat); so he drew up Roddy, Julian's battalion, and all the artillery except four guns and sent them back to Decatur. Between Guntersville and Blountsville there is a direct route which the raiders, if they succeeded in detaining the Confederates on the mountain, might take and make good their escape. He sent Anderson of the staff with Edmondson's regiment towards Guntersville. Anderson took a route to the north of and parallel to Streight and was quickly out of the way. For direct pursuit Forrest had left Biffle, McLemore, his escort, and his brother's scouts. This was a very small number, not quite half the strength of Streight; but they were veterans who had long been under his eye. He knew he could count on every man. And they knew that there were two liberties nobody, private or general, ever took with his temper—disobey his orders or leave the field in the presence of the enemy. He took the chance that Streight might discover how weak he was and turn on h'm. But it was not a great chance, for he had guessed his enemy's tactics: fighting and running.

With the escort and a company of the Fourth Tennessee, Forrest galloped ahead to bring the retreating column to bay. After a sharp gallop of half an hour, he overtook the rear. He had one general order: "Whenever you see anything blue, shoot at it and do all you can to keep up the scare." From now on it became a running fight, with Forrest pressing Streight a little harder each mile until he forced him to make another stand, ten miles from Day's Gap and seven miles from the scene of the last fight.

He drew up his men on Hog Mountain about an hour before sundown. The rat-tat-tat of the skirmishers' muskets soon grew into a steady roar. The sappy twigs and the young green of the trees dropped silently upon the soft, damp sand; then night covered the top of the mountain. "The pine trees were very tall, and the darkness of their shade was intense, the mountain where the enemy was posted was steep, and as we charged again and again under Forrest's own lead it was a grand spectacle. It seemed that the fires which blazed from their muskets were almost long enough to reach our faces. There was one advantage in being below them; they often fired above our heads in the darkness." So says one of Forrest's soldiers.

The lightning of the cannon flashed at regular intervals and illumined the tight faces of men peering down the long iron of their guns; or it showed them, crouching for the spring, their hats pulled low over their eyes; or it showed them looking towards that high shrill voice mounting above the roar of powder, the shouts of men, screaming animals, and the low moans of the wounded—its sudden light burning their eyes with his long arm and nervous fingers pointing south, oblivious to the hot lead balls curving in the dark.

Streight's men, well officered, knew how to fight. They repulsed every charge with the stubbornness that only veterans are able to command. For three hours this continued, and the dark blue raiders still knelt behind Hog Mountain.

At eight o'clock Biffle was ordered to take the reserve and move by the left flank and attack the mule holders. The escort, on a similar service, moved to the right. After some delay Forrest heard sounds of confusion far in the enemy's rear. The mule holders had been attacked. But his men, not knowing Roddy was well on his way to Decatur, thought it was he descending upon Streight's flank. With a fierce enthusiasm, they all swept forward.

Again they met only an intrepid rear guard to sweep from the field. The main body had skillfully escaped on their mules and horses. But Old Bedford got back his guns. They were spiked and the carriages were destroyed, but this did not matter. Their physical condition had already ceased to be of any importance. The matter of possession had become purely a question of moral ascendancy. The butternut riders buried them reverently in the sand and hurried away as the bugles sounded assembly.

"This battle closed about nine P.M., and shortly afterwards the moon rose in great splendor. . . . I walked along the line where they had been formed and found it littered from end to end with small bits of paper. It looked as if every man in their column must have employed the leisure afforded by that stop to tear up all the private letters found upon his person. It was clear their alarm had become serious."

Streight had thought it serious enough to remain with the rear in person. He strengthened it considerably. Colonel Hathaway, his best officer, was retained to fill the post of honor. "We had but fairly got under way," reports Colonel Streight, "when I received information of the enemy's advance."

The moon had by this time spread over the mountain top. This particular section of the plateau was covered by an open woodland, with here and there dense spots of undergrowth. The cold light falling down the smooth pines made the place good for an ambush. It set a double snare: It created false shadows about the thickets while it made the men moving along the open road into fine targets. In one of these thickets, not more than twenty paces from the road, Colonel Streight placed the Seventy-third Indiana.

To expect an ambush is to be prepared for it, and Forrest expected it. He threw Biffle forward with a small advance, ordering several men to move still ahead, mingle with the enemy, and reveal any position he might take up. With the rest of the command he followed in close formation, at a very slow pace. There was scarcely a sound. Only their critters' feet crunching in the sand. A limping horse might stumble in a hole, but he was quickly drawn up with a voiceless curse. The weird pines rose straight up from their needles to threaten the exhausted riders and keep them awake. The pivot men felt that death was lurking behind every sapling, and they drew tight their outer shoulders to meet it. But for four miles they heard only the crunch, crunch below their critters' bellies. Death still lurked in the Wilderness.

Private Granville Pillow, Biffle's command, had been one of those sent ahead; but he had failed to catch up. His mount, which had been moving at a stiff pace, suddenly stopped, threw up its head, pointed its ears, and sniffed the damp spring air suspiciously. Private Pillow, like all good scouts, had a profound respect for hoss sense. He galloped to the rear and reported to his lieutenant. The lieutenant sent him to Forrest.

This was the information the General had been waiting for. He brought forward the command and halted it a quarter of a mile from where Pillow's horse had balked. He then called for volunteers to draw the enemy's fire. He selected Pillow and two others. Taking out the horses, he had the artillerists push their guns, very silently, down the road.

The distorted shadows of three horsemen fell across the sand, into the piney woods, as Old Bedford's volunteers rode into the moon's full wash of light. They rode very carelessly—but their eyes were not careless. They were fixed in alert paralysis upon the tarnation thicket ahead.

They saw dark shadows behind the thicket rise from a prone position, and a few flashes from the metal on the Illinoisan barrels; then wheeled to the rear and, throwing their bodies well over the sides of their mounts, rode safely back to their buddies. The artillery was shoved a little closer. Private Pillow and Forrest showed the gunners where to point the mouths of their pieces. They were now at point blank range, and double-shotted with cannister. At the same time, McLemore crept around to the right until he was within one hundred and fifty yards of the thicket; to the left Biffle's men moved noiselessly over the pine needles.

At the signal, the lanyard was pulled. The cannister thinned out the thicket. The small arms rattled. For a few minutes the fire was heavy, but it did not last. The virtue of an ambush is surprise. Colonel Streight mounted his mules and fell back on the main body.

As soon as he could put his command in column, Forrest took up his steady drive against Streight's rear. He ran across a great deal of surplus baggage which the raiders were abandoning along the sides of the Old Corn Road. Niggers, who were becoming a burden, filled the woods. These signs looked mighty good to Forrest.

It was going on midnight, and the Confederates were drowsing in their saddles, when that familiar, "Move up, men" went down the lines. They shook the sleep out of their heads. The enemy had been brought to bay again. It was now about one A.M., May Day, six miles from the spot of the last skirmish. The enemy's position was strong, the southern bank of a swift, rugged stream. But again the ambush failed to surprise; and after another short engagement, Streight withdrew.

It was by this time two A.M., or two hours till sunup; so Forrest ordered his men to dismount and get what sleep they could until daylight. But Streight, not knowing whether he would be attacked again in the dark, still trudged along. The mules drawn at Nashville were constantly giving out and throwing his men on foot, but there was little straggling behind the rear-guard.

Up to this point all the odds of fatigue had been in Streight's favor. His march, since leaving Tuscumbia, had been broken by sleep; and his pace, although mules and mounted infantry mix very badly, had not been particularly stiff. On the other hand, the Confederates had had little rest by night or day since April 24. From Columbia, Tennessee, to Town Creek, Alabama, they had swung along in the rain. They had skirmished or had lain in line of battle all day of the twenty-eighth; and that evening, without sleep, they had set out after Streight. They made only two brief halts on the twenty-ninth, and they did not reach the vicinity of Day's Gap in time to get more than a few short hours' sleep, for at six A.M., the thirtieth, fighting began. And, including the intervals of pursuit, it lasted until two A.M., May 1. There is a limit to endurance; and if Forrest had to keep this pace, he would lose all his men on the side of the road. So, very subtly, he began shifting the odds. As his boys fed what corn they had left to their critters and lay down in their tracks, Colonel Streight's raiders rode or walked towards Blountsville, sleepless.

They reached this town at 10 o'clock and stripped for a quicker pace. After feeding and resting a while, they took all the corn in sight, transferred their ammunition and rations to pack-mules, bunched the wagons and set fire to them. But scarcely had smoke begun to rise from the pile when their rear videttes were driven in. As Streight's rear rode out of Blountsville on one side of the town, from the foothills near by Forrest swung in at a gallop, his escort and a squadron from McLemore's Fourth Tennessee behind him. They put out the fire, replenished their supply from abandoned ammunition and took up the enemy's trail, due east.

A few miles out, a scout dashed up and reported a column of Northern cavalry marching by a parallel route.

"Did you see the Yankees?" asked the General.

"No. I didn't see them myself, but while I was at the blacksmith's shop, a citizen came galloping up on horseback and told me he had seen them."

Before the dust raised by the horse had had time to settle, Forrest had jerked the scout to the ground and was beating his head against a tree.

"Now, God-damn you, if ever you come to me again with a pack of lies, you won't get off so easy."

It is ten miles from Blountsville to the Black Warrior River. Over this entire distance Streight had not a moment's relief. It was a running fight the whole way. The peril of his rear became so acute that, before he could cross the Warrior, he had to form in line of battle. This was about five P.M., almost dark this time of year. In his haste to get over, two of his pack-mules were drowned. Several of the hoss critters stumbled over the rocky-bottomed river to relieve them of their packs. One scrawny youth called out to his buddies as he struggled up the bank with a box of hardtack:

"Boys, it's wet and full of mule-hair, but it's a damned sight better than anything the old man's a-givin us now."

From the banks of the Black Warrior the second night march began. But Forrest did not move his whole command across the river. He picked a hundred of his best men and sent them under Biffle to "worry" the raiders, to see they got no sleep that night. The rest of his men were ordered to lie down until midnight. Streight was beginning to feel the steady, persistent drive of the man whose thunder he was stealing.

Just before dawn Forrest caught up with Biffle. He sent him and his men to the rear for a well-earned rest, while he, with his escort, took charge of the advance in person. He rode into the Mule Brigade feeding and resting near Wills Creek, fifteen miles east of the Black Warrior. Streight did not stand to fight. He threw his men across the creek as soon as his pickets were driven in. In fact, the passage was too hurried. In the deep fording a portion of his powder got wet.

Ten miles farther on, and four miles out of Gadsden, is a deep, narrow stream. It is called Black Creek. It got its name in the days before the Wilderness was cleared and planted in cotton. Now its banks are slippery clay, rising sharply above the deep, sluggish current, blood-black from draining the valley's gullied fields. It is crossed only by bridge or boat.

The chief reason for Colonel Streight's hasty retreat across Wills Creek was to reach and put this stream between Forrest and himself. Then he would be able to rest his command and prepare for the final push towards Rome, Georgia. To burn the bridges behind him at Black Creek would give half a day's advantage; to burn the bridge over the Coosa at Rome, one or two days. In this time his mounted infantry could recuperate from the terrific pace Forrest had set their mules and with fresh, well-fed mounts carry out Rosecrans's orders.

And in spite of the General's dogging, "worrying" tactics, the odds were still in Streight's favor, but not so decidedly so. All along he had gleaned the country of its stock and was always able to secure fresh mounts for his brigade, long fodder to feed them, and, by emptying the valley's cribs, plenty of corn. The gray riders, with a few exceptions, had to rely on the critters they had brought from Tennessee. So, in spite of the spirit of Forrest's veterans, more and more of Biffle's and McLemore's men were dropping behind, most of their mounts too exhausted ever to catch up. More and more were throwing their shoes, or dropping by the way from the effects of too little corn and too much April grass. But if his details were finding an increasing number of men asleep by the side of the road, and if they were unable to speed up the limping horses, these painful facts did not mean that the resources of Forrest's strategy were also exhausted. They grew more plentiful as the issue became more doubtful.

As soon as he hastened Streight across Will's Creek, he gave the entire command another rest. It had the look for awhile of an ill-fated rest: a lethargy of fatigue settled on man and animal from which they could not be aroused. But while the famished critters were eating what corn there was left to eat, Forrest walked through them, culled the weakest and sent them back to Decatur. He selected the best section of artillery and to it hitched the strongest horses he could find. He was now ready to attend to his men. After great difficulty he lined them up, and he spoke to them, warm words full of sympathy for their troubles, bold words to feed their pride; then his voice changed and it rang among them, calling for all who were willing to follow or fall in this, the last lap of the race. They forgot how dry-tired they were, and their hoarse throats shouted the right answer. In a few moments a bare six hundred were in the saddle, riding towards the horizon over which the enemy had disappeared ... six hundred riding down upon seventeen hundred.

About ten o'clock next day, May 2, a lone horseman dressed in blue was galloping at breakneck speed down the pike towards Black Creek. To his front he saw yellow flames leaping and covering the superstructure of the bridge; to his rear the quick gallop of gray riders, followed by the cry, "Halt! Surrender!" He faced about and threw up his hands. The Northern vidette had been caught between the works of his friends and the speed of his enemies. He handed over his gun to the foremost rider. This rider was General Forrest.

This time Forrest had been too slow. In spite of his terrific attention to the march, he was forced to sit his horse and watch the dark cedar smoke and sudden flames and reflect how pleased Streight must be to have placed such an obstacle in his path.

But it was not in Forrest's nature to reflect very long at such a time. To the left of the road, some two hundred yards from the bridge, he saw a simple dog-run dwelling. It belonged to the widow Sanson and her two daughters. Before the advance of the Confederates drew up the heads of their horses, the widow-woman had gone to pull her fence rails away from the bridge. Seeing them piled on the bridge and afire, she turned around and was on her way back to the dog-run when an officer rode forward:

"Ladies, don't be alarmed. I am General Forrest. I and my men will protect you from harm." And then, "Where are the Yankees?"

The widow Sanson told him they were across the creek, ready, if his men showed their heads above a small rise, to "kill the last one of you."

The skirmishers crawled to their places; the muskets popped, and the women returned to the shelter of their house. Forrest stopped the widow's youngest daughter, Miss Emma, as she was going through the gate. "Can you tell me where I can get across the creek?"

She told him of an unsafe bridge two miles away, but that was not what he wanted to hear; and then he heard her speak of an old ford, no farther away than a few hundred yards, and known only to her family. The cows, she said, used it to cross over in dry spells. If the General would saddle her horse, she would take him to it.

"There is no time to saddle a horse. Get up here behind me!" He rode against the embankment at the side of the road, and she pounced her calico on the lathered back of his charger.

The widow-woman called out in alarm, "You, Emma, what do you mean?"

"She is going to show me a ford where I can get my men over in time to catch those Yankees before they get to Rome. Don't be uneasy. I'll bring her back safe."

They rode across the field into a ravine which protected them from the farther bank. The branch in this ravine emptied into the creek just above the ford. Dismounting, the General and his girl-guide crawled through the bushes until they could see the ford, Miss

Emma going in front to show the way. By this time the skirmishing had grown heavy; so Forrest pulled himself in front. "I am glad to have you for a pilot," he said, "but I'm not going to make breastworks of you." She pointed out where he should enter and where he should come out on the other side and, amidstream, the shallow trail their cows had always taken. Then they crawled back out of danger. He asked her to tell him her name and asked for a lock of her hair.

In half an hour the flying artillery was up and the bank cleared of the enemy. The critters, belly-deep in the water, were soon picking their way over. The caissons were quickly emptied; and the men, from the backs of their mounts, held the ammunition high in the air. Old Bedford had no intention of letting his powder get wet. Next a long rope was attached to the shafts of the gun and caisson carriages and hitched to a team on the other bank. Into the water they splashed to sink plumb out of sight. Only the ripple on the top of the water told they were moving, until, dripping and sticky with mud, they traveled up the other bank to be returned to the hands of their keepers.

Streight, much to his surprise, as he was surrounding Gadsden to corral all the fresh horses and mules in town, heard the well-known thumps on the turnpike. He set fire to the small commissary stores and shook the clay-dust of Gadsden from his feet. "It now became evident to me," reports this officer, "that our only hope was in crossing the river at Rome and destroying the bridge . . ."

That night in the dog-run near Black Creek the widow's daughters sat up, holding wake for one of Forrest's men. Before he left, he had ridden up to Miss Emma to give her a piece of writing. "One of my bravest men has been killed, and he is laid out in the house. His name is Robert Turner. I want you to see that he is buried in some graveyard near here." With that he clipped a lock of her hair, told her goodbye, and rode away with his men, leaving the women alone with the dead.

Colonel Streight was growing a little desperate, but as yet his fortitude had not been shaken, although that of his command had been. Heretofore his men had not straggled behind his rear guard; but now a great number of men and broken-down mounts were constantly falling into Forrest's hands. His tactics was wearing them down.

At Gadsden, Forrest dispatched a courier to Rome with orders to fire the bridge. A little earlier Mr. John Wisdom had gone on a like errand. Leaving this town with an advance of three hundred of his strongest critters, the General bore down upon the straggling raiders. Twelve miles from Gadsden, at Blount's plantation, Streight stood at bay with his main body to protect the details while they fed his stock.

At this place the road, about forty yards broad, runs very straight for half a mile, turns sharply to the left; and, after going in that direction for several hundred yards, turns again to the right and splits apart open fields. On either side of the half mile stretch is a thicket of Oldfield pines. In these, Streight had scattered his sharpshooters; then, where the road makes the first turn, he closed it with a heavy barricade to force Forrest to move across the open field.

At the end of this field is a small rise. Lying behind it, five hundred Northern rifles and the brave Colonel Hathaway waited. Skirmishers were thrown half a mile to the front as if offering battle. The skillful way Streight had disguised his ambush showed that neither his resources nor his imagination had diminished on the run.

But Old Bedford had got so he could smell an ambush. He formed his three hundred in column of fours, with orders for the men to shoot to the right and left as they passed through the pine thicket. His bugler sounded the charge, and away they went, whooping and hollering and shooting as they had been told. They went at such a speed that the sharpshooters had no time to aim. With very small loss the Confederates galloped through the open field and up the rise. After a very bad handling, Colonel Streight withdrew, his men in great gloom, for Colonel Hathaway, his chief reliance for the rear guard's safety, had been killed.

Colonel Streight was now, for the first time, morally at bay. The last engagement had shown him that nearly all his reserve ammunition was wet and that much of that which he had issued to the soldiers had become useless. The paper had worn away and the powder had sifted out. He had also learned before reaching Gadsden that a very large body of Confederates was moving by a parallel route, with the probable intention of reaching Rome ahead of his column. This was Anderson with Edmondson's regiment moving, not to Rome, but between Streight and the river. But Streight did not know Anderson's orders. He, therefore, determined to make one mighty effort to get to Rome first, and towards this end dispatched Captain Russell with two hundred of the best mounted of the command to seize and hold the bridge across the Coosa.

In desperation, he proposed to do a heroic thing. Although his men could barely sit in their saddles, he intended to make his third all-night march. Only by such an effort did he believe he could reach the Coosa. A piece of misinformation he had gotten from a prisoner in the fight at Blount's plantation strengthened his purpose. He had captured a sergeant in McLemore's regiment, a youth so solemn and truthful-looking that the boys called him parson. When brought before Streight and questioned as to the strength of Forrest's command, he had answered with a saint's gravity that Forrest had, besides his own brigade, Roddy's, Armstrong's, and several others whose names he did not know. Streight took his answers, very likely, with a grain of salt. Nevertheless, he could not be certain he was lying. He knew that Forrest was a master at bluffing, but he also knew that his attacks for the last three days and nights had been too real and too heavy for bluffing. In the night, the sergeant escaped and returned to his command and reported the story he had imposed on Streight.

From the first stand beyond Day's Gap, Forrest discovered that ultimate victory would not depend upon the outcome of a pitched battle but upon pitched tents. The ammunition must be sleep, not powder. So far, he had shown himself superior in the tactical demands of such a campaign. For two whole nights he had "worried" his enemy into sleepless marches, and now with the cunning of the Wilderness he was driving Streight, weak from exhaustion, to the wall. He sent forward a skeleton squadron to "devil" him all night, while his own depleted regiments lay down for an all night's rest. Ten long, sweet, and delicious hours they slept while the Mule Brigade stumbled by starlight towards Rome.

But Colonel Streight, although he did not know it at the time, was never to cross this last barrier. Mr. John Wisdom reached the Georgia town before Captain Russell's squadron. The captain arrived on the third to find the bridge heavily guarded by Governor Brown's militia. Colonel Streight, after another ambush which was flanked by the "devilers," withdrew as silently as possible to push on to Rome. Unfortunately, the nearer he reached this city the more of his men were thrown on their feet. The remainder were so "jaded, tender-footed, and worn down, our progress was necessarily slow."

The Confederate advance took literally its orders. Outmarching the enemy, it squatted across the road in ambush near a village called Center. Streight, under the delusion that it was a part of the main body made a detour of three miles. As his tired brigade pulled back into the road, he was very pleased with himself, for not far to his front ran a branch of the Coosa. He reached it in high spirits. From the humours of his fatigue Rome rose before him, a mirage dazzling in his mind. But the mirage was quickly dispelled. The night mists of the Coosa's branch, and not the ferryboat, lay damp and chilling upon its waters. Captain Russell forgot in his haste to leave a guard at the ferry, and the boat had been spirited away.

But the Colonel made other plans. He learned that a bridge, some seven or eight miles away, spanned the stream near Gaylesville. He set out under new guidance to find and cross it. On the way he had to pass over an old coal chopping, "where the timber had been cut and hauled off for charcoal, leaving innumerable wagon roads running in every direction." In this maze of roads the command split into squads and wandered about the rest of the night, and not until daylight did Streight manage to get it together and across the river. Behind him, he left the Dyke bridge in flames.

He had scarcely got out of sight when the gray horsemen, refreshed by a whole night's sleep, galloped up and inspected the ruins of the bridge. Their inspection was interrupted by the arrival of Forrest. He looked at the river and gave a sharp, intense command. Soon men could be seen stripping; then into the water they rode. Its depth was discovered, and the entire body passed over, holding high above their heads their paper cartridges. The two guns and the empty caissons made the same underwater passage they had made at Black Creek. Small skiffs were found to carry over the contents of the caissons. By nine o'clock, after covering in four hours the same ground it had taken Streight eleven hours to make, Forrest came up with the raiders feeding and resting near a few houses, called Lawrence, strangely enough in what is called the *Straight-Neck Precinct*.

Throwing McLemore around the left flank, Biffle to the right, and his escort and a small detachment in the center, his line, in crescent shape, fringed a wooded ridge. This was most opportune. It masked the exact number of troops he brought to the field. His skirmishers opened a brisk fire.

There were barely five hundred Confederates on the ground, and one account places them as low as 420, when Forrest sent Captain Pointer forward with a flag of truce demanding immediate surrender, "in order to stop further and useless effusion of blood." He did not add that peremptory alternative, "or I will put every man to the sword."

He did not add it, because he knew the caliber of the man he had been chasing. The proud and gallant Streight would bring on a pitched battle before he would suffer any such indignity, and a pitched battle was the last thing Forrest wanted to happen. In his game of bluff his language had to be carefully weighed, firm enough to force a surrender but not too firm.

Colonel Streight's regimental officers had already expressed an opinion that if the enemy caught up with them again before reaching Rome, the chase was over. There was good reason for this opinion. That last night march had been the very heavy straw to break the back of their resistance. When what was left of the Mule Brigade halted that morning, the officers could not keep the men awake long enough to feed either themselves or their mounts. Nature was exhausted; they dropped in their tracks and lay there until the videttes were driven in. Their commander then, with what officers he could find who were fit for duty, dragged them into battle line; and there most of them lay with both eyes closed upon the gun sights, asleep in a heavy skirmish fire. To add to the Colonel's unhappy condition, a courier had just arrived from Captain Russell, announcing that he had failed to take the bridge over the Coosa; another reported a heavy body of the enemy marching by his left, which was then nearer Rome than he. To his front was a force he considered with certain misgivings to be three times his own number. Of the mules drawn at Nashville there were scarcely a score left; and the fresh ones he had impressed by the way were sorebacked and, being without shoes, limping with the tenderfoot. Besides these disabilities, most of his reserve ammunition was still wet. With these things in mind Colonel Streight went out to meet the white flag.

He and the General and several officers squatted in the road and discussed the matter. He seemed willing to surrender if Forrest would march out his command and show him they were at least equal to his own. Forrest told him, in effect, that he would not humiliate his men in an effort to persuade the enemy to surrender, an enemy they had been driving and whipping in every encounter for the last three days.

Colonel Streight was a hard-headed man. He still insisted on seeing for himself. Under the circumstances, it could not be granted. Forrest was in a delicate position. Streight then asked for twenty minutes' grace—to consult his officers. Forrest overflowed with generosity; his staff officers offered the Colonel a drink. Captain Pointer with rough banter, but to the point, told the Colonel he had better accept. It might be the last drink that would ever burn his throat. The

Confederates did their parts superbly: Colonel Streight had to be convinced that they were perfectly capable of storming his position. But Forrest wanted that twenty minutes' grace as much as the Colonel. In that time he felt he could prepare the stage to convince his enemy that four hundred men and a section of artillery could overwhelm fifteen hundred and two mountain howitzers.

In fifteen minutes, Streight was back. His officers had voted unanimously that the jig was up. But Streight, sensing the facts only too well, came back and demanded with stubborn despair to see that he was surrendering to a force the equal of his own.

Forrest was now prepared for this demand. Behind him was a small rise of ground. He had in Streight's absence sent back word for his two guns to circle the rise and give the impression that several batteries were coming up. He then so placed himself that his back and Streight's face would be turned in that direction. When the expected demand was made, Forrest repeated what he had said before, that discussion was useless, that he had known of the movement from its beginning, and was prepared to meet it; that he had now drawn tight the net, and that the only sensible thing for the Colonel to do was to admit his defeat. To reënforce his arguments, he pointed out that to Streight's left was a mountain, to his right a river, a large force in his front, and one in his rear which had been gaining strength every day.

"I seen him all the time he was talkin'," said the General to General Dabney Maury a year later, "lookin' over my shoulder and countin' the guns. Presently he said: 'Name of God! How many guns have you got? There's fifteen I've counted already.' Turnin' my head that way, I said, 'I reckon that s all that has kept up.' Then he said, 'I won't surrender until you tell me how many men you've got.' I said, 'I've got enough to whip you out of your boots.' To which he said, 'I won't surrender.' I turned to my bugler and said, 'Sound to mount!' Then he cried out, 'I'll surrender.' I told him, 'Stack your arms right along there, Colonel, and march your men away down that hollow.'

"When this was done," continued Forrest, "I ordered my men to come forward and take possession of the arms. When Streight saw they were barely four hundred, he did rear! Demanded to have his arms back and that we should fight it out. I just laughed at him and patted him on the shoulder . . .'Ah, Colonel, all is fair in love and war, you know.' "

The hoss critters were soon placed between the Yankees and their guns, for not until that moment did Forrest feel absolutely secure. He told his prisoners that as forage was scarce in Rome, he would send only one regiment and his escort for guard. Captain Pointer had already spread the report that the other brigades were camped at near distances, where they would remain rather than strain the hospitality of the Romans.

Captain Russell, returning from his unsuccessful attempt to seize the Coosa bridge, was informed of the catastrophe. With tears in his eyes he said he would rather die than surrender. He had returned too late for such a choice. There was now only one thing left to do— order his two hundred to stack their arms. This brought the total number of prisoners to 1600 or 1700 who that day, May third, fell into Forrest's hands.

Bragg's communications were out of danger. Rome and the state's manufactories could still serve the armies of the Confederacy; and Streight had learned what it meant to steal thunder. So had Rosecrans. Forrest taught these officers that he was as great a master at frustrating raids as he was at making them. In the future, Rosecrans would content himself with manœuvering his infantry.

Forrest's exploits were always satisfactory. His victories were never uncertain. There was something so complete, so final, about them. And to this part of the Confederacy, where the diet was still drawn battles followed by retreat, Forrest's name had a peculiar relish all its own. The capture of Streight, coming as it did after Stones River, had a moral effect far more stimulating than the capture of so small a body of the enemy would ordinarily have. For a month afterwards the press was filled with anecdotes and details of the campaign, and especially of the final stratagem which delivered 1700 Yankees into the hands of a bare five hundred. This made the fire-eaters' tales look conservative.

Again and again Forrest would win a minor victory after a major defeat or drawn battle. It informed the Southern people that the trouble with their defense was not with their soldiers but with certain of their generals.

When Rome heard the news, it went almost mad with joy. The town was filled with refugees and two thousand convalescents from the army hospitals. Among the refugees many of Forrest's men found their women folks and kin. This would have been reward in itself, but the Georgians threw the doors to their smoke houses and pantries wide open, and for men who had had saddles for pillows turned back the sheets on feather beds. There was at last rest for the weary, food for the "hongry," and praise for the brave.

The critters came in for their share. What corn and fodder the town had was theirs, but for these thoroughbreds the crib doors might as well have remained closed. The best blooded stock of Middle Tennessee and Kentucky, trained never to falter until the race was over, true to their breeding had kept their heads up until the end.

But the end of the race had been their end. They had been pushed beyond their strength. Of the five hundred and fifty horses which bore the gray riders into Rome that day and the next scarcely two hundred and fifty went out again. Taken with the scours and the cramps they dropped in their tracks by the score. The artillery teams suffered most of all. One hundred and twenty-five select animals had left Courtland attached to the guns and caissons. Twenty-five remained.

People began to understand how terrific Forrest's demands had been, but only those who had ridden with Old Bedford knew. Many commanders inspire courage and zeal on the battlefield, but the few great ones conquer fatigue. When the limit to endurance had been reached, Forrest then called on his men to make still greater efforts. And they always responded. It was this quality and his inscrutable strategy which was not understandable. When people are faced with phenomena they cannot explain by the reactions common to their experience, they resort to the supernatural. So hereafter, when they spoke of Forrest, they called him the Wizard of the Saddle.

There was much entertainment at Rome, and many gifts. The town presented Forrest a fine horse, and it planned a big barbecue for the sixth. Some of the Georgia people wanted to change the name of Union County to Forrest County. They could not do too much for their deliverer. Edmondson and Anderson rode in after the surrender and recuperated with the others and joined in the merriment.

Now that there was no danger from them, the Romans offered Streight and his raiders the hospitality of their town. But the brave, unfortunate commander of the Mule Brigade, as he thought about the ruse which had been practised upon his credulity, could not enter into the spirit of the entertainment. Captain Anderson, his face shiny and his flaxen hair all cleaned after his march, saw the Colonel's glum looks. He went over and, in a brotherly fashion, laid his heavy arm about the raider's shoulder.

"Cheer up, Colonel," he said, "this is not the first time a bluff has beat a *straight*."

CHAPTER XI

The Middle Tennessee Campaign

IT was not destined, however, that General Forrest and his hoss critters should fill the seats of honor at the Roman banquet. On the
night of the fifth, certain citizens arrived with the news that another
body of Yankees had penetrated Alabama and were then moving by
Elyton in the direction of Talladega. Mounting his tired troopers on
the captured stock, he retraced his steps as far as Gadsden. His own
couriers met him there with the information that there was no truth
to the report.

From Gadsden he took a leisurely pace to Decatur, sending back
two companies to pick up stragglers, the wounded, and abandoned supplies. There were many negroes mixed in with the stragglers. Streight
had made the mistake of loading down his flying column with slaves.

Forrest arrived at Decatur on the tenth and recrossed to the north
bank of the Tennessee. The next day he turned the command over
to Biffle and proceeded by rail to army headquarters at Shelbyville.
On the way, at Huntsville, the most important town in North Alabama, the whole population turned out to welcome and present him
with a fine horse. He now began to understand what the capture of
Streight meant to the people of the Southwest. They had watched
it like sportsmen, although they knew the stakes were more vital
than blue ribbons.

He found the same sort of reception at army headquarters. He had
shaken the dullness of winter quarters with a little excitement. Joseph
E. Johnston and Bragg had kept Richmond informed of his progress
as well as they could, and Bragg had ordered Dibrell to take post at
Fulton, Mississippi, to stop Streight should he return towards Corinth.
It was probably this regiment which alarmed the citizens into thinking another raid had been sent into the heart of the Confederacy.

The infantry, officers and men alike, of the Army of Tennessee
showed their gratitude in various ways. A Mississippi regiment sere-
naded his quarters and asked to serve under him. They told him they

understood he had captured enough horses to mount them. But even if Bragg had been willing to grant their request, there were no horses. Forrest had requested that the captured stock be returned to the people who had lost it. This was done, but out of sixteen hundred only four hundred and fifty ever reached their owners alive.

Bragg received Forrest with unusual warmth, almost with affection. He told him that he would urge his promotion to the rank of Major-General. He spoke of him as Chief of Cavalry. But Forrest told Bragg that another officer in his army was more suited to the duties of that position. While taking pride in his military prowess, Forrest did not have that self-conscious itch for distinction which had raised so many of the talented obscure from the dog-run to the mansion.

This change of heart on Bragg's part had been evident ever since Thompson's Station and Brentwood. But Forrest doubted its sincerity, for he had already measured the instability of his commander's character.

Before going south both Forrest and Jackson, the other division head, had conferred with the unfortunate Pillow and advised him to get himself put in Van Dorn's place. This general, while riding to parade in a buggy with Dr. Peter's wife, was seen by the doctor, who thought it one buggy ride too many. Later he shot and killed Van Dorn and escaped to the enemy's lines. This left a vacancy, and the hero of the Streight raid was ordered to fill it. Pillow, writing to Governor Harris, referred to the conversation in the following way: "Since, however, Forrest is assigned to the command, I am gratified at the result. He deserves the position, *though I had thought he would not be assigned to it."* *

This gave Forrest control over two divisions, Armstrong's and Jackson's; but shortly after he had assumed command, Jackson's division was detached and sent to Mississippi. This left him with two small brigades to guard the left flank of the Army of Tennessee.

Seddon, Davis's military adviser, had wired Bragg on the seventeenth to send Forrest or some other cavalry force to Mississippi. The situation there had become desperate. Grant had run by the batteries of Vicksburg and landed his army south of the armed town. He had then cut loose from his communications, supported himself off the country; and, striking Pemberton's scattered divisions in detail, had whipped them in separate battles. Pemberton then withdrew with some thirty-one thousand into the heavy fortifications of Vicksburg.

* Italics mine.

Joseph E. Johnston, the Commander-in-Chief in the West, had under his direction both Bragg's army and Pemberton's. But he failed to exercise the power he possessed, until his subordinate generals came to look upon themselves as independent of his control. When Grant crossed the river, Johnston wired Pemberton to concentrate and fight a pitched battle. Pemberton ignored the order and brought on the detailed reverses. When Johnston arrived on the scene and took charge of the troops at Jackson, two brigades only, he again sent Pemberton repeated orders to co-operate with him on an attack against Grant's rear. Pemberton disobeyed all of these orders. Grant, therefore, took Jackson and separated the commander of the department from his subordinate. When Pemberton finally withdrew into the fortifications, he received another order not to remain but to abandon the position and march northeast. Johnston knew that to remain meant to lose the town and what was left of the army. Pemberton, instead of withdrawing while there was time, called a council of war. The council decided that the army could not withdraw without destroying its efficiency as a fighting unit. Pemberton wired Johnston that he would hold Vicksburg to the end. Johnston then set himself the task of gathering in Grant's rear an army which would raise the siege.

The Yankee Government rushed troops to Grant. When he first crossed the Mississippi, Pemberton, if he had concentrated, could have brought between fifty thousand and fifty-five thousand men against Grant's thirty-three thousand; and if he had had any cavalry to keep him properly informed, he would have learned that in the very beginning the enemy had scarcely twenty thousand landed on the east bank. One of the greatest blunders made by the Confederate Government, and they made many in the West, was transferring Van Dorn's division to the Army of Tennessee. When it was too late, they rushed back Roddy's brigade and Jackson's Division. It was too late, because by June Grant's investing force numbered over seventy thousand men.

The Confederates were fast approaching the second great crisis of the war, the greatest since Fort Donelson. In the Trans-Mississippi Department a large army had been dissipated by incompetent generals. It was on the point of reorganization by Kirby-Smith, but at the moment it had only 12,500 ineffectives who could not neutralize the Yankees in Missouri and Arkansas, much less send aid to Johnston in Mississippi. There was Bragg lying behind Duck River in Tennessee. If he had been ordered immediately to Johnston, their combined forces working in conjunction with Pemberton's besieged army stood a reasonable chance of raising the siege. But this would mean giving up, at least temporarily, Middle Tennessee and very likely the whole state, besides parts of Alabama and Georgia. At that it would have required a bold, confident campaign under a general of the highest skill. And at the moment there was no such general available west of the Alleghanies. Both Bragg and Johnston, due to illness, psychological and physical, lacked at this moment the qualities necessary to such a campaign.

The hope of the Confederacy lay now, as it had never lain before, in Virginia. Lee's army, after the battle of Chancellorsville, was stronger as a fighting unit than it would ever be again. There was no immediate danger from the Army of the Potomac. If Lee had been sent with a great part of his army to the West and placed in command of all the armies in that territory, one hundred thousand men under his leadership would have crushed Rosecrans and left him free to invade the Northwest. This would have forced Grant to raise the siege and reëstablish his broken communications with his base.

Such a move, very likely, would have meant the fall of Richmond; but as this city had no real strategic value, the heart of the Confederacy being in the Southwest, its loss would have been slight in comparison with the great gains of such a bold campaign. Longstreet urged this plan of campaign on Davis and Lee. Davis favored it, as did Reagan, the Postmaster-General, and for a while Seddon, the Secretary of War. But Lee refused to go. He would not break up his fine army, and he would not for great gains abandon the State of Virginia temporarily to the enemy. He proposed to raise the siege of Vicksburg by an invasion of Pennsylvania, but victory in Pennsylvania required Jackson as well as Lee, and Jackson had crossed the river to rest in the shade of the trees. Lee did not realize at this time that the movement of his army, on the march and in battle, must be directed differently in the absence of his chief lieutenant. He would learn at Gettysburg, but the lesson would be a little late.

The other alternative, reënforcing Johnston with Bragg's army, alone remained. But Middle Tennessee was thought too precious to abandon even with so urgent a need; so the authorities, in a piecemeal way, sent Breckinridge's division, Ector's and McNair's brigades and Jackson's cavalry from Bragg's army, reducing an army already weaker than its antagonist without helping the relieving army under Johnston. He was never able to gather more than twenty-five thousand, too few and gathered too late, to help Vicksburg.

The Confederate authorities had repeated what Davis had done before the Battle of Stones River. At that time he had weakened the Army of Tennessee by sending ten thousand men under Stevenson to Mississippi. Rosecrans, as soon as he learned of the transference, had marched towards Murfreesboro. Now, again, as soon as he would learn that the Army of Tennessee had been reduced, Rosecrans would march against the fortifications at Shelbyville and the gaps around Beech Grove, Christiana, and Matt's Hollow.

In the meantime, an ominous inactivity settled upon all arms along Duck River. But behind it was the fear on the part of the Lincoln Government that not a part, but the whole of Bragg's army would slip away to Mississippi. To prevent this, Halleck was constantly urging Rosecrans to engage the Army of Tennessee and make such a move impossible. The tenor of Rosecran's replies was that it was not good strategy to risk two major engagements at once in the same theatre of war. If Grant were defeated before Vicksburg, his army, he argued, would be the only defense left to the Yankee Government; on the other hand, if Grant were victorious, then Grant could reënforce him sufficiently to make victory over Bragg certain. In the meantime, the best way to keep Bragg on his front was to lie opposite him.

On May 27, Lincoln wired Rosecrans: "Have you anything from Grant? *Where is Forrest's headquarters?*" (Italics mine.) Rosecrans wired back that Forrest was at Rigg's Cross Roads. Thinking the matter over, he sent out his cavalry to make sure he was there. When they failed to find any traces of him, Rosecrans became uneasy and wired Stanton: "Had you heard any news which prompted your question of last night?" Stanton answered that Lincoln's inquiry was to trace a rumor of disaster to Grant. "Much apprehension," he wired, "is felt in the North that the enemy would escape from your front and fall on Grant, and we were on that ground, also anxious to know where Forrest is, for reports say he has gone south for that purpose."

Other reports from Okolona, Mississippi, showed that he was expected there any day. To Davis and his government at Richmond, Forrest was just another efficient cavalryman. They had come to rely upon the Confederate horsemen to be victorious always. Stuart, Forrest, Morgan, Ashby, and Wheeler rarely sent in reports of failure; although Seddon and Davis were beginning to realize that Forrest was unique among his peers, they were too far removed from the Western Theatre to appreciate the strength of his arm. But this was not the case with Mr. Lincoln and his government. They more than appreciated it, for too often they had occasion to feel its weight. From this time on, with accumulative persistence, Forrest appeared as one of the greatest stumbling blocks to the success of their western campaigns.

But there was no danger of his removal to Mississippi. Bragg knew how much he meant to the Army of Tennessee. And there was another reason. One of the first official acts which Forrest did after his promotion to General Van Dorn's post was to have Lieutenant Gould, the officer who had abandoned the two guns on Sand Mountain, transferred to another command. The young lieutenant, although no reason was given for the action, knew that it was an official censure for his conduct. Feeling that it reflected upon his courage, he asked for an interview. General Forrest told him to come to the Quartermaster's office in Columbia at three o'clock that afternoon.

Both men were on time for the appointment. They went out into the hall and slowly walked up and down the corridor. The General listened in silence, twirling in his right hand a small pocket knife, the blades drawn to a point, making of it a triangle which twirled over and over his finger as they walked.

The Lieutenant's voice soon rose in excitement. He was asking the reason for his transference. His General told him that he would give him no reason and that, furthermore, he need not expect ever again to serve in his command. Gould, as the remarks he had heard on the battlefield returned and charged his quick temper, drew a pistol from an inside pocket and shot his commander. The ball entered the left hip, traveled in the vicinity of the intestines, and went out again.

Forrest reached out with his left hand, grabbed the pistol hand, and pointed the barrel away from his body. He raised his knife to his teeth and opened the largest blade; then, with very little conscious effort, struck Gould in the belly, ripping it open and perforating the bowels. Gould dropped the pistol and ran out into the street. Forrest walked to Doctor Yandell's office and dropped his trousers. The doctor examined the wound, pronounced it dangerous, and advised him to go to the hospital for treatment.

"No damn man can kill me and live." Saying this, Forrest ran out of the office, and snatched a pistol from a holster saddled to a horse tied in front of the building. As he ran, the warm blood pumped out of the hole in his side, curled down his hairy leg, and spattered on the streets.

Gould had fled to a tailor's shop and was lying on the counter bleeding profusely. A large crowd had gathered in and before the shop.

General Forrest's powerful form charged its outer edge. Somebody told Gould he was there, and he could hear. . . "Get out of my way. He's mortally wounded me, and I aim to kill him before I die."

Gould leaped out of the back window, some five or six feet to the ground. Forrest shot. Gould fell as if he had been done for. Voices cried, "You have killed him, General."

Gould, at his superior's orders, was carried to the Nelson House. Soon afterward Forrest grew faint and tottered.

In several days rumor had it that the General would recover, but the young lieutenant would not. Septic peritonitis had set in. Captain Morton, his immediate commander, passed between the two men. To him they both expressed their deep regret, and each man condemned his own haste in the matter. Two days later the doctor said Gould could not last much longer. He sent word to his commander that he wished to speak with him before he died and that, if it were possible, he would like to see him.

They lifted General Forrest's cot into the room and set it down close to the dying man's bed. Gould, when he saw who it was, reached over and took Forrest's hand and held it between both of his.

"General, I shall not be here long, and I was not willing to go away without seeing you in person and saying to you how thankful I am that I am the one who is to die and that you are spared to the country. What I did, I did in a moment of rashness, and I want your forgiveness."

Forrest leaned over the bed and "wept like a child." He told the young man he forgave him freely. He told him his own heart was full of sadness because the wound he had inflicted was about to prove fatal.

Self-preservation, the unconscious command of the wilderness, had made him kill one of his boys.

Through the rest of May and June there were daily affairs among the outposts, but nothing of particular importance. In the first week of June, learning that General Granger had transferred his headquarters from Franklin to Triune, about half way between Murfreesboro and Franklin, Forrest set out to discover what troops had been left in Franklin. He took and held the town long enough to release a number of political prisoners and impress a quantity of sutlers' supplies.

As he drew up before the place, signal flags wagged vigorously from the fort to call on General Granger for assistance. Mistaking them for flags of truce, Forrest sent his own in to receive the fort's surrender. To save time he went forward to meet it. Before he had gone very far an officer stood up behind a hedge and shouted, "General Forrest, you will retire at once. There is no truce. That is a signal flag."

Forrest raised his hat to acknowledge the courtesy and withdrew quickly to the rear. After retiring a certain distance, he turned on his horse and saw the officer and a detachment of soldiers still by the hedge, his eyes fixed on the retreating general. Forrest waved his hand to him; then galloped out of sight. The Federal officer had been captured by him at Murfreesboro in '62.

On the twentieth, Forrest attacked Triune to test its strength. As it had a heavy infantry force as well as cavalry there, he quickly retired. The fruits of the expedition, besides information, was a drove of cattle. Major Jeffrey Forrest managed this diversion with high success. Jeffrey was his youngest and favorite brother. He used to tell his men that Jeffrey was the only man on the face of the earth he feared. He told them this with pride and love, to raise Jeffrey in their estimation. He knew that, should the occasion present itself, he could not harm a hair of his head. Jeffrey, unlike the other brothers, had the polish of a classical education. Bedford had seen to that. With the disappearance of the border and its ways, he wanted Jeff to take his place among the leaders of the hardening culture of the Southwest. Now it was necessary for a young man of parts to know how to write a good letter, read Latin and Greek, and quote from Scott. When he was young and making his fortune, it was more important to know how to shoot straight, to know when to fight "fist and skull, or stomp and gouge."

On June 1, Forrest sent a message to Bragg: "My scouts report the enemy's cavalry all moved to the front of Murfreesboro. Rosecrans's headquarters are at Nashville. All the streets are being blockaded; cutting ditches and placing sandbags. They intend to move either forward or backward."

This dispatch gave General Bragg three weeks to prepare for the Yankee advance. But when it was finally made on the twenty-third, he was without the proper intelligence, alternative plans, or decision. Rosecrans made a feint on his entrenchments before Shelbyville and, throwing his heaviest columns through Liberty Gap, Hoover's Gap, and Matt's Hollow, turned his right flank. Bragg was taken so by surprise that Forrest was notified of the retreat barely in time to escape.

Wheeler held Guy's Gap, through which the Murfreesboro-Shelbyville road passed, with cavalry and artillery. Forrest was ordered to meet him at Shelbyville, but the enemy, massing his cavalry, drove

Wheeler so fast that he did not tarry in the town but put his brigades at once across the river. General Polk had already withdrawn his corps and the wagon trains, but the trains floundered in the mud, through a drenching rain, only a few miles out.

Having successfully held the enemy in check until the trains were safely across, Wheeler prepared to fire the bridge and assure their safety. Major Rambaut, of General Forrest's staff, dashed up at this moment and reported that his chief was within sight of Shelbyville and advancing rapidly to effect a crossing. Wheeler with five hundred men of Martin's division and a section of artillery countermarched across the bridge, determined to hold it for his brother-in-arms.

Before he could form a very effective alignment, the Yankees charged him in column of fours, ran over the guns and dispersed the five hundred. In the confusion a caisson was overturned on the bridge. Wheeler, seeing retreat cut off, shouted to his men to cut their way through; and, pointing the way, he urged his horse to the river bank and leaped fifteen feet into the churning waters below. His troopers, one by one, or in squads, followed after. The Yankees were taken so by surprise that they did not take immediate advantage of the situation. But soon, as horse and rider popped to the surface, carbines unloaded on the floundering targets. Wheeler and Martin escaped untouched, but it was estimated that forty or fifty of their men were shot or drowned.

Forrest, in the meantime, sensed the danger before him. He veered to the right and crossed over another bridge, eight miles away. He then took his place in the rear of the wagons.

If General Gordon Granger had ordered pursuit that night, as his lieutenant, General Stanley, wanted him to do, Bragg's train would have been at his mercy. Martin's division was temporarily disorganized and Forrest was cut off from the army. Each infantry division had detailed a brigade to guard the trains; and, well handled, it is possible they might have saved them. But infantry is no great check for cavalry, particularly when the wagons are floundering through the dark and the rain. It is a simple matter for a mounted man to ride by a wagon and drop fire in the hay lashed on behind.

At Tullahoma, his second line of entrenchments, Bragg called a meeting of his staff and corps commanders to decide upon giving battle. The enemy, on this day, June 29, had concentrated in front of Tullahoma and at Manchester, twelve miles to the northeast.

It is safe to say that the weather alone had saved Bragg. Rosecrans's corps commander, Crittenden, whose route ran by Woodbury to Manchester, had consumed four days in making seventeen miles. The armies were now operating in the Barrens, whose whitish, craw-fishy soil turned to quicksand under continuous rainfall. Crittenden had had to hitch his infantry to his wagons, sunk up to the hubs in the sucking soil. Some of his horses actually mired up and perished.

At the council Polk advised retreat. Bragg's communications had already been partially broken by Wilder's Mounted Infantry. But Wilder failed to reduce the garrison guarding the Elk River bridge, and Dibrell arrived and drove him away before he could destroy more than three hundred yards of the track. At the same time, Forrest with his escort and a part of a brigade moved towards Pelham to cut off his retreat.

It was raining very hard, and Forrest and the escort had galloped a good distance ahead of his support. Turning a bend in the road, he ran into a company of the enemy. Both were dressed in uninforming raincoats. Riding forward, Forrest asked with great friendliness "what command." It was a company of Wilders' Mounted Infantry. He answered that he was a part of the cavalry belonging to another Yankee division; and, saluting his brother officer, passed on. Thinking his regiments were only a short distance behind, he made preparations to block this company's retreat. But before he could do this, he discovered the enemy's main column trotting along the road. Quickly retracing his steps, he charged his one-time brothers-in-arms, captured some, and dispersed the others. When he brought up his demi-brigade, Wilder had escaped.

This activity had preserved the Confederate communications, but General Polk argued that they were still insecure, since the Army of Tennessee did not have sufficient cavalry to protect the communications and do other necessary duties. Bragg had allowed John Morgan to go on a raid into Kentucky with 2,500 of his riders, and Colonel Starnes, Forrest's best brigade commander, had been killed as he was guarding the Manchester road. This always, temporarily at least, makes a command less efficient. General Hardee then suggested that it would be well to have some infantry sent along the line to support the cavalry. This would allow the Confederates to wait for further developments before coming to any decision. It was agreed that this should be done, and with this the conference closed.

The truth of the matter was that General Polk did not want to risk another battle under Bragg. The rapid changes in the campaign only puzzled and confused him. The knowledge that his chief lieutenant and many of his generals had no confidence in his leadership, left Bragg helpless in the face of emergency. It had made him physically ill. His character, too frail to meet the responsibilities of his situation under the most propitious circumstances, now forced him to take counsel with men he despised. This shattered whatever power of action he had left.

On the thirtieth, Rosecrans got his army into battle order and began another turning movement, but Bragg, after deciding to fight, suddenly withdrew.

General Hardee, after the army had fallen back across the Elk, became greatly alarmed at the increasing hazard. He sent the following dispatch to Polk:

". . . If we have a fight, he (Bragg) is evidently unable either to examine and determine his line of battle or to take command on the field. What shall we do? What is best to be done to save this army and its honor? I think we ought to counsel together. . ."

But Hardee recovered from his alarm, for Bragg, after considering another fight at the base of the Cumberland Mountains, abandoned the idea and withdrew behind the Tennessee River at Chattanooga, Hardee moving through the gap at Pelham and Polk over the railroad through University Place.

In nine days Rosecrans had, with trifling loss, manœuvered the Army of Tennessee and its distraught commander out of the most productive basin of the state. It is true that he brought into the campaign some sixty-five thousand of all arms while the Confederates numbered forty-three thousand. But such odds were not unusual. The Confederate generals had often fought with a similar handicap. There were moments in the campaign when Bragg could have massed and met the segments of the enemy to his own advantage. But from the first he stood on the defensive and waited like an automaton the developing attack of his adversary. Any general who does this is sure of defeat, because he may know he will be well attacked.

On July 4, Vicksburg fell, and Pemberton turned over to Grant the position and what was left of his thirty-one thousand men. Port Hudson, at the other extremity of the river line, when it heard the news, capitulated and delivered up to the enemy over six thousand more men.

General Lee's attacks at Gettysburg came to an end on the same day, and although he withdrew to Virginia in safety, his failure to annihilate Meade was a great moral blow to the Confederacy. The

THE MIDDLE TENNESSEE CAMPAIGN 187

battle had been a drawn one tactically, but strategically the defeat was almost overwhelming. A war is not lost until a country's armies are completely destroyed. No matter how many repulses an army sustains, it can win back everything it has lost by one decisive battle.

But the blow seemed to be overwhelming. One of the Confederate armies had been destroyed; another repulsed; and the third driven one hundred and twenty miles in less than two weeks. Morgan, disobeying his orders which confined his raid to Louisville, swept into Ohio and was captured and his brigade dispersed, killed, or captured.

Northern hopes soared. They saw the end of the war in sight. Halleck sent Rosecrans peremptory orders to destroy Bragg. With Bragg out of the way, all could gather around the mighty Army of Northern Virginia. Fortunately for the Confederacy, Rosecrans had reached, for the moment, a deadlock. His men had to eat before they could either march or fight. To get at Bragg he had to cross an unproductive mountain range and the Tennessee River. In its wild expectations, the Government at Washington forgot these little obstructions.

The fate of the Confederacy hung to the banks of the Tennessee. Rising in the mountains around Chattanooga and moving through the narrow valley between Pigeon and Lookout Mountains, Chickamauga Creek twists in its valley to spill its mountain waters in the river above Chattanooga. Long years ago the Indians had fought from sun-up until sun-down along the banks of that stream. From then on they called it Chickamauga, the River of Blood.

Forrest, as he protected the rear of the army withdrawing over the mountains, was in constant conflict with the enemy's cavalry. Once he remained almost too long in their front and barely escaped capture.

As his detachment withdrew hastily through Cowan, the little town at the base of the Cumberlands, he brought up the rear riding like the wind. A sturdy hill-woman, one of the dog-run people, stood in her door and shouted at the troopers to turn and "whip them back." She saw the General straining his horse to keep up with his men. As he passed her door, she raised and shook her fist in his direction.

"You great, big, cowardly rascal, why don't you turn and fight like a man, instid of runnin' like a cur? I wish Old Forrest was here. He'd make ye fight."

CHAPTER XII

Rats in the Wall

AFTER Bragg had crossed the river into Chattanooga, he settled down to hide behind the mountains. When he discovered Rosecrans was not ready to follow, he went to the springs to recuperate his shattered health.

Forrest's division remained in camp around Chattanooga until the last of July. He was then sent to Kingston to guard the fords from that point down the Tennessee to Kelly's Ferry. The cavalry in East Tennessee, Pegram and Scott, was ordered to coöperate with him. Wheeler was held responsible for the river from Kelly's Ferry to Decatur, Alabama. Roddy, at Tuscumbia, guarded the fords as far as Corinth, keeping in touch with Wheeler's left. As the coming campaign developed, the East Tennessee cavalry formed a division in a corps under Forrest, and Roddy came directly under Wheeler's orders.

From Kentucky, General Burnside, now that his 9th Corps had been returned by Grant after the fall of Vicksburg, set out to invade East Tennessee with an army estimated by the Confederates to be twenty-five thousand men. East Tennessee was held by Buckner with two small divisions, Stewart's and Preston's, eight thousand nine hundred and fifty-five infantry and artillery, and five thousand, seven hundred and fifty-eight cavalry. After subtracting guards and details, Buckner could concentrate only seven thousand men for defense. It was the Federal's intention that Rosecrans and Burnside should close in from front and rear and crush the remaining Confederate defense in the Southwest.

Bragg's hasty retreat had convinced Rosecrans that the morale of his army was broken. Numerous deserters came in to sustain this opinion. "At Anderson seven prisoners were taken . . . desiring to take the oath of allegiance. They represent the mountains full of deserters, the rebel army much demoralized, and in nearly a starving condition."

Rosecrans's spies and scouts gave further evidence of this condition. One of them, R. Henderson, writes from McMinnville, "The army may be said to be demoralized, being but little, if any better than a mob. The common soldiers feel and say that they are not able to contend with Rosecrans's army, and the prevailing opinion with officers and men is that Bragg will retreat as soon as an advance is made, and they expect a movement in the direction of Rome, Georgia, which they all fear. Neither officers nor men have any confidence in Bragg's ability, and many doubt his courage."

"Men afraid of being conscripted (by Lincoln Government) if they desert. Mississippians anxious to get home, now Vicksburg has fallen." "The people seem to keep up good spirits, but are all finding fault with Bragg."

Much of this was true. There was serious difficulty with Buckner's East Tennessee and North Carolina regiments, so much so that it was contemplated transferring them to Lee's army or to Johnston in Mississippi. It was almost impossible to bring deserters from these regiments back, for they could hide in the mountain passes, or in the houses of Union sympathizers along the way. Over a hundred men from the Sixty-Fourth North Carolina regiment were absent without leave. Many of them lived openly at home and made crops.

Martha Revis wrote her husband a letter, which increased this regiment's desertion by one more. After telling him of affairs at home, she closed with, "You said you hadn't anything to eat. I wish you was here to get some beans for dinner. I have plenty to eat as yet. I haven't saw any of your pap's folks since you left home. The people is generally well hereat. The people is all turning Union here since the Yankees has got Vicksburg. I want you to come home as soon as you can after you git this letter . . . This is all I can think of, only I want you to come home the worst I ever did. The conscripts is all at home yet, and I don't know what they will do with them. The folks is leaving here, and going North as fast as they can.

Your wife, till death,

Martha Revis."

Whatever qualms Martha Revis's husband had against deserting, they probably toppled before the powerful suggestion of beans for dinner, although her array of seductions were massed to scatter the sternest resolutions. But in spite of this plentiful evidence of desertion,

Polk's corps, when it reached Chattanooga, was stronger by four hundred men than it had been at Tullahoma.

This Rosecrans did not know, nor did the deserters stay to find out. If the faint of heart could not stand the strain, there were many strong-minded veterans who could. The Army of Tennessee, winnowed of its chaff, lay behind Sand Mountain ready for battle.

But the idle army, under the best conditions, always dwindles, and Bragg was to remain idle for two months. General Polk, alarmed at this condition, wrote his friend Davis a letter. He advised a concentration of Johnston's Mississippi command, about twenty-five thousand of all arms, with Bragg's and Buckner's forces. This would give seventy thousand men for an offensive. His communication very subtly suggested that Johnston, being the senior general, would naturally take command. About the same time he wrote to Hardee, who had been detached to command a corps under Johnston, to sound the general out on the matter.

But Davis did not take to the suggestion. He and Johnston had become so estranged after the fall of Vicksburg that Polk's effort to bring about Bragg's removal failed. Instead of joining the two armies, Davis, after toying with the suggestion, wrote Bragg through his Secretary of War asking him if he would take the offensive provided he were strongly reënforced from Mississippi. Bragg replied that he would not undertake it. The reënforcements, after the necessary deductions for garrison duty, would give him only forty thousand infantry and artillery and ten thousand poorly equipped cavalry; and these were too few, he replied to Seddon, to attempt an offensive. And there, for the moment, the matter rested.

But there was no rest for Rosecrans. Slowly and steadily, while the Confederates crowed and pecked straws, he was pushing forward his communications over thirty miles of Barrens and seventy miles of mountains to the bank of the Tennessee. His army now must be fed entirely by rail, for there was no subsistence in this country. This long stretch of railroad gave him his only doubts about the oncoming campaign. He feared that Forrest might cross the river and break the lines and neutralize his advance, if he did not cause more serious damage.

He was constantly receiving reports of such a raid. General Hartsuff, in Kentucky, was also alarmed. He expected Forrest's appearance any day in the Blue Grass counties. One message brought the news that Major-General Forrest and four brigades were at Sparta. This raised flurries of alarm until it was discovered that it was Dibrell, not Forrest. He had been sent with his brigade to scout, forage, and let the men see their kin-folks.

Forrest was not ordered, nor is there evidence that he contemplated a raid on the enemy supply lines. It was more difficult to make raids now than it had been in the early days of the war. To begin with, Rosecrans's cavalry almost equaled that of the Army of Tennessee. And the odds in other ways did not favor it. Forrest would have to move over great distances, through a country rough and mountainous, and between two advancing armies. If Burnside could seize and close the gaps to his rear, he would be at Rosecrans's mercy, or be forced to make his escape by a circuitous route that would cut him off from the army. And his duty at the moment was to watch Burnside and Rosecrans and see that the Army of Tennessee was not surprised.

But these were not the chief reasons why no raid was contemplated. Forrest had turned his mind to other things. He had, like Polk and the other generals, seriously considered the future prospects of the army. A year ago he would not have thought of the cause in the terms he was to use from now on, but two years of battles and campaigning had changed his attitude towards his superiors and his estimation of himself.

Without any previous military training he had risen from the ranks to the commander of a division, and in the course of his rise he had mastered the various stages through which he had passed. In the beginning he had had a great respect for the professional soldier; but this respect had received many severe blows in the last six months. Most of the blunders in the Southwest could be laid to their doors. His direct association with the Army of Tennessee and his contingent operations had taught him that a West Pointer, as well as the layman soldier, had to be examined by the logistics and major engagements of a campaign before he could pass as an efficient soldier. But he had found that the West Pointer, himself, rarely took this view of the matter. The four-year passage through its halls, added to the garrison duty which followed, was to the professional a sort of divine right to command, a right Davis defended. But Forrest had found that the blessings of this power were not always sustained in action. The commander of the army, a West Pointer, had not brought victory, while he, not a professional before the war, had never been defeated. If the other West Pointers did not appreciate the full significance of this fact, the people of the Southwest did. For some time back, numerous letters had come to him from different parts of the South, asking him to come and free them from the enemy. Particularly had the people in West Tennessee and North Mississippi appealed for help. The esteem of his troops, his many victories, and this show of confidence by the citizens began to teach him his power. He had fought hard to win his victories and to protect the left of the army, and they had been costly in men and material. To a man of his temperament, it must have gone hard to watch Bragg's impotence throw away everything he had done for the cause.

So on August 9, he wrote to General Cooper, the Adjutant- and Inspector-General of all the Confederate forces. His letter, if the Richmond authorities had been able to interpret it properly, made manifest two things: his utter disillusionment as to Bragg's capacity to command an army and an understanding of his own powers. He proposed nothing less than a recovery of the Mississippi River.

He asked to be put in command of the forces from Vicksburg to Cairo, "or, in other words, all the forces I may collect together and organize between those points, say, in Northern Mississippi, West Tennessee, and those that may join me from Arkansas, Mississippi, and southern Kentucky."

In elaborating the details of his plan to reunite the Trans-Mississippi third of the Confederacy with its other parts—not a half as the Lincoln Government had claimed—he acquainted Richmond with his peculiar capacity to undertake the business. For twenty years before the war he had become thoroughly familiar with the territory and the prominent people of this country. He had on his staff and in his command officers who had rafted timber out of the Mississippi bottoms and who had a minute knowledge of every foot of the ground from Commerce to Vicksburg. He was confident that he could so move his men as to harass and destroy boats moving on the river, until only those heavily guarded by gunboats would be able to pass, while the miasmal swamps of the Mississippi bottoms, menacing with malaria and yellow fever to the unacclimated, would protect his small bodies of artillery and sharpshooters from the divisions of Grant and Sherman.

The possibilities of success were fascinating. He believed that in sixty days he could recruit from half-organized regiments, battalions, and companies between five thousand and ten thousand men.

"In making this proposition, I desire to state that I do so entirely for the good of the service. I believe that I can accomplish all that I propose to do. I have never asked for position, have taken position and performed the duties assigned me [His return from Kentucky into Middle Tennessee; West Tennessee, when he thought he was being sacrificed to Bragg's dislike; Second Fort Donelson] and have never yet suffered my command to be surprised or defeated. I should leave this department with many regrets, as I am well pleased with the officers in my command and with the division serving under me. I shall especially regret parting with my old brigade. It was organized by me, and a record of its past services and present condition will compare favorably with any cavalry command in the service, and nothing but a desire to destroy the enemy's transports and property, and increase the strength of our army, could for a moment induce me voluntarily to part with them. *There are thousands of men where I propose to go that I am satisfied will join me,* and that rapidly (otherwise they will remain where they are), until *all the country bordering on the Mississippi from, Cairo down is taken and permanently occupied by our forces."**

Although his express purpose indicated no more than a recovery of the Mississippi, these closing lines hinted at grander plans. There was at least the implication, intended or otherwise, that Forrest no longer belonged in a subordinate position.

His transference to other fields of duty would not materially weaken the Army of Tennessee. He proposed taking no more than four hundred men with him. With these as a nucleus, and the power of his name, he expected to go into country overrun by Grant and Sherman and raise an army under their very noses. After regaining all that had been lost by the expensive defenses of Fort Donelson, Island No. 10, Memphis, and Vicksburg—at least one hundred thousand men, not to mention loss of morale and treasure—this small army of five thousand or ten thousand might grow until "all the country bordering on the Mississippi from Cairo down is taken and permanently occupied by our forces."

He sent this communication by a friend to Bragg, to be forwarded through the proper channels to Richmond. Ten days later, he forwarded a copy direct to Davis, his reason appearing in a note attached: "Having understood that it was likely it would not be forwarded by the general commanding department, and believing the matter of sufficient importance to merit the consideration of your excellency, I have taken the liberty of sending a copy direct. . . . While I believe the general commanding is unwilling for me to leave his department, still I hope to be permitted to go where (as I believe) I can serve my country best, especially so as an experienced and competent officer,

* Italics mine.

Brigadier-General Armstrong, would be left in command of my division."

This copy contained certain rewording. The closing paragraph of the original, passed through Bragg, had the sentence: "I should leave this department with many regrets, *as I am well pleased with the officers in my command** and with the division serving under me." To Davis, this had been changed to read: "I shall leave this department with many regrets, *as I am well pleased with the officers in command** and with the division serving under me." Is it possible that he understood Bragg's sinister influence over Davis, or was this a loose copy of the first letter?

Davis's endorsement showed a complete misunderstanding of the possibilities of the plan's strategy and an ignorance of Forrest's military history. If anything, it was a matter that required immediate and decisive action; and he referred the *paper to Bragg for remarks.* This virtually meant a veto, for Forrest had already indicated that Bragg would be opposed to it.

But the Secretary of War, Seddon, probably having in his hands the original with Bragg's endorsement by August 15, understood the necessity for immediate action. He closed a letter to Joseph E. Johnston with,

"It is not of less importance that the use of the Mississippi River for trade should, if possible, be debarred to the enemy. If this could only be done effectually, it would deprive the North of most of the fruits of their late successes in Mississippi as an avenue of trade without peace and amity with the Confederate states. I should think, in the present low state of the water, field artillery with cavalry, under the direction of able and enterprising officers, might find ready access to the bank of the river for hundreds of miles, and render the passage of trading boats entirely impracticable."

Bragg's endorsement read: "I know of no officer to whom I would sooner assign the duty proposed, than which none is more important, but it would deprive this army of one of its greatest elements of strength to remove General Forrest."

This frustrated, as it turned out, the last chance the Confederacy had to "vex" further the Father of Waters, for when it reached Davis again, Rosecrans was crossing the river. Davis had never devised a general plan of operations for his Confederacy. He could only attend to his departments, like a feudal overlord, one at a time. Bragg's department, being at the moment the one most in need of attention, he

---

* Italics mine.

General Braxton Bragg

dismissed Forrest's proposition from his mind for future reference.

When, on August 28, it returned to him, he placed upon it the fifth and final endorsement.

Secretary of War:

The indorsement of General Bragg indicated the propriety of a postponement. Subsequent events have served to render the proposition more objectionable. Whenever a change of circumstances will permit, the measure may be adopted.

J. Davis.

The President did not consider—he was beginning to lose his sense of reality—that a change of circumstance might alter the chances of success, for in war, if in nothing else, success depends upon doing the right thing at the right time. And he had waited until subsequent events in the form of General Rosecrans had indeed rendered the proposition more objectionable.

While Davis moved along the page the close, meticulous phrases, signing away forever his rights to the Mississippi, Rosecrans was giving orders for his pontoons to be thrown over the Tennessee.

By the last of August his three corps, Thomas, Crittenden, and McCook, had begun the passage of the river at Battle Creek, Shell Mound, Bridgeport and Caperton's Ferry, opposite Stevenson, Alabama. Stevenson was thirty-six miles from, and south of, Chattanooga.

The south bank of the river was the Confederate side. Along it for miles Sand Mountain, known locally as Racoon Mountain, followed the river's course, at times rising abruptly from the banks itself, and again withdrawing some distance away, leaving coves and small valleys to be watered by the Tennessee's overflow. It was over the southern limits of this mountain that Forrest had pursued and captured Colonel Streight.

Several rough, but practicable wagon roads, led over its summit and down the southern slope into Will's Valley. This valley opened upon the river six miles southwest of Chattanooga, and was one approach to that town. The other wall to this valley was Lookout Mountain. Jutting abruptly upon the Tennessee River a little west of Chattanooga, it diverged from Sand Mountain and moved into Georgia.

A heavily wooded range, rising 2400 feet above the sea level, with sides of perpendicular rock cliffs standing straight up through steep, densely wooded bases, it presented very difficult problems of passage. It was surmounted, in a distance of fifty miles, by only two practicable wagon roads, the first twenty-six and the other forty-two miles from Chattanooga.

The first road ran through Frick's Gap and the second through Stevens's Gap, down into Lookout Valley and by easy ways over Missionary Ridge into McLemore's Cove. This cove was formed by Pigeon Mountain, a lateral spur branching off from Lookout forty miles below Chattanooga, as it extends to the northeast to flatten out into low hills near the road from the key city to Lafayette. In this cove the west branch of the Chickamauga has its source.

Chattanooga, itself, was in the mouth of the narrow valley formed by Lookout and Missionary Ridge. The Georgia State Railroad, passing around the northern extremity of the ridge, and down the valley of the east branch of the Chickamauga, by way of Ringgold, connected with the East Tennessee road at Dalton, thirty-eight miles from Chattanooga. The Georgia railroad was Bragg's main feed line, and Dalton, the junction of the two roads, would have been the landing place of reënforcements from Virginia, provided Buckner could hold Knoxville.

A road crosses Missionary Ridge at Rossville and moves southeast, through Lafayette, to Rome. If Bragg should retreat, as Rosecrans expected him to do, he would retreat by the state railroad and this wagon road.

McCook completed the pontoon bridge at Caperton's Ferry at one P.M., the twenty-ninth. He began at once to throw his divisions across. Only a few scattering cavalry disputed their passage. The rest of Rosecrans's army, using trestle-work at Bridgeport, rafts at Battle Creek, and captured boats at Shell Mound, was over by September 4. There was no opposition from Bragg, although for five days Rosecrans's movements were under observation of the Confederate signal corps.

Now that his army was safely across the river, Rosecrans made his next move to destroy Bragg. He ordered Crittenden to move up Will's Valley, take post at Wauhatchie and threaten Chattanooga. He was to make this movement without Hazen's and Wagner's brigades. These brigades supported by Wilder's Mounted Infantry and Minty's cavalry, about seven thousand in all, were to remain on the north bank and watch Chattanooga.

While this was taking place, Thomas, passing over Sand Mountain, was to seize Frick's and Stevens's Gaps on Lookout: and McCook to seize Winston's Gap, forty-six miles below Chattanooga and the nearest approach to Alpine and Summerville. The cavalry under Major-General Stanley was to proceed under support of McCook and make a raid on this road and cut Bragg off from his depot of supplies at Atlanta.

These various movements were completed by McCook and Crittenden on the sixth, and by Thomas on September 8. Rosecrans's contempt for Bragg had led him to believe that it was perfectly safe to scatter his corps beyond mutual support, in rough country, and through difficult mountain passes. Rosecrans was convinced that the Army of Tennessee, under its present commander, would not give battle.

But on August 22, Bragg had appealed to Richmond and to Joseph E. Johnston for help. Johnston promised two small divisions, nine thousand men. There was from Richmond, for the moment, an ominous silence.

Bragg expected Rosecrans to join with Burnside and cross above Chattanooga; so he withdrew Buckner and Forrest behind the Hiwassee at Loudon. They now formed the right of the Army of Tennessee. Frazer, with two thousand men, was left to hold Cumberland Gap.

For a week after the enemy's crossing Confederate headquarters were in ignorance of his force, his intentions, and his direction. General Daniel Hill had been sent by Davis from Virginia to take charge of Hardee's corps. Accustomed to the minute knowledge Lee had of every operation on his front, he was shocked at Bragg's ignorance; and the general feeling of the army caused him grave concern. When he reported to Bragg, he found him gloomy and despondent, and very nervous. He observed that Bragg had grown prematurely old. Hill had been a lieutenant in his battery at Corpus Christi, and it was natural for him to expect a cordial greeting. But Bragg received him with silence and reserve, and a slight suggestion of suspicion. Hill left with the fear that the campaign was to be a haphazard one on the part of the Confederates.

This impression was not confined to Hill alone. General Mackall, the Chief of Staff, who was more able to judge the mind of Bragg and the state of the army than any other, held the greatest fears for its safety. On the second he made a desperate appeal to Wheeler for accurate information. "The passage at Caperton's Ferry broke the line, and a week has passed and we don't know whether an army has passed. If this happens on Lookout tonight, and the enemy obtain that as a screen to their movements, I must confess I do not see myself what move we can make to answer it."

On September 3, Buckner's cavalry was definitely put under Forrest's orders, and he was drawn down towards Chattanooga. Scott's brigade was left at Loudon to guard the bridge there, with orders to burn it and retreat when Burnside appeared before it in force. Buckner's corps was ordered to remain a few days longer along the Hiwassee.

The brigades of Hazen and Wagner, still on the north bank of the Tennessee, had left the impression that a corps still remained on the other side. Forrest went to Bragg with a plan to destroy it in its isolation. There had been a two months' drought, and the river was fordable at certain places.

At ten A.M., on the fourth, Bragg wrote Hill and informed him of this body's isolation. "If you can cross the river, now is our time to crush the corps opposite. What say you? Or if we could draw the enemy over. We must do something and that soon. We have a pontoon bridge here, but it is not fordable, and the crossing would be under fire. By selecting fords Forrest promises to cross the infantry on horses." He wrote this, acting on the assumption that the other two corps were at Caperton's. But he wrote they were completing their passage of the Tennessee.

He had advised Hill to consult with Cleburne, leaving the project to their judgment. He, the general of the army, in a matter which he considered to entail a great victory, left the decision entirely in the hands of a corps and division commander.

Hill, as ordered, advised with Cleburne, who answered that the corps opposite ought to be crushed. Expecting the enemy to be fortified at the foot of the mountain, Cleburne asked how the artillery could be put over. Neither general asked for Forrest's advice, although the original suggestion had been his.

It took a whole day for Hill and Cleburne to pass letters between their different headquarters. In the meanwhile Bragg had decided to evacuate Chattanooga. Either the inability to cross the artillery, or his vacillation had caused him to drop the matter and pass on to something else.

A few days before the crossing into Will's Valley, Bragg had complained in a petulant mood, "It is said to be easy to defend a mountainous country, but mountains hide your foe from you, while they are full of gaps through which he can pounce upon you at any time. A mountain is like the wall of a house, full of rat holes. The rat lies hidden at his hole ready to pop out when no one is watching. Who can tell what lies hidden behind that wall?" said he, pointing to the Cumberland range across the river. It is significant that Bragg did not see himself in the rôle of the cat.

By the eighth all the Confederate troops were out of Chattanooga and in the vicinity of Lafayette. On the ninth Crittenden took peaceable possession of the town, the objective point of the campaign. His residence, however, was not yet assured.

Rosecrans's expectations were high. He ordered McCook to push vigorously ahead by Alpine and Summerville and throw his divisions across Bragg's line of retreat, for he pictured him fleeing in haste, if not in panic. He ordered Thomas to cut through the gaps in Pigeon Mountain; Crittenden to pursue through Rossville.

He threw Stanley forward to break through the railroad line. He told him that Forrest and Wharton were in the neighborhood of Chattanooga, and that therefore the way was open. Stanley was not so optimistic, but assisted by a diversion under Wilder on Bragg's right at Tunnel Hill and Ringgold, he moved through Will's Valley, climbed Lookout and descended into the valley. His thirteen small regiments looked smaller the farther he went towards his goal. When he reached the foot of the mountain, he discovered that Rosecrans had misinformed him. Forrest, with a portion of Wharton's division, was in his front.

On the sixth Forrest, who had filled the enemy's lines with his "deserters" with conflicting evidence of his position, was at Ringgold; but on the morning of the eighth he was before Alpine. On that date he wrote to Wheeler: "Have arrived at Gowers. If I hear nothing from the enemy today, I shall cross the mountain and get in their front. If the enemy do not advance on us *we must move on them.*" *

Stanley did not wait for this move. He reclimbed the mountain and returned to a safer position. Forrest learned of his withdrawal and countermarched to Ringgold. He arrived there on the tenth and found that two divisions of Crittenden's corps had crossed the Chickamauga at Red House bridge and were isolated from the other portions of the army.

But how very great was the isolation Forrest did not, at the moment, know. McCook was now at Alpine, forty-six miles from Chattanooga; Thomas had pushed Negley into McLemore's Cove; and Crittenden's other division, Wood, was at Lee and Gordon's Mill, ten miles from Ringgold. In other words, Rosecrans had not only scattered his corps, but he had gone a step farther: he had scattered the divisions of the

* Italics mine.

corps. His army was completely at Bragg's mercy, for the Army of
Tennessee was concentrated behind the mountains, in a position to
turn upon Crittenden and Thomas and annihilate them in detail.

Forrest immediately informed Bragg and Polk, who was only six
miles away, of Crittenden's position. Assured in his own mind that
Bragg would fall upon Crittenden, Forrest procured guides and made
preparations for a circuit to the rear and the seizure of the Red House
bridge. He communicated this, also, to his superiors. Crittenden's condition was so obviously critical that the pickets and the men around
the camp fires spoke of his destruction as an affair foredoomed.

But Forrest waited until midnight, and no word came from his
superiors. He could stand the delay no longer; so, mounting a horse,
he galloped to interview Bragg and find out what was the matter.
He found Bragg was no longer on the field, but had gone to Lafayette.
All the infantry, about half the army, then in the vicinity of Lee and
Gordon's Mill was under orders to follow after. Bragg had decided,
first, to fall upon Thomas in the Cove.

Forrest returned to his command and threw Scott's brigade, nine
hundred strong, across Crittenden's front and Pegram with the remainder of the division between Lafayette and the enemy's right
flank. Doggedly throughout the following day these men resisted
the advance of two divisions, delaying them at one time two hours.
Forced to give way in the end, Forrest fell back to Tunnel Hill and
there made another stand. Dibrell joined him there. This brought his
strength up to three thousand.

Dismounting the men and using them as infantry, he made as
obstinate a fight as General Hill had made at South Mountain before
the battle of Antietam. His division commander, Pegram, displayed
unusual skill in holding their strong position. Crittenden finally retired
to Ringgold where, as if bent on destruction, he turned his column
towards Lee and Gordon's Mill and camped on the same grounds
Polk and Buckner had just left. But Crittenden was now closer to
his other division, Wood.

In the meantime, on the tenth, Negley's division of Thomas's
corps, with Baird supporting, crossed Missionary Ridge and descended
into McLemore's Cove. From a distance of ten miles Bragg sent
orders to Hill and Hindman to move through Wortham and Dug
Gaps, fall upon the enemy in the cove, and crush him. Bragg did not
know, or had forgotten, that the gaps were obstructed, although
Wheeler had reported their condition to headquarters. These obstruc-

tions delayed Hill, and as the attack was to be a combined attack, it did not come off.

The roads were so dry that Negley's march could be seen for fifteen miles, as he was winding down the ridge into the cove's bristly bowl. Buckner was now sent to Hindman's assistance. Before noon, the eleventh, Hindman with his own troops and this corps, about fifteen thousand men altogether, deployed in line of battle from Pigeon Mountain across the cove, ready to move against Negley and Baird. In other words, fifteen thousand Southerners had ten thousand Northerners backed up against the walls of a mountain.

Hindman had driven in Negley's skirmishers and was preparing to advance his whole line when a courier galloped up with the following order from Mackall:

If you find the enemy in such force as to make an attack imprudent, fall back at once on La Fayette by Catlett's Gap, from which obstructions have been moved.

The tone of this note delayed the attack. An hour later, another dispatch came from Mackall. It asked Hindman if he was certain he could retreat by way of the gap. Hindman replied that he could, but that he had ordered an advance. Shortly afterwards he received still another dispatch informing him that twelve thousand or fifteen thousand of the enemy were forming line of battle in front of Dug Gap.

These overcautious notes from headquarters had all been misleading, and the last one on top of all the others led Hindman to believe that this large force was in *addition* to the force in his immediate front. He stopped the forward movement and made another reconnaissance. If Bragg had been on the line of battle, this confusion would not have resulted. To send orders to the front from a position miles to the rear is to invite defeat, particularly when the commander is not sure of his information. Hindman, knowing Bragg, probably decided it was unwise to move ahead, especially since it had been the commanding general's habit to seek a scapegoat for his own failures.

Hindman undoubtedly played safe, but if Forrest had been in his place, he would have "given them a dare, anyway." He thought less of his reputation than of the enemy's defeat; nor did he doubt his capacity to extricate his command from perilous positions. But Forrest was away, stinging Crittenden's front and flanks.

Hindman ordered a retirement through the gap that had concerned Mackall so much, but before it could be executed, he learned that the enemy was retreating towards Stevens's Gap. He followed, but it was too late. Baird and Negley escaped. About dark the ineffectual pursuit was called off by Bragg.

But Hindman believed that there was still an opportunity to destroy the enemy. His corps and Buckner's and Cleburne's division of Hill's corps were now united at Davis's Cross-Roads, the place originally appointed for the junction; and the enemy was at Stevens's Gap, the point where the original attack was to have been delivered. So Hindman, when he reported to Bragg, suggested that it was not too late. But Bragg replied, "We can't stay here," and galloped off to the rear. He left orders for the command to march that night, and with the least possible delay, to Lafayette.

Bragg was retreating before a hypothetical enemy. He evidently considered that Thomas's and McCook's entire corps were near by, and that they had thrown out Negley as bait to lure him into the cove so that Crittenden might close in on his rear. It is certain that he did not grasp the actual situation. On the thirteenth, Lieutenant Baylor of Wharton's division reported to Hill that McCook had encamped the night of the twelfth at Alpine, twenty miles from Lafayette. When Hill delivered verbally this piece of information to Bragg, he received the excited answer, "Lieutenant Baylor lies! There is not an infantry soldier of the enemy to the south of us."

But Lieutenant Baylor did not lie. McCook had been ordered to Summerville, eleven miles south of Lafayette, but when he discovered that Bragg was not hastening towards Atlanta, he became cautious, ordered his wagon train back to the top of Lookout, and halted at Alpine until the thirteenth to wait and see what was going to happen. Hill's signal corps on Pigeon Mountain throughout the eleventh and twelfth had reported the march of a heavy column to the Confederate left and rear, but this also was discredited by Bragg. He refused to believe that the greatest part of Rosecrans's army was not hidden somewhere behind Stevens's Gap, waiting the time to pounce upon him.

On the thirteenth Rosecrans discovered his perilous situation, and by midnight McCook had received his order to countermarch with all possible speed and rejoin Thomas in McLemore's Cove. The distance was fifty-seven miles, by tortuous roads and rocky passes and through dust so thick that it was difficult for the teamsters to see how to drive. McCook made heroic efforts; but, in spite of them, he did not reach McLemore's Cove until the seventeenth, thus allowing Bragg four more days to retrieve his blunders and crush the still separated enemy.

Bragg had failed in the Cove; so now he turned his attention to Crittenden. On the eleventh two of Crittenden's divisions were at Ringgold; the other was at Lee and Gordon's, where it remained alone and unsupported until late in the day of the twelfth. Bragg had known of the separation in this corps as early as the tenth, but he did not order Polk to take position at Rock Spring until midnight eleventh-twelfth.

Rock Spring was four and a half miles from the Mills and seven miles from Ringgold. It therefore offered a force placed at it a chance to strike Crittenden's two camps in detail. It took Polk all of the twelfth to concentrate his corps and Walker's division. At six P. M. that night Bragg ordered him to fall upon Wood in his isolation next morning and destroy him; and afterwards to assail the others who would then be at his mercy. But this was impossible, for by nightfall of the twelfth Wood was no longer isolated. Palmer and Van Cleve had, in the meanwhile, closed up in easy supporting distance. At eight o'clock, having found not one but three divisions and Wilder's cavalry brigade confronting him, Polk asked for reënforcements to the extent of Buckner. How many more of the enemy lay behind Crittenden's line ready to sustain him Polk did not know; but he feared "a considerable accession of force from Chattanooga," which Rosecrans will not fail "to send forward." Buckner was needed "so as to make success sure." Polk was painfully aware of the confusion at headquarters and the ignorance as to the enemy's position and intentions. Besides this, he had witnessed the army's concentration in McLemore's Cove against what was reported by a member of the signal corps to be only two brigades. He had justification for thinking that most of Rosecrans's army might be in front of his position.

Bragg, unaware of Crittenden's concentration—Polk had indicated only an aggressive approach by different roads—reiterated his order at midnight to strike "him at the earliest moment and before his combinations can be carried out." He assured Polk that he would send Buckner but admonished him not to delay the attack waiting for his arrival. Thirty minutes later he sent another order to make a quick and decided attack in the morning.

Next morning Polk had disposed his troops for battle, but it could not be delivered. Crittenden had already moved his reunited corps over the Chickamauga out of immediate reach. Bragg then arrived on the field ahead of Buckner, and his presence there automatically relieved Polk of the initiative. He was chagrined to find the enemy removed from Polk's front, and he blamed this general for its reunion and escape when, if anybody was to blame, it was his own tardy decision to begin the movement. He had given his subordinate orders which were physically impossible to obey.

But there was still plenty of time to destroy this corps of Rosecrans's army. All day of the thirteenth and the morning of the fourteenth it remained at the Mills in utter ignorance of a larger force to its front. Since Bragg was on the field and had had information of the absence of Thomas and McCook, he should have forded the creek and delivered battle. He had on hand two-thirds of his army. But instead of taking the "action, prompt and decided," which he had urged on Polk, he placed "the trains and limited supplies in safe positions, when all our forces were concentrated along the Chickamauga *threatening the enemy in front.*"

Bragg was acting like a man so hardened by misfortune that he dared not grasp the sudden prospects of Good Fortune for fear they were a snare to trick him into greater misery. But his men were anxious to meet the enemy. On the soft and sandy roads they tramped barefooted, hanging their footgear with veteran economy to the barrels of their guns for rougher wear. As they moved up and down the valley, they looked eagerly for the enemy's destruction at the end of each choking march. Their good cheer was strengthened by the rumor that a part of Lee's army was on its way from Virginia.

In the meantime, McCook on the seventeenth brought two of his divisions into the cove. To make room for them, Thomas, gaining distance northward, closed in that direction on Crittenden.

Rosecrans's army was now practically out of danger, although there were still gaps between his different wings. As soon as McCook made his appearance, Crittenden was ordered to take up his old position at Lee and Gordon's Mills; Thomas to support him with a division at Crawfish Springs, and with the rest of the corps to move by the Widow Glenn's to the Rossville-Lafayette road, his left spreading obliquely across it at Kelly's farm, nine miles from Chattanooga. McCook was to close up on Thomas's division at Crawfish Springs and protect Crittenden's right. But the movements were so slow that by dark, September eighteenth, McCook had gone no farther than Pond Spring, a position opposite Catlett's Gap; and Thomas had barely reached Crawfish Springs.

Now, after Lee's strategic defeat before Gettysburg, all eyes were turned upon Tennessee. What had been true all along was being partly recognized at Richmond, that the Army of Tennessee was the key army of Confederate defense. Lee's dissolution, discounting the moral effects of such a disaster, could mean only the loss of one state; Bragg's annihilation, the ruin of the Confederacy.

With this in mind, and again at the insistence of Longstreet, a Georgia man, Lee went to Richmond in August and there decided to send two divisions, Hood and McLaws, some ten thousand men, and Alexander's twenty-six guns, to Bragg's relief. What had been advised as a whole before Vicksburg and Gettysburg was now being executed in part. For the first time in the war the interior lines were about to be used.

Lee followed Longstreet to his horse to see him off and, as he mounted, said to him: "General, you must beat those people."

Longstreet's answer was significant: "General, if you will give your orders that the enemy, when beaten, shall be destroyed, I will promise to give you a victory, if I live; but I would not give the life of a single soldier of mine for a barren victory."

Lee replied, "The order has been given and will be repeated."

But there were rats in the walls of the Confederacy. In the White House at Richmond, and in the Valley of the Chickamauga, they scurried and gnawed.

CHAPTER XIII

Chickamauga

The First Day

M cLEMORE'S COVE, extending to the northeast, widened into a large valley through which the west branch of the Chickamauga wound to spill into the Tennessee River above Chattanooga. This stream separated the two hostile armies from each other. Its course would serve as the eastern boundary of the battlefield. The country to its front was heavily timbered, so dense in places that movements fifty feet away might be heard but not seen. Narrow dirt roads turned through its forest in the direction of the various fords and bridges, passing clearings, a few good-sized farms, and Jay's Sawmill to the front of Reed's bridge. Four square miles of such terrain marked the limits of the battle to come.

For on the seventeenth Bragg finally decided to take the initiative, although he had informed the army on the sixteenth that they would be thrown over the creek. He issued a circular order of battle, instructing Bushrod R. Johnson's improvised division to cross at Reed's bridge, face to the left, and sweep up the Chickamauga; Walker to cross and join the line two and a half miles lower down, at Alexander's bridge. Buckner was next to take it up at Thedford's Ford. Polk with the largest corps in the army, if the battle line cleared the way, was to cross at Lee and Gordon's Mills; otherwise, he was directed to move down stream and follow Buckner at Thedford's. Hill was to remain on the extreme left and protect that flank from the enemy in the Cove. If he should discover that Rosecrans was reënforcing at Lee and Gordon's Mills, he was to cross over and take him in flank.

As a battle order, it was good enough; but Bragg, as he gave it, was ignorant of the number and the exact position of the enemy. Lee had been forced to the issue at Gettysburg with the same handicap, but with him it was not from choice. Stuart, the eyes of his army, when to see was a crucial matter, was absent on a raid in Meade's rear. But this was not the case with Bragg. The eyes of his army were present, and one of them, at least, was sharp and discerning.

Forrest and Wheeler had present for duty eight thousand cavalry, a body slightly superior to the enemy's; but the general commanding was as a man who, having eyes, would not see. He neutralized Wheeler in the gaps of Pigeon Mountain, and the scattered condition of his infantry divisions led him to dismember Forrest's corps to guard the fronts and flanks of these segments. "One of the greatest elements of strength" to his army might as well have been in Mississippi for the use he was put to before the battle. Besides deliberately ordering his corps against the thickets of a wilderness, Bragg could not be certain they would cross in time to support each other.

After he had lost the several priceless opportunities to strike Rosecrans in detail, it probably would have been wiser for him to have concentrated his divisions on strong ground and waited for the reënforcements he knew were on the way from Virginia. Then, if he was not attacked, he might move in superior numbers upon the Army of the Cumberland. The only good reason for an immediate attack was the hope that Rosecrans was still divided. His retention of Hill on the extreme left seemed to support this view.

But by the morning of the eighteenth Rosecrans had brought together in the valley of the Chickamauga the bulk of his army. At the moment Bragg, counting the reënforcements from Mississippi, numbered some sixty thousand of all arms; Rosecrans, fifty-seven thousand —but counting stragglers, especially in McCook's corps, he probably fell two thousand or three thousand short of this. So, even at this late date, if the actual movements of Bragg's army had conformed to his orders, the Confederate general could have struck Crittenden with overwhelming numbers and hurled his broken lines back on Thomas's divisions arriving to succor him. McCook, in spite of his arrival in the Cove, would have been of little help. It took him until nightfall to reach Pond Spring.

But Bragg had not considered properly the difficulties of the narrow roads, his scattered corps, and the usual delays which attend a concentration. Many of his divisions got into position, but they were prevented from crossing by their orders to follow from right to left. Bushrod R. Johnson, not sufficiently forewarned, did not pass over Reed's bridge until late in the afternoon, and then not until Forrest had cleared the way with one hundred infantry and dismounted cavalry in a charge and a hand-to-hand fight on the bridge.

So, on the evening of the eighteenth, after a heavy skirmish with Wilder, Bragg had placed upon the west banks of the creek only ten small brigades of infantry and sixteen hundred cavalry. The greater part of his army bivouacked that night on the east bank, leaving his advanced brigades exposed and without easy support, although Buckner had so arranged his corps that quick passage of the creek was possible. Bushrod R. Johnson kept his men under arms all night and one-third of them awake.

That evening, about nine o'clock, General Hood and General Forrest, Hood having arrived late that day with two brigades, Robertson's and Law's, rode to headquarters for orders. Bragg told Hood that he would command the right—Johnson's division, his own under McLaws, and Walker's corps, about fifteen thousand infantry and sixteen hundred of Forrest's cavalry. The orders to Forrest were explicit. He must make a reconnaissance to the right and front in the morning. If he brought on a general engagement, he was promised the support of Walker.

But while Bragg had been moving up the Chickamauga, Rosecrans had shifted, and was shifting, his three corps down the creek. While the Southern generals were discussing the next day's work, Thomas's men had fallen in to take up the march. By daylight of the nineteenth the head of the column, Baird's division, reached Kelly's farm and took position at the cross-roads facing Reed's and Alexander's bridges. Therefore Hood, who camped the previous night near Alexander's bridge, could not take the initiative without a change of orders.

It was Thomas who took the initiative. Colonel Wilder, commanding the mounted brigade of Reynolds's division, reported to his corps commander and informed him that the Southern army had crossed in force at the two bridges the evening before, driving him away from those crossings beyond the Chattanooga-Lafayette Road to the heights east of the Widow Glenn's house. This meant that there was a wide gap between Baird's right and Wilder's left. Thomas expected to fill it with Reynolds's two other brigades as soon as they came up.

In the meantime, Brannon arrived with his division. Thomas posted it to the left of Baird, along the roads leading to the two bridges.

Now, Colonel McCook, of the Reserve Corps, five thousand men under Granger holding the Rossville Gap, reported to Thomas that he had been stationed the previous night near Reed's bridge, and he believed only an isolated Southern brigade was west of the Creek. He had destroyed the bridge behind it, and it was now cut off and at Thomas's mercy.

Thomas had, therefore, received two contradictory reports of the enemy's position: Wilder reporting that he had crossed in force; McCook that only a brigade was to the west of the Chickamauga. Dividing Brannon's division, Thomas advanced two brigades on the road to Reed's bridge and the other one, Croxton's, by way of the Alexander bridge road, to support the movement. Thomas inclined to accept McCook's report, and he gave Brannon orders to capture the brigade. Baird was told to advance his right to be more in line with Brannon. As his right still hung in the air, Thomas warned him to look to this flank.

The morning of the nineteenth a heavy fog dripped from the trees and shrubs, but Forrest was in the saddle by daylight, feeling his way through it. Turning to the right, he galloped towards Reed's bridge. As the fog lifted, he found himself in the vicinity of Jay's Sawmill, due west of the bridge. At this point, between nine and ten o'clock, he ran into Brannon. At once he rode forward with General Pegram to reconnoitre. He discovered two heavy lines moving through the woods. Their left was in his front; their right extended as far as he could see towards Crawfish Springs. He saw at a glance what had happened to Bragg. The Southern right had been outstepped. He hurried this information to Bragg and requested immediate and strong reënforcements.

While he had been occupied in this examination, Davidson's brigade of Pegram's division, his only force on the field, had been struck on its left before it could form line of battle. Forrest and Pegram soon hastened to its assistance, and all the available force was "soon well posted under the general direction of General Forrest."

Forrest realized that before Bragg could readjust his divisions to meet the changed situation, Rosecrans had it in his power to crush his flank and roll up his army like a wet blanket. He determined to give Bragg the necessary time to make the readjustments. But he had only one brigade on hand. Sending Captain Anderson after Armstrong's division, some six or seven miles to the rear with Polk, he dismounted Davidson—all except Rucker—and drove the enemy skirmishers back upon their main line. Anderson soon returned with Dibrell's brigade—Polk felt he could spare no more—and Forrest dismounted it and threw it into line with Pegram. From behind trees,

shrubs and rises in the ground these woodsmen poured an accurate
stream of lead into Croxton, until his infantry halted in its tracks. Brannon's center and left as they progressed upon the supposed right of the
lone brigade, ran upon Dibrell and the two batteries of Huggins and

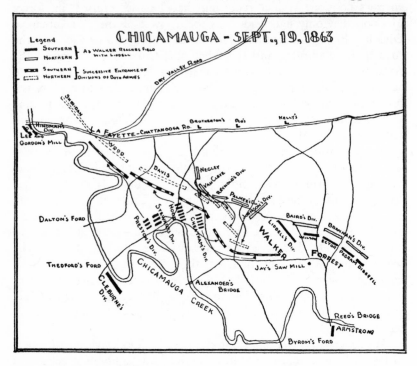

Morton. So furious was his reception that he reported two divisions
confronting him.

But the weight of numbers began at length to tell. Doggedly, under
the eye of Davidson, Pegram, Dibrell, and Forrest, the horse infantry
fell back towards the creek. The artillery, pushing forward in line,
scattered its canister and grape and made up, to some extent, for the
numerical weakness in men.

In spite of Forrest's repeated messages, the infantry heads seemed
not to appreciate the danger to their right flank, and time was precious.
Forrest realized that unless he got more reënforcements he would
be thrown back into the creek. So, ordering Pegram to hold the
present position "no matter what happens," he galloped off to the
rear and brought up Wilson's brigade of Walker's corps. It deployed,

and the regiments, with the precision of a well-oiled machine, moved forward and drove in Croxton's first line. Forrest then sent orders down the line to halt. His right was unable to keep pace with Wilson, and the stubborn resistance made by Brannon's whole division told him it would waste his men to no advantage to continue the advance with his present force. Besides being outnumbered, he had lost heavily. Pegram obeyed literally his previous orders to hold his ground, and upon it one man in every four had fallen.

Therefore, without asking Walker's permission, Forrest ordered up another brigade, Ector's, and threw it between his dismounted cavalry and Wilson's infantry. This pushed his dismounted men over towards the enemy's left flank and rear. As the issue now stood, Forrest had not only managed to hold his own in the presence of two divisions, but he was planning a counterstroke.

But before it could be executed, Wilson's right was turned. This general sent a messenger to the rear to call up Ector. Finding that brigade no longer behind him, he rallied his breaking left and center in the woods east of an open field. His two right regiments swept forward in the charge which Forrest and Ector now made.

They pierced Brannon's center, but they could not divide it, for Thomas strengthened it with most of Baird's division. In the heat of the struggle General Ector called an aide, C. B. Kilgore, to his side and directed him to go to General Forrest and urge him to be very vigilant in the protection of his right flank. Kilgore galloped to the right, where the batteries were placed, as he had been told he might find General Forrest there. A red haze of smoke and dust hung low over the Chickamauga woods, filtering out of its sinister clouds down upon the tops of the trees, quivering where the batteries exploded, making whirlwinds from the exhaust of each fresh round. Where the lines were close together, the circles of smoke almost met in neutral ground.

"General Forrest, General Ector directed me to say to you that he is uneasy in regard to his right flank."

"Tell General Ector he need not bother about his right flank. I'll take care of it."

The aide returned to his command, and an hour later the news came in that Wilson had been hard hit and driven back. Ector sent Kilgore back to Forrest, announcing this time fears for his left flank.

Kilgore "found him near the same spot, right in the thickest part of the fight, the battery blazing away and every man fighting like mad.

I told him what General Ector had directed me to say, and this time he got furious. He turned around on me and shouted, loud enough to be heard above the terrible din that was in the air:

" 'Tell General Ector that, by God, I am here and will take care of his left flank as well as his right.'

"It is hardly necessary to add that we were not outflanked on either side." But one good reason for this was the arrival of Walker with the rest of his corps, Liddell's division, which he hurled in a vicious attack on the very position Ector and Wilson were being forced to give up. His fresh gray lines this time broke through, captured several batteries, and separated Brannon's right from his left. Croxton was pushed off the field, his ammunition exhausted.

Rosecrans now listened to Thomas's repeated calls for help and rapidly sent Palmer's and Johnson's divisions and the rest of Reynolds's to his left. Johnson arrived and formed on the right of Brannon's reorganized troops. They fell together on Liddell's small division and pressed him slowly and deliberately back to his original position. Armstrong had come upon the field in the meantime with his other brigade. Forrest threw it far to the right, but it was carried back along with the rest of the line. Rolled back to their original position, the Confederates stopped and re-formed. The roar of the battle had become terrific. The ends of the Southern line were bent, and were bending, to the rear. How much could it bend without breaking, questioned the mind of every general officer. Thomas's wing had now five divisions, three of his own and one each from the other corps. The Southerners, two divisions and the cavalry, used up in detailed assaults, were still fighting with determination. They had convinced Thomas that he was engaging great odds. But Walker looked anxiously, and repeatedly, to the left for Cheatham. As soon as he had arrived on the field he had sent for Cheatham.

This general had effected his crossing of the Chickamauga by seven A.M. and was ready to move when the battle opened, but it was eleven o'clock before he received his orders to go to Walker's relief. He arrived at twelve o'clock with his five brigades, three in front, two behind, and moved to the attack just after Liddell had been taken out.

Brannon and Baird were badly broken by these Tennesseans and were driven three-quarters of a mile to the rear. A concerted attack at this moment might have given Bragg the victory; but Cheatham was left, as Walker had been, as Forrest had been, to fight the enemy alone. Cheatham replaced his front line with Strahl and Maney, but scarcely did they take position when Palmer, Reynolds and Johnson fell upon and overpowered them. As they fell back, Jackson and Smith of the first line took their places. They formed on either side of Turner's battery, and with the excellent practice of these guns were able to bring the enemy to a stand. With a rapid, accurate fire of grape and canister, great masses of Thomas's attacking went down.

Forrest, on his part of the field, saw the emergency. He pushed Morton's and Huggins's batteries up to gun shot range and poured in an effective fire on the enemy's flank. These batteries were protected by two small regiments of Dibrell's brigade.

The cannons' fan of lead swept whole squads to the ground. The steady plunges of ramrods, and the blue line's charge was thinner. A jerk of the head, paper cartridges off with a bite, and powder juice spilled down the worn tobacco creases of the butternut men. The enemy hestitated, halted, fell back and re-formed in the skeleton thickets.

But in spite of this obstinate resistance, Cheatham, Forrest and Walker must eventually have been swamped but for the timely arrival of Stewart's three brigades. This general, after manœuvering to the left of Alexander's bridge, received an order from one of Bragg's aides to move to the point where firing had commenced. As this seemed from its sound to be far to the right and somewhat in his rear, and as there were other troops nearer than he, Stewart went to Bragg for specific instructions. But the general commanding had none to give. He only knew Walker was much cut up and that his flank was threatened. Bragg was one division behind: it was Cheatham, not Walker, who now needed aid. He told Stewart that Polk was in command and that he must be *governed by circumstances.*

From Thedford's Ford, east of north, Stewart took up his march. As the steady roar of musketry increased in volume, his men quickened their pace. Mangled horses lay upon the ground, kicking blood from their wounds; others with a wild look dashed upon the closed gray ranks, riderless. Stretcher-bearers passed on their way to the rear. One of the wounded, his bowels pouring out of his belly, raised himself up on his litter and waved a piece of a hat, "Boys, when I left we were driving 'em." The column stiffened its pace.

After marching about a mile, it reached a cornfield. Beyond this field the firing was the heaviest. Stewart sent a messenger to find Polk; but, not having been told where this general might be found, he could not direct his aide specifically. After waiting some time fearing to waste any more daylight, he threw his brigades across the field, one at a time. They moved forward gallantly and threw back Palmer's flanking mass which threatened Cheatham's overthrow; then met Van Cleve hastening to Thomas's assistance and threw him back. They recaptured the battery Wright's brigade, Cheatham's left, had lost; but as there was no superior officer to marshal the division in unison with the others, it wasted its strength on piecemeal attacks.

First, Clayton's Alabamans dashed forward—it was their first engagement—remained an hour, lost four hundred men, and were taken out. Next, Brown's veterans filled the opening, drove in the enemy's first line, seized the crest of a ridge, but met with a terrific artillery fire from fourteen guns massed near the Lafayette road. They fell back, and forty-eight horses of Carnes's battery being killed, they did not bring off all the guns. They came out with heavy losses and no permanent gains.

Besides the ghastly jumble of dismembered horses and men about Carnes's battery, the woods caught fire; and at a crucial moment the staff ran into a large number of yellow jacket nests. The mad jackets fixed their stingers in horse and rider, and the plunging, ungovernable horses almost broke up one of the lines.

Bate was now thrown in. The gun fire he received was still terrific, but his attack was so impetuous that it forced the enemy, already weakened by the other charges, to abandon one position after another, losing and recapturing a piece of artillery and retaking a standard which had been lost by one of Wright's regiments. Clayton's brigade was again brought forward, and the two brigades kept up the pursuit, driving Van Cleve half a mile across the Lafayette road to the tanyard and the burning house (Poe's).

But Thomas, now that the pressure had ceased on his extreme left, removed the much reduced Brannon and Baird to strengthen his right. On their appearance Bate and Clayton fell back leisurely about sundown, re-forming on the east of the road.

Preston's, Buckner's other division, took no part in the day's fight, but maintained a threatening attitude on the extreme left, perpendicular to the general battle line; but Hood and Bushrod R. Johnson, once to be the Confederate right, now the left, entered the fight in the middle of the afternoon and crushed the right center of Rosecrans's army, capturing artillery and seizing the Chattanooga road, until from Brotherton's to Poe's field his lines were broken. But the Southerners, after this early success, had to meet the fresh divisions of Wood,

Davis, Negley, and a part of Sheridan, and were themselves thrown back east of the road.

About three o'clock Hill received an order to report to the commanding general in person and to push Cleburne forward to the same place. When Hill arrived at the ford, he learned for the first time that Rosecrans had outflanked Bragg. The commanding general gave him orders to go to the right with Cleburne and enter the battle.

Cleburne got into position about sundown, several hours after the right had shot its bolt. He moved through the underbrush, over the bodies of the slain, with a brisk pace. Night fell before his men had a chance to do any great damage, but with Key's and Semple's batteries pushed to within sixty yards of the Northern lines they managed to sweep them back three-quarters of a mile, capture three hundred men, three guns, two standards and several caissons. Darkness, with its confusing cover, interrupted pursuit and brought an end to the first day's engagement.

The field was left in the hands of the Army of Tennessee, but the battle had not been decisive in any way. It had been brought on by accident. Thomas, since Rosecrans had determined to stand on the defensive, had only expected to pick up the lone brigade, not to bring on a general engagement. In such circumstances, victory usually falls to that general who is first able to rush the most troops to the field. Rosecrans, at Thomas's insistence, lost no time in transferring his right and center to the left; but it was late in the day before Bragg seemed to realize what had happened. When, on Forrest's information, he discovered that Rosecrans's line was not where he had expected to find it, he went to pieces. Instead of going to the right at once to make a realignment in face of the changed circumstances, he remained all day at Thedford's Ford, waiting for his paper orders to be fulfilled; and in the meantime, except for a few frenzied commands, allowed the flow of battle to suck a great part of his army into its ungoverned flood.

Hindman, Preston, and Breckinridge never got in the battle at all; and Cleburne just before dark, too late for any effective use, whereas all of Rosecrans's army except two brigades had been put "opportunely and squarely into action." Therefore Bragg, with the largest force present, actually fought with the odds against him. Rosecrans, like Bragg, had not been on the field in the morning; but, unlike Bragg, he had delegated his authority to capable hands. Thomas was to him what Jackson had been to Lee. Bragg, later in the day, did order Polk to take charge of his right, but this was too late to organize the parts into an aggressive whole.

The fact that the Confederate right was not turned and overwhelmed by the heavier forces confronting it was due to Forrest's immediate appreciation of the danger and his prompt action in calling forward one of Walker's divisions. Bragg had, by pure accident and in spite of himself, an officer as stubborn as Thomas and as quick as Thomas was slow to take charge of his right and snatch the initiative from Rosecrans. Forrest took Brannon's cautious advance by surprise and struck it with so much vigor and persistence that Thomas, thinking he was facing overwhelming odds, was thrown on the defensive. It was very possible that Forrest had caught Rosecrans and his generals at a time when they were laboring under a severe psychological strain. The shock to their judgment, when they found the Army of Tennessee concentrated and heavily reënforced and not, as they had thought, fleeing in panic, was so great that it impaired, unnecessarily, their present conception of the changed conditions. Forrest's bold assault was to Thomas evidence of the reënforcements from Mississippi and Virginia.

But the opportunity was lost when the control of the right passed from Forrest's hands. Afterwards, though fierce and resolute, it became a battle, so far as the Southerners were concerned, by driblets. Never once massed and hurled with any sort of plan upon the enemy, corps, divisions, and even brigades, fought separate, and usually unsupported battles, each fresh division or brigade coming on the field in time to prevent the dissolution of the one retiring, but too late to support its advance.

The fury of these attacks almost made up for the absence of tactical direction. The veterans of the Army of Tennessee, encouraged and shamed by the arrival of aid, were determined to be done with retreating. They had never felt themselves defeated, and they were growing desperate about their repeated withdrawals. There now seemed to grow among them a subconscious resolution to make up by valor what their commanding general lacked in skill and, it was hinted by some, in courage. He had been nowhere seen that day on the firing line.

But Forrest had been there, on every part of it, rallying the infantry as well as the cavalry. They all saw him, wrapped in a linen duster, his pistol and sword buckled on the outside where it would be most handy, galloping up and down or standing beside a battery peering through the powder like a hawk, his ears attuned to the right and left, listening to the vast orchestration of noises to translate their complex meaning into action.

Silently, after Cleburne's assault, the lines were adjusted for the morrow. No fires were allowed, though the night was cold. The moon was shining, but its light was meagre as it penetrated the dense woodland, falling upon the wounded and the dead. The men crept through the shattered cornfields, looking for food. A few nubbins were found for the horses, but no corn for the men. One man turned over a dead comrade and took the crackers out of his haversack. He found their edges soaked with blood. He chipped off the soggy parts and crunched the rest. Log breastworks were thrown up in a few places; at the same time the noise of axes was heard across the thickets. The wounded cried for water, or they moaned thickly through their swollen tongues. The stretcher-bearers moved through the strange light in their direction. Those who could not call out must be left to die.

A Northern officer, Colonel Vonschrader of Thomas's staff, rode into the Southern lines and was captured. Soon it was whispered along the bivouacs that General Preston Smith was dead. In a dense thicket a Southerner ran upon a man in blue sitting bolt upright against the trunk of a tree, one hand on his gun which rested across his thighs, the other tightly grasping the brim of his hat drawn well down on one side of his face to shield his eyes from something. From under the knee of one leg a pool of clotted blood was frozen to the ground. In places, where the woods had caught fire, the bodies of the dead were charred and twisted. As much of the legs and thighs as was not burned off was drawn tightly against the stomach, and the stumps of the blackened arms against the chest. There was a calm and beautiful expression on the smooth and beardless face of a slender boy, and a hole in his brain. Near a field hospital a lone man was walking, his jaws firmly set, his face hard and fixed with pain. He was walking up and down, holding tight to his amputated arm. The story went the rounds of a Tennessee regiment that Bud Loranz, a fresh recruit from Rutherford County, when his whole line dropped to reload, looked around him in wonder and said, "Great God, the first shot and got 'em all but me!"

Longstreet reported at eleven o'clock with two more brigades. He lingered several hours around Bragg's campfire. Bragg told him that he was reorganizing for the next day's battle. There would be two wings. Polk would command the right wing, he the left wing. The assault was to begin at daybreak, beginning on the extreme right and taken up successively to the left.

In the meantime, on the other side, in the consultation at the Widow Glenn's, Rosecrans was convinced that he was greatly outnumbered and that he must expect to fight next day for the safety of his army and for Chattanooga.

He appealed to Burnside by wire, "Johnston is with Bragg with a large portion of his force and reënforcements have arrived from Virginia. We need all we can concentrate to oppose them. Let me hear from you." And later with fatal resignation, "It is of the utmost importance that you close down this way to cover our left flank. We have not force to cover our flank against Forrest now; we may want all the help we can get promptly."

CHAPTER XIV

Chickamauga

The Second Day

SEPTEMBER 20 dawned a brisk, clear autumn Sunday, although over the battlefield its appearance was disguised by a fog, heavy with stale powder smoke that held the stinking odors of yesterday's battle close to the earth and turned the light in the woods to a sultry red. The troops on the left of the Southern battle line were under arms and ready. Many had been unable to sleep through the night for thinking of this dawn. Now that the day had come they were nervously expectant.

A lone horseman, without staff or escort, rode up from the rear and shook hands with Stewart. An overcoat was buttoned over his stars and wreath, hiding his rank. The boys wondered who the stranger with the broad, impassive face and elephant eyes could be. It was Longstreet meeting his old West Point roommate. He had come to say to Stewart that his three brigades would form the right of the Left Wing, and he would be under his command that day.

He now moved through the woods, inspecting his ranks. He found Bushrod R. Johnson next to Stewart, Hindman next to him, and Preston posted on the extreme left of his line. Hood was withdrawn in reserve, near Johnson's rear. He took out Preston, a fresh, untried division, and put Hood's Texans in the front line between his two right divisions. He adjusted until his line was satisfactory. Where there were three brigades to a division, one was put in reserve, two when there were more than three. He had reconnoitered his wing, had organized it to act as a whole, and was ready for battle, or almost ready. General Lee told Mrs. Page that it always took three rounds of the enemy's cannon to arouse him to action, but that after this little prelude he was terrible.

The instructions from Bragg were for the battle to begin on the extreme right, the divisions taking it up successively to the left. This meant a turning movement to the left, the end of Longstreet's wing acting as pivot.

As the ears on this part of the field were strained to catch the sound of firearms from the direction of Chattanooga, McLaws's two other brigades arrived from Catoosa Station. They marched up in splendid order and made a fine showing in their new uniforms. The ragged Tennesseans had not seen since the beginning of the war such an array of fresh clothes. They made it plain that the purty breeches would be dirty before the day was over. The Virginians made it just as plain that they had come over to show the Tennesseans how to fight, and as they moved off to the positions assigned them, a few of Bragg's men began to scratch among their rags.

The sun had been up two hours, and there was still nothing to break the silence except a steady noise from the west of axes felling trees. Staff officers were galloping restlessly along the lines. It was said that Bragg, half an hour ago, had been seen going towards the right.

This was true. He had gone to see why the battle had not begun at day-dawn. He found the Right Wing in confusion. General Polk, shortly before midnight, had sent orders to Hill, Cheatham, and Walker to begin the attack at the appointed time. Hill's corps and Cheatham's division were directed to attack at once, with Walker in reserve. Cheatham and Walker received their orders, but Hill, due to a complicated set of reasons, missed all the couriers who had been sent to find him.

The Wing Commander, having waited until the sun was up without communicating with Hill, then sent direct orders to Hill's division commanders, Cleburne and Breckinridge, to attack at once. Polk sent these orders without examining his lines and on the assumption that Hill's corps was ready to advance, although neither he nor Hill had told the division commanders to prepare for any such movement.

When Polk's orders reached these officers, Hill was with them, having just arrived after a futile effort to find his two superiors. The two papers were placed in his hands. Aware that the essential preparations for a battle had not been made, and could not be made without the presence of the Commander-in-Chief or at least the Wing Commander, he countermanded Polk's orders to his inferiors. He explained his reasons to Polk in a note.

He then set his men to feeding, some of them not having eaten for twenty-four hours. Breckinridge's wagons had been lost in the night. He ordered them up. In an emergency soldiers can do without food, but Hill saw no reason why they could not eat while the battle line was being adjusted. He did not know that Bragg had intended to bring on the battle without making this readjustment, without reconnoitering the enemy, and without placing any cavalry on the flanks.

But on the other side, as soon as there was sufficient light, Rosecrans with his chief of staff and aides, began the inspection of his entire army.

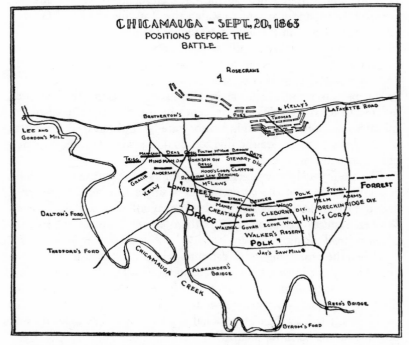

He found gaps and weak points, especially in McCook's corps. He gave minute directions to eliminate these defects and to close up his line.

Cheatham, who was to follow Hill into the fight, was at right angles to this corps. Hill pointed this out to Bragg and got the reply that Cheatham was in his right place.

Hill had spent a great part of the previous evening examining his position, and he had discovered that the breastworks Thomas's men were building were open to a turning movement. To be able to make this movement he had ordered Breckinridge to place his division on the extreme right, but if Cheatham remained in his present position, Breckinridge could not go as far as was necessary.

During the delay General Forrest and General Adams made a personal reconnaissance and reported that the enemy's left was without cavalry protection, the only protection to his flank being a long line of infantry skirmishers.

At Hill's request Forrest was now ordered to protect the extreme right. He dismounted Armstrong, all except two regiments reserved for the extreme right flank, and marched him into line with the infantry. Pegram, who suffered heavily the day before, he placed in reserve; and Scott's brigade was sent to watch the Rossville road and Gordon Granger's division in the gap at Missionary ridge.

By 9:30 the Southern right at last moved forward. First Breckinridge, then Cleburne, set out to find the enemy. Armstrong's mounted and dismounted men kept pace with Breckinridge.

There was some confusion in Cleburne's division. He had been ordered to dress on Breckinridge. Since he did not move until fifteen minutes later, his right caught up too rapidly and jammed his left as it was closing up. Before the division could be straightened out, parts of it had found the enemy.

The moment the movement began, Hill sent a staff officer to Polk, reminding him that the corps was in a single line without reserves, and if broken at one point was broken at all points. Polk ordered Walker, instead of supporting Cheatham, to form his reserve so as to echelon Breckinridge.

When the time came for Cheatham and his five thousand Tennesseans to join the advance, his men had not gone a hundred paces before they ran into Stewart. To prevent him from overlapping the right of the Left Wing he was taken out and put in reserve. The military evils which result from a lack of personal supervision before a battle were now beginning to show themselves.

By ten o'clock, although unevenly dressed, the Southern right, eight brigades strong, had struck, or was striking, the enemy behind his log works. Forrest with Armstrong and the mounted men, about one thousand eight hundred, swept forward and turned to the left. Coming next, from right to left, Breckinridge's brigadiers, Adams, Stovall, and Helm (Lincoln's brother-in-law), about four thousand men, their breakfasts still working in their stomachs, struck the works. Cleburne, with five thousand veterans under Polk, Wood, and Deshler, followed next.

These eleven thousand men, bent slightly forward, dressing on their flags, moved bravely to their work. Due to Cheatham's withdrawal the impetus of their attack was only two-thirds of what it ought to have been. If Cheatham had not been thrown out of line, Cleburne would now be marching in Breckinridge's place,and Breckinridge would be so far to the right that he and Forrest would have overlapped Rosecrans's right fully a mile, and be in a position to take the whole line in reverse.

As it was, the two right brigades of infantry and Forrest's men swung behind the left of the breastworks, Adams and Dibrell actually reaching their rear. From this point of vantage, they drove the enemy before them, ran into Beatty's brigade of Negley's division coming up from the Northern right, drove him back upon several regiments of Palmer's reserve, Van Derveer's brigade, and a portion of Stanley's brigade. The fighting here was fierce and a good supporting line would very likely have produced decisive results. But there was none: Walker's reserve and Cheatham's five thousand were idle in the woods near the creek. Bragg was at Thedford's Ford listening to the noise of battle.

Adams was wounded. He fell into the hands of Van Derveer's men, and Stovall's left was hard hit when it charged the retired portion of the breastworks; so the two brigades fell back in some confusion. Adams's brigade re-formed behind Slocomb's battery and checked pursuit.

Hill, happening in this quarter about the time of the advance, saw a body of men advancing in splendid order. He called Captain Anderson of Forrest's staff and asked him:

"What infantry is that?"

"That is Forrest's cavalry, sir."

Hill looked incredulous. "Can I see General Forrest?"

As they approached his position, Forrest rode back to meet them. General Hill raised his hat. "General Forrest, I wish to congratulate you and those brave men moving across that field like veteran infantry upon their magnificent behavior. In Virginia I made myself extremely unpopular with the cavalry because I said that so far I had not seen a dead man with spurs on. No one can speak disparagingly of such troops as yours."

Old Bedford thanked him, waved his hand; and, wheeling his horse, galloped to take position near his artillery which had just been advanced to the open field in front of Cloud's Spring.

Very soon after he fell back with the infantry, but not until his mounted men had captured the road and the enemy hospitals.

Helm's brigade, a little to the left, was the first to mount the log works. His regiments were met by a fire equal to the speed of repeat-ing rifles. The front ranks of Thomas's men fired, while those in the rear did nothing but load. Helm was killed and his brigade cut up. It was thrown back into the bushes in fragments. This made it pos-sible for Thomas to enfilade Stovall's left. The fire was more deadly than usual, because Stovall did not reach the works until Helm's men were on the point of falling back.

Hill, seeing the danger to the whole attacking body, sent to the rear for Gist's brigade to take its place. The order was misunderstood, for instead of the single brigade Polk brought up Walker's entire com-mand. But by this time an hour had elapsed, and the Northerners had planted themselves firmly in the gap. This gave them an enfilade fire both to the right and the left and was largely responsible for the failure of Hill's attack.

Two brigades, Walthall and Gist, were quickly hurled against the angle, but they could not disturb Thomas's men. They came out badly cut up.

Opposite Cleburne's right and right center, Polk's brigade and Low-rey's regiment of Wood's brigade, were halted within one hundred and seventy-five yards of the breastworks by a deadly artillery fire. Here Polk's men lay along a crest of a ridge and kept up a destructive fire for an hour and a half, until, their ammunition exhausted, they were ordered to retire to a position four hundred yards away from the enemy.

In the meantime Wood, in unison with Stewart's division of the Left Wing, pushed through the woods around the southern face of the works and seized the Chattanooga road. Wood's left had reached the remains of Poe's house, when from the front and upon his flanks musketry and artillery knocked his men down by the companyful. To his right the breastworks were hidden by thick bushes and scrub oak timber, and the fire from that end took him by surprise. He fell back in confusion, leaving upon the ground six hundred officers and men.

His withdrawal left Brown's brigade of Stewart's division open to this same enfilading fire, but Brown pushed forward fifty or seventy-five yards farther, until, unable to stand the thick stream of lead, his two right regiments broke and ran back to their original position. His center and left, however, ably supported by Bate and Clayton, dashed ahead and drove the enemy beyond the cornfield and the burnt house, across the road for some two hundred yards and into the second set of works parallel to the Lafayette road. But these works they could not carry, for here, as on all parts of the fortified line, there were five or six loaders and one firer. There was no let-up to this steady small-arms firing, and it was supported by artillery. So the rest of Stewart's division fell back to re-form on the ground occupied before the charge.

Deshler had not been in the fight at all. Longstreet, to make way for Hood in the front line and to eliminate a gap which Stewart had informed him existed between the two wings, ordered Stewart to close up towards the right. This movement had already thrown Cheatham out of line. It now threw Deshler out of line, and into the rear of the Left Wing.

Cleburne, finding him here, moved him by the right flank to connect with Polk after Wood's withdrawal. But the connection was not made, as it was observed that Polk's brigade was barely holding its own on the ridge seventy-five yards from the log works. It was about this time that Cleburne sent Polk and Wood four hundred yards to the rear. This left Deshler *en echelon* with the rest of the division, and to the front, advanced to the crest of the low ridge Polk and Lowrey had held. Here he rested for some hours. Deshler had himself been killed while in the act of placing his men, a round cannon shot passing through his chest, tearing his heart and ribs out of his body.

Hill's whole corps had failed in its attack. Breckinridge lay at the end of the field marked by his dead and wounded; and Cleburne, the finest division commander in the Army of Tennessee, had made even less of an impression on the twelve Northern brigades lying behind the logs and rails Thomas had thrown up. Stewart's three brigades, following the Right Wing into the fight, had punished Palmer and Reynolds, but at great loss and without permanent gain; and two of Walker's brigades had wasted their strength in vain against the bloody angle, although Helm's lifeless body and most of his brigade lay before it to urge them forward. Forrest, thrown back beside the infantry, hovered near the Chattanooga road, dangerously near the enemy's flank and rear, which once that day he had tramped around.

But although this offensive on the Right Wing had been a tactical failure in itself, it had had a most important strategic bearing on the final outcome. It fell with such violence and, while it lasted, was sustained so vehemently, that Thomas now doubted his ability to stave off a return attack. He set up, as on the day before, loud calls for assistance.

At 10:10 Garfield, Rosecrans's adjutant, wrote to McCook to be prepared to support the left flank "at all hazards even if the right is drawn wholly to the present left." At 10:30, about the time Cleburne was fully engaged, he sent in another call, and Sheridan's division was ordered to him. Still again, at 10:45, a courier from Thomas appeared before Rosecrans with the same appeal, and Van Cleve's division was soon on its way "with all dispatch."

After sending these two divisions to Thomas's part of the line, Rosecrans filled the interval left by Negley's withdrawal with Wood's division. There were now, on the Federal side, two divisions in motion and eight in line, in the following order from left to right: Baird, Johnson, Palmer, Reynolds, Brannon, Wood, Davis, and Sheridan.

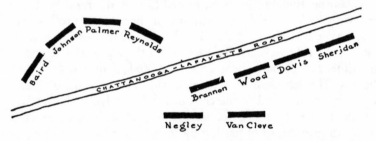

In the meantime, another aide of Thomas's, on his way to Rosecrans, saw what he thought was a large gap in the line. He informed the general commanding that Brannon was out of line and that Reynolds's right was exposed. As it happened, Brannon was not out of line but was *en echelon* and slightly to the rear of Reynolds. But Rosecrans, without verifying this piece of information, sent an order to Wood to close up on Reynolds's right. Wood, instead of closing up to the front of Brannon, obeyed the order literally by moving to the rear of Brannon. The aide who brought the fatal piece of misinformation returned to Thomas with the word that he should be supported if it took the entire corps of McCook and Crittenden to do it. It was not long before he became involved in the ruin he had helped to bring about.

By pure chance it happened that the whole Confederate Left Wing had just been set in motion. Wood had advanced little more than a brigade length when Bushrod R. Johnson, Hood, and Hindman, advancing in three solid gray lines, burst through the forest into this opening. In a very short time Rosecrans's entire left flank was churning with panic. The rear of Buell's brigade, Wood's brigade, was cut off and destroyed. Hindman surrounded Davis, front, flank, and rear, and dismembered his division.

In the rout which followed, he captured twenty-seven guns and one thousand prisoners. Brannon's right was thrown back and two of his batteries were taken in flank by Bushrod R. Johnson and driven through two brigades of Van Cleve, then on a march to the left, throwing this division "into confusion from which it never recovered until it reached Rossville." Sheridan's entire division—two of his brigades were on their way to fill the gap left by Wood—was cut up and scattered. One of his brigadiers, Lytle, was killed as he attempted to rally his men near Snodgrass Hill. Six Northern brigades were swept off the field, about eight thousand in all in a rout which was fast becoming a panic. Forty pieces of artillery fell into Longstreet's hands, and several thousand stands of abandoned arms.

At the time, Mr. Dana, one of Lincoln's assistant-secretaries of War, was asleep on the battlefield. He said he was awakened by "the most infernal noise I ever heard. I sat up on the grass, and the first thing I saw was General Rosecrans crossing himself. . . . 'Hello,' I said to myself, 'if the general is crossing himself we are in a desperate situation.' I had no sooner collected my thoughts and looked around towards the front, where all the din came from, than I saw our lines break and melt away like leaves before the wind. Then the headquarters around me disappeared. The graybacks came through with a rush, and soon the musket-balls and cannon-shot began to reach the place where we stood. . . . My orderly stuck to me like a veteran, and we drew back for greater safety into the woods a little way."

He soon came upon aides halting fugitives. "They would halt a few of them, get them into some sort of line, and make a beginning of order among them, and then there would come a few rounds of cannon-shot through the treetops over their heads, and the men would break and run. I saw Porter and Drouillard plant themselves in front of a body of these stampeding men and command them to halt. One man charged with his bayonet, menacing Porter, but Porter held his ground, and the man gave in."

After advising Wilder's mounted infantry to go to Thomas, he turned his horse in the direction of Chattanooga. "Everything on the route was in the greatest disorder. The whole road was filled with flying soldiers, and here and there were piled up pieces of artillery, caissons, and baggage wagons." McCook and Crittenden became involved in the confusion and were carried off the field. Rosecrans hastened to Rossville, then to Chattanooga, to prepare for his broken army.

But this turned out to be unnecessary. He could have rallied it two miles from the battlefield, for there was no pursuit. About three o'clock, Bragg sent for Longstreet. He told Bragg of the satisfactory progress of the battle, why he had changed the wheel from left to right. He asked for troops that had not been so severely engaged as his, to allow him to pursue down the Dry Valley road the fragments of the enemy he had scattered, and at the same time to throw a column between Thomas and cut him off from Chattanooga.

Cheatham had remained idle all morning on the Right Wing with five thousand fresh men, but Bragg told Longstreet that the troops on that part of the field had "no more fight left in them" and that he must hold his present position.

The rout of Rosecrans's right seemed not to have penetrated the Confederate commander's mind or to encourage him to rise to the occasion. The failure of his paper plans, which seemed more decisive than it actually was because he had not been on the ground to witness it, apparently convinced him that the battle was lost. He rode away without giving Longstreet any instructions, saying, "General, if any-thing happens, communicate with me at Reed's bridge."

This lull in the battle had given Thomas sufficient time to stiffen his line and rally the fragments which had drifted his way from the right. With these, Brannon's division, and two and a half brigades of Wood's, he formed a new line along the crest of a very strong hill, known as Horseshoe Ridge, perpendicular to the former line of battle. The new battle position had the conformation of a horseshoe, the two flanks bending backward from the old left, now the center.

General Gordon Granger, commanding Rosecrans's reserve at the Rossville Gap, gathered from the direction of the firing that the day was going against his side. He decided to assume the responsibility and march to the sound of the firing. He had some five thousand men under his orders; but he brought only four thousand with him, leaving one brigade at McAfee's Church to cover the Lafayette road.

As soon as he had set out, Forrest's vigilant scouts brought the news. Hill had just renewed the assault on Thomas's right with a part of Walker's small corps. Unfortunately, his left had been unfilled by Jackson's brigade of Cheatham's division, this officer for some reason failing to close up properly, and it suffered from the same enfilade fire that Breckinridge had encountered much earlier in the day. The right also became exposed to the discharges of cannon, and the attacking brigades again were driven east of the road.

Hill surmised that this second repulse probably saved the troops from destruction, "for that ever watchful officer, General Forrest, reported to me soon after that a heavy Yankee column was coming from the direction of Chattanooga."

Forrest, after making the report, had already taken steps to cut Granger off, although his command was outmatched two to one. Borrowing a section of artillery from Breckinridge, he massed fourteen guns across Granger's path and threw a constant stream of lead and iron into his brigades. He manœuvered his horse infantry, and for two hours Granger was delayed on his way to Thomas.

All this time Cheatham lay idle, and Hill refused to take any of the other troops out of line to assist in Granger's capture. Polk did make an ineffectual attempt to send Cheatham, but it was irresolute. When Cheatham finally drew up within acting distance, Granger had already carried his superior numbers through, and just in time to stay Hindman's division, at that moment pouring over the top of Horseshoe Ridge into Thomas's rear. If Bragg had sent Polk word of the rout on the left, the right could have acted with greater confidence. But Bragg was busy at Reed's bridge with plans to receive his shattered divisions.

The battle was now to be fought out with the commanders of both armies off the field. Rosecrans was at Chattanooga, Bragg at Reed's bridge. On the Northern side Thomas held the interior lines, the advantage of a strong defensive position, and over two-thirds of the army, further strengthed by four thousand extra men under Granger, totaling some thirty-five thousand or forty thousand of all arms. He labored under the disadvantage of the defeat on his right. He had received orders from Rosecrans to retreat to Rossville, but he decided to hold on until nightfall.

On the Southern side, each wing under separate commanders prepared to fight it out in two different engagements. Polk, still not being informed of Longstreet's success, was not able to take advantage of the changed conditions. It was therefore impossible for them to act in concert. Rosecrans's absence on the Northern side, after all, made no great difference, for he had left one single commander on the field; but, on the Southern side, Bragg was still nominally in command; and when he refused at three oclock to organize his wings for common action, he doomed the Army of Tennessee to the impotent policy of detailed assaults.

Longstreet threw column after column up the steep slopes of

Horseshoe Ridge, but Thomas's men, now assisted by Granger, held to the crest with desperation. Near sundown, Longstreet put in Stewart and his reserve under Preston, while Buckner, who had arranged twelve guns in a position opposite the Right Wing, began an enfilade fire down the enemy's center. The combination was well-timed and arranged. Preston, with the nervous valor of the untried, dashed up the hill. Stewart flanked a reënforcing column and captured a large part of it. Buckner's artillery did not have an immediate effect, its range being nine hundred yards; but its fire was so steady and so withering that a body of men directly under it threw down their arms and surrendered. Preston and Stewart met Granger's eager resistance as well as Wood and Brannon. The lines swayed both forward and backward, and still the enemy held to the hill. But he had been badly broken in places, and Buckner's steady-crashing guns began to be felt. Thomas decided it was time to withdraw. The sun was falling over the rocks on Lookout.

On the Right Wing, Polk ordered a general advance at three-thirty o'clock. It got under way at four P.M., and by five o'clock the men "who have no more fight in them" were throwing themselves recklessly against the logs that had withstood their previous divided assaults. Brigadier-General Polk took the bloody angle, and Breckinridge, supported by Cheatham, charged the rear. Forrest, stronger by Biffle's regiment just arrived from West Tennessee than he was in the morning, crept by Van Derveer's left and formed for assault there and on his front. Longstreet reorganized his men, and together both wings of the Army of Tennessee, without orders from a common commander, charged the enemy as he was retreating from his works. A simultaneous and continuous shout rose up from the whole line, such as one officer said he had never heard before, and followed the rear of the enemy as it hastened to Rossville.

Forrest and Breckinridge had more difficulty than the troops on the left and in the center, for they came in direct contact with the guard ordered to protect Thomas's rear. When the enemy discovered that Forrest had passed Van Derveer's left, he withdrew his left to meet it. This formed an obtuse angle opening towards the front. "Into this, and heavily against the left of it, Forrest hurled his columns, four deep. On came these men in gray in magnificent lines, which showed clearly through the open forest, bending their faces before the sleet of the storm, and firing hotly as they advanced. As they came within range of the oblique fire from Van Derveer's right, they halted within forty yards of his left, and for a few moments poured in a destructive fire. A wheel of Smith's regular battery, and a section of Church's guns, which had reported, brought them where they poured a nearly enfilading fire of canister down these long lines, standing bravely there and fighting almost under the mouths of the guns."

It was now dark. General Hill called a halt. The darkness might lead to an engagement between the two wings of the Southern army, as Longstreet was pressing northward, Polk southward. Although the moon came up and made the night almost as bright as day, there was no pursuit. Nobody had thought it necessary to inform Bragg that his army had won a victory—Longstreet said he thought the rebel yell was sufficient notice—so Thomas was allowed to retreat to Rossville without molestation. Forrest said the time to whip an enemy is when he is running.

Wheeler, after a slow start, followed that afternoon down the Dry Valley road, capturing one thousand prisoners; but night forced him to return before he had had a chance to make of the rout a panic.

The next morning Forrest was up by four o'clock and in the saddle. He called together Pegram, Dibrell, and Armstrong and gave them each a separate line of march. He decided to go with Armstrong and four hundred of his riders. Soon they came upon Northern cavalry hovering near Rossville. "Armstrong, let's give them a dare." Armstrong agreed. The charge was sounded, and the two generals sped at the head of the four hundred down upon the cavalry to their front.

The enemy fired a volley and turned to gallop in the direction of Chattanooga. It did not stand to meet the dare. One of the balls broke an artery in the neck of Forrest's charger. The pressure of the gallop pumped the blood in all directions, spraying the clothes and the face of the General. At this rate, he would soon be on foot; so he leaned over, rammed his finger in the wound, and the horse galloped bravely on. After the chase was ended, Forrest removed his finger and dismounted. Presently the horse fell in the road and wallowed in its blood. This was the second animal he had had killed at Chickamauga. The fine animal the citizens of Rome gave him was shot on the first day.

Swinging into another saddle, he pushed on to Missionary Ridge. Climbing a tree about seven o'clock, he looked in all directions. The view, as it spread out below him, was very satisfactory. The scene was wild with chaos. Wagons and teams, cannon, stragglers, columns of infantry, and squads of cavalry were all mixed up together in their haste to reach Chattanooga. He climbed down and sent a dispatch to Bragg.

Going on farther, he saw a Northern captain and two men in an observatory. Calling them down, he took their glasses and looked in every direction, sweeping his eyes over the town, the river, Chattanooga Valley, and Waldern's Ridge far to the north. He called down to Anderson to take dictation.

Genl:

We are in a mile of Rossville—Have been on the Point of Missionary Ridge—Can see Chattanooga and everything around. The enemy's trains are leaving, going around the point of Lookout Mountain.

The prisoners captured report two pontoons thrown across for the purpose of retreating.

I think they are evacuating as hard as they can go.

They are cutting timber down to obstruct our passage.

I think we ought to press forward as rapidly as possible.

Respectfully,

To Gen'l Polk   N. B. Forrest

Please forward to Gen'l Bragg.

Longstreet had, in the meantime, conferred with Bragg. He had suggested that they move above the town, fall upon Burnside; then cross the river and force Rosecrans to retreat. Longstreet said that Bragg seemed to agree that this was the thing to do. In fact the movement was begun at four o'clock, Hill's corps moving toward the Chickamauga. It was then halted. Longstreet, seeing this message of Forrest's years afterwards, remarked that "it was this dispatch which fixed the fate of the Confederacy. General Bragg had decided to march around Rosecrans, leaving him in Chattanooga, when the dispatch was received which caused Bragg to think that the place would be abandoned on the night of the twenty-second, when he decided to turn back and march through Chattanooga."

But it was not this note which fixed the fate of the Confederacy, because it did not cause Bragg, as Longstreet thought, to retrace his steps. This and another dispatch reached Bragg before four P.M., the time Hill's corps set out for the Chickamauga. If he had expected to pursue through Chattanooga, he would not have allowed Hill to go in the other direction, or have allowed the Left Wing to follow the Right the next day at daylight. Bragg gave as his reason for not following the enemy the absurd excuse that he was without supplies. This was an excuse to hide the real reason. The battle of Chickamauga presents a condition unparalleled in any war, a victorious army losing the fruits of victory because its general was suffering from the illusion of defeat.

When the army failed to move, and while Rosecrans was using every precious hour to restore order to his corps and strengthen the already powerful works around the town, Forrest sent another imperative dispatch to Bragg. "Every moment lost is worth the life of a thousand men." But Bragg still did not move. In desperation Forrest threw his cavalry against the fortifications at Rossville. McLemore penetrated to within three miles of Chattanooga. He was soon among a mass of Northern soldiers, but they did not see him. Forrest recalled him from his exposed position, and he came out burdened with prisoners.

That night Forrest mounted a horse and rode to Bragg's headquarters. As he moved along the road, he was sick with the thought of what had been lost that day; and he was going to make a direct appeal to his commander. He found him in his tent, sound asleep. He had an orderly arouse him and, going in, he tried to impress upon Bragg what he considered the helpless condition of the enemy. He told him that if they pursued at once, capture was certain. Bragg asked him how he could move his army without supplies.

"General Bragg, we can get all the supplies we want in Chattanooga."

To this, Bragg made no answer. Nor did his subordinate argue further. He was not given to argument, and he rarely volunteered advice. He turned, and, bending his powerful body under the flap of the tent, stalked out into the dark. Although no words had passed between them, there was more insolence and contempt in this silent departure than he could have put in a studied invective.

He was in the saddle and soon in a swinging gallop. Opportunity wasting away, the helplessness of a powerful man through the more powerful weakness of another in authority, the terrific effort to control his anger . . . all released themselves in the long strides of his animal's legs.

His orderly asked if the army was going to advance. Terrific profanity—then, "I have written to him. I have sent to him. I have given him information of the condition of the Federal army.—" Another stream of profanity. "What does he fight battles for?"

The next day, the twenty-second, he attempted to take the matter
into his own hands. Assembling the whole cavalry corps on Missionary
Ridge, he descended into Chattanooga Valley and drove the infantry
and cavalry pickets to within half a mile of the town. For two miles
his men moved forward on foot in a thin gray line, too few to make
any impression. He took up a position covering the roads to Rossville
and Cleveland and the road around the end of Lookout. Dibrell lost
fifty men and several officers at that point. Forrest sent in flags of
truce demanding "unconditional surrender."

McLaws's division came up on picket duty. Forrest went to his
headquarters and proposed that they, together, venture an attack on
the Northerners. That day with twenty troopers he had ridden within
seventy-five yards of the works on the Rossville road. The volley he
provoked was so uncertain that not a man was touched. But McLaws
was unwilling to assume the responsibility.

While Forrest was trying to persuade McLaws to end Bragg's
blundering in an irregular way, Longstreet was turning in his mind
a more regular way to the same end. On the twenty-sixth he wrote to
Seddon and explained how the fruits of victory had been lost by aim-
less movements up and down the Chickamauga Valley for two and
a half days, while Rosecrans had been busy restoring order and re-
enforcing fortifications already strong.

"To express my convictions in a few words," Longstreet's letter
read, "our chief has done but one thing that he ought to have done
since I joined this army. This was to order the attack upon the
twentieth. All other things that he has done he ought not to have done.
I am convinced that nothing but the hand of God can save us or help
us as long as we have our present commander. . . . Can't you send us
General Lee? . . . You will be surprised to learn that this army has
neither organization nor mobility, and I have doubts if its commander
can give it them. . . . When I came here I hoped to find our commander
willing and anxious to do all things that would aid us in our great
cause, and ready to receive what aid he could get from his subordinates.
It seems that I was greatly mistaken. It seems that he cannot adhere
to any plan or course, whether of his own or of some one else. I desire
to impress upon your mind that there is no exaggeration in these statements. On the contrary, I have failed to express my convictions to the
fullest extent. . . ." On the arrival of this letter Davis packed his bags
for another trip to the West.

About this time, at Longstreet's headquarters, "an old woman

❑ Please send me a free copy of
Schreiner's Iris Mini-Catalog!

Name_____

Address _____

City _____

State _____ Zip _____

Schreiner's
IRIS GARDENS
3625 QUINABY ROAD NE
DEPT 34
SALEM OR 97303-9720

PLACE
STAMP
HERE

áressed in an ancient black silk dress and very remarkable bonnet, approached the table, and stopping a few paces off, asked if General Longstreet was there. He replied: 'Yes, is there anything I can do for you?' 'Is there any harm to come here?' (She wanted to know.) She said she had walked eight miles since she had breakfasted and that she did not now have up in the 'settlemint' what she used to have and she believed she would take a bite. While at breakfast she was very lively, telling of her adventures during the war. She spoke of the cavalry as 'Mr. Forrest's critter company,' and of a line of battle as 'a string of fight.' After she had breakfasted she informed the General that the object of her visit was to get him to give her a little tobacco to smoke. Her pockets were filled with *Lone Jack,* and she was sent home rejoicing in an ambulance."

On the twenty-third, the critter company was gradually relieved by infantry pickets. Hungry men and exhausted, shoeless horses retired to Byrd's Mills to recruit. But they were allowed to rest for only a day. Orders came to Forrest to proceed at once to Cleveland with Armstrong and Davidson and meet the advance of Burnside's army, then reported moving down from Knoxville.

Without wasting any time, although the ribs of his horses were chaffing their hides, Forrest crossed the Hiwassee in the face of enemy cavalry and drove it, Wolfords and Byrd's brigades, to Philadelphia. While in the midst of the pursuit, the following order reached him:

Missionary Ridge, Sep. 28, 1863.

Brigadier-General Forrest, near Athens:

General:—The general commanding desires that you without delay turn over the troops of your command, previously ordered, to Major-General Wheeler.

This was the last straw. Forrest's decision never to serve again under Wheeler was known to the army and to Bragg. In view of this, he could take this order only as a personal affront. Such humiliating treatment, coming so soon after the painful aftermath of Chickamauga, was more than his patience, never too good, could bear. At the height of a terrific rage he called his aide, Captain Anderson and, before his temper had time to cool, dictated a letter to his superior. Anderson's script was smooth, well-rounded, and full of flourishes; but it could not disguise the hard, uncompromising content of the letter. It accused Bragg of double-dealing, and gave him the lie. It told him that Forrest would call at his headquarters in a few days to repeat to his face what he had written. Before closing he made it very clear that he expected to shirk no responsibility which his charges might imply.

The letter was read, signed, and sealed; and as a courier rode away with it, Old Bedford remarked to his aide, "Bragg never got such a letter as that before from a brigadier."

He not only never got such a letter as that before from a brigadier, but he had never before been treated with such open contempt by any officer. It must have taken him completely by surprise, for in the past he had always taken advantage of military organization to cover his blunders by shifting the blame to subordinates, and usually to subordinates whom he disliked. He was very busy with this business now. He had arrested Polk and Hindman and removed them from command, and Hill was soon to follow. These gentlemen retired with dignity to Atlanta. Their conduct was regular and what Bragg expected them to do.

But in this instance he had outplayed his hand. It was not in Forrest's nature to submit to injustice in any such way. For once Bragg could not hide behind technical regulations. Forrest had put his chief in a dilemma whose horns bent to a single point. He had told him he would call on him in a few days to say in person what had been said in writing. In other words, Bragg must be prepared to act and without relying on the Richmond Government to sustain him.

The usual procedure, when cavalry passed infantry on the march, was for the footmen to greet the horsemen with insulting jeers:

Infantry. "Mister, did you ever see a Yankee?"
Cavalry. (Sharply) "Yes."
Infantry. "Did he have on a blue coat?"
Cavalry. (More Sharply) "Yes."
Infantry. "Did you stop to look at him?"
Cavalry. (Still more Sharply) "Yes."
Infantry. (Very Earnestly) "Mister, please tell me if your hoss wuz lame, or if your spurs wuz broke?"

But the men who rode with Forrest enjoyed a singular position in the army. They were heroes even to the infantry. So all they had to do to stop such chatter was to suggest that they belonged to Forrest's Cavalry. The foot soldiers at once became respectful. They asked about Old Bedford's raids, where they had been, where they were going, how he did it. They knew that Wheeler's name or any other cavalry officer's name could not give them the same position of respect in the army.

So when his boys heard that Bragg had transferred them to Wheeler, great discontent, almost mutiny, spread among them, especially through the Old Brigade. They made it known that if he said the word, they would obey no commands but his. But he complied with the peremptory orders, and the brigades were soon on their way to Wheeler. He now made his preparations to pay Bragg the promised visit.

Dr. Cowan, Chief Surgeon to the corps, was left in charge of the hospital at Alexander's bridge. He notified his commander that he was ready to report back for duty, and Forrest directed him to meet him next day at Ringgold. From Chickamauga Station the two kinsmen rode in the direction of Missionary Ridge in silence. This was so unusual that Dr. Cowan looked out of the corner of his eye and found upon his chief's face, "an expression which I had seen before on some occasions when a storm was brewing."

There was plenty to set a storm brewing. Forrest had protested that his regiments were in no condition for the hard duty ahead of them, that they were out of ammunition, and short on subsistence. They had had no rest since the Chickamauga campaign and little food. The horses were almost broken down. Wheeler found that "the three brigades from General Forrest were mere skeletons, scarcely averaging five hundred effective men each." These were badly armed, he said, with but a small supply of ammunition, and mounted on horses who were in "a horrible condition, having been marched continuously for three days and nights without removing saddles. The men were worn out, and without rations." Bedford Forrest, on his way to the ridge, thought of this bad treatment. It was adding injury to insult, for he knew the consequences of beginning a raid with men and mounts in a broken-down condition. He could stand personal injustice, and he could stand to have his men and their critters driven to the limit or killed by the score when he knew that they were strong enough to gain some important objective, but he had never been able to submit to the injuries they received at the hands of a blundering superior.

The two men pulled up in front of Bragg's headquarters. Forrest dismounted, threw his reins to an orderly, and strode by the sentry without returning his salute, something so unusual that it set Cowan to thinking as he followed him into the tent.

Bragg rose from his seat and offered his hand; but it remained thrust into the air, untouched. Bedford Forrest had drawn his powerful body to its full height and crossed his arms like a Choctaw chief. The pupils of his eyes, two hard, glinting points, focused in an iris of shattered steel; a dull, bronze flush gathered in his cheeks; and, as he spoke, the beard on his chin fell upon his collar in quick, precise jabs—"I am not here to pass civilities or compliments with you, but on other business."

Bragg's hand fell to his side, and he went to the other end of his tent and sat in a chair behind a little field desk. The blood had drawn into his beard, his mouth was closed; and, as he listened, not a muscle moved in his face.

"You commenced your cowardly and contemptible persecution of me soon after the battle of Shiloh, and you have kept it up ever since. You did it because I reported to Richmond facts, while you reported damned lies. You robbed me of my command in Kentucky, and gave it to one of your favorites—men that I armed and equipped from the enemies of our country. In a spirit of revenge and spite, because I would not fawn upon you as others did, you drove me into West Tennessee in the winter of 1862, with a second brigade I had organized, with improper arms and without sufficient ammunition, although I had made repeated applications for the same. You did it to ruin me and my career.

"When in spite of all this I returned with my command, well equipped by captures, you began again your work of spite and persecution, and have kept it up. And now this second brigade, organized and equipped without thanks to you or the government, a brigade which has won a reputation for successful fighting second to none in the army, taking advantage of your position as the commanding general in order to further humiliate me, you have taken these brave men from me.

"I have stood your meanness as long as I intend to. You have played the part of a damned scoundrel, and are a coward, and if you were any part of a man I would slap your jaws and force you to resent it.

"You may as well not issue any more orders to me, for I will not obey them. And I will hold you personally responsible for any further indignities you try to inflict on me.

"You have threatened to arrest me for not obeying your orders promptly. I dare you to do it, and I say to you that if you ever again try to interfere with me or cross my path, it will be at the peril of your life." [1]

[1] Cowan's account to Wyath. Major Cliff verified the rumor of this meeting by asking Forrest.

He dropped his long finger, which he had been shaking in Bragg's face, and abruptly left the tent.

"Well, you are in for it now," Dr. Cowan said, as they rode away.

He stood in his stirrups and turned to Cowan, "He'll never open his mouth. Unless you or I mention it, this will never be known."

He knew that if the things he had said to Bragg became public, Bragg was a ruined man, for he had refused to take the only kind of action an officer and a gentleman can take in such a circumstance. Forrest was shrewd enough to understand this, but in the end it was he, not Bragg, who had overplayed his hand. He would pay a great price for settling his bile—he would make the South pay a great price —for he had done the Southern cause such an injury that all his genius would be powerless to repair it. Bragg's bloodless cheeks did not run white from fear alone. He would be satisfied for this mortal insult. In the end, the man who is ambitious and designing always triumphs over a man like Forrest.

In the Wilderness panthers know by instinct they can't mess with pole-cats.

PART FOUR

THE ATLANTA CAMPAIGN IN NORTH MISSISSIPPI

PART FOUR

THE ATLANTA CAMPAIGN IN NORTH MISSISSIPPI

CHAPTER XV

Raising a Command Within Enemy Lines

PRESIDENT DAVIS was at headquarters, trying to settle the disputes between Bragg and his lieutenants, when Forrest denounced his commander. It is said by some that Bedford sent in his resignation to him, by others that he did not, for fear it might be construed that he was trying to shirk the responsibility for his action. At any rate, the President took no official notice of the incident.

He wrote Forrest that he could not dispense with his services and asked him to meet with him at Montgomery. At the same time Bedford was led to understand that his entire command would be returned to him when Wheeler's expedition into Middle Tennessee was over.

He asked for a ten days' furlough and went to visit his wife, then at Rome, Georgia. An order from Bragg reached him there on October third, placing him directly under Wheeler. He ignored it and met Davis at the appointed time in Montgomery. They had a long, satisfactory talk, which ended in Davis giving him permission to raise the independent command in North Mississippi and West Tennessee.

Returning in the President's suite as far as Atlanta, he got together the nucleus of men he was allowed to take with him, fewer than he had been promised, and sent them overland to Okolona, Mississippi.

Field and staff	8
Escort	65
McDonald's battalion	139
Captain Morton's battery	67
Total effectives	279

His old brigade, the one he had taken into West Tennessee in '62, the one that had followed him in pursuit of Streight, sent in a petition to go with him. The petition was not granted.

When the time came for him to leave, he drew them up for the last inspection. He rode along the ragged squadrons of Starnes's Fourth, Biffle's Fifth, Dibrell's Eighth, Edmondson's Eleventh, Cox's Tenth, and Freeman's battery, then out to front and center. He did not trust himself to say much, but he told them the things they wanted to hear and then said goodbye.

The western counties of Kentucky, all of the State of Tennessee between the Mississippi and the Tennessee Rivers, and North Mississippi—this was the country Forrest proposed to occupy for the Confederacy. Southern and Western Kentucky had not been in Southern hands since the fall of Donelson; West Tennessee since his raid against Grant's communications; and at present North Mississippi, above a line drawn between Panola on the Mississippi Central Railroad and Okolona on the Mobile and Ohio Railroad, was disputed territory.

General Hurlbut, one of Sherman's Corps Commanders, held it for the North. With headquarters at Memphis, he had distributed the Sixteenth Army Corps in garrisons along the railroad from Corinth to Memphis and up the Mississippi River to Columbus.

Tuttle's division, 3,300 strong, had its headquarters at La Grange. The Fifth Division, under Veatch, was at Memphis; General Stevenson commanded the District of Corinth with a strong force. The Sixth Division held the District of Columbus under General Andrew J. Smith, while Grierson's Division, four brigades of cavalry and mounted infantry, had its headquarters at Memphis, although its troops were scattered in garrisons and in the field. Hurlbut commanded some twenty thousand men, but between Corinth and Memphis there were no more than ten thousand.

The interior of West Tennessee was empty of enemy forces, but this strong cordon, ten thousand men on the southern border, the Tennessee River on the east, General Smith at Columbus, and the Mississippi on the west, held it firmly subjected.

On November fifteenth, General Nathan Bedford Forrest arrived at Okolona, alone, to bring this territory again under the authority of Richmond. His army, two hundred and seventy-nine men and four guns, did not arrive until three days later.

On his way he had stopped at Selma, the largest arsenal in the Southwest, and ordered a small battery. He called on his new commander, General Joe Johnston, and explained in full his views and his intentions. General Johnston ordered Stephen D. Lee, recently assigned to command his cavalry, to give Forrest every possible aid.

Lee had already written to Forrest a letter of welcome. He told him of hearing with regret of the separation from his old command, "with which you have rendered so much service to the cause. No longer than yesterday I wrote General Bragg stating that if you were unpleasantly situated West Tennessee offered a good field . . . I am confident that five thousand men can be raised in West Tennessee . . . I take this occasion to state, General, that whether you are under my command or not, we shall not disagree, and you shall have all the assistance and support I can render you. I would feel proud either in commanding or co-operating with so gallant an officer as yourself and one who has such an established reputation in the cavalry service."

Johnston also ordered Richardson's brigade of two thousand West Tennesseans to report to Forrest; but when he arrived at Okolona, he found that at the muster on the thirtieth only two hundred and forty were present for duty. The others had gone home, without leave, to see their kin and to get warmer clothes.

This was a heavy blow, but Forrest had made up his mind he was going into West Tennessee. Lee promised to get him through the lines. With his fierce energy he pushed forward his preparations. He was soon ready, but the arms Davis promised him did not arrive. He waited, but the days passed and the arms still remained unissued. The ordnance department was waiting, apparently, for Forrest to show the men first. He found, also, that the march across the country had so blown the horses of his "army" that he would be compelled to leave fifty men and two of his guns at Okolona.

There was no evidence that the Confederate authorities appreciated his capacity to carry out his plans. He was still the raider, and therefore not to be taken very seriously. Johnston's doubt was revealed in a dispatch to Davis. He asked for General Hampton to command the cavalry in the northern part of his department so that he might withdraw Lee farther south. Davis was scarcely enthusiastic, although he had Forrest appointed a Major-General on December 4. Major-General Stephen D. Lee was the only man who understood the value of his service, and he helped him in every way.

Hurlbut received early information of Forrest's appearance in Mississippi, and he said he expected him to put a little more "dash" into affairs. He remarked rather indifferently that Forrest would probably escape into West Tennessee, but this did not seem to give him any concern. His immediate fears were that Lee would snatch up the Federal garrisons along the Memphis and Charleston Railroad. Sherman had warned him not to let this happen.

It was very likely that Hurlbut's lack of concern was due to Sherman's indifference. He assured his subordinate that "the enemy will not penetrate much north of the road, save as a maraud, and we should so dispose matters that they maraud their own people. It is none of our business to protect a people that has sent all its youth, and arms, and horses, all that is of any account to war against us. Forrest may cavort about that country as much as he pleases. Every conscript they now catch will cost a good man to watch." This dispatch of Sherman's did much to clear his way.

Despairing of his arms, Forrest ordered his four hundred and fifty riders, two guns, and five ordnance wagons to march to New Albany and form a junction with Lee's convoy, Ferguson's and Ross's brigades. He had already sent ahead Colonel Bell, a prominent West Tennessean he had met in Bragg's army, to spy out the land and tell the people he was on the way.

It had been raining for forty days, and the bottoms were soaking, the rivers and creeks high or out of their banks. It began again on the twenty-seventh, and it poured all that day. The Tallahatchie at New Albany was now past fording. A raft was ordered, but it was abandoned; and the men were set to work repairing an old bridge. The bridge was finished by the thirtieth, rations were issued for six days, and the whole command was over by December first.

Ferguson's brigade led the march to Ripley. The advance met a small enemy scout. Skirmishing grew heavy five miles north of Ripley, where the enemy increased to one thousand. Ferguson drove them within fifteen miles of Pocahontas; then gave up the chase.

Saulsbury, on the Memphis and Charleston Railroad, twenty-seven miles northeast from Ripley and seven miles east of Grand Junction, was the place selected to let Forrest through the lines. On December 2, the command moved in that direction. A picket of thirty or forty men fired on its advance; then dashed off in the direction of the town. Nor did they stop there, for when Lee and Forrest entered, they found it held by one white soldier and one black. Hurlbut was protecting his garrison at Pocahontas.

The way was open. Forrest took his leave of Lee and the convoy and moved rapidly north. That night he camped at Van Buren, ten miles on the road to Bolivar. General Stephen Lee assaulted Moscow and prevented pursuit.

On the sixth, Forrest arrived at Jackson. His march, all the way, had been like a triumphal procession, with plenty of food, forage, and entertainment at every halt. At Bolivar there was a big wedding; at Jackson a round of parties, dinners, and gaieties. Stevenson reported to Hurlbut on the tenth that "Forrest made a speech on his arrival in Jackson, in which he said he had not come into West Tennessee to make a raid." He had come to stay and he meant to hold West Tennessee "if he had to fight a battle three times a day. Rebel gas." This was not exactly the cavorting Sherman had expected.

But Hurlbut still refused to be alarmed. He told Stevenson that he had been *advised in advance of Forrest's plans,* and that as soon as the rivers fell and the roads were practicable, he would attend to him. He had asked Grant to reënforce Smith at Columbus; and, when this was done, Smith would move down from above and he would send others up from below. Forrest would be caught between the two forces and crushed.

While these leisurely preparations were going on in Hurlbut's lines, Forrest's agents were spreading through the country like fire and water. He sent Richardson to Brownsville to recruit between Fort Pillow and Jackson. Colonel Logwood gathered men under the shadows of Memphis. He scattered Colonels Newsom, Wilson, Greer, and Russell through the towns and the bottoms. They all found that Colonel Bell had done his work well. On the sixth, the day Forrest arrived at Jackson, he wrote General Johnston that he had already about five thousand men. He promised that if he was not molested he would have eight thousand effectives by the first of the year. He was allowing men to volunteer until that time. Afterwards, he told them, he would begin to conscript for the infantry.

"I have never seen a more healthy spirit manifested anywhere than is shown by the people here. . . . The Federals are and have been conscripting in Southern Kentucky, and of one hundred and thirty conscripted at Columbus over one hundred have escaped and joined my command. They are coming in daily at the rate of fifty to one hundred per day, and as soon as it becomes known that my command is here, large numbers will leave the Federal lines to join us."

He found that provisions were abundant, except where the railroad and main roads had been in continual use by the troops of both armies. There were from four thousand to six thousand head of good beef cattle to be driven out for the army, thousands of pounds of bacon, leather, lead, and clothing ready to be taken. He wrote General Cooper at Richmond by special messenger, Major Galloway, and told him "I am satisfied we can hold the country and secure for the army a vast amount of provisions and supplies not to be obtained in like quantity and at so little cost anywhere else."

He sent Bragg the same information, adding that there were from five thousand to six thousand men belonging to the Army of Tennessee in West and Middle Tennessee that could be sent out. He said he was already aiding his commissary department. He asked for General Pillow and Armstrong to help him organize his recruits.

But he warned them all that he could not hold West Tennessee and serve their armies with empty-handed men. They must rush through his promised arms and enough money to buy quartermaster supplies and wagons for transportation. His scouts informed him daily that the enemy combinations were forming to close upon him. The Memphis and Charleston road must be destroyed. This out of the way, it would be an easy matter to send out men and supplies. He asked Johnson to send Lee up with his arms, his other section of artillery, and the small Selma battery. Together, then, they could tear up the road.

But, in the meantime, Rosecrans's army, now under Thomas, had been reënforced by Grant, Sherman, and Hooker; and Bragg had been routed at Missionary Ridge and driven back to Dalton. This calamity made everything else seem insignificant to Richmond. Bragg resigned on December 2, and Hardee was left temporarily in command of the Army of Tennessee. On the sixteenth General Johnston was ordered to turn over his command to General Polk and proceed to Dalton and take charge there. This change in the command produced the usual confusion, and no immediate action was taken to supply Forrest's wants.

He repeated his call on the eighteenth for one hundred thousand dollars for the paymaster and one hundred and fifty thousand dollars for his quartermaster. He wrote Johnston that he had already spent twenty thousand dollars of his private funds, and to inform him of the need for quick action he said, "From the movements of the enemy I am of opinion they are preparing to move against me, and that they will do so by the twenty-fifth instant or soon thereafter.

"I shall have at least one thousand head of beef-cattle ready to move south by that time, and I write to ask that General Ferguson's and General Chalmers's brigades be sent up without delay to aid in taking the cattle out and meeting any expedition of the enemy against me. I can collect together in two or three days at least one hundred thousand pounds of bacon, and if wagons are sent over with the troops asked for, will load them out with bacon. . . General Roddy has written me that he would move in from Tuscumbia at any time to my assistance. I will have boats prepared for crossing the Hatchie at Estenaula and will have forage gotten up and ready for them. (Ferguson and Chalmers.)"

He wrote directly to Lee for assistance, for "you are aware that with my force of raw, undrilled, and undisciplined troops it will not do for me to risk a general engagement with a superior force. I have been gathering up the cattle and will, I fear, have to abandon them unless I get your assistance."

Time grew precious, and he got no reply to these letters; so he started Colonel Russell on his way with twelve hundred of the raw, unarmed troops. Russell was directed to arm himself; then return with the equipment for the rest of the men. By taking unused byways and by traveling only at night Russell eluded the enemy, marched near and through Purdy, east of Corinth, back to Iuka, and on to Pontotoc.

Stevenson reported this to Hurlbut on the eigthteenth and closed with "Part of Roddy's command yesterday were on the other side of the Tennessee River driving cattle and hogs in direction of East Port; they were just below Savannah. The beef and hogs were for Bragg's army. You certainly underestimate Forrest's strength. I am most outrageously imposed upon by my scouts if his force does not approximate five thousand." Russell's escape right under Stevenson's nose was a sort of "rebel gas" which should have been a warning to Hurlbut.

Both the Northern and Southern scouts had been unusually active and accurate, with this difference: Forrest's men had been more consistently accurate. And Hurlbut's spies worked at a disadvantage. The General's men were scattered in the deep, confusing bottoms, or in the heaviest part of upland forests in small detachments of twenty-five or thirty each. For weeks they bivouacked under the rude shelter of shebangs, a pole resting on two forks, over which a blanket or captured oilcloth was stretched. The conscripts ordered to these places were well guarded by the volunteers.

But the complacency of the Northern generals was at last thoroughly disturbed. Grant had sent Smith 5,500 men in one week. He had directed his Chief of Cavalry, Sookey Smith, to take two divisions and make "a heavy raid through Mississippi, to free that state entirely, if possible, of cavalry." Hurlbut wrote on the nineteenth, "I think we shall cure Forrest of his ambition to command West Tennessee."

He had good reason to believe he possessed the cure. Smith, so strongly reënforced, was moving down from Union City with a body of mixed troops, 7,500 strong. From below he had divided Grierson's cavalry division, three thousand, into two parts. One part was moving from Corinth, by way of Purdy, to Jackson; the other part from La Grange, by way of Bolivar, to Jackson. The first body was supported by a brigade of infantry under Mower; the other by a brigade under Morgan.

When these various columns gathered dangerously near, Forrest gave orders for his command to assemble in Jackson. He had waited until the last minute for the promised arms. In his front the Hatchie River, rising about Bolivar, flowed west and emptied into the Mississippi above Fort Pillow. Near the Northern garrisons the Wolf, also rising near Bolivar, swept in the same direction and fell into the Mississippi above Memphis. Their swollen waters added to the peril of his position.

His young boys piled out of the bottoms into the town. They were as gay, as self-confident, as if the war had just begun. They knew nothing about Hurlbut's dispositions and cared less. They knew Old Bedford could "whup" the boots off "ary" man alive. Jackson itself reflected their mood. The ladies sent word there was to be a farewell dance in the courthouse that night.

But all of Forrest's men couldn't be there to "dossy-do" or to swing corners. Old Bedford's orders were falling thick and fast. Early that morning he sent Richardson to Estenaula. There, scuttled and sunk in the Hatchie, was a frail ferryboat. Richardson had orders to raise it, cross the river, and hold a position on the other side until the main body of recruits and the train arrived. About the same time Colonel Prince, of Grierson's command, was sweeping west with five hundred men. He was looking for the ferry too. Richardson had only three hundred who were armed.

Jeff Forrest's regiment, reduced to one hundred and fifty, had arrived at Jackson under Lieutenant-Colonel Wisdom's command. In the afternoon Forrest ordered him, McDonald's battalion, and a detachment of Kentuckians, about five hundred in all, to move southeast and hold Meisner of Mower's command in check until Jackson was completely evacuated.

This left Bell's men, the train, Morton's section of artillery, and the escort in Jackson. All but the escort had orders to march at dawn.

The ladies had been as busy as the men. Fires on the kitchen hearths had been going at full blast. The kettles sizzled, the ovens filled with cake batter were set in the ashes and covered with hot coals; the whites of eggs foamed; red whiskey poured into the yolks and cooked them for the nog. By evening all was ready. The square was lighted by bonfires and pine torches. The courthouse had been cleared, the candles lit.

The fiddles were tuned, the bows drawn across the strings, and a loud vibrant voice called the partners to their places. Some treaded the Virginia reel; others treaded through the mazes of a quartet, but most every trooper favored the square dance. The fiddles whined, the prompter called the figgers, the floor shook, and the booted feet swung corners, set to partners, circled to the left, until the east was gray with dawn. A clear bugle call, "Boots and Saddles," brought the rhythmic tromp to an end; and before the sun was an hour high Bell with the train, the recruits, and the artillery was on the road to Estenaula, eighteen miles away. Last of all, the General, staff and escort pulled out about six o'clock that evening.

Just as the dance came to an end, Colonel Wisdom surprised Meisner at Mifflin, fifteen miles southeast of Jackson. The enemy rallied, and the fighting was brisk all day. In the charge Major Phil Allen was unhorsed. Private Argyl Powell saw his embarrassment and called out, "Wait a moment, Major. I'll bring one from the Yankees yonder!" In a short while he rode back with a fine horse and its rider. "Here's the horse I promised you, Major, and a Yankee to boot."

But Meisner soon drew out his line and enveloped the much shorter Southern line. Wisdom then retreated in the direction of the Hatchie. Major Allen covered the rear with McDonald's battalion. The enemy did not follow, but withdrew to Purdy. Colonel Wisdom had served the purpose for which he had been sent. There was no rear attack on the trains.

In the meantime, Richardson had crossed the Hatchie at Estenaula about one P. M., the twenty-fourth, just in time to meet Colonel Prince from Bolivar. Prince was a vigorous officer, and he got to work at once. He drove in Richardson's advance and prepared for a charge. Richardson, to forestall him, lined up the men who were armed and made a counterattack; but, in face of a larger number, his men wavered and fell back in confusion. Neely, one of his colonels, covered the retreat at the river crossing. Prince followed, but he did not attempt the second position. The sun went down. He drew off in the direction of Summerville. Neely sent a detachment to reconnoitre his movements. It was now Christmas eve and a full moon rose, bright and clear, shedding almost the light of day on the river.

The General arrived with his escort and crossed the Hatchie about dark. He learned that Prince had gone into camp some distance ahead near Miller's house. He ordered sergeant Boone to take ten men from the escort, move down the road, and ride through everything until he found something solid. In a few minutes he followed with the rest of his escort; Richardson followed him; and Bell began the slow work of ferrying the train.

About two miles from the Hatchie, Sergeant Boone dug his spurs into his critter, rode over the first picket, pellmell into the reserve, forty strong. He and his ten men were going with such speed "We could not check up in time to avoid a collision even had we so desired. Taken by surprise, and evidently thinking we were more numerous than we really were they also broke and ran towards their main camp. We soon saw, just in our front, their camp fires scattered on both sides of the road, and slowed up for a minute or two, until General Forrest arrived with the balance of the escort under command of Lieutenant Nathan Boone."

Forrest ordered Lieutenant Boone (the Sergeant's brother) to reconnoitre with the entire escort while he went back to bring up Richardson. "As we moved forward to the edge of the cornfield towards the enemy's camp, Lieutenant Boone, with the reckless daring which was so characteristic of him, determined to take matters into his own hands, and, forming us into as long a line as we could be stretched into, there being about ten paces between each member of the escort, he told us he was going to charge into that camp, no matter what it cost; that he wanted each one of the lieutenants and sergeants to give orders as if commanding a company, and in as loud a voice as possible, and when all were ready he would give the order to charge. In the meantime we could see by their camp fires that they were in considerable disorder, trying to mount their horses and forming in line. At this moment Boone gave the order, 'Forward, brigade; Charge!' and we swept across the cornfield, making a tremendous racket. It was a clear, frosty night, and as our horses' feet trampled the cornstalks down they made noise enough, with the yells we were giving, to represent at least a regiment. The Federals evidently believed that we were upon them in force, for they broke and ran in great disorder. We dashed through the camp, and though many of us would have liked to have stopped and helped ourselves from the pots of meat that were on the fire, we kept on after the enemy. It must have been at least two miles beyond the camp before the pursuit was stopped."

The weather was intensely cold, and the freezing mud and water almost unbearable, but, under the inspiring eye of Colonel Bell, the frail ferry made all that night regular trips back and across the Hatchie. Forty wagons and their teams were transferred to the other bank, two hundred head of beef cattle, three hundred hogs, and the recruits. Only one wagon of bacon was lost. It tumbled into the river, and the icy water closed forever over its driver and its team. Colonel Wisdom finally brought up the rear, after riding thirty miles in eight hours. By noon on Christmas day, Forrest's entire command had crossed safely the first formidable barrier.

Most of the troopers were allowed to rest during the afternoon, but not the scouts. They reported that Prince was at Summerville with a force increased to seven hundred and fifty. At Bolivar there was a body one thousand strong, as many at Middleburg on Mississippi Central; other troops were massed on the Memphis and Charleston east of Moscow. At La Grange three trains were filled with infantry. The steam was kept up, the engines ready at an instant to move in either direction. Hurlbut had ordered all the bridges destroyed from Moscow to Memphis. He now had Forrest between the rivers. The Hatchie was behind him, the Wolf to his front. Around Corinth, where the streams were shallow, Hurlbut had massed. He expected Forrest to break through in this direction, because further west the Wolf, slow-moving and sullen, was no longer spanned by bridges.

Forrest's veterans were alert: his recruits did not know the facts, but some information sifted down through their ranks. They grew nervous. That afternoon, marching orders were given. The direction was Summerville.

Richardson's brigade was stronger now by fresh recruits. Forrest ordered him to move southeast, then at the proper moment turn west and take Prince in flank, while he with the escort, McDonald's battalion, and Wisdom's men, moved directly on Summerville by the Memphis Road. The train, the cattle, hogs, and a large body of recruits followed under Bell. It was understood there was to be no let-up, night or day.

Richardson bivouacked that night at Whiteville before the great, blazing fires of the town, in their warm beds, and at their tables. This put his command in good humor. Next day, on the Bolivar road, he ran into Prince withdrawing from Summerville. According to orders, he avoided an engagement. He skirmished at long range with his riflemen, while the unarmed men were hidden behind a hill.

Five miles away, Forrest heard the firing to the south. He turned in that direction and pressed down the hard-frozen pike at such a gait that he arrived in Prince's rear with little more than one hundred and fifty men. These let out a yell as he ordered the charge. At the same time Colonel Greer formed Richardson's unarmed men on a hill, and they charged with a shout. Prince, deceived by numbers, gave way. The escort struck hard and fast. Sergeant Boone was killed; his brother, the Lieutenant, was wounded. Harry Rhodes, a seventeen-year-old private, ordered three of Prince's troopers to surrender. They turned on him; a ball crashed his underjaw, and he was thrown to the ground. They beat him over the head with their pistols until he appeared either insensible or dead. Then, watching from the corner of his eye for the right moment, the boy sprang to his feet and killed two of the men and captured the third.

Prince broke so rapidly that he left behind seven dead, thirty wounded, and eighty captured. He lost his train of six wagons, loaded with subsistence and ammunition, one ambulance, and one hundred horses and mules. In the pursuit of a party of these fugitives, one of Forrest's officers, as he was about to turn back shouted after them, "Get out of our country, you worthless rascals." In the rear of the Northerners, on a horse slower than the rest, a trooper turned and in the brogue of his country called back, "Faith, and by Jasus, an't that same we're trying to do jist as fast as we can?"

Gathering his booty together, Forrest now moved through Summerville and bivouacked that night six miles westward, at Whitehall. Bell made connection with the train and went into camp at the same time. If Forrest made his escape, it would have to be done the next day. He must decide that night where he would break through.

The next morning early, Grierson had his patrols out in all directions between Corinth and Moscow. They were very alert. The trains still puffed their steam, but no orders came to move. Hours passed, and Forrest did not make his appearance where the enemy had expected him. Then at last he was discovered moving towards La Grange, but when Grierson attempted to wire the news, he found the wire was cut.

It was cut, and for a very good reason. Forrest was not where he seemed to be. What seemed to be Forrest was a body of two hundred gray riders sent especially to throw Grierson off the scent while he crossed the Wolf—in the unexpected direction of Memphis. Colonel Logwood had discovered, while recruiting near the river, that the bridge at La Fayette had only been partially destroyed by fire and that it had been reclaimed by a Northern officer. The floor boards only had been removed, and they were piled on the southern bank under the protection of a small fort.

So, at dawn on the twenty-seventh, Forrest divided his force into three parts. He sent Faulkner, guided by Major Strange, with seven hundred recruits directly on Memphis. Within four miles of the city they were to cross over the Raleigh Ferry, make a feint on the town, then sweep south as fast as they could go. Bell took two hundred veterans and the other body of recruits and left for La Fayette with orders to seize the bridge. Forrest took personal charge of the train.

Several hours later, Bell, under cover of a deep woods, crept close to the water's edge; then gave the order to charge. His men rushed forward with a yell, tripped across the bridge timbers, and drove the enemy out of the fort. He relaid the flooring, and the recruits marched over. He sent fifty men moving in the direction of Moscow to make a show of pursuit. They came upon a trainload of troops moving in their direction, fired upon it, and forced it to reverse its wheels. The track was torn up on either side of the bridge.

The bridge was taken at eleven o'clock in the morning. By four P. M. Forrest appeared with the train, his cattle and hogs, and his recruits. They were quickly thrown across and sent with orders to march all night for Holly Springs, by way of Mount Pleasant. When Grierson recovered from his surprise, he wired Major Coon, "Forrest has gone south like hell."

But Old Bedford was not as far away as Grierson thought. He knew that his heavy train was still in great danger. The Coldwater and the Tallahatchie were still to his front, and to be crossed. The fair Christmas weather had not continued: for twelve hours it had been raining. This helped, however, to cover his tracks and to hide his weakness.

So with his escort, three hundred men, and the artillery, he attacked Collierville with vigor. He sent another detail to make a feint on Moscow. The detail had orders to break towards Memphis and draw in that direction all enemy troops away from his train. He left at La Fayette some of his older men to pretend they were farmers and further delude the pursuing columns. His Chief Engineer, Captain Mann, was fortunately captured. He gave out the information that General Lee had joined Forrest.

In the meantime, it had ceased to rain; and, the wind changing to the north, the weather turned freezing cold. Forrest now followed his train and withdrew through Holly Springs. He reached Como by short, slow marches. Faulkner and Strange arrived the first day of the new year without the loss of a man.

Colonel Morgan, one of Grierson's supports, reached Mount Pleasant on the twenty-ninth. He sent forward an advance; then prepared his brigade to continue the pursuit. But his preparations were without spirit, because as he said in his report, "Forrest is certainly far away."

Forrest was indeed far away, and he always would be far away when he had pitted against him such commanders as Hurlbut. He summed the matter up with characteristic brevity. "Whenever I met one of them fellows who fit by note, I generally whipped hell out of him before he pitched the tune."

CHAPTER XVI

"Sookey" Smith Does Not Reach Sherman

THE Wizard of the Saddle had again done the unexpected and the impossible. At this stage of the war, when Southern desertions were crippling all the armies in the field, Forrest, almost alone, had moved through the Sixteenth Army Corps and raised in *twenty-one days* four thousand two hundred men and plenty to feed them. No such confidence had been shown in any leader, Lee not excepted, since a nervous hand had set off the gun at Sumter.

Bu. Forrest had worked too fast for his friends; so he had not been able to hold West Tennessee. At the same time he had worked too fast for his enemies, for he had brought out this mob of recruits when there had been no more than eight hundred arms in the entire body. He would never again combine in any operation such skill, daring, and luck, although he would be skillful, daring, and blessed with luck. His contempt for Hurlbut, Grierson, and their subordinates filled these generals with shame and respect. They tacitly admitted they were now on the defensive.

Forrest spent the month of January organizing his command. It was divided into four brigades: Richardson's, fifteen hundred strong; McCulloch's, sixteen hundred; Bell's, two thousand; Jeff Forrest's, one thousand, making a total of some 6,000 of all arms. McCulloch and Jeff Forrest were formed in a division under Chalmers. His commission of major-general reached him, and he was formally assigned to the Department of West Tennessee and North Mississippi. He asked Richmond to revoke all previous authority given to officers to raise troops, so that he might combine the numerous detachments into companies. The permission was granted, and General Polk saw to it that he got his arms and ordinance supplies.

But there was discontent. Too many had desired commissions, and there were not enough warm blankets and winter clothing. Desertions followed. Men left in large squads. He sent his veterans in pursuit, and they brought many back; but the task was difficult. It took all the peculiar genius of Forrest's nature to make the freest men on earth content with military discipline. Most of them were young boys, but some were deserters from other armies. There were squads of bushwhackers, partisan groups, and men who early in the war had decided they couldn't kill all the Yankees anyway and had left for home. There were gentlemen, with and without classical education. There were the reckless tavern loafers, and the plain men. Finally the issue came to a head one day when nineteen marched off in a body.

These were quickly captured and brought into camp. Forrest gave orders for their execution. Their coffins were made, the graves dug, and they were told to make their peace with their Maker and the world. The ladies of Oxford, the clergy, all petitioned the General to spare their lives. Some of his officers hinted at mutiny. But he was firm. He would make an example of them.

On the day set Bell's brigade, mounting and moving out into a large field, was formed in line on three sides of a hollow square. The culprits, blindfolded and seated on their coffins, occupied the center of the other side. Behind each coffin was a grave, flanked by a mound of fresh, red dirt. The firing squad in position, the condemned were ordered to rise. There was a moment of silence; then sharply the voice of the commanding officer—"Present arms! Make ready! Take aim . . ."

Then the noise of a galloping horse. A staff officer pulled up and stopped the proceedings. He turned to the culprits. "General Forrest has requested me to say to you that it is unpleasant to him to shed blood in this manner, and that, through the petitions of the clergy, the prominent citizens of Oxford and your officers, if you will now promise to make good and faithful soldiers, he will pardon you."

There were nineteen loud shouts, "We will! We will!" This was followed by a louder cheer from the entire brigade. But the lesson was not lost. All believed that next time he would not be so lenient.

His headquarters were at Oxford, and his troops were scattered from Panola east, behind the Tallahatchie. Since he had taken charge in North Mississippi, General Ferguson's brigade was moved south into Lee's territory. But Ferguson had one regiment, the Second Tennessee under Barteau, who had applied to serve under Forrest. They felt that if they moved south, they would never see home again during the war and they knew Old Bedford expected to spend a great deal of time in Tennessee. Sergeant Hancock reported in his diary their anxiety. "The brigade was to start south the next morning. Dark came, yet no transfer. 'What will we do?' 'Colonel Barteau, can you not help us out of this trouble?' 'Don't despair, men, perhaps we will be transferred yet.'

"Eight, nine, and ten o'clock came, and yet no transfer. Some lay down to rest, though, perhaps, too much troubled to sleep. Finally, about eleven o'clock 'The Second Tennessee is transferred to Forrest' spread like lightning through the camp. Those who had been trying in vain to while away the time in sleep now sprang from their tents to unite with the rest in yelling, hallooing, shouting, and such another jollification as they had from then until daylight next morning had never been witnessed in the camp before. . . . We had no cannon by which we could give Ferguson a parting salute: however, some of the boys got up a right good substitute by boring holes in logs and filling with powder."

Forrest immediately ordered them into West Tennessee to destroy the Memphis and Charleston and to capture or drive the notorious Colonel Hurst out of the district. Colonel Barteau said in his notes: "This seemed more like work than anything we had been commanded to do from the battle of Corinth, under Van Dorn, up to that time; and the regiment, feeling that a more glorious career was foreshadowed, undertook, with a new vigor, the fulfillment of this order." But Barteau's work was not done. He ran into a heavy body of cavalry concentrating under General "Sookey" Smith.

Even after it was clear that Forrest had made more than a "maraud" in West Tennessee, Sherman wrote to Admiral Porter—"Forrest is not hurting us . . . I propose to strike at large armies and large interests, and let the smaller ones work out their salvation."

He was now about to strike at one of his "large interests." He proposed to take four divisions, about twenty thousand men, march directly east from Vicksburg to Meridian, destroy the Confederate railroads, burn their supplies, and wreak havoc generally. He had given General "Sookey" Smith seven thousand of the best Northern cavalry in the service, twenty guns, excellent mounts, and efficient officers—and orders to march from Collierville into the rich prairie country and join him at Meridian. It seemed practicable, they would then march together towards Selma and the heart of the Confederacy, or turn south and reduce Mobile. He explained to Smith just the kind of officer Forrest was, for he assured Smith that he would certainly meet him on his march. His explanation went into detail—into too much detail.

North Mississippi was basically a red-clay country. It was largely a country of the plain people. The plantations were few in comparison with the Delta, for the cultivated land was chiefly the highlands, sufficient for a homestead, but not for a large establishment. The hills were surrounded with low forests and swamps. In wet weather the country was difficult.

The dividing line between the hill and flat country was Okolona, the Indian for Queen of the Prairie. The Prairie produced corn in such abundance that it was called Egypt Land. Along the Mobile and Ohio Railroad there were hundreds of bins filled with corn for the armies of the Confederacy. Each bin belonged to a farmer, and it was his duty to keep it filled at fixed times. Besides, the depots were crammed with meal, bacon, white beans, and hundreds of thousands of bushels of corn in the shuck. And in the flat, black soil thousands of acres of corn were standing in the fields, brown and frozen. Two streams, the Tombigbee River and the Sookatoncha Creek, bound together this granary. The "Bigbee River" flowed north from Columbus; the Sookatoncha, northwest. Meeting near Columbus, they formed a perfect cul-de-sac into which any army might be drawn. Forrest knew this.

Sherman began his march on February 3, and he reached Meridian on the fourteenth without much opposition. He had expected to find Smith there, as he had ordered this general to march on the first. But the cavalry detachment did not start until the eleventh, a day after it should have been at Meridian. Smith had delayed, waiting for Waring's brigade to come from Columbus, Kentucky.

With an infantry brigade Smith made a feint on Forrest's front around Wyatt and Abbeville, then swung east and marched through Holly Springs, New Albany, Pontotoc, and so on to Okolona, which place he reached by the eighteenth. Here he began a systematic destruction of the supplies, the road, gin houses, cotton, barns, and dwellings. Escaped slaves, mounted on their masters' stock, flocked to him to the number of three thousand. Then he turned south, towards West Point.

Forrest was not confused by the feint on his front at Abbeville. He ordered Chalmers to move from Oxford to Houston and keep on Smith's flank, while he dropped back to Grenada and crossed the country with Bell, his escort, and the artillery to Starkville. He reached this position the same day Smith began his destruction around Okolona. Jeff Forrest's brigade had already been sent ahead, across the Sookatoncha to Aberdeen. It was now Forrest's purpose to hold the enemy between the two streams until Stephen Lee could arrive from the south. General Polk wrote Lee that Forrest was in high spirits.

Jeff Forrest began skirmishing around Aberdeen and fell back slowly towards West Point, almost the point of the cul-de-sac. The General made his dispositions. He ordered Barteau, now commanding Bell's brigade, to cross the "Bigbee" at Columbus, move up the stream to Aberdeen and prevent Smith from crossing to the east bank. At daybreak, the twentieth, Forrest, himself, left Starkville with Mc-Culloch's brigade, his escort, and six hundred of Richardson's men under Neely. He arrived at Ellis's bridge at two P. M. In its front, Colonel Forrest was skirmishing heavily.

To the right of the Northern advance spread the Sookatoncha swamp, to the left the Oktibbeha swamp. Both were soaking, as it was the rainy season. By the road which Forrest had moved the Sooka-toncha could be crossed only at Ellis's bridge, the only approach to it being over a long, narrow, thrown-up causeway, while the banks of the stream on either side were miry and steep. Forrest pushed across; then retreated over the bridge. It was not his purpose to fight yet. He was waiting for Lee.

That night he took McCulloch's brigade and galloped to Siloam, four miles higher up the creek, where it was reported the enemy had crossed. He found the detachment by the light of a building they had fired—a small body of the Fourth Regulars. He captured twenty-three and killed a few others; and afterwards returned.

Nightfall found all of his forces, except Bell's brigade, stationed along the west bank of the creek, the head of Smith's column at and around West Point, and Barteau throwing Bell's brigade to the west bank of the Tombigbee, near Waverly, some twelve miles east of West Point.

The next morning Jeff Forrest's brigade was thrown back across the bridge, and he was soon engaged in another heavy skirmish with Major Coon of Smith's advance General Chalmers, seated upon his horse, had taken a position on the south bank of the creek, near the bridge. He said, "I had considerable curiosity to observe General Forrest, but up to nine o'clock that morning he had not appeared upon the scene. Suddenly, out of a cloud of dust, accompanied by an orderly, he came dashing up the road towards the bridge. As he approached me and reined up his horse, I noticed that his face was greatly flushed, and that he seemed very much more excited than I thought was nec-essary under the circumstances. In rather a harsh, quick tone he asked

me what the condition of affairs was at the front. As I had not been
on the firing-line, and did not know anything definite excepting that
the firing indicated quite a severe skirmish, I replied that Colonel
Forrest had reported nothing to me beyond the fact that there was
some skirmishing going on at the front, and added that I thought it
was not a very severe affair. Forrest said quickly, and with evident
impatience: 'Is that all you know? Then I'll go and find out for
myself.'

"It was about four hundred yards from the bridge to where Jeffrey
Forrest was in line, and a portion of the Federal advance had now
reached a position where their shots were falling pretty thick in the
road, and where they could readily fire at anyone crossing on the
bridge. Even as we were conversing, the bullets were falling about us,
and I thought, even there, we were unnecessarily exposed; but as
General Forrest and his orderly dashed across the bridge (it seemed
to me then in a spirit of bravado), I followed him, more out of
curiosity to observe him than for any definite purpose.

"As we galloped over the bridge and up the road, the enemy's
skirmishers singled us out and commenced firing directly at us. We
had proceeded not more than a hundred yards in the direction of the
skirmishers when I noticed, coming at full tilt towards us from that
direction a Confederate soldier, who, dismounted and hatless, had
thrown away his gun and everything else that could impede his rapid
flight to the rear. He was badly demoralized and evidently panic-
stricken. As he approached General Forrest, the latter checked up his
horse, dismounted quickly, threw the bridle-reins to the orderly who
accompanied him, and rushing at the demoralized soldier, seized him
by the collar, threw him down, dragged him to the side of the road,
and picking up a piece of brush that was convenient, proceeded to give
him one of the worst thrashings I have ever seen a human being get.
The terror and surprise of the frightened Confederate at this unexpected turn in affairs, at a point where he thought he had reached
safety, were as great as to me they were laughable. He offered no resistance, and was wise in this discretion, for the General was one of
the most powerful men I ever saw, and could easily have whipped him
in a free-for-all encounter. At last he turned him loose, faced him again
in the direction of his comrades, and thundered at him: 'Now, God-
damn you, go back to the front and fight: you might as well be killed
there as here, for if you ever run away again, you will not get off so

easy.' . . . the news of this incident spread rapidly through the command and even through the Southern army, and, almost as soon, it appeared in one of the Northern periodicals of this time, which came out in illustrated form, and was entitled, 'Forrest breaking in a conscript.' "

Smith had expressed himself as being anxious to "pitch into Forrest wherever he found him," and now at last, he was where he could gratify his wish. But instead of pitching in, he began to think about Sherman's description of Forrest and the more he thought, the weaker grew his resolution to advance. He inspected the swamps and found them alive with rebels. He learned from "deserters" that Forrest's numbers had miraculously increased; that Lee was on his way to add others. He forgot what Sherman had told him, that all the Southern cavalry in the state would be less than his seven thousand. And finally, out of his picked troops, he found "there was but one of my brigades that I could rely upon with full confidence." So he decided that since he had got such a late start, even if he should manage to reach Meridian, Sherman would have no use for him. He gave orders to retire.

Shortly after Old Bedford had "broken in his conscript," he noticed the enemy withdrawing from his brother's front without apparent cause. He concluded that Smith was withdrawing to turn his flank farther east. Sending back to Chalmers, he ordered that officer "to send him two of the best companies in his division to make a forced reconnaissance." Captain Tyler reported with one hundred and fifty Kentuckians.

The General ordered Tyler to follow the enemy and find out what direction he was taking. The escort had heard their commander's order; and they overlooked Tyler's men as they rode up to report. Some of them growled out in disgust and contempt—"Jesus Christ, those are the Kentucky Go-rillers. They won't fight." Colonel McCulloch was near by, and he called back,—"Go with them one time and see."

Tyler was soon galloping north near West Point, he captured a few of the enemy, found out Smith was retreating, and sent a courier to Forrest. Six miles beyond West Point, Smith made a stand at the end of two open fields lining both sides of a lane and just in rear of a heavy woods. Tyler halted his two companies under cover to the south of one of the fields. Soon the Kentuckians heard a bugle sounding the charge. Looking around, they saw Old Bedford at the head of his escort, its flag stiff with the wind, bugle blowing, the General himself well in the lead, bearing down in a sweeping gallop upon the mouth of the lane.

Tyler formed in column and swung in line. "It is death, General, to attempt to go through that lane." His commander snapped, "Fall in behind and follow me." "No," said Tyler, "We will ride with you, but we will not ride far." But Old Bedford knew more about war than his captain. They rode far enough to make the enemy fall back.

"You appear to have a pretty good lot of boys with you," said Forrest, "and you handle them well. I will give you another lot— the best soldiers on earth, my escort under Lieutenant Thomas Tate. Follow up the enemy and harass their rear as you have been doing, and I'll hurry up Chalmers's Division."

Forrest then turned in a gallop and disappeared to the rear. Tyler inspected the escort critically. "Boys, let's see whether this escort is composed of crowing cocks, or fighting cocks."

Together they drove Smith from Watkins's place to the cotton gin on Evans place, where a full regiment had made a stand. Tyler flanked them out of position, and it became a race for the mouth of Randle's Lane a half mile away. Galloping in column eight abreast, it looked as if Tyler would head them off—when a terrific volley not fifty feet from the lane, from behind a snake fence and snakier timber, brought him to a sharp halt.

The fire was too heavy for men to stand, and Tyler was on the verge of ordering a retreat, when above the roar of battle he heard a familiar voice, "Close in with your revolvers, Tyler, I am here."

It was Old Bedford, charging down the road with sabre drawn, full thirty feet ahead of McCulloch's brigade. McCulloch dismounted and followed him and Tyler across a narrow, slippery causeway and bridge spanning a *slash* which could not be turned. The fighting was terrific. Forrest killed a man in personal combat, but the four thousand Northern riders had orders to withdraw; and they did so, followed by one thousand of the butternuts. The pursuit was called off in the night, and Forrest bivouacked in the Northern camp, filled with fodder and pots of meat fourteen miles south of Okolona.

In the meantime, by eight o'clock in the morning Barteau had crossed Bell's brigade to the west bank of the Tombigbee; and all day he had swept forward on the enemy's left flank. That night he went into camp near Egypt Station with a brigade reduced to some twelve hundred men. His bold movements had much to do with Smith's steady withdrawal, although he had been in an exposed position all day and open to destruction.

At three o'clock the next morning he was again in the saddle and, as the Northerners were rushing through Okolona, he took a position in the open Prairie about three-fourths of a mile southeast of the railroad running through that town. He gradually advanced his line until he was six hundred yards from the railroad.

Forrest was also in the saddle at an early hour. He divided his two brigades. He sent his brother on a left-hand road with orders to move quickly over to the Pontotoc road and cut off Smith's retreat. McCulloch was ordered to follow directly into Okolona. Forrest himself swept ahead with his staff and escort to discover the condition of affairs in front.

He soon made contact with the Fourth Regulars and drove them into Okolona. Smith had already retired his First Brigade and the Second. The third Brigade was formed in line across the Prairie to protect the Fourth Regulars on its extreme right. Smith ordered the Seventh Indiana to reënforce the Regulars. Grierson was on the field and in charge.

About this time Forrest made his appearance and took in the situation. Before him Barteau's thin line was stretched across the open Prairie with the enemy overlapping both his flanks. It was a moment of great peril. He threw the escort upon the flank and rear of the Regulars; then galloped around the town to Barteau's position. He arrived in advance of his staff. The anxious Tennesseans saw him. Sergeant Hancock wrote that "the effect was profound. Every countenance irradiated with confidence, courage, and enthusiasm, which found immediate expression in loud cheers and prolonged shouts of mingled joy and defiance, in recognition of which Forrest lifted his hat and politely bowed to us as he passed our front, from left to right, at a gallop, saying mildly, "Mount your horses."

His only question to Barteau was, "Where is the enemy's whole position?"

"You see it, general, and they are preparing to charge."

"Then we will charge them," he said.

In a moment the three regiments were wheeled into column of platoons, and they dashed into Okolona by two different streets. Within one hundred and fifty yards of the enemy the Southerners began firing with their long guns. But the breech-loading rifles of Grierson's men were more effective, and Barteau's brigade staggered.

Seeing this, Forrest dismounted Wilson's and Russell's regiments and ordered them to charge on foot. He placed himself at the head of the Second Tennessee, mounted, and called out "come on, boys." As he expressed it later "I saw Grierson make a bad move, and I rode right over him."

Grierson's bad move was on his right. He detached a regiment to go to the rear to the assistance of the Fourth Regulars. The regiment made a tactical error and Forrest acted upon it before it could recover. The Fourth Regulars, the Seventh Indiana, and the third Tennessee (Union) broke and left the field in confusion. In a few moments, Wilson and Russell struck that part of the line that had held, and it melted into the general rout. The flight of the Third Brigade and parts of the Second crowded a battery of five guns into a ditch. Lieutenant Curtis of the artillery reported, "We had not proceeded very far from Okolona when we were unexpectedly surprised by the presence of flying cavalry on both sides of us. They were in perfect confusion; some hallooing, 'Go ahead, or we will be killed!' while some few showed a willingness to fight."

Colonel Waring, with his brigade five miles west of Okolona, received a message from the rear informing him of the disaster and ordering him to form and fortify the first available position. "I formed my brigade in line, with skirmishers far out on each flank, and remained until the Third brigade had passed through, portions of it in such confusion as to endanger the morale of my own command." Waring then retired to a stronger position called Ivey's Farm.

At Okolona, Forrest used the identical tactics Frederick the Great had used at Leuthen and Zorndorf, with this difference: his battle order had been spontaneous. In the pursuit, the regiments became intermingled; so the brigade was halted and re-formed. McCulloch and Jeff Forrest now came up, their movement incomplete because of the muddy roads.

Waring's position was on the crest of a ridge which sloped down into the marshes of the Talaboncla Swamp. The Federals were drawn up in two formidable lines, behind the houses of Ivey's plantation, rail fences and scrub oak timber. Jeff Forrest's brigade, reënforced by Russell's regiment from Bell's brigade, received orders to charge to the right, McCulloch to the left. They were to move forward in column until within three hundred yards of the enemy, then change into line. McCulloch galloped down the road to take position; and, as his men swung by Jeff Forrest's brigade, thinking they were to go into action first, they jeered unmercifully. But at the sound of the bugle, both columns galloped forward together.

The attack was furious, and the two brigades carried the first line; but the fire from the second was terrific. It cut great holes in the Southern ranks, and it dropped the officers from their horses. Colonel Jeff Forrest fell to the ground with a bullet through his neck, not more than fifty yards from the enemy. The General was informed; and he rushed to the spot, leaped to the ground, and picked up his brother in his arms. Words tumbled from his mouth. Colonel Russell saw that "the moment was too sacred for angry passion to have sway, and catching its inspiration I ordered the men to cease firing, that all might join in sympathy with the suffering general." The enemy took advantage of this calm to withdraw.

In a few moments, Forrest was himself again. He mounted in stern silence, quickly but carefully overlooked the field, and shouted in a loud, hoarse voice to his favorite bugler, "Gaus, sound the charge!" He fell with his escort and his brother's brigade upon the mass of the retreating enemy with such fury that Major Strange thought Jeffrey's death had driven him to rash madness. Dr. Cowan said, "I had just reached the spot where Jeffrey Forrest was lying dead, when Major Strange said to me as I rode up, 'Doctor, hurry after the General; I am afraid he will be killed.' Putting spurs to my horse, I rode rapidly to the front, and in about a mile, as I rounded a short turn in the road, I came upon a scene which made my blood run cold."

Forrest and his escort, about sixty strong, had outridden all support and were, at the moment, in a hand-to-hand conflict with five hundred of the enemy. "Horrified at the situation," said Dr. Cowan, "I turned back down the road to see if help was at hand, and, as good fortune would have it, the head of McCulloch's brigade was coming in full sweep towards me." But when they saw the peril of their general, they hesitated. It seemed certain death to rush into the trap that had been drawn about him. McCulloch had been shot in his hand, and the bandage was red and dripping with blood. He raised it high above his head and shouted at the top of his voice, "My God, men, will you see them kill your General? I'll go to the rescue if not a man follows me!" He dashed forward, and the Missourians and Texans followed to a man.

But before they arrived Bedford Forrest with his own hand had killed three men. The enemy fought well; but the gray riders were fighting for the life of Old Bedford, and they gradually threw Smith's rear back to another strong position, reënforced by houses and fences. Forrest was soon upon them. As he passed to the front, he heard the cries of a Northern soldier. He rode up to the man and found that his surgeon had abandoned him, leaving the amputating saw caught in the marrow of his bone. He dashed a cloth of chloroform to his nostrils and ordered Cowan to complete the operation.

When Cowan rejoined him, he found him greatly exposed. "General, I think you should get out of the road; it is not right unnecessarily to expose yourself."

"Doctor, if you are alarmed, you may get out of the way. I am as safe here as there."

"At this moment," continued the doctor, "a piece of artillery which had not been observed opened upon us, and the General's horse fell dead. I dismounted at once and offered him my own, but he said, 'No, I will take Long's (calling to a member of his escort by name), and he can go to the rear.'"

But in a few minutes this horse was also shot, and its saddle shattered by five bullets. Again on foot, Forrest picked up a musket and, gathering a few men about him, charged through the back yard of a house. Then "King Phillip," a large gray gelding, was brought up. This horse, twelve years old, had gone through the Vicksburg campaign and had been given Forrest by the people of Columbus. Sluggish on ordinary occasions, he became superbly excited in battle and was as quick to detect the presence of a bluecoat as any of Old Bedford's riders. And he was as ready for battle. Whenever he saw the enemy, he lay back his ears, threw up his tail and, leaping forward across the field, snapped his teeth at anything blue.

The enemy again broke and crowded to the rear. They made their final stand on the northwest side of an open field. Here Forrest found them "in three lines . . . at intervals of a hundred paces, and the rear and second lines longer than the first. My ammunition was nearly exhausted, and I knew that if we faltered they in turn would become the attacking party, and disaster might follow. Many of my men were broken down and exhausted with climbing the hills on foot and fighting almost constantly for the last nine miles. I determined, therefore, to rely upon the bravery and courage of the few men I had, and advance to the attack." Only about three hundred men had kept up. With these he charged and then fell back behind a deep gully, banked with willows and running across the center of the field.

The first line of the enemy, the Fourth Regulars, dashed to within sixty yards of Forrest's position, broke, and re-formed to the rear. The second line, bugles blowing and men yelling, reached to within forty yards; but they, too, broke and fell back. But the third line dashed across the gully and charged the dismounted gray coats. Forrest's three hundred were now without ammunition; so they threw down their guns and drew their six-shooters, and with these repulsed as Forrest reported "one of the grandest cavalry charges I had ever witnessed." McCulloch had been forced to leave the field, but his brother came up at this time with the brigade; he captured some of the Regulars who had broken through and were in rear of Forrest's advance line.

Lieutenant Tate, of the escort, in personal combat with an enemy officer, was on the point of death, for his only weapon was an empty carbine. Just as the Northern officer was about to shoot him, Forrest rode up and, with a sweep of his sabre, almost severed the Northern officer's head from his shoulders. The man toppled to the ground. Tate grabbed his revolver as he was falling, swung into the empty saddle, and plunged into the battle.

This was the last fight of the retreat. General Gholson arrived with seven hundred state troops and kept up the pursuit, but Forrest's men were too exhausted to follow. In the engagements on the twentieth, the twenty-first, and the twenty-second, the Southern losses were: 27 killed, 97 wounded, and 20 missing,—total, 144. Smith's losses were, 54 killed, 179 wounded, and 155 missing—total, 388.

But the enemy's actual loss in men and material was slight in comparison with the great blow to his morale. Colonel Waring, commanding a brigade, said: "The retreat to Memphis was a weary, disheartening, and almost panic-stricken flight, in the greatest disorder and confusion, and through a most difficult country. The First Brigade reached its camping ground five days after the engagement, with the loss of all its heart and spirit, and nearly fifteen hundred fine cavalry horses. The expedition filled every man connected with it with burning shame, and gave Forrest the most glorious achievement of his career."

Sherman never forgave Smith. "I wanted to destroy General Forrest," he said, "who was constantly threatening Memphis and the river above, as well as our route of supplies in Middle Tennessee. In this we failed utterly, because General Smith, when he did start, allowed General Forrest to head him off and to defeat him with an inferior force near West Point, below Okolona." Sherman would never again refer to Old Bedford as "one of the smaller ones."

General "Sookey" Smith, as Forrest's men called him, did his best to explain to Sherman and the War Department in his report. He told of destroying two million bushels of corn, numerous dwellings, gins, public buildings, and other supplies; but it was evident to his superiors that he was trying to make his pen do, what his generalship had failed to do—make of his expedition a success. His case was very plain. He had been whipped by the name of Forrest, for he had had under him as fine a body of cavalry and mounted infantry as the Northerners had up to that time put in the field. They had been anxious to fight, and one of their brigadiers, Waring, was unafraid. But the fears of their commanders soon shook their self-confidence and turned a formidable body of troopers into a panic-stricken mob.

Forrest's raw soldiers fought well. The sight of the burning buildings stiffened their resolve. They were also anxious to behave well in Forrest's presence, and he was everywhere on the battle front. His command to Barteau's men, "Come on, boys," was significant, and it was one of the keys to his success on the field.

His command gained in morale what Smith's divisions had lost. It sustained his reputation of success. There is no way to measure in numbers and war material the value of such a commander's army, for its blade is double-edged. It makes such a leader's own people dare the impossible; and it places the enemy commander on the defensive, inclining his conduct to rashness or overcaution.

But General Stephen D. Lee was disappointed. He had hoped to take part in the fight. But General Polk was pleased at the turn of events, so pleased that he gave Forrest three depleted infantry regiments, seven hundred strong. They were Kentuckians, and only one-third arrived mounted. General Abe Buford came with them. Their arrival allowed Forrest to reorganize his corps into two divisions: Chalmers's and Buford's. But many of the Kentuckians and some of his other men lacked horses. Richmond informed him they had none to issue; so he decided to go where he had always gone for his mounts— to the enemy.

CHAPTER XVII

Holding West Tennessee for the Confederacy

GRANT was made a lieutenant-general and placed in charge of all the armies of the North. He transferred his headquarters to Meade's army to take direct charge of the Army of the Potomac and crush Lee. He left to Sherman the command in the West. It was his duty to drive Johnston back to Atlanta. By disposing of Lee and Johnston, Grant hoped to bring the war to a close. The operations of the Northern forces had now one head; the South's control was still divided into feudal departments.

But if the military situation of the North promised more decisive action, the political affairs of its government were none too good. Kentucky was beginning to realize that Lincoln's promises of slaves and the Union too were only promises. Their slaves were already gone, and the Union which the Kentuckians had cherished, they discovered, was not the Union they had been fighting for. When Kentucky and the other border states made this discovery, there was the rise of the Democratic Party and the talk of McClellan for President. Lincoln's party referred to them as the Copperheads. It soon became evident that unless Grant and Sherman won decisive victories, Lincoln could not be reëlected in the fall campaign; and the failure of his reëlection would mean very likely the triumph of the Confederacy. There was already strong evidence that the North was tired of the war. It had been expensive in men and treasure, and for all its recent victories there was, to the people of the North, no evidence that the South was weakening. It had lost territory, but its two principal armies, the Army of Northern Virginia and the Army of Tennessee, were still intact. Sherman's Meridian Expedition, where he began as a matter of policy to make war on the non-combatants, was a tacit admission that the Northern armies could not win primarily in the field.

At this time the right tactics for the South was a Fabian policy. Lee and Joe Johnston realized this, and they both prepared to wear out the patience of the North. To succeed they must impress Davis with their ideas. Davis had brought Bragg to Richmond and made him his military adviser.

Many of the Northern divisions had been furloughed. It was hoped they would return to the ranks with an added zeal for war, after reviving the enthusiasm at home. Their departure had necessarily weakened the forces in the field, particularly in West Tennessee.

It was about this time, March 15, that Forrest set out to mount his Kentucky brigade, to secure more supplies, and to get rid of the bushwhackers and armed deserters who were preying on the people. Before leaving, he relieved Chalmers and Richardson of their commands and ordered McCulloch to take charge of the First Division and remain in Mississippi and gather in the deserters there. He took with him Buford's Division, Bell's and Thompson's brigades, two thousand two hundred and fifty-eight rank and file, and the Seventh Tennessee Cavalry, McDonald's battalion, and his escort . . . altogether about twenty-eight hundred men.

On the twentieth he reached Jackson with the advance. On the twenty-second he moved towards Trenton with the Seventh Tennessee, his escort, and the Twelfth Kentucky. The next day he ordered Colonel Duckworth to take five hundred men and reduce Union City. With the rest of Buford's division he moved north, in the direction of Paducah.

Colonel Hawkins, who had surrendered to Forrest in '62, was in charge at Union City with a force equal to Duckworth's. This officer arrived and invested the place in the dark of the morning of the twenty-fourth. The light from a burning building soon convinced him that without artillery the position was too strong to carry. He skirmished heavily until ten o'clock; then decided to try a ruse. He had his men shout as if receiving reënforcements, while he dashed up with a group of officers, made a hasty inspection of the works; retired and sent forward a flag of truce demanding unconditional surrender, with the usual threat attached. Duckworth signed Forrest's name.

Colonel Hawkins asked to see the commander in person before he decided. This put Duckworth in a dilemma, for Forrest was by this time well on his way to Paducah. But he acted boldly. He rode forward and told Hawkins that Forrest was not in the habit of meeting with his inferiors in rank and that he had delegated his authority to Duckworth. While this was going on, some of the men had mounted a black log on the forewheels of a wagon, hitched two mules to it, and with a box fixed on the other wheels to serve as a caisson moved about some bushes as if looking for a suitable position for artillery. Hawkins was impressed by this and by Duckworth's conversation. He asked for time and was granted five minutes. Much to the chagrin of his men, he surrendered when help was near at hand. General Brayman, with two thousand men and a battery, had been stopped by a burned bridge only six miles away. He heard of the capitulation and returned in disgust to Columbus. In his report he said:

"I heard with great pain and surprise that Colonel Hawkins had surrendered at eleven A.M., and had, with his force, been removed, and his fortifications destroyed. The force of the enemy does not appear more than one-fourth the number reported (seven thousand), and without artillery. The number of men surrendered is probably five hundred (475), some seventy-five having escaped. All were armed and equipped; about three hundred mounted. . . . I learn that Colonel Hawkins's command had been recently paid for over a year's service, and that the aggregate of individual loss will reach some sixty thousand dollars."

The next day, after a hard ride of twenty-six miles, Forrest arrived in front of Paducah with Thompson's and Bell's brigades and a small battery of popguns. He quickly seized the town, drove the enemy into the fort, and demanded a surrender. But Colonel Hicks was a more determined man than Hawkins. He refused. Then, without orders, Colonel Thompson, and four hundred Kentuckians charged the works and were repulsed with heavy loss. Thompson was killed almost within sight of his home. His enthusiasm had been too great.

After holding the town for ten hours, burning a transport and cotton piled on the wharf, relieving the various warehouses of their supplies and the barns of their stock, Forrest gradually withdrew. Moving southward to Mayfield, he disbanded most of Buford's men and many of the West Tennesseans and allowed them to go to their homes, see their kin, improve their clothing and their mounts. His command was now well scattered over West Tennessee, Kentucky, and North Mississippi.

While on his way to Paducah, Forrest had sent orders to Chalmers, who had been reinstated in command of his division by Polk, to send the First Brigade under Neely into West Tennessee. Neely met Hurst's partisans at Bolivar on the twenty-ninth and completely routed them. Chalmers, in a congratulatory address, told his soldiers that "Colonel

Neely . . . drove Hurst hatless into Memphis, leaving in our hands all his wagons, ambulances, papers, and his mistresses, both black and white." What was more important, he left behind fifty thousand rounds of ammunition. This small victory was a source of great satisfaction to the people of this part of the state. Hurst was a renegade Tennessean who had carried on a bitter partisan warfare.

Again a body of Chalmers's Division distinguished itself. On April third, Lieutenant-Colonel Crews with sixty men of McDonald's battalion met Grierson on the Summerville road, twenty-five miles from Memphis. He manœuvered his small body and charged so vigorously that Grierson mistook it for the advance of a stronger force under Forrest and withdrew his two regiments to Memphis, burning the bridges behind him. He reported to Hurlbut that "Forrest was a little too strong for me."

On April ninth and tenth, Forrest met his division commanders, Buford and Chalmers, and some of the Brigade commanders in Jackson to decide on the next move. At the conference Buford told of reading in a Northern newspaper that the horses and mules Forrest took away from Paducah belonged to the citizens, and that the government horses had been hidden away in an old foundry. He asked and Forrest gave him permission to return and capture them. It suited the General's entire plan for his next move, the reduction of Fort Pillow. He ordered his officers to make a simultaneous demonstration on Columbus, Paducah, and Memphis, while he struck Fort Pillow in earnest.

He ordered Neely to march on Memphis from the northeast and spread the rumor that Forrest's whole command was moving in that direction. At the same time, he sent a messenger south with orders for Colonel McGuirk to push up from Mississippi and spread the information that Lee was advancing north with his whole force. Buford was to throw out false signals before Columbus and Paducah.

Buford marched north the same day that Forrest and Chalmers set out towards Fort Pillow. He detached Captain Tyler and a staff officer with one hundred and sixty men to invest Columbus, and on the fourteenth he arrived in front of Paducah and drove the enemy into the fort. Ever since the eleventh, Colonel Hicks had been "looking and waiting for Messrs. Forrest and Co. There is an awful shaking among the timid," he wrote, "but the righteous are bold as a lion."

Buford sent Colonel Faulkner to the foundry, where he found one hundred and forty excellent horses and their equipment, but most of the subsistence and other supplies had been carried across the river to safer ground. After employing several ruses to hold Hicks in his fortifications, Buford withdrew with his plunder. In the meantime, the squadron under Captain Tyler had made the impression on the garrison at Columbus that Buford's whole division was investing. For a while Tyler thought he would be embarrassed by capitulation, but the commander finally declined to surrender. Tyler rejoined Buford and on April eighteenth fell back with him to Dresden.

Forrest's strategy, in its execution, was successful at every point. Each Northern garrison chief, from Hurlbut on down, thought he had settled his especial attention on him. Even Sherman believed "the object of Forrest's move is to prevent our concentration as against Johnston, but we must not permit it. Until McPherson's veteran volunteers assemble at Cairo I cannot make my plans to attack Forrest where he is."

Sherman had already done everything he could to make Hurlbut move out of Memphis and fight. He said he knew Hurlbut had plenty of men: Buckland's brigade, two thousand; dismounted men, three thousand; Grierson's cavalry, twenty-five hundred; the Blacks at the fort, twelve hundred; others, two thousand; and in a tight, three citizen regiments—all told, thirteen thousand six hundred men. But Hurlbut felt the safety of Memphis was in danger.

Finally Veatch's Division, as it moved east to concentrate, was ordered to take post at Purdy and be a support for Grierson. Veatch waited a few days, got no news of Forrest; then left for other parts. Sherman was furious; said Veatch left without orders, and feared he would endanger Grierson. But Grierson was careful not to let this happen. He withdrew in plenty of time to Memphis. These withdrawals left the way open for Forrest to send out six hundred prisoners and a great part of the supplies he had gathered during his stay.

On the thirteenth Sherman dispatched, "Forrest is reported again to be attacking Columbus, Kentucky, and also trying to cross the Tennessee near Hamburg. He seems to be omnipresent, but I think his cavalry is scattered over between the Mississippi and the Tennessee stealing horses and feeding them."

Sherman had guessed Forrest's original purpose, and about this time the garrisons in West Tennessee recovered from their fright. They all decided Forrest had been bluffing. Hurlbut wrote Booth, the commander at Pillow, that he believed the rebuff received at Paducah would cure Forrest from again attempting the river forts. He believed the Confederate was about to cross the Tennessee and pay Sherman a visit.

But on Sunday the tenth, "that devil Forrest" gave Chalmers orders to move with Bell's and McCulloch's brigades, fifteen hundred men, and Walton's battery across the Forked Deer—in the direction of Fort Pillow. Chalmers set out at once from Jackson with McCulloch. But as Bell was in camp near Eaton, some thirty miles from Jackson, this officer did not get his brigade in motion until nine P.M.

Forrest, leaving Jackson with his escort, early next morning overtook Chalmers in Brownsville at two P.M., twenty-eight miles distant. He ordered Chalmers to push ahead and surprise the fort. It was thirty-eight miles away, and the night settled down drizzly and murky. But by dawn, the morning of the twelfth, Chalmers and McCulloch captured the picket before Fort Pillow. One or two escaped to the fort. Bell was not up. He arrived about nine o'clock, after riding all Sunday night, Monday, and Monday night. His men had had one hour's sleep in sixty. Many were nauseated from the great strain of their march.

Chalmers made a partial investment on the south side. Booth and his adjutant were killed in this preliminary skirmish. Forrest arrived on the scene shortly after and began an inspection of the position. Near the river, on a high ridge, the enemy had thrown up earthworks covering an acre of ground. Surrounding it was a ditch six feet deep, twelve feet broad. The works were six high and eight feet through. There were six guns, each with an embrasure. The old Confederate fortifications surrounded this inner work.

Forrest personally conducted Barteau's regiment to the northeast side, near the mouth of Coal Creek, which emptied at this point into the Mississippi. He now turned back and threw forward Russell's and Wilson's regiments to the left of Barteau. He sent word and asked McCulloch if he could take a group of cabins and a rifle pit a short distance from the inner work, on the south side. McCulloch answered with a charge. The enemy, as they retired, tried to burn the buildings. They succeeded in burning one row. Bell now advanced, and Bradford, the commander since Booth's death, withdrew into his works on the river.

Forrest, with McCulloch on the left and Bell on the right, now had the fort completely invested, but at long range. His sharpshooters, placed on two high ridges east and northeast of the fort, commanded the works and the five hundred fifty-seven black and white troops inside. There were, besides the regular garrison, over one hundred citizens and some women and children. Many of the troops were known to be deserters from the Confederate armies, and they all had been a menace to West Tennessee. Before Forrest ever decided to invest the place, his soldiers appealed to him to leave a brigade for the protection of their women. In the gray ranks there was one man who had a personal score, a very strong one, to settle with Major Bradford.

Forrest doubled his line of sharpshooters; then with his guide, Shaw, and Captain Anderson he set out to make a closer study of the ground. He noticed the fort had three sides—north, south, and east. From its east face the land sloped down gradually for forty or fifty yards, then sharply into a narrow gorge. The gorge turned westward and ran in that general direction for four or five hundred yards until it struck Coal Creek. The slope, itself, was broken by several deep and crooked gullies. Thus, on the east and north sides of the fort, Forrest saw there was protection for his men anywhere from thirty to one hundred yards of the ditch. On the south face the ground also fell off gradually for two hundred yards; then rapidly into a narrow valley whose course was perpendicular to the river. This valley was seamed by a ravine which offered a good hiding place for a storming party. McCulloch's men had already taken the buildings occupying this valley. It was so deep that the artillery of the fort could not be deflected to rake its sides.

The inspection took an hour, and it was two hours before the ammunition wagons came up. Forrest had scarcely begun the reconnaissance before the rifles of the fort singled him out. His horse was mortally wounded, and it reared with pain and fright and fell over on him. He mounted another and continued his inspection. Anderson warned him that he should finish his inspection on foot. "I am just as apt to be hit one way as another, and I can see better where I am," he said. Two other horses were shot from under him, but the bullet molded to strike General Forrest was not in that fort that day.

It was now one o'clock, and Bell received orders to advance his brigade. By moving with caution along the face of the Coal Creek bluff, Barteau managed to place his regiment, not without loss, however, in the ravine on the north side. Under cover of sharpshooters, Russell and Wilson consumed more time in taking their positions. As Bell's troops rushed over the exposed places, the sharpshooters opened a heavy fire against those in the garrison who exposed their heads and shoulders above the parapet. A gunboat, the *New Era,* shelled the Confederates; but the shells did little damage.

Fort Pillow was now invested at close range. To prevent, if possible, the cost of an assault, Forrest called Captain Goodman of Chalmers's staff and sent him forward with a flag of truce and the following note:

"As your gallant defense of the fort has entitled you to the treatment of brave men, I now demand an unconditional surrender of your force, assuring you at the same time that they will be treated as prisoners of war. I have received a fresh supply of ammunition, and can easily take your position. Should my demand be refused, I cannot be responsible for the fate of your command."

After some minutes he received in return the following: "Your demand does not produce the desired effect."

"This will not do," exclaimed Forrest. "Send it back, and say to Major Booth—whose name was attached—that I must have an answer in plain English, yes or no!" And he added grimly, "You can tell that Federal officer that if I am compelled to butt my men against their works, it will be bad for them."

The Federal officers who had met the flag wanted assurance that Forrest was present. He rode forward to satisfy their doubts, and then back again, out of range of the fort, for some of the negroes had been shooting during the truce. Others had been jeering, making grimaces, and doing insulting things with their hands. Behind the ravines and the shanties the gray men lay without reply, but their anger seethed like a strong steam in a rusty pipe.

While the communications were passing to and fro, several steamers loaded with Northern soldiers made an effort to land. Forrest ordered Anderson to take two companies and slip in behind the fort and "fight everything between wind and water until yonder flag comes down." After one volley the steamboat withdrew.

The flag returned a second time, and Bradford asked for an hour to reach a decision. He was given twenty minutes. This was peremptorily refused. They thought Old Bedford was bluffing.

Forrest called an orderly. "Go to Colonel Bell, commanding on our right, and tell him when he hears my orderly bugler sound the charge, to go over these works if he gets killed and every man in his command, and tell him I don't want to hear of Tennessee being behind." Turning to another aide, he repeated: "You go to Colonel McCulloch, commanding on our left, and tell him when he hears my orderly bugler sound the charge, to go over the works if he is killed and every man in his command, and tell him I don't want to hear of Missouri being left behind."

He had already sent minute directions about the storming. He ordered some of the men, as soon as they dropped into the ditch, to stoop down and serve as a ladder for the others. He thought of the smallest details, because success or failure often hangs on just such details. The men would not now waste time wondering how they were going to get out of the six-foot ditch and up the parapet.

He gave his orderlies plenty of time to reach their separate commanders; then turned to his favorite bugler, the little German. "Gaus, ride your horse up that ravine until you reach about the center of our lines; then sound the charge."

Gaus galloped to the top of a ridge, where all could see him, and raised the bugle to his mouth. There was an explosion of fire from the fort, but a more terrible sound mounted the noise of battle. It was the rebel yell, a cross between a hog-call and a fox-hunter's shout.

There was no second volley from the enemy. Forrest's sharpshooters saw to that. Bell and McCulloch reached the center of the works about the same time, but they were behind their men. For ten minutes there was a terrible slaughter; then the blacks and the whites ran down towards the river. The gunboat had promised Bradford to steam up and cover his withdrawal. But, instead of this, the blacks and whites met a devastating fire from Anderson on one side and a company of Barteau's regiment on the other. In desperation many threw themselves in the river, to drown farther out in its treacherous current. In the meantime, the flag of the fort still floated from its staff.

The garrison was now practically without officers. Major Bradford was hiding below the bluff, and his men were running about in a drunken daze. Squads surrendered; then broke away to resume the fight. There were barrels of ale and beer scattered inside the works, and buckets of whisky with dippers attached. All the hatred and vengeance of partisan warfare was loosed on top and beneath the steep clay bluff. Forrest arrived on foot as soon as he could reach the fort. He had the flag cut down and two of the captured guns turned on the gunboat. Firing ceased almost immediately, but there was some work of private vengeance afterwards. But under the circumstances, the insults of former slaves, the drunken condition of the garrison, and the lack of a competent commander, made the slaughter greater than it ordinarily should have been.

About three P.M., just after the firing had ceased, Forrest was standing among a large group of officers and men. Pointing to the high ground where Gaus had sounded the charge, he said, "When

from my position on that hill I saw my men pouring over these breastworks, it seemed"—he placed his right hand on his left breast—"that
my heart would burst within me. Men, if you will do as I say I will
always lead you to victory. I have taken every place that the Federals
occupied in West Tennessee and North Mississippi except Memphis,
and if they don't mind I'll have that place too in less than six weeks.
They killed two horses from under me today, and knocked me to my
knees a time or two, so I thought, by God, they were going to get me
anyway."

Bradford was caught and brought in. He was allowed to bury his
brother; then put in McCulloch's tent for the night on his word of
honor that he would not escape. He slipped away in the dark, but
was caught later trying to make his way to Memphis. This time he was
put under strong guard, and in the squad of guards was the man he
had wronged. It was reported later that Bradford had been killed while
attempting a second escape.

Forrest turned the command over to Chalmers with orders to bury
the dead, give up the enemy wounded to a passing boat, and hurry
away with the plunder, six guns, several hundred horses, and the
prisoners. Chalmers carried off as prisoners: unwounded officers, seven;
enlisted men, two hundred and nineteen—thirty-six negroes and one
hundred and sixty-three whites. This meant over half the garrison was
killed, drowned, or mortally wounded. For the unknown camp followers who belonged to no command, there was no way of reckoning the
loss. The total deaths may be roughly set down at three hundred and
fifty. Forrest pushed ahead to Brownsville, and he found all the women
of the vicinity gathered on the courthouse steps to thank him. They
sent him a pair of silver spurs, made from their thimbles.

The threats at Columbus, Paducah, Memphis, on the Tennessee
River, and the complete fall of Fort Pillow filled the enemy camps
with fear and rage. They began to speak of it as the Fort Pillow Massacre, and they discovered members of the garrison who were willing
to swear that negroes were burned alive, that the great loss of life came
after the surrender, a surrender which was never made. There were
even reports of men being buried alive. A correspondent of the New
York *Tribune,* writing from Knoxville, under date of April 18, gave
a colorful background to this "massacre" for the Northern audiences.

"These Forrests," he wrote, "the oldest of whom, General Bedford
Forrest, has by this and other atrocities, obtained such a record of
infamy, were all negro traders. There were four brothers—Bedford,

who kept a negro pen for five years before the war, on Adams Street, in the rear of the Episcopal Church, Memphis; John, a cripple and a gambler, who was jailer and clerk to Bedford; Bill Forrest, an extensive slave trader at Vicksburg; and Aaron Forrest, general agent to scour the country for the other brothers. They accumulated large sums of money in their nefarious trade, and Bedford won by that and other influences a natural promotion to Brigadier in the woman-whipping, baby-stealing rebel Confederacy.

"He is about fifty years of age, tall, gaunt, and sallow-visaged, with a long nose, deep-set, black snaky eyes, full black beard with a moustache, and hair worn long. He usually wore, while in the "nigger" trade in Memphis, a stove pipe hat set on the back of his head at an angle of forty-five degrees. He was accounted mean, vindictive, cruel, and unscrupulous.

"The slave pen of old Bedford Forrest, on Adams Street, was a perfect horror to all negroes far and near. His mode of punishing refractory slaves was to compel four of his fellow slaves to stand and hold the victims stretched out in the air, and then Bedford and his brother John would stand, one on each side, with long heavy bull whips, and cut up their victims until the blood trickled to the ground. Women were often stripped naked, and with a bucket of salt water standing by in which to dip the instrument of torture, a heavy leather thong, their backs were cut-up until the blisters covered the whole surface, the blood of their wounds mingling with the brine to add torment to the infliction. One slave man was whipped to death by Bedford, who used a trace chain doubled for the purpose of punishment. The slave was secretly buried, and the circumstance was only known to the slaves of the prison, who only dared to refer to the circumstance in whispers.

"Such are the appropriate antecedents in the character of the monster who murdered in cold blood the gallant defenders of Fort Pillow."

As a piece of propaganda, this was a masterpiece. It was copied all over the North and set burning anew in abolitionist bosoms the hatred for the "woman-whipping, baby-stealing Confederacy." The fall of the fort also had a very decided military effect. It happened just as the Northern officers were beginning to believe Forrest's demands for surrender were bluffs. The next day Hurlbut urged General A. J. Smith, whom Sherman had ordered from Louisiana to attend to Forrest, to make haste. "It is of prime importance," he wired, "that the orders sent you by General W. T. Sherman to return be promptly carried out. With your forces here I can rapidly clear West Tennessee and reopen the river; without it, we in Memphis are practically in a state of siege."

Sherman had not yet heard of Pillow's fall, but on the fourteenth he dispatched Grant's Chief of Staff at Washington, "Forrest still is up between the Tennessee and Mississippi, and is reported today crossing the Tennessee at Hamburg; also attacking Columbus. I admire his skill but he can't do that. . . . I will not let Forrest draw off my mind from the concentration going on."

The next day Grant wired Sherman: "Forrest must be driven out, but with a proper commander in West Tennessee there is force enough now. Your preparations for the coming campaign must go on, but if it is necessary to detach a portion of the troops intended for it, detach them and make your campaign with that much fewer men.

"Relieve Maj. Gen. S. A. Hurlbut. I can send General Washburn, a sober and energetic officer. . . . Does General Hurlbut think if he moves a part of his force after the only enemy within two hundred miles of him that the post will run off with the balance of his force?"

Sherman replied by telegram, "I don't know what to do with Hurlbut. I know that Forrest could pen him up in Memphis with 2,500 men, although Hurlbut has all of Grierson's cavalry and 2,500 white infantry, 4,000 blacks, and the citizen militia, 3,000."

Later he referred to it again. "I have sent Sturgis down to take command of that cavalry and whip Forrest, and, if necessary, to mount enough men to seize any and all the horses of Memphis, or wherever he may go.

"The forces of Fort Pillow are not on my returns. I broke it up. It does seem as though Forrest has our men down there in cow, but I will try new leaders, for I believe our men will fight if led."

General Dodge, at Athens, Alabama, wrote his chief, McPherson, "Reports from West Tennessee indicate that Forrest is making out of the country. I have followed him enough to satisfy me that infantry cannot even get a shot at him, unless it is so weak a force that he is satisfied he can whip it. He watches this country very closely, especially the river from East Port north, and no doubt anticipates a movement from this direction. . . .

"He takes everything without regard to former principles of the owners, and that entire country is feasting him and his officers. I know of a large number who have professed 'great' love for our flag who have outdone themselves in toadying to Forrest. It would be a just judgment on West Tennessee if the troops sent there were given orders to burn the entire country, take everything that can walk, and destroy any and everything a rebel can eat or drink or be of any benefit whatever to them." Dodge did not say how this was to be done, or who would do it. He is arousing himself on the mere prospect of a visit. The multiplication of 'atrocities,' the vindictive attitude towards people who honored Forrest, indicated one thing—a great and growing fear of him. If at this time Davis could have had the inspiration to recognize in Forrest the capacity for high command, the situation might yet have been saved.

Davis, with a clear mind, recognized Robert E. Lee when all others were calling him the general who hid behind breastworks. It was possible he might discover Forrest. There was, however, one great impediment in the way. General Braxton Bragg had the President's ear, and Bragg was beginning, very subtly, to undermine all his enemies behind their backs. The chief ones were Forrest, Polk, and Joseph E. Johnston, Johnston because he had become the idol of the Army of Tennessee. But he had greater reason to dislike Polk and Forrest.

These two officers feared this. It caused Forrest to write personally to Davis and inform him of his successes. He sent a letter by Mr. William McGee on April 15. In it was one very important paragraph: "I am ordered back to Okolona, Mississippi, by General Polk with my command to meet, in conjunction with General Lee, an anticipated raid through Alabama from Middle Tennessee. It is my opinion that no such raid will be made from Decatur or any point west of there. General Lee has about seven thousand cavalry, and with our forces united *a move could be made into Middle Tennessee and Kentucky which would create a diversion of the enemy's forces and enable us to break up his plans,* and such an expedition, *managed with prudence and executed with rapidity,** can be safely made.

This paragraph showed that Forrest had a thorough grasp of the oncoming campaign—he had written Polk that it was clear the enemy was concentrating before Richmond and at Chattanooga—and he was offering to Davis a plan to frustrate their objective. It was what Sherman and Grant feared would happen, and later those in high position in the Southwest tried to impress upon Davis that Forrest was the key to victory before Atlanta.

Davis read the letter but he did not act on the suggestion. He referred it "to General Bragg for his information and remarks." The remarks were full and illuminating.

* Italics mine.

"The statement of the strength of this command is very surprising after the verbal reports sent here of the number of men raised in the first visit to West Tennessee. Two of the four brigades were transferred under Brigadier-General Chalmers from General Lee's command, one (Richardson's) was raised by him and Colonel Bell *before Forrest went to the department,** and one large regiment (It was actually 150 men) and one battalion of five companies were sent by me from the Army of Tennessee, and General Polk has assigned three small regiments of Kentucky infantry. *But little is left for the men raised by General Forrest.** The movement into Middle Tennessee was, and I consider is still, of utmost importance. The breaking up of the marauding bands of the enemy is very gratifying, if it is not to be followed by similar organizations claiming to be in our service. If Mr. William McGee, General Forrest's messenger, belongs to a Louisiana battery, he is employed by the general without authority, and is one of the cases of men enticed from their commands and employed in violation of orders. He should be arrested and sent to his proper command, and General Forrest made accountable for his unauthorized absence.

"BRAXTON BRAGG,
"General."

For fear the raid, suggested by Forrest, would be made and very likely under his command, orders were sent to Polk to place Forrest directly under Lee's orders. Heretofore Lee and Forrest had occupied separate departments. Lee protested against the order—he preferred an active command in the field and said, "I will take this occasion to state that I am not aware as to what influences were brought to bear to cause the order to be issued."

Polk was not aware, either, of the influences brought to bear; but he had very strong suspicions. He wrote to General Hodge, who had recently inspected his department. "I send you reports of General Forrest of his operations in West Tennessee. . . . I desire to call your attention to them and to ask that you, in your correspondence, call attention of the President to them, *with a request from me that he will read them.*" And later, he added, *"May I ask you to see that the President receives my letter?"* *

Forrest felt that he could do Sherman a great deal of damage. He openly talked of this move into Tennessee. One of Dodge's spies in-

* Italics mine.

formed his commander "that he heard Forrest say that he was about played out trying to get us to send a force to West Tennessee after him. He supposed that if we did not come after him, he would have to go to us, and he did not want to get where they could pit him or any of his force against Wheeler again, as his men had no confidence in him."

Disgusted with the failure of Hurlbut and his subordinates, Sherman finally shook up all the officers in West Tennessee and West Kentucky. Washburn replaced Hurlbut at Memphis, and Sturgis was put over Grierson. Both of these officers left for their commands with a great deal of assurance and self-confidence. But Washburn no sooner arrived than he began to feel the influence of Forrest's strange magic. His reports to his superiors became at once more cautious, and they were full of requests for reënforcements.

Sherman, with resignation, answered Washburn with, "I cannot understand General Hurlbut's reports. He took a short leave of absence when I first came to Memphis, and hearing that Forrest was above Memphis, wrote me that Grierson was after him, supported by infantry. Every report since, the strength of the cavalry has fallen off more and more, until now you report it down to one thousand one hundred. . . . Do the best you can, but *try and not exaggerate the forces of the enemy or your own weakness,* but use your force to the best advantage. Don't let Forrest insult you by passing in sight almost of your command. . . . I don't see how our cavalry destroy so many horses. When I left Memphis, Grierson had full five thousand horses. Not one has been drawn away, and I want to know what has become of them." Sherman's astute conception should have told him the answer was not far to seek.

Washburn acted, however, with a great deal more vigor than Hurlbut had ever shown. He organized a mixed force—three thousand five hundred cavalry, two thousand infantry—and sent it out to prevent Forrest from returning to North Mississippi. Sturgis was in command.

But Sturgis left a little too late. Forrest, after beating the country for conscripts, sent Chalmers and Buford south with a heavy ox-drawn wagon train, loaded down with supplies, liquors, leather, and eight thousand or ten thousand pounds of lead which had been collected at Corinth. The Kentucky brigade entered the campaign, 1,004 strong; it now had over 1,700 to answer the roll call; Bell's brigade had been increased from 1,254 to over 1,700. Chalmers's Division, in spite of losses, was much stronger, for the General's dragnet had brought into the service a great many men. Forrest followed his brigades on May 2, joined Colonel Crews with enough men to make a force of three hundred, and with them held Sturgis off until a heavy train escaped south; then followed it and arrived in Tupelo a day ahead of Buford.

Washburn put in a call for more troops. Hurlbut grew sarcastic and protested bitterly that since he had been removed for "marked timidity," Washburn should be forced to deal with Forrest with the same number of men that were at his disposal. His protest was not sustained, but Sherman wrote Washburn that "We want you to hold Forrest and as much of the enemy as you can over there, until we strike Johnston. *This is quite as important as to whip him.** You should have a good force of infantry of about 4,000 men as a solid column against which Forrest could make no impression by his bold dashes. Don't calculate on a force moving inland from the Tennessee River now, as we cannot spare it, but rely on your own command, which make as strong as possible. We cannot judge at this distance as well as you can, but don't let Forrest move about in that country as he has done."

McPherson gave Washburn more explicit orders: "You may not be able with the troops at your disposal to assume the offensive with as much boldness as is desirable against an enemy like Forrest, and force him to fight or be driven out of West Tennessee. It is of the utmost importance, however, to keep his forces occupied, and prevent him from forming plans and combinations to cross the Tennessee River and break up the railroad communications in our rear."

Sherman added the last warning: "follow him wherever he may go, and not be stopped unless Forrest shall be reënforced by a largely superior force."

In the Northern camps the issue was clear: Grant must crush Lee; Sherman, Johnston. Sherman outnumbered Johnston, but he had a very long line of communication, and one that would grow longer if he succeeded in pushing his enemy back upon Atlanta. The rat in his meal barrel was Forrest. If the Richmond authorities realized this soon enough, there was going to be serious trouble in Sherman's rear; and serious trouble there would mean possible disaster to Grant's grand strategy.

Two days after Forrest returned to Mississippi, on May 6, to be exact, the Confederate Congress resolved that:

"The thanks of the Congress are eminently due and are hereby cordially tendered to Major-General N. B. Forrest and the officers and

* Italics mine.

men of his command, for their late brilliant and successful campaign in Mississippi, West Tennessee, and Kentucky; a campaign which has conferred upon its authors fame as enduring as the record of the struggle which they have so brilliantly illustrated."

In his office at the Capitol, General Braxton Bragg, the President's friend and his military adviser, picked up the message from his table and read it carefully through to the end.

CHAPTER XVIII

Brice's Cross-Roads

GENERAL STURGIS, after turning back from his race after Forrest, wrote to Washburn on May 7: "Upon reaching Ripley I found that the rear of Forrest's command had passed through that place nearly two days before. . . . It was here that I had hoped, almost against hope, to intercept him. . . . Although we could not catch the scoundrel we are at least rid of him, and that is something." A week later, back in Memphis, he made a report to General Sherman—"My little campaign is over, and I regret to say Forrest is still at large. . . . I regret very much that I could not have the pleasure of bringing you his hair, but he is too great a plunderer to fight anything like an equal force, and we have to be satisfied with driving him from the state. He may turn on your communications—I rather think he will, but I see no way to prevent it from this point with this force."

General Sherman gave Washburn orders to see that Sturgis had a sufficient force, for if there was anything Sherman wanted, it was Forrest's hair. He suggested a command of six thousand men, but Washburn, to make sure of the scalp, added two thousand more. It was even a finer body of men than "Sookey" Smith had taken out of Memphis in February. Grierson had a division of cavalry, three thousand, three hundred strong, divided into two brigades; one of one thousand, five hundred men and six guns, under Colonel Waring; another, one thousand, eight hundred men and four guns under Winslow. Waring had been with "Sookey" Smith and was known as a hard fighter and a clear-thinking officer. Winslow had been with Sherman on the expedition to Meridian. Besides the cavalry, there was a division of infantry, three brigades strong: Wilkins's, two thousand, with six guns; Hoge's, one thousand, six hundred, with four guns; Bouton's, the negro brigade, one thousand, two hundred men and two guns. The division was commanded by Colonel McMillin, a very determined man. Sturgis's total, including the artillery was: Grierson, three thousand, three hundred; McMillin, four thousand, eight hundred; artillery four hundred—eight thousand, five hundred officers and men, and twenty-two guns. To support this body, there was a train of two hundred and fifty wagons, twenty-five ambulances, all stocked with medicines, ordnance and rations to last twenty days. The command was short on one thing, forage. Smith had carried off last February the people's slaves and stock, and laid waste their country to such an extent that Northeast Mississippi was almost a desert. At the crucial moment, the result of Smith's raid was beginning to work a greater hardship on the North than it ever could on Forrest.

On June 1, Sturgis set out with this fine army of veterans to destroy the Mobile and Ohio Railroad and to get Forrest's hair. Sturgis may not have known it, but if there was one thing Forrest was proud of, it was his hair. He was known to keep it always brushed and combed, even on the march; and in camp its thick locks were never allowed out of place. But Sturgis had made a promise, and the night before his departure from Memphis, he celebrated in great fashion. This was a bold gesture, entirely in keeping with the tone of his letters to his superiors. Some of his officers, however, were unkind enough to say that he had chosen the wrong time to celebrate.

In the meantime, Forrest had spent the month of May organizing his command into an efficient fighting unit. He gave Chalmers three brigades—Neely's, McCulloch's, and Rucker's; Buford two brigades—Bell's and Lyon's. Lyon now commanded the Kentuckians. He placed Captain John Morton over the artillery; a battalion of four batteries, Rice's, Thrall's, Walton's, and his own: sixteen guns. Altogether there were twenty regiments, four battalions, five independent companies, and sixteen guns, numbering nine thousand, two hundred and twenty officers and men. Since many of the new men were deserters from other armies, and he had to turn a great number over to the War Department, this reduced his small army. Under him they would make excellent fighters; sent back to their commands, they would only desert again. One private who had joined the escort was such an excellent soldier that Forrest sent him across country with seven recruits to exchange for himself.

His order books of this date showed his internal administration to be as vigorous and as intelligent as his action on the march or on the battlefield. He acted very promptly in a matter that had caused all Southern commanders a great deal of worry. The principal defect of the Southern Staff was its subsistence department. It was directed by a pedant at Richmond who was independent of the commanders in the field, and this was the principal reason the Confederate armies were short of supplies. They often starved in the midst of plenty. One of these petty sovereignties was erected in Forrest's department. They speedily collided, and Forrest delivered the following ultimatum: "I am directed by the General Commanding to say, that he understands you are at Okolona, and several of your men loitering around here, instead of being up at the front attending to getting out cattle. He further directs me to say that, if the matter is not given your attention, he will withdraw his cavalry, who are to aid you, and report the fact to the proper department. If there is anything hindering you from giving this matter your immediate attention he desires to know it at once, and expects that you and all your men will be at work while you have the opportunity. No enemy in the country, and force sufficient to protect you.

"(Signed) CHAS. W. ANDERSON, A.D.C."

On May 26, Chalmers was detached with Neely's and McCulloch's brigades and Walton's battery and sent on an expedition into the interior of Alabama. On the thirtieth, Forrest, himself, was directed to go to the relief of Roddy who was expecting a raid from the direction of Decatur. Roddy wired that the danger had passed; so Lee thought it was time for his lieutenant to make a raid into Middle Tennessee. Therefore, the day Sturgis moved out of Memphis towards Mississippi, Forrest left to strike Sherman's communications, which were growing longer as the Army of Tennessee was flanked out of one position after another and forced back on Atlanta.

Forrest reached Russellville, Alabama, when a courier arrived from Lee ordering his return to meet a heavy column of the enemy moving down through North Mississippi. He countermarched and rode into Tupelo on June 6. It was discovered here that Sturgis was moving on Corinth. Forrest was unaware of his own importance and naïvely thought that this was another body on its way to reënforce Sherman. To interrupt the march he threw his brigades up the line of the Mobile and Ohio Railroad in the direction of Corinth. Lee had already ordered Rucker, who was at Oxford, to move east and rejoin his commander. Rucker ran into Sturgis's advance near Salem, drove it two miles; then, when darkness ended pursuit, reached for Booneville, the second station below Corinth.

On Grierson's report, that the country in the immediate vicinity of the railroad was even more barren than the country to their front, Sturgis changed the order of march to the Ripley-Guntown Road. Burdened by his heavy wagon train, his progress was slow; and he reached Ripley on the seventh in a cheerless mood. If he had been offered just one lock of Old Bedford's hair, he would have returned to Memphis without hesitation.

He called together his division commanders for advice, for there was "a serious question in my mind as to whether or not I should proceed any farther. The rain still fell in torrents. The artillery and wagons were literally mired down, and the starved and exhausted animals could with difficulty drag them along." Grierson agreed with his superior, but McMillin, the infantry commander, was in favor of going ahead. He pointed out that Sturgis had already given as excuse for turning back on his other expedition the condition of the country. He was in favor of going ahead, even if they did get whipped.

Sturgis gave orders to advance, but gossip sifted down to the ranks that he had said he did not expect to save his train. This news was anything but cheering to the men. On the night of the ninth he camped at Stubbs Farm, twelve miles east of Ripley and eight miles from Brice's Cross-Roads. At Brice's house the road from Ripley to Guntown intercepted the road from Baldwyn to Pontotoc.

That same evening Forrest's command was scattered along the Mobile and Ohio. Bell's brigade, two thousand, seven hundred and eighty-five, was at Rienzi, the first station below Corinth. Rucker, seven hundred strong, bivouacked at Booneville. Below Booneville, at Baldwyn, there were two brigades, Johnston's, five hundred, and Lyon's eight hundred. Johnston had just made a forced march from North Alabama with his brigade of Roddy's command. His march had been so swift and the roads were so heavy that he had lost half his men on the way. Forrest placed his headquarters at Booneville, and Morton's and Rice's artillery were there, reduced to eight guns. General Lee had held a conference with Forrest, at which he decided to meet the enemy farther south. He withdrew four guns with Ferrel, the baggage trains, and all surplus supplies. He ordered Forrest to concentrate in Sturgis's front and draw him to Okolona, where, at the proper moment, they would fall upon and destroy him. Lee did not actually forbid his lieutenant to deliver battle beforehand.

Late in the evening Forrest called a council of his officers, more to discuss the reports he had received than for any other purpose.

General Buford, Colonel Rucker, and Captain Morton were present. Bell was at Rienzi, seven miles to the north; Lyon at Baldwyn, twelve miles to the south, so these officers were absent. Forrest told his officers that he had reliable information that the enemy were in camp at Stubbs Farm, on the Ripley Guntown road, and that while he preferred to get them in the open country, "where he can get a good look at them," he added that he might be obliged to deliver battle before joining Lee at Okolona. As soon as the meeting was over, orders reached Bell, Lyon, Rucker, Morton, and Johnston to march at dawn in the direction of Brice's Cross-Roads.

Bell was twenty-five miles away; Rucker and the artillery eighteen miles; Johnston and Lyon six miles. Sturgis's entire command was only eight miles distant from the point where Forrest expected to run into it. There were only one thousand, three hundred Confederates who were nearer to the point of expected contact than the enemy. It had rained all day of the eighth, the ninth, and on the evening of the ninth it fell in torrents. But the clouds broke at midnight, and at sun-up the sky began to clear.

Grierson was in the saddle by 5:30 A.M., and his three thousand, three hundred riders moved southeast, down the narrow, heavily wooded road. Their horses were soon lifting their feet in the slimy mud of the bottoms which surrounded the south prong of the Talla-hatchie. The infantry had orders to march at seven o'clock, after the cavalry had cleared the way.

As soon as it was light, Forrest's troops were in motion. At Carroll-ville, a small settlement six miles from the Cross-Roads, Old Bedford ordered his march. Lyon's eight hundred took the lead; Rucker's seven hundred followed next; and Johnston's jaded horses followed him still farther to the rear. Bell, the largest brigade, had the greatest distance to make, and Morton was urging forward the artillery.

The sun was now high and sucking at the wet roads and forests. The road pulled at the horses' fetlocks; and, steaming and wet, the sultry air stuffed the lungs of the riders with humid breath. Thousands of hearts, heavily pumping, threw the sweat, popping in great drops, upon their foreheads and tickling down their backs. Lather gathered under the saddles; white beards foamed at the chins of the critters and fell in the mud and water under their feet. The strong stench of unwashed men and the leathery smell of horses hovered above the moving columns, doping the riders' minds with its strange odor and overloading an atmosphere already saturated. The sun was a nasty

Grierson and His Staff

bronze. In a few hours it would dry the forests and the roads and press its sticky heat through the low places. General Forrest, sitting high on his big sorrel, looked up at the sky as he rode alongside Colonel Rucker. It was not yet eight o'clock.

He told Rucker he meant to attack Sturgis at the Cross-Roads. "I know they greatly outnumber the troops I have at hand, but the road along which they will march is narrow and muddy; they will make slow progress. The country is densely wooded and the undergrowth so heavy that when we strike them they will not know how few men we have. Their cavalry will move out ahead of the infantry, and should reach the Cross-Roads three hours in advance. We can whip their cavalry in that time. As soon as the fight opens they will send back to have the infantry hurried up. It is going to be hot as hell, and coming on a run for five or six miles over such roads, their infantry will be so blowed we will ride right over them. I want everything to move up as fast as possible. I will go ahead with Lyon and the escort and open the fight."

But Lyon had already opened the fight. A mile beyond Brice's house, on the Baldwyn road, his advance and Waring's collided. The road, enclosed by a worm fence on either side for a quarter of a mile, split the center of a cleared field. The field was shaped something like the State of Tennessee, and like the road it was surrounded by worm fences with tops further strengthened by poles and brush. On all sides a dense forest of scrub-oak and black-jack thickets closed about the fences. The leaves were so thick and the bushes so stubborn that it was impossible, almost, for cavalry to operate on the ground. Grierson dismounted Waring's brigade, now one thousand, four hundred and fifty men, and threw it on both sides of the Baldwyn road, just at the edge of this field and well protected by the thickets.

Messages from Lyon's advance flew to the rear with the information that a large force had driven them back. Forrest sent word to "Fight on, men, and keep fighting till I come." Shortly after, he and Lyon arrived with the rest of the brigade. Lyon quickly dismounted the Third Kentucky and threw it forward; next, the Seventh, with the exception of two companies which were placed, mounted, on the flanks. The Eighth was kept in reserve in the center of the line. Lyon drew a heavy fire and, seeing the enemy mass as if for an advance, fell back behind his rail fence. Forrest now ordered alternate rails moved, to leave an impression that he was about to resume the offensive. He was, in fact, praying for time and the arrival of his rear

brigades. He sent Captain Anderson in a flying gallop to Old Carroll-
ville with orders to "Tell Bell to move up fast and fetch all he's got."
His instructions to Morton were to put his artillery in a gallop. Rucker
was still two miles from the field, and Johnston was in his rear.

In the meantime, Grierson's other cavalry brigade, Winslow's
one thousand, eight hundred men, arrived. It was dismounted and
placed on the right of Waring. The Northern line, in the form of a
fan, began a little to the north of the Baldwyn road and extended
in a circle to and beyond the Guntown road, touching on that road a
bald prairie which is still to be seen a little ways below the Bethany
School House. Grierson now had over three thousand cavalry hidden
in the black-jack thickets, with four guns in position and in reserve
near Brice's house. The wooded land sloped down behind the Cross-
Roads onto two corn fields, one on each side of the road. The fields
touched the southern banks of Tishomingo Creek. Its narrow flow
was spanned by a single wooden bridge.

Rucker, two miles from Lyon's position, heard the sound of firearms and put his command in a gallop. He soon reached the field.
"When we got there" recounted one of the men, "the old soldier was
sitting on his horse in the center of the road. . . ."

"What is it, General?"

"Yankees, and lots of them."

"Is it a battle?"

"Yes, it is a battle. Never took a dare from them yet, and won't do
it today."

With these words he ordered Rucker to dismount and take position
on Lyon's left. The Seventh Tennessee formed on Lyon's right, and
Chalmers's Mississippi battalion next to it. Duff's Mississippians were
sent, mounted, to guard the extreme left. All told, there were now
some one thousand, six hundred gray men on the field, to oppose
Grierson's three thousand, two hundred.

The bugle sounded, and the line charged with a shout through
the muddy cornfield. After heavy firing, the Confederates retired again
to their original position, Chalmers's battalion in disorder. He had gone
too far and received a terrific enfilading fire from Winslow's right.
Just as Lyon and Rucker returned, Johnston's Alabamans galloped onto
the field. Forrest sent them to the right. After a feeble attack lasting
five minutes, Johnston fell back to and dressed on Lyon.

It was now eleven o'clock, and although Bell and the artillery were
still on the way, Forrest prepared to carry out the first part of his

plan. He rode along the lines, telling the men that when the bugle
sounded again he expected them to rise and go forward; he told them
the next attack was no feint; it was to be desperate work, and at close
quarters.

There was a moment of quiet; then the shrill, peremptory notes
of the bugle. The three skeleton brigades dashed forward, Johnston

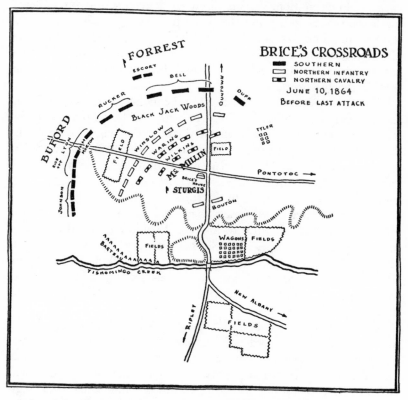

on the right, Lyon in the center, and Rucker on the left. Each command vied with the others in an effort to reach first the sturdy blue
men concealed in the black-jack screen. Rucker made the first impression. He struck the fence fully one hundred yards ahead of Lyon
and Johnston, and the enemy concentrated a terrific fire on the Seventh
Tennessee and Chalmers's battalion. The men staggered, dropped
flat upon the ground; they hid in small gullies. Lieutenant-Colonel
Taylor and Rucker dashed up and down ordering the men back in
line. They rose, and, bowing before the storm of lead, again rushed

forward. And again they hesitated. The fire was still as deadly, and
the fence was before them. Somebody cried out, "Pull out a tree,
boys." A bushy-topped blackjack was jerked bodily into the cornfield,
and the Seventh Tennessee hurried headlong through the gap to
mix with the unseen enemy.

Pistols were drawn, muskets were used as clubs, and the stubborn
enemy held its position. Waring threw in the reserve of two regiments,
the Second New Jersey and the Seventh Indiana; but it was no use.
Rucker would not retreat. It was said he had a bulldog look that day.
His horse was shot five times, and a bullet struck him in the abdomen,
but he stayed on the field. Lyon and Johnston soon relieved the
pressure on his front.

The Color Sergeant of the Seventh Tennessee, Perkins, "The Un-
lucky," had been ordered to remain with the horseholders. It was
feared the flag might be torn in the thickets. But when he heard the
shouts and the noise coming out of the black-jacks, he forgot his orders
and ran forward with the old flag, placed himself to the front of the
troops and waved them on. He was shot in the leg—for the fifth
time—and had to be carried to the rear.

Waring's center slowly gave way, and he hastened to form a
second line a short distance to his rear. Winslow dropped back and
formed on the new line. The Northern cavalry was now beaten at
all points; and although intact, there was little fight left in them.
For the last two hours Grierson had been sending urgent requests
for the infantry to come up. Sturgis sent orders for them to double-
quick to the Cross-Roads.

They arrived at 1:30, none too soon, for Waring's extreme left had
quit the field without "orders." Sturgis was forced to send in his own
escort to make a show of having a line at that extremity. Hoge's brigade
arrived first. It replaced the center. Wilkins came next on the field
and formed a second line in rear of Hoge, although some of his regiments were thrown forward to the right and left of Hoge. For the
last six miles of their march they had been urged forward at a trot,
and the last mile was made at a run. Many dropped by the side of the
road exhausted or senseless with sunstroke. Some were so blown they
were unable to lift their hands to load their muskets. Bouton's negro
brigade had been left to guard the wagons.

Forrest's weapons had in the past been varied, but this was the
first time he ever conscripted the sun to serve in his ranks. He did

not at the moment know how well it had served him, for the heavy green forest covered McMillin's arrival. So, in spite of his success, Forrest's situation was perilous. In the last attack he had about two thousand men on the ground; but, after deducting horseholders, he was able to bring on the field only some one thousand, seven hundred. And these had lost heavily. The Seventh Tennessee, alone, was reduced one-third in killed and wounded. And Lyon's loss was almost as heavy. Chalmers's ranks had been considerably thinned. A determined counter-stroke might have brought disaster.

For some time past Old Bedford had been casting his eyes to the east, looking for Morton and Bell. Now at the crucial moment, the artillery rolled up, was unlimbered, and placed to the right of the Baldwyn road in Lyon's rear. It had come at a gallop for the last six miles through the thick mud, and the bellies of its teams were bloody from the spurs. Soon after, Buford galloped up with Russell's and Wilson's regiments of Bell's brigade. Barteau, according to Forrest's orders, had been detached at Carrollville to move through byways and fall upon the enemy's rear. Old Bedford ordered Buford to take charge of his right and center, and he led Bell's men to the left and put them in line beyond Rucker. They now extended to the west of the Guntown road. Captain Tyler had two companies mounted on the extreme left to support Duff.

Both sides, as if by common consent, prepared for the final struggle. Sturgis had, discounting the losses of battle and those who fell by the roadside, almost eight thousand men present; Forrest just half so many. But at the moment Grierson's cavalry division was withdrawn behind the battle line to re-form. This left with McMillin about three thousand, four hundred infantry to meet about 3,200 Southerners. Bell's two regiments were the freshest men on the ground, fresher than the Northern infantry. But Rucker, Lyon, and Johnston had been fighting since ten o'clock in the morning, and fighting is exhausting work.

For half an hour there was a lull, as the two forces readjusted their positions. There was no more open ground, except a few acres around the Brice house in the angle of the Cross-Roads. Forrest noticed that the enemy was massing heavily in front of Bell and Rucker. He sent Buford this information, told him that everything was ready on the left and that when the attack opened, he must push Lyon hard against McMillin's left and throw Johnston around his flank, to get as near as possible to the Ripley road behind the Cross-Roads. Duff and Tyler were told to charge the other flank and ride their horses up to pistol-shot range.

This was his usual battle order. A heavy assault on the front, supported by as heavy an assault on the flanks; and if Barteau reached the field in time, there would be an attack on front, flank, and rear. There was to be a feint at no part of the field, but earnest, deadly work on all parts.

About two o'clock Bell moved forward, and the battle reopened. The Confederates knew the Northern infantry had come on the field, for the small shrubs and bushes were being cut off close to the earth. Bell's men held their ground for a while, but his regiments were wasting away. Forrest had remained on this part of the field because he expected the deadliest fighting to be here. He saw Bell's men break and Hoge take advantage of it and order an advance all along the line.

Old Bedford got down from his horse, dismounted his escort under Captain Jackson and Gatrell's Georgians who were on headquarters duty. He slung these at the breaking line, and it stiffened. With Bell's help, the backward movement was stopped. At this crucial moment Lieutenant-Colonel Wisdom arrived with two hundred and eighty of Newsom's regiment. Forrest threw him in on the left, and Hoge's advance was definitely checked in Bell's front.

The weight of the enemy's attack had fallen against Bell's right and Rucker's left. When Rucker saw the enemy's bayonets sticking through the foliage, he called out to his thin line, "Kneel on the ground, men, draw your six-shooters, and don't run!" This command was an inspiration. The shrubbery had been cut off close to the ground; and, while the bodies of the enemy were hidden, their legs were visible. Bullets from the navy sixes in the hands of Rucker's men began breaking bones: thighs, shins, kneecaps, and ankles. A pistol was as good as a repeating rifle at close range, and in the hands of Forrest's men it was better. The blue infantry reached Rucker but rebounded.

Lyon and Johnston had struck as hard. In the enemy command word went back to McMillin that the attack on the right was the real attack. The feint was on the left. A few minutes later the commander on the left informed McMillin that he was receiving the real attack and he was positive the feint was on the right. Both officers were partly correct: there was no feint on either flank. Slowly Forrest was bending Sturgis's command back upon the Cross-Roads.

It was now four o'clock. The battle had shaken the forest for two hours. Very soon it must be settled one way or the other. At this crucial moment Buford sent a message to his chief. From the open position which he occupied on the extreme right, he had observed a sudden movement of the Northern cavalry near Brice's house to the rear. Vaguely and then distinctly he heard the sound of musketry off to his right, near Tishomingo Creek. This was what Old Bedford had wanted to hear. It was Barteau, with the Second Tennessee. He knew that, if the battle was ever won, it must be won now. The sun was not many hours high.

Both sides, as if by common consent, drew back just far enough for the intervening trees to obscure the vision. A private of the Seventh Tennessee reported: "Our men still in line of battle lay on the ground for a much needed rest. Here we had a bountiful supply of water from the rills, which had been fed by the recent rains. I never tasted better. The cessation of battle was as grateful as the water, but there was intense anxiety to know the final result. An order to retire from the field would have brought no surprise."

Barteau, spreading out his two hundred and fifty men in a line three-quarters of a mile long, sent his bugler up and down the line sounding the charge. His arrival was the decisive stroke of the day. It drew off to this quarter Waring's and Winslow's brigades of cavalry just as they were about to be thrown back into the line as support to the infantry.

But that order to retire from the field was never given. Private Hubbard continued, "But Forrest and his brigade commanders were better informed. Mounted on his big sorrel horse, sabre in hand, sleeves rolled up, his coat lying on the pommel of his saddle, looking the very God of War, the General rode down our line as far as we could see him. I remember his words, which I heard more than once: "Get up, men. I have ordered Bell to charge on the left. When you hear his guns, and the bugle sounds, every man must charge, and we will give them hell.""

Forrest reached Morton's guns, and the young Captain whose twenty-first birthday came during the battle of Chickamauga, impulsively warned his superior, "General, you'd better get down the hill. They'll hit you here." Suddenly aware of his rashness, he apologized; and to his surprise Forrest replied, "Well, John, I will rest a little." He dismounted and lay down on the root of a tree some thirty yards back of the guns. Before he retired, he told Morton he believed he had the enemy whipped, but that they were holding on with considerable stubbornness at the Cross-Roads. He told him that in ten minutes he was going to order the charge all along the line and "double 'em up on the road right up yonder where that piece of artillery is." When the charge sounded, he told Morton that he wanted him to hitch up his guns and charge too, *without support* and "Give 'em hell right up yonder where I'm going to double 'em up."

Rice, the other battery commander, overheard the order. He thought there was some misunderstanding. "Captain Morton, do you reckon the General meant for us to charge sure enough without support?"

"You heard the order, Captain Rice. Be ready."

In a few minutes, Old Bedford was again mounted and riding towards Buford's position. He gave him final instructions and told him what part the artillery was to take in the charge. Buford suggested that it was dangerous to throw the guns forward without support and he received the quick reply, "Buford, all the Yankees in front of us can't get to Morton's guns."

He stopped in front of Lyon and gave him orders. "Charge and give 'em hell; and when they fall back keep on charging and giving 'em hell, and I'll soon be there with you and bring up Morton's Bull Pups."

He hurried back to Bell, sent his two escort companies to strengthen the extreme left, and gave Gaus the signal. The Confederate line, now much shorter and therefore much stronger, leaped to its work with a shout. Morton's four guns, double-shotted with canister, charged down the road and unlimbered just as a heavy blue line came out of the woods. The guns threw charge after charge of canister and round shot into the enemy until he fell back in confusion. The artillerists pushed the guns forward by hand and increased the slaughter. Johnston swept far to the right and threw the guard of the wagon train into commotion. The wagons, parked in a field west of the Ripley road and near Tishomingo Creek, were moving out to the rear. Lyon, Rucker, and Bell, first slowly then rapidly, rolled the enemy back to Brice's house. As both sides moved towards this angle, the Confederate line grew increasingly stronger, the Federal, weaker, for it was only a much shorter skirt to a heavy mass which could not be brought into action. As the Confederate artillery poured into this seething mass, it overflowed to the rear and towards Tishomingo Creek. A dismounted regiment of cavalry, reënforced by a negro regiment, attempted to stem the tide; but it was useless. Morton captured six guns at the Cross-Roads. He immediately turned three of them on the panic-stricken enemy. Sturgis, whipped before he ever reached the field, now fled before his defeated army. A wagon turned over on the bridge and blocked the retreat and cut off a great part of the train. The enemy crawled over, swam the creek, or drowned in it. The escort had passed over a quarter of a mile above the bridge. They charged into the mob and made large captures of men and wagons. Morton's guns were finally worked over, and he recognized the escort's flag in time to reserve his fire in that direction.

Two miles from the field, at the Reverend Agnew's house which commanded a slope, one thousand, five hundred of the enemy made a stand. They threw back the first line of the advancing Southerners, but when a section of artillery was brought up, they dissolved in the general rout. Mrs. Agnew's daughter told me that "As the negroes passed the house going down to the battle, they shook their fists at the ladies on the porch and said they were going to show Mr. Forrest they were his rulers. Coming back, with tears in their eyes, they asked my mother what they must do. Would Mr. Forrest kill them?" They also cut the well rope. Coming back, they were glad to drink slop. As they fled, they tore off badges marked "Remember Fort Pillow."

The sun went down, but the pursuit kept up. Forrest came upon a squadron of his men at a small creek. He asked what the trouble was, and they told him the Yankee rear guard was at bay several hundred rods ahead. He took a candle from his pocket, lighted it, and held it above his head. His men were terrified. "What is that?" He asked, pointing to an object in the water. "A wagon." . . . "And that?" . . . "A gun!" . . . "Come on, men," he shouted. "In a rout like this ten men are equal to a thousand." He plunged in the creek, and they after him.

The horseholders were sent to the front to keep up the pursuit, and he allowed the rest of the command to sleep from one o'clock until three the morning of the eleventh, then struck Sturgis again at Stubb's Farm and drove him to the Hatchie bottom. Here Bouton attempted to hold the rear until the train was crossed. Bouton went to Sturgis and asked for a white regiment to help him lift the wagons on to better ground, but Sturgis answered, "For God's sake, if Mr. Forrest will leave me alone, I'll leave him alone. You have done all you could and more than was expected of you, and now all you can do is to save yourselves."

But Mr. Forrest had no idea of leaving him alone. As he said to

Morton next morning, the way to whip an enemy is to "git 'em skeered, and then keep the skeer on 'em." He captured the rest of the wagon train, many ambulances, and fourteen guns; then flanked Sturgis out of Ripley, where there was an attempt to organize the men into companies and regiments. Forrest now directed Buford to pursue on the direct road, while he took a short cut to Salem. He hoped to cut off and capture the remaining fugitives there. Buford moved so quickly, however, that when Forrest came up, he had passed Salem. Perhaps the reason for Forrest's delay was his physical condition. A mile from Salem he dropped from his saddle and lay unconscious for an hour. The terrific strain, mental and physical, broke for a while a will almost as terrific. The Southern sun which he had conscripted to undo the enemy had almost overpowered him. When he came to, he mounted and ordered his men to come on.

He threw out regiments on either side of the road to gather in the enemy who were wandering in the woods. A citizen of Ripley said the "White soldiers were afraid to be caught with the niggers, and the niggers were afraid to be caught without them." A squad came upon four or five that night squatting on a log like chickens gone to roost. They lighted candles and held them above their heads as they called out, "Don't shoot, don't shoot." The citizens along the road pointed out the hiding places of others, or often it was only necessary to level guns on thick clumps of bushes and call out, "You blue-bellied sons-of-bitches, come out of there before I shoot."

At last the pursuit was abandoned, and the enemy straggled into Collierville. Washburn sent a brigade to protect them there. It took Sturgis ten days to reach the battlefield. He made the return trip in sixty-four hours, without, however, the impediment of his artillery and his train.

On June thirteenth, Parson Agnew noted in his diary: "Find many dead horses . . . and the stench is great. General Forrest passed back today. I noticed nothing special in his appearance. Understand he is in a bad humor, having been informed that the citizens have been stealing the articles from the Yankee wagons. General Buford also passed. He is a large, chuffy man. General Lyon also went down. A good many troops passed down today. . . . Eight hundred Yankee prisoners passed down today under guard. It is impossible to find one who will acknowledge that he ever plundered. One remarked as he came up—"here is the man that caught your turkeys." Another was heard to say,

"Here's the place where we got the wine." Some officers were among them. Nice looking men they were. A few negroes brought up the rear. The most of the negroes were shot, our men being so incensed that they shoot them wherever they see them.

"June fourteenth. . . . negroes are covered with very little dirt. The stench from dead horses almost insupportable. It is sickening to pass along the roads."

The Confederates did not crush Sturgis without paying a heavy price. In Rucker's brigade the loss was twenty-three, in Lyon's twenty, per cent. Dr. Cowan reports 492 killed and wounded in the entire little army.

General Sturgis, in his official report on June twenty-fourth, gave his loss as 2,230; but his brigade and regimental commanders showed it to be much higher: two thousand, six hundred and twelve. Besides this, Forrest reported the capture of two hundred and fifty wagons and ambulances, five thousand stands of small arms, five hundred thousand rounds of ammunition, and all the enemy's baggage and supplies. But many of the wagons were destroyed, and Sturgis sent back before the battle forty-one wagons and four hundred sick. Forrest's quartermaster gave a revised statement: wagons and ambulances, 182; his provost-marshal lists 1,618 prisoners. Five of the ambulances were loaded with precious medicines and sent under guard to Johnston's army in front of Atlanta.

On the return from Ripley, Old Bedford rode up to his Chief of Artillery and laid his hand on his shoulder. "Well, John, I think your guns won the battle for us." Flushing with pride, young Morton says, "General, I am glad you think so much of our work, but you scared me pretty badly when you pushed me up so close to the infantry and left me without protection. I was afraid they might take my guns." Forrest answered as he rode off, "Well, artillery is made to be captured, and I wanted to see them take yours."

He established his headquarters at Guntown and began to clear the field. He sent to a citizen and asked to borrow his mules to help remove the plunder to the railroad. "Yes, sir," replied the man, "General Forrest can get anything I have except my wife."

Sherman wired Stanton that he had just received news of the disaster to Sturgis, "whose chief object was to hold Forrest there to keep him off our road. I have ordered A. J. Smith not to go to Mobile, but to go to Memphis and to defeat Forrest at all cost. Forrest has only his cavalry; I cannot understand how he could defeat Sturgis with eight thousand men."

He did not understand, because, like many others, he regarded Forrest only as the boldest raider in the Confederacy. He was that, certainly; but if Sherman had studied his movements in North Mississippi and West Tennessee, he would have learned that Forrest had fought his men chiefly as infantry. Brice's Cross-Roads had enough men on both sides to be raised to the dignity of a battle. At least future military critics so regarded it. Marshal Foch took it as the text of a lecture at Chaumont.

It has been said that "marches, when conducted properly and in accordance with strategical principles, prepare the way to success, battles decide it, and pursuit renders it complete." There is no finer example to prove this rule than this battle. Forrest foresaw where he was bound to meet the enemy. He put to use his knowledge of the country; concentrated his troops, scattered anywhere from eight to twenty-five miles from the field; defeated the enemy cavalry before the infantry arrived; then turned on the exhausted infantry—his strategy had exhausted them—and defeated it. Barteau's appearance at the crucial moment drew off Grierson, who had rested sufficiently to serve as a reserve to the main line. Forrest was bravely and intelligently served by his officers and his men, but it was he who planned, executed his plans, and then saw to it that the *fruits of the victory were gathered*.

There is no other battle in the Civil War that shows harder fighting on both sides or a more crushing victory. One army was magnificently led; the other very badly. Forrest used his horses as a means of quick transportation. His men did not carry sabres. Only the orderlies and officers. He used the most efficient weapons he could find, the Navy six-shooter and the short Enfield—a sawed-off long Enfield. In the excitement of battle men frequently shot their ramrods away. He had the ramrods attached to the rifles so that the weight of his attack would never fall off for any such reason. So, he had the three arms of the service: infantry, artillery, and cavalry, unusually, but more efficiently, organized. It was no wonder that the West Pointers were confused.

On June fifteenth Sherman communicated again with the Secretary of War: "I will have the matter of Sturgis critically examined, and if he should be at fault he shall have no mercy at my hands. I cannot but believe he had troops enough. I know I would have been willing to attempt the same task with that force; but Forrest is the devil, and I think he has got some of our troops under cower. I have two officers at Memphis who will fight all the time—A. J. Smith and Mower. The latter is a young brigadier of fine promise, and I commend him to your notice. I will order them to make up a force and go out to follow Forrest to the death, if it costs ten thousand lives and breaks the Treasury. *There will never be peace in Tennessee until Forrest is dead!"*

CHAPTER XIX

Harrisburg

THE drama of personalities, which was to have such a decisive bearing on the final outcome of the struggle, was fast drawing to a climax. Forrest's fine display of skill at Brice's Cross-Roads, his crushing defeat of Sturgis, served to bring in strong relief one of the greatest strategic blunders ever committed by those who directed the Confederate war policy. On May tenth, the return of Forrest's cavalry showed his strength to be 9,220. If he had been turned loose on Sherman's communications in Middle Tennessee with one-half this number, he could have broken them so effectively that Sherman would have had to retire. His railroad guards were mostly negro soldiers, and there were not a great many even of those. Never again in this campaign would Sherman's communications be so vulnerable. Stephen D. Lee seemed to understand the importance of the move, for Forrest was on his way to Middle Tennessee when he was recalled to repulse Sturgis.

Unfortunately, Lee had sent Chalmers's division out of the state; he had detached Gholson's brigade to the southern part of his department. He had, as well, scattered other regiments. If he had kept Chalmers in Mississippi, he could have concentrated enough troops to meet Sturgis without recalling Forrest. This was his blunder, and after he had committed it, to protect his department there was nothing left for him to do but to order Forrest's return.

But, even so, it would have served the cause better to have let Sturgis overrun a part of Mississippi, as rich in supplies as it was, when Forrest's move promised to affect so vitally the movements of Johnston's army in Georgia. His defeat would mean that the crops in Mississippi would no longer be of use to the Confederate armies, for Johnston's defeat meant the ruin of the Confederacy. And this is where Davis should have intervened and relieved Lee of the responsibility, but Davis did not rise to the occasion. He did not meet Grant's grand strategy with a grand strategy of his own. He abandoned his interior lines of communication to his dispersive departmental system. When it was crystal clear to the best minds in the Confederacy that every other front should have been neglected in the interest of North Georgia and Virginia, Davis held to his departments with a fatal jealousy.

The month of June passed, and General Johnston appealed through Bragg four separate times, the third, the twelfth, the sixteenth, and the twenty-sixth of June, to have Forrest thrown into Tennessee. On the thirteenth he sent a request directly to Davis, and he made one final appeal to him on July sixteenth. General Cobb, Davis's friend, and the Governor of Georgia added their petitions, but they were refused. "I regret," replied Governor Brown on July fifth, "that you cannot grant my request. I am satisfied that Sherman's escape with his army would be impossible if ten thousand good cavalry under Forrest were thrown in his rear this side of Chattanooga, and his supplies cut off. The whole country expects this, although points of less importance should be for a time overrun in the destruction of Sherman's supplies. Destroy these, and Atlanta is not only safe, but the destruction of the army under Sherman opens Kentucky and Tennessee to us. Your information as to the relative strength of the armies in northern Georgia *cannot be from reliable sources.** If your mistake should result in the loss of Atlanta, and the capture of other strong points by the enemy in this state, the blow may be fatal to our cause, and remote posterity may have reason to mourn over the error."

This acid reply was flashed at once from Richmond: "Your telegram of yesterday received. I am surprised to learn from you that the basis of the comparison I made on *official reports and estimates is unreliable.** Until your better knowledge is communicated I shall have no means of correcting such errors, and your dicta cannot control the disposition of troops in different parts of the Confederate States. Most men in your position would not assume to decide on the value of the service to be rendered by troops in distant positions. When you give me your reliable statement of the comparative strength of the armies, I will be glad also to know the source of your information as to what the whole country expects and posterity will judge."

Governor Brown had already suggested that his "official reports and estimates" were unreliable. He should have made the issue clearer by stating explicitly that Davis preferred certain of his official reports to others: in other words, he preferred Bragg's to Johnston's.

The truth was, that Davis had by this time lost all sense of reality.

* Italics mine.

He had withdrawn into his shell at Richmond and refused to meet the growing crisis. His skin was too tender. Every fly speck sank to the bone and lay there to canker. In the beginning, when his policy should have been aggressive, he had rested on the defensive. Now, he had completely reversed himself. For weeks past, with the desperation of despair, he had insisted that Johnston take the offensive. Bragg was at his side and urged it, a thing he was unable to do when he commanded the Army of Tennessee. He completely dominated the President, whose feminine mind demanded the support of another. And there was the personal animosity between Davis and Johnston, made green again by the whole situation—Bragg, forgetting that Johnston supported him when he was his superior, now turned against him. He could not bear to see Johnston popular with the army whose confidence he had lost, a confidence so great that the army cheered Johnston even in retreat. Its spirit had never been better, for it knew that it was, at last, in capable hands. The tactics of his retreat were masterly. The army was in condition to turn on Sherman, if he could be forced to fall back by a broken line of supply.

But Forrest was not permitted to bring this about. He became one of the points of contest between Davis and his general, and Davis and Bragg were subconsciously determined to ruin Johnston even at the expense of the ruin of the Confederacy.[1]

Davis had already sent Bragg west to spy on Johnston and to plot his downfall. Hood was to be the willing tool of this conspiracy.

Sherman and Grant took it for granted, as the obvious thing to do, that Davis had ordered Forrest to Tennessee. They realized that the Sturgis disaster was expensive, but it had served its purpose. They now set to work to send out another expedition, even stronger and better officered, to hold Old Bedford where he could do no harm. One of the brigadiers, Mower, was promised a Major-Generalcy if he succeeded in killing Forrest. Sherman wrote to Lincoln and asked him to make his promise to Mower good if he should succeed.

In the meantime, Forrest, unaware that all this fuss was being made over him, prepared to defend his country from the ravages of the enemy. He had driven back "Sookey" Smith with seven thousand men, Sturgis with eight thousand; and now, he prepared to do the same with the present expedition under "Baldy" Smith. It was double in strength the first Smith's force.

Forrest made his preparations, but he wrote General Stephen Lee

[1] See Allen Tate's *Jefferson Davis* and Eckenrode's *Jefferson Davis*.

that he was in no physical condition to take active charge in the field. His tremendous energy, after his active campaigning, and particularly after the exhaustive work at Brice's Cross-Roads, was beginning to flag. Boils had broken out all over his body, and Dr. Cowan told him he must take a rest. Lee, however, felt he could not spare him.

General A. J. Smith, with two divisions of infantry, the negro brigade, and a division of cavalry, a force "amply sufficient to whip him," left La Grange on July fifth, the day Brown and Davis were burning the wires with their telegrams. The column moved in the form of a parallelogram directly south—Grierson's cavalry, 3,200; eleven thousand infantry under General Mower and Colonel Moore, and five hundred artillerists with twenty-four guns.

It moved in close formation, well protected by flankers and the cavalry, to Ripley, New-Albany, and Pontotoc. Here it met its first real opposition on the morning of July eleventh. Buford's and Chalmers's divisions lay directly across its path.

Two miles out of Pontotoc, on the Okolona road, a treacherous swamp spread between the two armies. The Confederates had felled trees and placed other obstructions to an advance. Smith tried this front; then withdrew suddenly. Forrest and Lee became convinced that Smith had no more stomach for a fight than the other Northern generals, and they prepared to close with him here.

But they had misjudged their opponent. Smith's caution was not fear. He had studied the causes of the last disaster, and he was determined to leave no weak places in his line of march. When Forrest, with his escort and Mabry's brigade, drove the rear of Smith's army into Pontotoc, he found the main body had turned directly east and was then moving towards Tupelo. Chalmers and Buford were ordered to fall upon his flank while Forrest drove his rear. Chalmers managed to attack his wagon train, but he was severely repulsed after killing twenty-seven mules and forcing the enemy to burn seven wagons and a few ambulances.

By the night of the thirteenth, Grierson's cavalry had seized Tupelo and destroyed four miles of track. Smith had halted the main body just west of this place at Harrisburg, an abandoned town. His position was strong, a high ridge circling two miles from the north of the town to the east. Most of the buildings of Harrisburg were literally torn away to strengthen the already strong position.

The day had been choking hot. The roads were inches deep in burning dust. There was not a cloud in the sky to obstruct the direct rays of a July sun. The wells were low, and no water flowed in the wet-weather streams. Only their cracked beds, slick and brown, with here and there a little green scum dampening the low places, taunted the swollen tongues of the riders. Out of the parched woods the gnats swarmed to drink the salty sweat streaming down their faces; and horse flies dug their spurs in the horses' backs just out of reach of their tails. In the fields by the roads the fodder on the cornstalks was curling, and the ears were swelling in the silk and popping at the top with an ashen-gray smut. Just before sundown General Lee, hot and tired, dismounted and sat down on the trunk of a tree. Forrest, with his sleeves rolled up, threw his coat on the ground and lay down on it. The day had been wearing; Smith had outmanœuvered him, and his boils were throbbing. Suddenly he got up, put on his coat, and called Lieutenant Donelson. They mounted their horses and rode off together.

After they had been moving half an hour, Forrest remarked that he had left his pistol behind. When Donelson offered one of his, he replied, "It doesn't matter much anyway. I don't think we will have any use for them." The two men rode on in silence, until the twilight thickened into a dark night; then Forrest turned his horse's head directly towards the enemy's camp. He and Donelson passed around the pickets and were presently riding casually among the wagons. Nobody challenged them, and Forrest made, leisurely and thoroughly, an accurate inspection of the position Smith had taken up and the means he was using to strengthen it for tomorrow's battle which he apparently regarded as inevitable. Having completed his reconnais-sance—the personal reconnaissance which was one of the secrets of Forrest's success in battle—he and Donelson turned to seek their own lines. Presently they were challenged by a picket. Without halting, Forrest rode directly up to him and in a harsh, commanding voice said, "What do you mean by halting your commanding officer?" Without waiting for an explanation, the two Confederates rode off into the night; then, bending low over their horses' necks, galloped away. The confused picket fired a volley, but the shots went wild. Forrest related the adventure with great pride. He said that a bullet would have done him good; it might have busted one of his boils.

He returned from the reconnaissance with the belief that Smith's position was too strong to be attacked, and it was rumored among the camps that Forrest favored a flanking movement. He met Captain Morton and told him to see that his men got well rested during the night, for they would have hot work before them on the morrow.

But Forrest was not the superior officer on the field. Bragg had seen to that. And, besides, he was not well. At an infomal conference the next morning, General Lee decided to force the issue that day. If he could not draw Smith out of his works, he proposed to make an assault. Lee seemed to recognize that this would mean meeting the enemy on his chosen ground, but in spite of it, he was determined to make the attack. There are matters of controversy that have never been cleared up, but if anything is clear, it is that Forrest was in favor of waiting and forcing Smith to take the offensive. Buford entered his protest. But at the moment, Lee, the department head, interfered with Lee, the tactician. He was thinking about the threat against Mobile, and the enemy moving from Vicksburg towards the center of the state. He did not known that these were feints to draw him off from the main objective, the destruction of Forrest. So he prepared to commit a grave military error: fight the battle of Harrisburg prematurely so that he could rush back and protect Mobile. No battle should ever be fought in a hurry. Every battle should be delivered as if it were the only battle —the decisive battle of the war. This was one of the few secrets of Forrest's invincibility—he never struck the enemy except on his own terms, and when the enemy was too strongly fixed, he always managed to find a weak spot, or to manœuvre him into a false position.

The Confederates had, on the morning of the fourteenth, the following troops on the field or marching in the direction of Harrisburg:

Chalmers's Division—McCulloch's and Rucker's brigades.	2,300
Buford's Division—Bell's, Lyon's, and Mabry's brigades..	3,200
Roddy's Division—Patterson's and Johnson's brigades....	1,500
Lyon's Infantry Division:	
Beltzhooven's battalion of infantry	900
Gholson's dismounted brigade	600
Neely's dismounted brigade	600
Artillerists, 20 guns	360
Total	9,460

Lee, seeing that most of the brigades belonged to Forrest, offered him the command. He declined it and chose to serve with Roddy's Division. He declined because he did not acquiesce in the resolve of his superior. Forrest's temper, as always, when he thought his men were being wasted, was none too good. James Hancock, in Roddy's

Division, overheard a conversation which threw an unhappy light on the state of the Confederate command.

General Lee, "Let Roddy's Division form on the left and Buford's on the right."

General Forrest, "No, I want Buford's Division on the left and Roddy's on the right."

General Lee, "As Roddy is here, why not let him form on the left, and Buford can fall in on the right as he comes up?"

General Forrest, "No, I want Buford on the left."

General Lee, "Very well, have your own way then."

There was little doubt but that Lee felt uncomfortable in directly commanding Forrest or his men. Particularly was this so when he could see that Forrest did not agree with his battle order. Lee's military training also warned him that frontal attacks, especially parallel frontal attacks, against breastworks manned by a superior force were almost doomed to failure. He relied, apparently, upon Forrest's great prestige, upon his success with inferior forces, to do the trick. But he forgot that Forrest fought his battles and won them in his own way. Forrest's troops under Lee could not be expected to act as they would under Old Bedford; and yet Lee seemed to hope they would.

This was a forlorn hope. In the first place, neither Lee nor any other man except Forrest could control them. His hard and unbending will, their feeling of perfect safety in his hands, their respect for his generalship—such things made of his wild and desperate lot the best soldiers in the West, if not in the Confederacy. As Colonel Kelly, the fighting parson, said: "He knew both men and horses; knew how to treat them; knew the full measure of the capacity of each; what was the utmost limit of endurance and what were the best methods of re-cuperation. When exertion had reached the limit, when camp life was monotonous, he was glad for man and horse to drill, though he never learned any of the technical manœuvers. When, however, he was preparing for a long march or resting from a raid, he demanded abso-lute rest for man and horse. There was from the first no detail of equipment, no element of supply which did not receive his most minute attention. He so carried in his capricious brain every detail that no other general kept his men and equipment up to such high grade. In this as in his capacity for long marches and precipitate attacks he had but one rival in our struggle, Jackson. If Jackson overmatched Forrest in knowledge of military science, Forrest more than made up this disparity by his quickness of perception of position, his unerring reading of the mind of his foe so as to tell with prophetic certainty the effect of a given movement on his part. He could deceive, mislead, and destroy with the certainty of a hunter who has given his life to the study of the peculiarities of his prey."

"Day or night," wrote another one of his veterans, "winter and summer alike his indomitable energy never slackened or tired. He was everywhere, and fell upon his enemy like a thunderbolt out of a clear sky. He was more than a born soldier—he was a born god of battle. He, in a large measure, infused his own splendid spirit into his entire command. The commonest soldier under his eye became a hero. I think he would have accomplished substantially the same marvelous results with almost any body of men that might have been given him. Who of his soldiers can ever forget the electrical effect of his presence on the battlefield or the danger-beleaguered march? I can now see, by the flashes of lightning in the dark night, while the rain falls in torrents, the dispirited column as it struggles through the indescribable swamps of Mississippi, men and beasts worn out with the loss of sleep and with work and hunger. But see how every eye flashes wide-open and how each bent form straightens itself in its saddle—how the very horses whinney with pleasure and recover their strength, at the sound of that strange, shrill voice, and at the sight of that dark form, the incarnation of storm and battle, that rides by on his big gray war steed, his legs swinging like pendulums on either side of the saddle, and followed by his famed body guard. Each man is suddenly awake, and invigorated as by the first fresh breath of dawn. All apprehensions of defeat slink away at his approach. His commission as general was not only signed by Jefferson Davis, but by the Almighty as well, and his soldiers knew it."

This confidence in him was now about to cause a great slaughter among his men. Roddy was on the right. Crossland's Kentucky brigade held the center; then Bell, next in line, took position across the Pontotoc road. Mabry held the extreme left of the line. Chalmers's Division was in a second line, and the infantry under Lyon was still farther to the rear. The three lines contained about five thousand in the first, two thousand, three hundred in the second, and two thousand, one hundred in the third. The artillery, twenty guns, was scattered out among the brigades. Morton suggested to Lee that he concentrate them and bombard the left center of Smith's works and prepare the way for a quick rush, but Lee did not agree. He had not ordered a flank attack.

The assault was supposed to be simultaneous, but Forrest had a mile to go to reach Roddy's position. The day was even more scorching than the day before; the charge must be made across open fields. There was little or no protection. Lee ordered the left and center to advance slowly after half an hour's artillery preparation, but before Forrest could reach Roddy and support the movement on the left, Crossland's Kentuckians felt that Old Bedford had arranged everything on the right. They felt invincible, merely because he was on the ground and, with a loud yell, broke ahead and dashed for the works. Their officers could not restrain them. The artillery and small arms of fourteen thousand Northerners concentrated on this one gallant, fearless brigade, eight hundred strong. It was broken and thrown back. Now Bell and Mabry made separate attacks. The Kentuckians rallied and swarmed to their support, but the withering fire of the enemy threw them again back to the edge of the woods. Lee had lost control of the battle, if he ever had control. Forrest, on the left of Roddy, galloped among the Kentuckians, grabbed a standard, and rallied them. He did not order Roddy forward. The premature assault on the left would now leave him open to the same treatment. He moved Roddy over to the front of Crossland, called Chalmers to his aid, when Lee had already ordered Chalmers to the left. When he saw Forrest's order, Lee divided the division, leaving McCulloch to Forrest and sending Rucker to Buford. After two hours of such fearless, piecemeal attacks, Lee ordered a withdrawal and prepared his lines to receive a counterstroke. But Smith had never before seen such reckless bravery; he had never seen men so contemptuous of lead or the sun, which struck down those the bullets had missed. He remained behind his breastworks.

Mabry and Crossland had lost a third of their brigades, Bell almost as much. The entire loss in Buford's Division for the whole campaign was over one-third. Roddy's loss was light, but Chalmers, who had scarcely done more than cover the withdrawal of Buford's shattered division, reported over three hundred killed and wounded. The fierce heat made the repulse more painful. Eighty of Buford's men were carried off, insensible and suffocating. Forrest observed the useless blunder, but he said nothing. His relations with Lee had been so pleasant; and Lee had, heretofore, done so much to assist him that the usual revolt was controlled. But one of his soldiers, Joe Smith, living in Tupelo, Mississippi in 1930, told me that General Forrest rode by him after the repulse, and he said that the General was "so mad he stunk like a pole-cat."

Early in the evening Forrest took Rucker's brigade and his escort and, crossing to the Tupelo-Verona road, made a spirited attack on the left of the line. He was met with one of the heaviest fires he had witnessed during the entire war. It was not damaging, however. The enemy overshot Rucker in the dark.

During the battle the Calhoun place was used as a Confederate hospital. It belonged to John C. Calhoun's brother William. The name was such a hated one among the enemy that a squad of Grierson's cavalry came out to shoot the old man. His wife made such an earnest entreaty that his life was spared, and later in the day she boiled a kid, seasoned it well, and fed it to the wounded. Three hundred were placed in her halls and parlors, and eighteen died there. The kid was all she had on the place, for the enemy had cleaned the countryside. So many arms and legs were cut off that they made a large pile outside her windows. A stray hog got through a hole in the fence and rooted and sniffed among them.

Later in the evening a meeting of the general officers was held at a house in the rear of the lines. General Forrest did not at first attend. He sent word that he was unwell. But General Lee sent back for him to come. Mr. William Wesson said that Kelly and Chalmers, who were present, described the conference to him. Forrest stomped in, saluted, and folded his arms Indian fashion as he sat down. He remained silent while the others discussed the situation. Finally Lee was forced to turn to Forrest. "General, we are in a bad fix." "Yes, we are in a hell of a fix," came the abrupt answer. Kelly and Chalmers saw what was coming and hastily turned the conversation. After some minutes of idle talk Lee again turned to his subordinate. "General Forrest, have you any ideas on the subject?" "Yes, sir, I've always got ideas, and I'll tell you one thing, General Lee. If I knew as much about West Point tactics as you, the Yankees would whip hell out of me every day." His voice then choked up. "I've got five hundred empty saddles and nothing to show for them."

The active direction of the command was turned over to him with the instruction to do the best he could. The next day, about noon, the information came in that Smith was retreating. He gave as his reason that his bread had spoiled. Pursuit was made by parts of Buford's and Chalmers's divisions, but at Old Town Creek, four miles out of Tupelo, Smith's rear under Mower turned and struck the Confederates a heavy blow. Chalmers made a flank movement with Kelly's brigade and saved Buford's horses and his artillery. Forrest was shot in the foot. He turned over the command and went to the rear to have the wound dressed.

The rumor spread rapidly that he had been killed. When he heard that such a report was going the rounds, he mounted his horse and, without taking time to put on his coat, rode to the front and galloped along his weary, disheartened lines. "The effect produced upon the men by the appearance of General Forrest is indescribable. They seemed wild with joy at seeing their great leader still with them."

The wound in his big toe, though painful, was not serious. He did not give up his command; but, seated in a light buggy, with foot propped up on the dashboard, he went about the business of reorganization. Riding over the battle-ground as the burial squads were at work he spoke to the men. "This is not my fight, boys. When it's my fight, you'll know it."

It was not his fight, but he had to pay for it. The tone of his command never quite recovered from the battle, and he was never able afterwards to fill up his depleted ranks. He was particularly crippled in officers. All of his brigade commanders but Bell were taken off the field, and all of his colonels were either killed or wounded. Out of a total loss of 1,347, over one thousand men fell in Buford's Division. The percentage of mortality was much greater than it appeared, for some five thousand men never took part in the day's work. It was another case where his troopers had been badly handled by a blundering superior.

The enemy rejoiced. They apparently considered it a victory merely to return to Memphis in good formation. Mower, who was to receive the Major-Generalcy if he managed to kill Forrest, was rewarded with the promotion, although he had only shot him in the toe. But Grant and Sherman were not entirely pleased with Smith's conduct. His orders had been to destroy Forrest, and he had only knocked him off his horse and put him in a buggy; but Forrest in a buggy was better than most men mounted. Sherman and Grant knew this, and they sent orders for Smith to return and keep Forrest occupied. Affairs before Atlanta were about to reach a crisis, and Sherman did not want it disturbed from Mississippi.

CHAPTER XX

One Foot in the Saddle

IT is the duty of the Government to direct the general plan of operations. It is no less its duty to leave the plan of campaign to the general intrusted with operations. This, Jefferson Davis was unable to do. He felt the crushing weight Sherman and Grant were throwing against his two armies, but he did not discover the true meaning of the political dissatisfaction in the North. The Northern people could not see that Sherman and Grant were wearing away the strength of the Confederacy; they only saw the long lists of killed and wounded, particularly in the Army of the Potomac, with no decisive results in return.

On July fifteenth, Bragg wired Davis from Atlanta: "I have made General Johnston two visits, and been received courteously and kindly. He has not sought my advice, and it was not volunteered. *I cannot learn that he has any more plan for the future than he has had in the past. . . ."* (Italics mine.)

About the same time a committee from the Confederate Congress visited General Johnston. The Senator from Missouri, Vest, in afteryears gave the following version of the conference to Harry M. Todd, a New York journalist.

"The committee informed the general of President Davis's attitude and he became very indignant. 'You may tell Mr. Davis,' he said, 'that it would be folly for me under the circumstances to risk a decisive engagement. My plan is to draw Sherman further and further from his base in the hope of weakening him and then cutting his army in two. That is my only hope of defeating him.'

"'But,' said Mr. Vest, 'Mr. Davis feels that you have it in your power to deliver a crushing blow, and if you succeed, it will turn the tide of affairs, so far as the Confederacy is concerned. As a military man he believes that if he were in your place he could whip Sherman now.'

"'Yes,' was Johnston's answer, 'I know Mr. Davis thinks that he can do a great many things that other men would hesitate to attempt. For instance, he tried to do what God had failed to do. He tried to make a soldier of Braxton Bragg.'

"While we were talking, a courier came in with the information that a part of Sherman's army had crossed the Chattahoochee, and another division of it had been thrown across Peach Tree Creek. Johnston immediately arose and said: 'Gentlemen, the time has come to strike. Sherman has cut his army into three pieces and I believe now, by rapid movements, I can whip him in detail.'"

Johnston had already chosen high ground looking down into the valley of Peach Tree Creek upon which to place his army. If Sherman exposed his communications in crossing, he expected to deliver battle. "If successful," wrote Johnston, "we should obtain important results, for the enemy's retreat would be on two sides of a triangle and our march on one. If unsuccessful, we could take refuge in Atlanta, which we could hold indefinitely; for it was too strong to be taken by assault, and too extensive to be invested."

If Johnston could not, as he hoped, hold Atlanta indefinitely, he at least could hold it long enough for the Confederate Government to order Forrest to Sherman's rear. Davis, faced with a definite crisis, would be compelled to act, for it would then be clear that the only hope of relieving Atlanta would be to break Sherman's one-track railroad, which was vulnerable for five hundred miles. The conditions would not be the same which Grant faced at Vicksburg. There he was close to his base, the Mississippi River, and cavalry could not injure him. The only hope for Vicksburg was a large relieving army. How different was the situation before Atlanta nobody knew better than Sherman. He said " . . . (we) saw him (Johnston) fairly across the Chattahoochee on the tenth, covered and protected by the best line of field intrenchments I have ever seen, prepared long in advance. No officer or soldier who ever served under me will question the generalship of Joseph E. Johnston. His retreats were timely, in good order, and he left nothing behind. We had advanced into the enemy's country one hundred and twenty miles, with a single-track railroad, which had to bring clothing, food, and ammunition, everything requisite for one hundred thousand men and twenty-three thousand animals. The city of Atlanta, the gate city opening the interior of the important state of Georgia, was in sight; its protecting army was shaken but not defeated, and onward we had to go—illustrating the principle that 'an army once on the offensive must maintain the offensive.'"

But just at this moment, when Johnston had his adversary at the greatest disadvantage since the beginning of the campaign, Davis, desperate and made more desperate by the telegrams Bragg was sending from Atlanta, wired Johnston on July sixteenth: "I wish to hear from you as to present situation, and your plan of operations *so specifically as will enable me to anticipate events*." * Johnston was a general of an army, not a prophet; so he answered: ". . . As the enemy has double our number, we must be on the defensive. My plan of operations must, therefore, depend upon that of the enemy. It is mainly to watch for an opportunity to fight to advantage. We are trying to put Atlanta in condition to be held for a day or two by the Georgia militia, *that army movements may be freer and wider*." *

Freer and wider movements meant nothing to Davis. He wanted to hear that Johnston intended to take the offensive and destroy Sherman; so the next day he relieved Johnston from command; and Hood, raised to the temporary rank of general, took his place. Johnston, in turning over the command, wired the Secretary of War. . . . "Confident language by a military commander is not usually regarded as evidence of competence."

"At this critical moment," wrote Sherman, "the Confederate Government rendered us most valuable service. Being dissatisfied with the Fabian policy of General Johnston, it relieved him, and General Hood was substituted to command the Confederate army. . . . The character of the leader is a large factor in the game of war, and I confess I was pleased at this change, of which I had early notice. I knew that I had an army superior in numbers and morale to that of my antagonist; but being so far from my base, and operating in a country devoid of food and forage, I was dependent for supplies on a poorly constructed railroad back to Louisville, five hundred miles. *I was willing to meet the enemy in the open country, but not behind well-constructed parapets*." *

Hood, on July twentieth made the assault Johnston had planned, but it was only a partial assault. Hardee, who had been senior to Hood, resented the change in commanders and he made such a feeble attack on his part of the line that the Confederates failed to injure Sherman. They were forced back into the parapets of Atlanta.

And now, Sherman, feeling great self-confidence in the changed conditions, wired Washburn that the crisis of the Georgia campaign was nearing, and that Forrest had to be occupied in Mississippi. Even with Hood in command, the fruits of his advance might still be lost,

* Italics mine.

if Forrest eluded the divisions ordered to keep him far away from Georgia.

Forrest's wound had given him more trouble and it had been more painful than any other he had received during the war, but he kept the field in his buggy, leaving Chalmers in active charge at the front. His men rapidly recuperated the last two weeks of July. He scattered them out where they could get plenty of vegetables, corn bread, and hog meat. The corn crop was abundant, and in that state of maturity best suited to recruit jaded horses. The fat meat actually was lined with pieces of lean, and it quickly greased up the "jints" of his hard-driven riders. Plenty of rations and plenty of good rest did much to restore the tone of Forrest's Cavalry and make it forget the disaster at Harrisburg.

General Stephen Lee had been withdrawn to command a corps in Hood's army, and General Dabney Maury was placed temporarily in charge of the department. He was the first superior to understand how Forrest might best serve the cause. He wrote him, telling him that he would send him supplies, but that he did not propose to interfere with his defense of North Mississippi, for "I reflect that of all the commanders of the Confederacy you are accustomed to accomplish the very greatest results with small means when left to your own untrammeled judgment."

One evening the two of them were sitting on the veranda of Maury's headquarters at Meridian, when the escort came by on its way to water. Maury said, "General, that is a fine body of men and horses." "Yes, it is," replied Forrest, "and that captain is the eighth captain who has commanded it. The other seven have all been killed in battle."

Smith, assembling his forces at La Grange, repaired the railroad to Holly Springs and early in August began to invade the state. Forrest sent Chalmers to obstruct the fords and rivers and build fortifications. But as his command had been reduced to a little over five thousand men, and these being very short of officers, he did not expect to be able to meet Smith and defeat him in battle, for his army this time outnumbered Forrest four to one. He had four thousand cavalry under Grierson; ten thousand infantry; three thousand negroes and three Minnesota regiments sent from St. Louis.

But Forrest had no intention of letting the enemy overrun his department. The greater the odds brought against him, the greater were his latent resources found to be. He had one general order: "Whenever you see a Yankee, show fight. If there ain't but one of you and a hun-

dred of them, show fight. They'll think a heap more of you for it."
Smith thought so much of him for it that his second invasion made
very slow progress. The weather, too, had a lot to do with his wary
advance. August was a rainy month, and the Tallahatchie rose a little
higher each day.

The distance from Holly Springs to Oxford was thirty miles, and
the Tallahatchie was crossed about half way between these two places.
General Chalmers destroyed the bridges and trestles below Holly
Springs and took a position south of the river. There was constant
skirmishing between the two forces, and Forrest from his headquarters
at Okolona wired his lieutenant to "Contest every inch of the ground.
Do not give back unless forced to do so."

But by the tenth, Chalmers was pushed into Oxford; and there,
with one foot in the stirrup, he found Old Bedford. He had come up
with Bell's and Neely's brigades and Morton's artillery. An advance
was immediately made as far as Hurricane Creek. After heavy fighting
for three days the Confederates found themselves outflanked on the
thirteenth. Again they retired to Oxford.

By the evening of the seventeenth Henderson's scouts reported that
Smith had repaired the railroad as far as Abbeville, had collected supplies, laid a pontoon across the Tallahatchie, and was ready to advance
south in earnest.

Everybody realized the inability of the Confederates to cope with
the superior forces to their front. At any moment they might be flanked
out of their position and driven back. The suspense in the rank and file
was great. Then, at the height of this anxiety, the order went through
the camp for two thousand men to cook rations and prepare for an
expedition. Buford, who was guarding the prairie at Pontotoc, received orders to repair to Oxford.

The camps took on new life. The direction of the expedition was a
mystery, but it was whispered that Old Bedford was going to Memphis. There was a rigid inspection of the men, and the weak, sorebacked horses and jaded riders were ordered to fall out. Then, on
August eighteenth, on a night as black as ink and in a pouring rain,
the General, fifteen hundred men, and four guns, slipped out of Oxford riding west. Unable to stop Smith from the front, he was on his
way to attack his base and accomplish by strategy what he could not
by tactics.

By morning the command had reached Panola. Here there was a
short rest to let the column close up. There was another culling of

worn-out horses, and Captain John Morton was sent back with one hundred men and two guns. Details had been sent ahead to have the women along the way cook up a lot of cornbread. This was issued; the sun came up, and the riders' spirits rose with it. After this short delay that familiar command, "Move up, men," went down the line, and the raiders swept due north. That night they reached Senatobia, twenty-three miles away, and well in Smith's rear.

It was found here that the command was so worn by the march that an all-night rest would be absolutely necessary, particularly since two streams, Hickahala Creek and the Coldwater, lay to its front.

The next morning, as the column drew near to the Hickahala, the boys began to discuss among themselves the difficulties of crossing this stream. They knew there was no bridge spanning it, and the slow passage by ferry might hazard the success of their raid, for everything depended upon a rapid, secret march. A little ways out the command was halted and Old Bedford rode back where all could hear him. "I want ten men from each regiment," he said. That was a familiar command, too; and the most daring always volunteered. Quickly the details rode up and faced him. Between him and his privates there was always a great deal of familiarity, although he allowed none from his officers. He required them to obey the strictest rules of military etiquette. He looked the boys over and said, "You think you're mighty fine roosters, don't you. You all think you'll get out in the country and drink a gallon of buttermilk, don't you. Well, I hope you do. I hope you drink two gallons. But I'll tell you what I want you to do. I want you here to go to every ginhouse in this country and strip up their floors—they are loose, you won't have any trouble—and I want you to go to the cabins and strip them too; then carry the planks to the Hickahala Ferry. Now, skedaddle. Now, you others. I want you to cut down these telegraph poles and drag them up to the ferry."

"General, we can't drag no poles up to the ferry. We ain't got no single-trees."

"Yes, you have! You've got your horses' tails. Plat 'em, and hook the poles to 'em. A horse's tail is the best single-tree a body'd want."

A few hours later, the command had reached the Hickahala. A detail, sent ahead, had already cut down two trees on each side of the creek. And they had stripped from the forest a large number of grapevines. These vines, as tough as any leather, were now stretched from tree to tree across the sixty-foot creek. As the central pontoon, the ferry, about twenty feet long, was anchored midways. Two rafts, made from the cedar telegraph poles and tied together with muskedine cables, were next floated into the current on each side of the ferry and fastened to the main cable. On top of this large, but light, pontoon the men laid other telegraph poles, and over these the flooring was spread. The bridge was finished in an hour, and the command began immediately to cross over. Forrest had brought a wagonload of corn out of Senatobia. He ordered it dumped, and carried over by hand. He was the first man to pick up an armload. The riders followed in column of twos, the men dismounted and leading their critters. By the time the last of the command had passed over, the bridge had sunk well into the water; but it had served its purpose. The Cold Water, seven miles beyond was crossed in the same way; but it took three hours to build the bridge there, as the stream was twice as wide. The last regiment crossed a little before sundown, and it closed up the rear at Hernando, ten miles away, after nightfall.

Here Forrest met several of his scouts. They gave him accurate information of the strength and position of Washburn's forces. Allowing the column a short rest, he now took the direct road to Memphis, twenty-five miles away. All was quiet there, without the least suspicion of the impending danger. Forrest was far away and busy with Smith.

In spite of the mud, darkness, and the great fatigue of the horses, the command drew rein about three o'clock Sunday morning four miles south of Memphis. By this time his scouts, as thick as flies, had been swarming out of the city with information. He knew the exact location of the three generals, Washburn, Hurlbut, and Buckland, where the five thousand troops, mostly hundred days' men, were scattered, and where the horses and mules were quartered. He called his general officers and explained to them fully what parts various detachments of their regiments would play, and these in turn called up the detachments and delivered the definite and comprehensive instructions.

Captain Bill Forrest was to overpower the picket, dash by the most direct route into the heart of the town and capture General Hurlbut at the Gayoso House. Colonel Logwood, with another detachment, was to follow behind him and place detachments at the junction of Main and Beal, Shelby and Beal, and at the steamboat landing. Colonel Jesse Forrest was ordered to move down De Soto to Union and capture General Washburn. Colonel Bell, with parts of Newsom's, Russell's, and Barteau's regiments were held in reserve; Colonel Neely was to attend to the hundred days' men. The men were told to keep silent until the center of the town was reached, and officers were ordered to shoot plunderers.

When everything was ready, the command moved forward about daybreak. A heavy fog covered the movement. Captain Bill preceded the rest of his company some sixty paces with ten picked men. Through the thick, damp fog came a sharp "Who goes there?"—"A detachment of the Twelfth Missouri Cavalry with rebel prisoners."—"Advance one."

Captain Bill, covered by the fog, rode stealthily forward. His men followed slowly but closely behind him. He reached the picket, struck him one blow with his heavy revolver, and the man tumbled to the ground. At the same instant his men sprang forward and captured the reserve. But one gun was fired. General Forrest, moving with the main body a hundred yards behind, heard this discharge with no little anxiety.

The entire command now pushed rapidly towards the city, but it struck a long deep mudhole in Mississippi Avenue. In the dim light it looked interminable. The men in the rear crowded those in front, and for a moment confusion spread through the eager column. The command soon reached firmer ground, and from the front Captain Bill's men let out the rebel yell; the entire command, although it was strictly against orders, took it up. It was too much to ask them to keep from whooping and hollering. What was a raid for anyway? Forrest now ordered Gaus to sound the charge.

Captain Bill galloped to the Gayoso and, without the formality of dismounting, rode into the lobby. One officer resisted and was shot. Some of Hurlbut's staff were captured, but the general escaped. His convivial habits had led him to spend the night away from his quarters. Buckland was aroused by his sentry, "General, they are after you." "Who is?"—"The rebels." He jumped out of bed, dressed, and ran to the barracks to rally his men. Washburn received the same notification, but he did not take time to dress. He leaped to his feet and slipped out the back door. Colonel Thurston, the inspector-general, says in his report that "the general ran away for a safe place in the fort, which was fully a half-mile from his home, when he was but three squares away from the provost-marshal's office; and all this without giving any orders or commands as to what should be done by the troops."

Buckland took charge of them and they were soon gathered and made a strong resistance. Neely met as serious a resistance from the infantry, one thousand in all. General Forrest seeing his check, turned their flank and they retired into the Female College. The General there charged and dispersed the cavalry and captured a good many horses.

By nine o'clock the resistance was well organized, and the boys were recalled to the outskirts. A battery which Bill Forrest had run over but had not stopped to spike now gave the retiring raiders trouble, but they were soon withdrawing from the city with their captures, about six hundred men, a number of horses and mules, and private plunder. Colonel Jesse Forrest did not deliver Washburn into his brother's hands, but he brought him his clothes. The General had these returned by flag of truce; and Washburn, to show his appreciation of this little courtesy, had Forrest's tailor make a handsome, new uniform, which he sent out to his enemy. He also sent a large bolt of gray cloth, and a suitable amount of lace to his staff. Major Strange received a beautiful sword.

Forrest halted at Cane Creek and sent Major Anderson in with a request that Washburn send out clothes and food for the prisoners, many of whom were convalescents and in no condition to make the return march. Washburn refused to exchange prisoners, but he sent out two wagons filled with food. Two days' rations were issued to the prisoners, and there was food left over for the raiders.

Forrest had cut the wires; so Washburn was delayed in informing Smith of what had happened. His directions when they did get through, were a little contradictory, and Smith was a little confused. "Then we heard of Forrest's raid to Memphis, but could not believe it. I soon received your dispatches of the twenty-first and was induced to believe from your last telegram and information received at Oxford that Forrest would retreat through Holly Springs." He ordered his cavalry to this place, and Old Bedford slipped back to his own lines by the same route he had taken on the advance.

Although Forrest was well on his way south, the garrisons were stampeded in Memphis on the twenty-third by the report that he was back in town in force. They remained under arms all day. Sherman wired Washburn, "If you get a chance send word to Forrest that I admire his dash but not his judgment. The oftener he runs his head against Memphis the better." Sherman also sent orders for Smith's return. By the twenty-ninth Forrest wired Maury, "Enemy left Holly Springs at two o'clock yesterday, marching rapidly in the direction of Memphis and La Grange. They say they are ordered to reinforce Sherman."

This was true. Forrest's descent upon Memphis, his complete surprise of the town and Smith's surprise at his departure, set Sherman to thinking. If Forrest could slip away so silently and make a raid on Memphis, he might slip away just as silently and make a raid into Tennessee. So he recalled Smith to Tennessee not to reënforce him against Hood, but to steal a march on Forrest. Smith never reached Sherman. He was diverted to assist Rosecrans in the Trans-Mississippi, but later, when Forrest did make a raid into Middle Tennessee, Sherman wired Webster at Nashville: "Ask Rosecrans for me if he cannot spare A. J. Smith, and explain to him that he may be needed. *I wanted him for this very contingency, which I foresaw.*" *

Chalmers, by his stubborn contest of the ground around Oxford, made the expedition a success, for he handled his troops so well that not once did Smith suspect that Forrest had left the front. General Maury wired Forrest, after the raid was over. "You have again saved Mississippi. Come and help Mobile. Fort Morgan was captured by the enemy yesterday. . . . We are very weak."

Hurlbut, who had been on a party in North Memphis the night of the raid, remarked next day with a great deal of satisfaction: "Well, they removed me from command because I couldn't keep Forrest out of West Tennessee; but apparently Washburn can't keep him out of his bedroom."

* Italics mine.

CHAPTER XXI

A Great Success that Failed

ATLANTA fell on September second. Hood's appointment had forced him to take the offensive. He made two sorties in July, and both failed. Sherman then threw the bulk of his army across his line of communications and forced him out of the impregnable works around Atlanta. Hood took up a position west of the town and changed his base to Jacksonville, Alabama.

Maury had recently been superseded by Lieutenant-General Taylor, a son of old Zachary's and a brother to Davis's first wife. Taylor had, to protect his department, the garrison at Mobile and Forrest's command. This meant that Forrest was the only combat force outside of Hood's army. Events, in a time of disaster, were forcing the Confederate authorities to understand the importance of the only man in the West who had never been defeated.

On September fourth, in answer to Maury's urgent call for help, Forrest sent McCulloch's brigade to Mobile and he was himself moving by train with Rucker's brigade when he learned that Taylor had taken charge of the department. Taylor says "an hour later a train from the north, bringing Forrest in advance of his troops, reached Meridian and was stopped, and the general, whom I had never seen, came to report. He was a tall, stalwart man, with grayish hair, a mild countenance, and slow and homely of speech. In a few words he was informed that I considered Mobile safe for the present, and that all our energies must be directed to the relief of Hood's army, then west of Atlanta. The only way to accomplish this was to worry Sherman's communications, north of the Tennessee River. . . ."

"To my surprise, Forrest suggested many difficulties (although he himself had just suggested this movement to Davis), and asked many questions: how he was to get over the Tennessee; how he was to be supplied; what should be his line of retreat in certain contingencies;

what he was to do with prisoners if any were taken. I began to think he had no stomach for the work; but at last, having isolated the chances of success from causes of failure, with the care of a chemist experimenting in a laboratory, he rose, and asked for Fleming, the superintendent of the railway, who was on the train by which he had come. Fleming appeared—a little man on crutches, but with the energy of a giant—and at once stated what he could do in the way of moving supplies on his line, which had been repaired up to the Tennessee boundary. Forrest's whole manner changed. In a dozen sharp sentences he told his wants, said he would leave a staff officer to bring up his supplies, asked for an engine to take him back north twenty miles to meet his troops, informed me he would march with the dawn, and hoped to give an account of himself in Tennessee."

When the engine brought him back to his troops, he ordered the trains to countermarch to Tupelo; then, going to the back-end of his coach, he sat down, folded his arms, and dropped his chin on his chest. His staff withdrew to a respectful distance. The General was at work, and they knew better than to disturb him. He was planning the raid: how much ordnance he would need, how many supplies, the expected obstacles, the route of march, reports of his scouts, movements weeks ahead—every detail which he could possibly foresee passed through his powerful mind and was put in its proper place. At such a time his imagination, rooted deep in a concrete brain, was too much for his nerves. The slightest interruption turned them, raw and jangling, from his thoughts to his muscles.

A lady who knew him well happened to be on the train and, seeing him all alone, could not resist the temptation to while away the journey in such distinguished company. A member of the staff told her he was very busy; that at such times he was not quite himself; and that it would not be wise to bother him. But the lady persisted. The officer then suggested that she might find the staff an entertaining group of men; but she let it be known that she never took bread when she could get meat. Passing the empty rows of seats, she greeted the General cheerily. The sound of a growl rose above the noise of the train, and the lady fled back to the amused staff, her eyes flashing, her face red, and her pin feathers bristling. "I've never been spoken to before like that by any man. General Forrest is a boor!"—"I told you, madam, you should not disturb the General."

Shortly after this episode, the General rose up and rejoined his staff. He greeted the lady as if he were seeing her for the first time. Her anger melted, and they were soon busy with compliments. When the inevitable lull came, the lady asked, "General, why is it the hair on your head is gray and your beard is black?"

"I don't know, ma'm, unless it's because I work my head more'n I do my jaws."

The lady lapsed into silence.

When Forrest reached Tupelo, he found that he could not march with the dawn. There were inevitable delays, and among them there was discontent in Rucker's brigade. In a recent reorganization of his entire command Forrest had placed all the Tennesseans in one brigade, and he definitely assigned Rucker to the command. As Rucker was junior to certain of the colonels, there was great excitement in the camp at Sookatoncha Bridge. Chalmers made a politic speech, and the waters were calmed; but the officers made it known that they would not obey Rucker's orders. This was open defiance of Old Bedford; so he arrested Colonels Duckworth, Green, Neely, and Major Phil Allen and sent them to Mobile. Just before the move into Middle Tennessee he mounted a platform, built for the purpose, and addressed the men. He told them he was going to their home country, and he told them what he expected them to do. Part of his speech referred to the mutinous officers in harsh, bitter language. He let it be known that he was commanding and that he intended to be obeyed by officer and private alike.

On September 16, all was in readiness for the raid. The command was to march in two columns. Forrest would move by rail with four hundred and twenty dismounted men up to Corinth, and from Corinth to Cherokee, Alabama, while Buford would move the main column, over three thousand strong, across country and over a more direct route. The General was walking up and down the Tupelo depot, with his hands under his coat, clasped behind him, his coat tails bobbing up and down, his head bent over in thought. As he paced the flooring, he was oblivious to the bustle and the noise of departure. A lieutenant-colonel whom he had offended walked up and planted himself across his path. "General Forrest," he said, "I want a conference with you. You have grossly insulted me, and I want an apology or satisfaction."

Forrest halted his pacing a moment, looked at and through the man, and without speaking moved on to the other side of the depot. The officer ran through the door of the station and confronted him again. "Oh, no, you can't get away from me that way, sir—" When he came to "that way," Forrest's left hand shot up to the scruff of the colonel's neck. His feet flew into the air, and unconscious he lay flattened out upon the station floor. Without a word, without looking at him, the General continued his pacing to and fro, his coat tails bobbing, his head bent over in thought.

Presently four long trains of supplies and men were rolling out of the station. There were frequent halts, as the track had to be repaired in numerous places. The men cut enough wood along the way to heat the boilers, while others took buckets and filled them from the running streams. On the eighteenth the command reunited at Cherokee Station. Chalmers had been left behind with Mabry's brigade to guard Mississippi in Forrest's absence.

Forrest had been told that Wheeler would assist him on his raid, as well as Roddy; but Wheeler had recently returned from a disastrous raid upon Sherman's communications in Georgia. He had been driven into East Tennessee and had barely made his escape through Middle Tennessee. On the twentieth Forrest wrote Taylor:

"General: I have the honor to state that I met Major-General Wheeler today at Tuscumbia. His command is in a demoralized condition. He claims to have about two thousand men with him; his adjutant-general says, however, that he will not be able to raise and carry back with him exceeding one thousand men, and in all probability not over five hundred. One of his brigades left him and he does not know whether they are captured or have returned, or are still in Middle Tennessee. He sent General Martin back in arrest, and his whole command is demoralized to such an extent that he expresses himself as disheartened, and that, having lost influence with the troops, and being unable to secure the aid and co-operation of his officers, he believes it to the interest of the service that he should be relieved from command. General Roddy is sick, but has ordered three regiments—I suppose about nine hundred men—to report to me. You will see, therefore, that I can expect but little assistance, but will nevertheless go ahead; am all ready and will move in the morning and have my command across the river to-morrow night. General Wheeler has turned over to me what he has of my old brigade, *numbering sixty men.** When I left it with him last November it then numbered over two thousand, three hundred for duty. I hope to be instrumental in gathering them up. I am satisfied that many will flock to me and I shall greatly need the arms telegraphed for to-night."

After Forrest had crossed the river and his raid was well under way, he received a reply from Taylor telling him how much he relied

* Italics mine.

upon his skill and energy to accomplish the objects of the raid; and to this end he directed him to be guided by his own good judgment, *"reporting directly to me and acting independently of any officer, regardless of rank,** with whom you may come in contact." Taylor had no intention of repeating the mistakes of the past, "for the nature of the service in which you are now and in future likely to be engaged renders it desirable that you should not be tied down to or burdened with the details of a district command...." At last he was to be given freedom to confuse the plans of the enemy. But this freedom, perhaps, would be given too late to restore the failing fortune of the Confederacy. Atlanta had fallen, and its fall had assured the election of Lincoln.

But, on the morning of the twenty-first, Forrest began the passage of the river he had crossed so many times. Major Anderson was put in charge of the wagons, the artillery, and the dismounted men with orders to use the boats at Colbert's Ferry. At Ross's Ford, at the lower end of Colbert's Shoals, the cavalry was lined up in column of twos to make the dangerous one-mile trip to the other side. The river at this point was seldom fordable, but a careful guide led the long, winding column through the shallows and around the treacherous holes. At one time the gray riders and the stumbling horses stretched from bank to bank. They were soon over without the loss of a man and on their way to Florence, twenty-five miles away. They bivouacked that night within two miles of the town. Colonel Johnson reported the next day with one thousand of Roddy's men, bringing the entire force up to forty-five hundred men and eight guns.

In the early forenoon of a perfect day, Forrest, in a handsome new uniform, mounted on "King Phillip," rode in from the west at the head of his escort. He turned into Court, then into Tennessee Street; and from the walks, crowded with convalescent soldiers, women, children and old men, a mighty yell rose to greet him. He took off his hat, "Kink Phillip" began to prance, and the escort and staff swelled with pride as the hero of the Southwest bowed to the people of Florence. No one thought of the desperate condition of the Confederacy when Old Bedford rode through town.

One of his privates on furlough watched the reception, and he compared it to his first meeting with the General, thirteen years ago. "Why the first creosote I ever saw he put into an aching tooth of mine, when on one of his trading expeditions he was camping in front of my father's house on the road from Grenada to Greensboro. He was a

* Italics mine.

man to impress even a stripling, as I was then. I should have carried
his image in my mind to this day even if there had never been a war.
A stalwart, who habitually went in shirt sleeves. A man of commanding, but pleasing personality, with grayish-blue eyes, who spoke kindly
to children. A broad felt hat, turned up at the sides and surmounting a
shock of black hair. . . ."

At ten o'clock the night of the twenty-second he ordered his brother,
Colonel Jesse, and Colonel White to take their regiments and capture
a corral at McDonald station, between Decatur and Athens. The next
day before sundown he surprised the garrison at Athens with the main
body of his command and drove them into a fort three-quarters of a
mile from the town. He sent Colonel Barteau and Major Anderson
with the Second Tennessee and his escort to capture a train, then
whistling at the station, and to cut the telegraph wires and the track.
Barteau, with his usual efficiency, set to work. He deployed his men
in line—about two men to a cross tie—along the road, and when the
command "All Together" was given, a portion of the track the length
of the regiment was lifted from its bed. He kept this up for several
hours; then rejoined Bell at Athens, bringing with him one hundred
horses and their equipment.

In the meantime, Forrest surrounded the town and three sides of the
fort. It rained during the night, and some of the ammunition was injured. The next morning three hours were taken to put the command
in a position for assault. Reënforcements for the enemy were reported
coming from Decatur. Colonel Forrest and Colonel White, having
returned from their detached service, were thrown across the road to
prevent this junction. Forrest, to save "the effusion of blood," sent
Major Strange forward with a flag of truce demanding the surrender
of the fort. Colonel Campbell, the commander, declined. Forrest now
prepared to make the assault, but he could not bring himself to expose his men; so he requested Colonel Campbell to meet him outside
the fort at any point he might designate, and he would convince him
that he had sufficient force to storm the works. Campbell consented.

The two officers began at once to review the investing body. The
first troops displayed were the dismounted cavalry, deployed as infantry. Some six hundred yards rearward the horse-holders were drawn
up and so disposed as to appear four thousand strong. Colonel Campbell was next shown the artillery, and while he was inspecting its
positions, the cavalry, now mounted, dashed into view and deployed.
Next he was shown another body of infantry, the horse-holders this

time; then more artillery. His report showed that he saw Morton's eight guns twenty-eight times. Campbell was thoroughly convinced that Forrest had eight thousand or twelve thousand troops; and as he commanded negroes, he thought it best to surrender.

Major Strange and Major Anderson returned with Colonel Campbell with orders to make the surrender as speedy as possible, as the relieving body at that moment was fighting its way through from Decatur. So the garrison, fourteen hundred rank and file, was marched out about one o'clock and made prisoners of war. Just at this time the reënforcements from Decatur pressed within sight of the fort. Seeing it was in Southern hands, after a most valiant effort to relieve their friends, they threw down their arms and surrendered—about four hundred. Colonel Forrest was wounded in the thigh shortly before this.

Two block-houses remained to be reduced. One surrendered at once, (85 officers and men) on the same terms which were granted to Colonel Campbell; but the other fortalice was commanded by a stubborn officer. So stubborn was he that when private West tied his handkerchief on a stick, he fired upon it. West afterwards remarked that his handkerchief was so dirty that perhaps the enemy mistook it for a black flag. The commander, a Dutchman, finally stuck his head out of the works and replied: "Shoost tell Sheneral Forrest dot I vill nefer shurrender. I haf but vun debt to pay to mein Godd, und I pay heem in mein block-house. And do you git away from here damn qvick, or I'll haf mein gunners shoot your damned head from your shoulders off!"

When the arrogant reply reached General Forrest, he made the air blue. "Does the damn fool want to be blown up? Well, I'll blow him up, then. Give him hell, Captain Morton—as hot as you've got it, too."

The first shot did little damage, merely tearing away a large log on top, but the second plowed between two logs and raised a fog of planks, dust and puncheons. Inside two were killed and one wounded. Instantly a white flag appeared at one of the port holes. Morton ordered firing to cease.

"Go on, John. Go on. That was bully. Keep it up!"

"Why, General, I see a white cloth from a porthole. Look yonder."

"Well, I don't see any. Keep on firing. It'll take a sheet to attract my eyes at this distance."

A few more shots were fired, when the surrender was received. The Dutchman was a valuable prize. He was sent in with the demands for surrender at other block-houses, and his account of the attack on him was so forceful that it usually brought capitulation without the firing of a shot.

The complete captures of the day were some nineteen hundred officers and men, two pieces of artillery, a large amount of small-arms, thirty-eight wagons, two ambulances, three hundred horses, mostly equipped, and a considerable amount of ordnance, quartermaster's, and commissary stores. The prisoners and the captured property were immediately sent back to Cherokee under care of Colonel Nixon. This was accomplished with the loss of five killed, twenty-five wounded.

After burning the block-houses and everything that could not be carried off, the head of the column was now turned towards the Sulphur Trestle, eleven miles from Athens. The trestle was a costly structure, spanning a deep ravine four hundred yards broad and seventy-two high. It formed a vulnerable link in the communications between the Northern forces in North Alabama and their base at Nashville. Accordingly, it was well protected by a square redoubt three hundred feet in length. This was furnished with two twelve-pound howitzers which swept all possible approaches. It was garrisoned by four hundred white cavalry and about six hundred and twenty negroes. There were also two block-houses which strengthened the defenses.

Rucker's brigade, now under Colonel Kelly, supported by Roddy's men, dashed across an open field and charged the rifle pits. The enemy, after a short skirmish, withdrew into the fort. General Forrest now made a close reconnaissance, and the works seemed impregnable to his force, especially since the block-houses were built in a ravine and sheltered from his artillery. But after several hours he managed to place most of his men within one hundred yards of the breastworks, and under the protection of a ravine. Captain Morton had also found four positions for his artillery, about eight hundred yards away. Forrest sent forward the usual demand for surrender. An hour passed before Major Strange returned with a definite refusal.

The Confederate artillery was soon put in position, and the firing began. Morton's practice was excellent. Every shot fell and exploded in the fort. The commander, Colonel Lathrop, was killed early in the day. The enfilading fire gave the garrison no cover, as they were seen to run from side to side in an effort to escape the exploding lead. Many ran into some light-framed buildings inside the redoubt, but the shells soon crushed these in or set them on fire. At first the Northern artillery did good work. Particularly the gun on the north side. Morton watched its practice closely and noticed that the gunners moved it to the port hole, discharged it, then withdrew it to reload. He ordered Sergeant Zaring to reserve the fire of his gun, while he watched carefully the answer from the fort. Just as the troubling gun was pushed back to its position, Zaring fired. His ball struck the lip of the cannon, exploded and killed five men, including the major of the fort. Soon the remaining artillery was dismantled and the garrison, now demoralized, was at the mercy of the Confederates.

Forrest ordered the firing to cease and sent forward another demand to surrender. This time it was acceded to without delay. The interior of the fort presented a sickening spectacle. Eight hundred rounds of artillery had been used, and over two hundred Northern officers and men lay mangled and dead within the works. The place had the appearance of a slaughter pen. So deadly was the work of the Confederate artillery that no more than thirty were wounded. This left nine hundred and seventy-three officers and men to capitulate; the plunder, two injured guns, twenty wagons and teams, three hundred and fifty cavalry horses, with their equipment complete, some ammunition and commissary stores.

The trestle was thoroughly destroyed, the dismounted men were all mounted and well equipped, and the prisoners sent back under escort. Also four pieces of artillery were added to the cavalcade. Forrest had used so much of his ammunition that only about four hundred rounds was left for the four pieces he retained.

Just before the cannonade, Barteau's men had captured a negro as he was fleeing from the fort. As soon as he found he was not to be killed, he gave his reasons for taking cover: "When dat letter come in dar wid Mr. Forrest's name to it I node dat was no place for dis nigger. I node Mr. Forrest before the war. I node him as well as I node Mas Jim—he was hard on niggers."

The command now swept down the road, destroying block-houses, culverts, and the track until it drew near Pulaski. The Northern pickets were encountered a mile beyond Richland Creek and pushed back a mile, where the main force, about six thousand strong, was found drawn up in strong position. Forrest threw Buford's division and Johnson's brigade forward on foot, while Rucker's brigade under Kelly made a detour to gain the rear. The enemy fell back gradually, and retired within its works around Pulaski. Forrest soon realized that these were too heavy to carry by storm; so that night he had his men build a long line of campfires; then about ten o'clock withdraw quietly in the direction of Fayetteville and the Nashville, Chattanooga Railroad, Sherman's main supply line.

The roads were boggy from recent rains, but the command marched thirty miles and bivouacked at dark, the twenty-eighth, five miles beyond Fayetteville on the Tullahoma road. Early next morning it pressed forward to within fifteen miles of that place, when Forrest's scouts reported that heavy columns of the enemy were converging on him from every direction.

Sherman had been planning his march to the sea, but Grant wired him, "It will be better to drive Forrest from Middle Tennessee as a first step, and do anything else that you may feel your force sufficient for." Sherman replied . . . "Have already sent one division (General Newton's) to Chattanooga, and another (Corse's) to Rome. Our armies are much reduced, and if I send back more I will not be able to threaten Georgia much," and for that reason he asked Grant to hasten the troops from Indiana and Ohio to Nashville. A large army, some thirty thousand, under Thomas, Rousseau, Schofield, Steedman, Croxton, Webster, Granger, Washburn, and A. J. Smith, was gathering to "press Forrest to the death," for "there will never be any peace in Tennessee until Forrest is dead." General Thomas said: "I do not think we shall ever have a better chance than this."

Rousseau, when he discovered Forrest's ruse of campfires, moved rapidly by rail to Nashville, and from there to Tullahoma. On the same day, Steedman with five thousand men crossed the river near Chattanooga and moved towards the same point. Morgan's corps was started on the twenty-ninth to reënforce Thomas, who was attempting to run down "an enthusiastic cavalry command led by one of the boldest and most successful commanders of the rebel army." "Forrest has got into Middle Tennessee," and Sherman was certain he would "get on my main road to-night or to-morrow, but," as he wired Halleck, "I think we can prevent his making a serious lodgment. His cavalry will travel one hundred miles in less time than ours will ten. I have sent two divisions up to Chattanooga and one to Rome, and Thomas started to-day to clear out Tennessee, but our road should be watched from the rear, and I am glad General Grant has ordered reserves for me to Nashville. *I can whip his infantry, but his cavalry is to be feared."* *

Rousseau confirmed Sherman in his analysis of the danger—"Forrest struck the road at Athens, and destroyed it to within a few miles of

* Italics mine.

Pulaski, where I had repulsed him on the twenty-seventh. He is here to stay, unless driven back and routed by a superior cavalry force. Infantry can cause him to change camp, but cannot drive him out of the state. Forrest's movements are much more cautious than formerly. He has attacked no place held by white men, but every post held by colored troops has been taken, and his destruction of railroad was most thorough. I have here about three thousand cavalry, not enough to fight him without support. This is much more than a raid; *I regard it as a formidable invasion,** the object of which is to destroy our lines, and he will surely do it unless met by a large cavalry force, and killed, captured, or routed. The cavalry, supported by infantry, can fight and defeat him, but he must be caught. He will not give battle unless he chooses to do so."

Since Forrest, with four thousand five hundred men, created such concern after the fall of Atlanta, which liberated the troops Sherman was able to send back to drive him out, it was clear what he might have done before, when Johnston commanded an army of enthusiastic veterans waiting for the opportunity Forrest could have furnished.

But it was now a physical impossibility for Forrest to break the main road. His command was reduced by battle and the large details sent back with the prisoners to about three thousand men. In other words he had one man to the enemy's ten. These odds were too great, even for him; but if he went ahead and sacrificed his entire force to break the road, the loss would not justify the sacrifice. It would not starve Sherman out of Georgia. In July the corn was too green to be eaten, but now the broad Georgian fields were waiting to be robbed. Nor was Hood in any condition, after his three desperate offensives, to do more than watch Sherman, although he and Davis were planning brave things.

So Forrest ordered a right-about. He divided his men into two parts. Buford, with portions of his own division, Kelly's and Johnson's brigades, was ordered to proceed to Huntsville, reduce that place if possible, destroy the road from there to Decatur; then retreat to Florence. With the balance of the troops, parts of Lyon's and Bell's brigades, the Seventh Tennessee, and Forrest's old regiment, Forrest moved over an obscure road in the direction of Columbia. He reached Spring Hill on October first.

Here, seizing the telegraph office by surprise, he found the line in operation from Pulaski to Nashville. He intercepted several official dis-

* Italics mine.

patches which gave precise information as to the location of the various bodies which had taken the field to run him down. One dispatch annoyed him particularly. He learned that Steedman was moving by way of Huntsville to cut off his retreat to the Tennessee River. Sending several confusing wires to the enemy, he destroyed the line and turned in the direction of Columbia.

On the road he found four block-houses, four bridges, a large government sawmill, thirty oxen, forty mules, six wagons, a stage-coach, and large quantities of wood for the locomotives. He summoned the first two block-houses to surrender. Forrest's artillery had gone with Buford; so he actually had no way to reduce them. When his demand for a surrender was promptly refused, he requested an interview with the commander. This was agreed to, and they met and inspected his forces. The officer could see he was without artillery, but as they approached Forrest's ambulance, Old Bedford assured him that he had the means in his power to destroy his block-houses without artillery. He called his driver and told him to bring a vial of "Greek Fire!" Forrest took it and broke it against a fresh oak stump. The fluid spread in a running blaze over the still green bark; the boys broke into a cheer for "Greek Fire"; and Forrest, taking advantage of the tumult remarked that as his men were growing excited it were best to retire, which they did before the Northern officer could observe the positive effects the "Fire" had had on the stump. The officer said he was satisfied that it would be foolish to resist under the circumstances and surrendered the two little forts and sixty-five men. They were immediately destroyed, and the truss bridges 150 feet long, which they guarded were given to the flames. The next two block-houses, after apparent hesitancy, capitulated, and the bridges were given to the flames. But another could not be fooled into surrender; so in the dark of night, Colonel Bell called for volunteers to burn the bridge. "Ten gallant men," as Forrest reports, "were marched forward, and in the face of the murderous fire applied the torch" (another vial of Greek Fire). "The night was dark, but my command marched until ten o'clock by the light of the burning ruins, which illuminated the country for miles."

He next made a feint on Columbia, and then turned south. He carried with him a great many recruits, and large numbers of men whom Wheeler had left behind. He arrived at Florence on the fifth and found that Buford had reached the ford thirty-six hours ahead of him and had already sent across the wagons, artillery, and a part of his command.

The rains had been heavy in the mountains; the river was high for the season, and rising. The wind, whipping the surface into good-sized waves, made the trips backward and forward perilous; so Forrest first ferried over the weakest men and horses, for the process was slow, as he had only three ordinary-sized boats and ten light skiffs.

Colonel Windes, of Roddy's command, was now thrown out on the Huntsville road to hold Steedman in check. Barteau with parts of the Second, Sixteenth, and Seventh Tennessee took position on the Nashville road. Hearing Windes was being pressed back, Barteau joined him; and they both retreated through Florence to Martin's bluffs, a strong position commanding the direct road leading to the lower ferry, which Forrest had moved to. Here, Barteau held the enemy at bay until the eighth. By this time, everything was over the river except about one thousand men, not counting those with Barteau.

The situation had grown suddenly embarrassing. It was almost a question of hours when Forrest must confront the enemy, for Steedman, reënforced from Nashville, had on hand some twelve thousand men. He immediately began to flank Barteau. Forrest, informed of this, now dropped down to an island below Florence and some seventy yards from the north bank. To this island he quickly transported the last of his command, swimming the horses, and hid them well in the cane-brakes on the southern side. The banks of this island were high on the north side and allowed Forrest to ferry his men over to the southern bank of the Tennessee without being seen. No fires were allowed, although the night was cold, for three hours after he had cleared the mainland, the enemy made their appearance. They turned back in disgust, not realizing that a hundred head of beef cattle and a thousand graybacks were hiding within seventy yards of their forces.

All that night the ferries plied back and forth across the river, and the next morning the pickets were called in. Fearing that some had been overlooked, Forrest made a personal inspection. He found four men still in the driftwood. "I thought I would catch some of you damned fools loafing back here in the cane as if nothing was going on. If you don't want to get left all winter on this island you had better come along with me. The last boat is going over right away."

"When we reached the boat," reported one of the four, "we were all made to take our turn at the oars and poles, and do our share of the work in ferrying across the river. The General, evidently worried and tired out, was on the rampage, and was showing considerable disregard of the Third Commandment. There happened to be standing in the bow of the boat a lieutenant who took no part whatever in the labor of propelling the craft, noticing which, Forrest said to him: 'Why don't you take hold of an oar or pole and help get this boat across?' The lieutenant responded that he was an officer, and did not think he was called upon to do that kind of duty. As the General was tugging away with a pole when this reply was made, he flew into a rage, and, holding the pole in one hand, with the other he gave the unfortunate lieutenant a slap on the side of the face which sent him sprawling over the gunwale and into the river. He was rescued by catching hold of the pole held out to him and was safely landed in the boat, when the irate General said to him: 'Now, damn you, get hold of the oars and go to work. If I knock you out of the boat again I'll let you drown.'"

In the meantime, Barteau was cutting his way through the surrounding enemy. Forrest had given him orders to disperse and cross the river the best way he could. The men had been trained in this sort of thing; so, taking to the hills, they moved camp daily until they had eluded all pursuing columns. Splitting into groups of companies, or into single companies, they all crossed at separate points.

Companies D and E of the Seventh Tennessee had gone into the service together, and so they stuck together in such time of trouble. Private Hubbard tells of their escape: "When these two companies got over into the hills of Wayne County, we hired a guerrilla guide, whom his followers called 'Captain' Miller, to show us a place on the river where we could cross. His remuneration was a thousand dollars in Confederate money, which was likely more money of any kind than he had ever seen in one lump. The people along the route cheerfully furnished us with supplies. I remember, we went down Trace Creek and across the headwaters of Buffalo, and reached the river at the mouth of Morgan's Creek, in Decatur County. Here was a booming river about a half mile wide, and no means of transportation but a large 'dug-out' some eighteen or twenty feet in length. We had grown about reckless enough now to try the impracticable and test the impossible. Three men with their horses and trappings were to make the first trip, two to bring back the boat, then three more with their horses, to go with the two who had brought the boat back, and so on till all had crossed. Everybody worked. Two men took their places at the oars, while I sat in the stern, where I was to hold each horse by the bridle as he was pushed from the bank, which was four or five feet sheer down to the water. Little Black was the first to make the plunge. He made one futile effort to touch bottom, and sank up to his ears. I pulled him up by the reins, and slipped my right hand up close to the bits, so as to keep his nose above the water. He floated up on one side and became perfectly quiet. I soon had the noses of the other two close up to the boat. The men at the oars pulled for dear life against the booming tide, the swellings of which we could feel under the boat. Our object was to make an old ferry landing several hundred yards below. We had no fear for the horses now, for they were behaving admirably. Though the men at the oars exerted themselves to the limit, we missed the landing, and were carried some distance below it. When we did pull into shallow water, I turned the horses loose. My own horse was the first to mount a steep, slippery bank, where he shook himself, and, looking back, gave a friendly nicker."

The campaign was now over, but Forrest ordered Colonel Kelly to make a parting blow at East Port where the enemy, moving from Memphis with two gunboats and three transports, were on the way to cut off his return to Mississippi. Kelly masked Walton's section of artillery and hid his brigade at the landing. The enemy was in command of one of Forrest's old opponents, Colonel Hoge. The colonel disembarked innocently, and Kelly gave the order to fire. The artillery had plenty of time to get a perfect range on the transports. One of the gunboats, the *Undine,* was disabled and dropped down the river. The *Key West* followed her. This left the transports without great protection; so Hoge ordered the troops to reëmbark. He went on board the *City of Peking,* when a shell exploded in a caisson on the *Kenton,* and set the transport on fire. Another shell exploded on the *Aurora,* bursting her steam pipe and setting her on fire. Hoge's whole expedition was now in confusion. The boats, in spite of his commands, backed into the water, leaving a battery of four guns and about two-thirds of his command on the shore. By marching under the bluffs, most of it escaped later; but the battery and twenty-five prisoners fell into Kelly's hands. Hoge's total loss was: eighteen killed, thirty-one wounded, and twenty-five missing—total, seventy-four. Besides this, Kelly captured sixty small arms, twenty horses, four boat cables, and artillery harness.

The entire command now marched to Corinth, and the raid was officially at an end. Forrest had marched and fought his men five hundred miles in twenty-three days. The qualities which usually distinguished his generalship had, on this raid, reached their greatest development. The Confederates generally, and Davis particularly, began to understand what their enemy had known for two years, that Forrest was one of the most powerful and most successful military commanders in the entire Confederacy, and that he always won his campaigns and at a ludicrously small price. He had on this raid put *hors de combat,* including the prisoners, some three thousand five hundred of the enemy, almost one man to every man in his command. He had done this at the cost of forty-seven killed, two hundred and ninety-three wounded, or a total of three hundred and forty. Besides this, he had brought out eight pieces of artillery with their caissons and some ammunition, nine hundred head of beef cattle, and about one hundred wagons (most of them were destroyed), three thousand stand of arms and accoutrements, and unusually large stores of commissary, ordnance, and medical supplies, the very supplies the South was most deficient in. For once his men had plenty of sugar and coffee, a luxury that the Confederates rarely enjoyed at any time, and certainly not in the last months of '64.

He destroyed six large truss railroad bridges, nearly one hundred miles of road, two locomotives, fifty freight cars, several thousand feet of heavy railroad trestling, a saw mill, a large amount of board lumber, five thousand cords of wood, and ten block-houses which were considered impregnable to ordinary field artillery.

He, as well, brought out with him one thousand men added to his immediate command and six hundred or eight hundred who had straggled from Wheeler. And he had done most of this not with fighting but with successful strategy. It was this one thing, above all others, that made his men cheerful and self-confident when the veterans of other Confederate armies were growing fatalistic.

But this great success had come too late. The right thing done at the wrong time, it did not assist in the establishment of Southern Independence. The Georgia Campaign in Mississippi was to Sherman all he had hoped it would be, although the price he had to pay was heavy—Forrest's several invasions of West Tennessee, "Sookey" Smith's repulse, Brice's Cross-Roads, Harrisburg, Memphis, and now the Middle Tennessee Campaign. It was one of the strangest anomalies of the entire war that Sherman won in Georgia by losing five battles in North Mississippi. But those failures in Mississippi, added together, made one grand success, because they neutralized the powers of the most dangerous military wizard in the entire Confederacy, the one man whose very name struck more terror to the hearts of the Northern generals than any other man below the line. But for the Confederates it had never been the Georgia Campaign in North Mississippi. One part of a piece of grand strategy, never combined with the other part,

Johnston's Army of Tennessee before Atlanta, it was left to spin out a separate conclusion; and its empty victory could only make more bitter the failure of the whole, a failure due, to state it in its simplest terms, to the feminine mind of Davis. The tragic flaw of the Confederacy was Davis, and this flaw's core, Bragg, insignificant as it was, was sufficient to destroy it. One drop of buttermilk in a well of pure water will make it stink like death.

CHAPTER XXII

Gunboats and "Hoss" Marines

ON September 28, 1864, Davis appeared unexpectedly at Hood's headquarters at Macon. He had come to give his advice, his military advice. After a conference, he and Hood decided between them that the best way to drive Sherman from Georgian soil was to move the Army of Tennessee, now reduced by casualties and desertions to some forty thousand effectives, from Sherman's front to his rear. He made a speech to the army and told the men that Hood would lead them to Sherman's communications and make of his retreat a second Moscow. This was quickly reported to Sherman, who was undecided what next to do, and allowed him to make his preparations to receive Hood. In the political world Davis had treated his fellows with military dictation; now, he appeared before the army and tried to move it to victory by political appeal. Each method was madness, and Hood was out of reason to let him announce to the enemy his plans. This evasion of Davis's was, probably, the key to his character. He could not, in political life or in military affairs, face the issue squarely, concretely; and there are no two other professions which are more concrete.

And yet Davis, still mixing his modes, had apparently lost confidence in Hood and saw that his appointment had been a mistake—if he had not, the loud cries from the army "Give us Johnston" informed him of his blunder—for he appointed Beauregard over the whole Southwest. The appointment of Beauregard meant that he had learned nothing, for to be of value Beauregard should have replaced Hood as head of the army. As department commander he was little more than Davis's political viceroy.

While this was going on in Georgia, Forrest was resting his command in Mississippi from the strain of the last raid. He wrote to Taylor that he was worn out and that he must have rest. Taylor replied that affairs were in too precarious a condition to give him leave and that he must go to West Tennessee instead and carry out his suggestion of interfering with the enemy transports. After this, he might rest.

So, Forrest set his brigades in motion for West Tennessee to give one other blow to Sherman's communications, not realizing that the blow might be hurtful but not fatal. On the sixteenth, Bell set out from Corinth. The next day Buford took Lyon's brigade and Morton's and Walton's batteries, and Forrest brought up the rear with Rucker's brigade, still commanded by Kelly. He met Chalmers with remnants of Mabry's and McCulloch's brigades, about seven hundred and fifty men, at Henderson; and then moved towards Jackson. Forrest now discovered that the supplies were scarcer in West Tennessee than he had expected to find; he also found that the last raid had been harder on man and critter than he had thought. Many horses gave out on him, and many dropped dead in their tracks. The rest were badly shod, and every mile the barefooted began to limp. The men noticed this and wondered what Old Bedford was going to do about it. It was certain they could not march much farther in the present condition. About the time the speculations had become general, the command was halted and the old familiar call for ten men from each regiment went down the line. There was never any trouble to get volunteers, and soon the men were crowded around Old Bedford.

"Well, you think you're mighty fine roosters, don't you?" They knew it was coming. "You think you'll git out and drink a gallon of buttermilk, don't you? Well, I hope you do. I hope you drink two gallons. But I'll tell you what you must do. Now, you there—down such and such a road you'll find a bunch of wagons in a barn lot. Strip off all the ties and bring 'em back, and before sundown. Now you go up that road to the west until you come to a cross-roads. You'll find a blacksmith there. It's full of iron. Bring it all back, and before sundown."

The details galloped off, and they were all back before sundown, loaded to the guards, with iron hanging over their saddles, wheel hoops around their shoulders, and in their saddle bags. The smiths in the command worked all night beating wagon ties into shoes, and by morning the two brigades were on their way to Jackson all shod.

Buford had gone ahead and planted batteries at Paris Landing, at Fort Heiman, five miles below, and another section of Morton's battery six hundred yards below that. They were all masked and waiting for the rich transports carrying supplies up the river to Johnsonville to be transported by train to Sherman and the garrisons in Tennessee. Presently four transports were seen coming down the river. Just as the men were ready to open fire, General Buford slipped up and said, "Keep quiet, men, keep quiet, don't fire a gun. These are empty boats going down after more supplies. I want a *loaded* boat, a richer prize. Just wait until one comes up the river and then you may take her if you can."

The gunners were itching to pull the lanyards, especially the gunners of the two twenty-pounder Parrotts brought up from Mobile for this very purpose; but they waited.

The next morning, about half past eight, the transport *Mazeppa,* heavily laden and with a barge in tow, churned into sight. They let her pass the first battery; then about nine o'clock the middle section opened on her. The Parrotts followed. In a few minutes her machinery was disabled, and she drifted to the other side and was deserted by the crew.

The problem was now how to get her over to the right bank of the river. This was quickly solved. Private Claib West had prepared for such an emergency. He stripped to the waist, pushed a slab into the river, used a chunk for a seat, tied his pistol about his neck, and with a paddle he had made with his knife, began to navigate the river. The captain, who had remained with his boat, helped him on board; and the two of them re-crossed in a yawl. General Buford stepped in with a detail and paddled back to take possession.

A hawser was attached and the *Mazeppa* was soon resting at anchor on the west bank. The prize was particularly rich in flour, shoes, blankets, hardtack, axes, and other stores. After supplying one brigade, there were left to be divided out among the others, nine thousand pairs of shoes and one thousand blankets. Private West found a demijohn of good French brandy. Buford saw him and ordered it turned over into the proper hands. At this, away went West with Buford after him. West succeeded, however, in getting out of sight long enough to fill his canteen. Buford now mounted the Hurricane Deck with the jug. The boys called to him not to drink it all, but to save them some. The Kentucky general shook his head—"Plenty of meat, boys, plenty of hardtack, shoes, and clothes—all for the boys, but just enough whiskey for the General."

Three gunboats now made their appearance and, as most of the supplies had been removed, the *Mazeppa* was fired. The next morning, another transport, the *Anna,* hove into sight and was fired upon. She agreed to surrender; then after the firing ceased, skipped out of range. Several hours later the gunboat *Undine* came in sight, conveying the transport *Venus* and two barges. They were permitted to pass the first battery, when it opened on their vital parts. Bell's sharpshooters drew their beads on the portholes. The boats dropped down the river, out of range of the first battery only to run into the Parrott guns at Fort Heiman. These were too much for them. About this time Colonel Barteau's regiment reached Paris Landing. Colonel Morton, when he reached the position assigned him, improvised the order for his battalion—"Halt! Dismount and prepare, on foot, to fight gunboats!" The men spread out along the shore, at fixed intervals, just in time to bring to the *Cheeseman,* another transport whose machinery had been disabled at Paris Landing by the artillery. The *Cheeseman* had a small freight of commissary stores, such as coffee, candies, nuts, and a quantity of furniture. The furniture was given to the people living in the neighborhood, and the boys split the coffee, the gumdrops, and the long-johnny.

About noon General Chalmers arrived with Rucker's brigade, commanded by Rucker returned from sick leave. They soon made the transport *Venus* surrender, and the *Undine* was driven to the opposite shore in spite of her eight twenty-four pounder howitzers. Colonel Kelly boarded the *Venus* with two companies and steamed over to take possession of the gunboat.

Forrest had done about every kind of fighting known to war, but he had never fought on water. Going up to Captain Morton, after complimenting the officers on their prizes, he said, "John, how would you like to transfer your guns to these boats and command a gunboat fleet?"

"Not at all, General. My whole knowledge is of land batteries. I know nothing of water, and I prefer to stay on terra firma."

But Forrest was not to be thwarted. He commandeered Captain Gracey, an artillerist and one time steamboat captain, to take charge of the *Undine.* Colonel Dawson was ordered to walk the poop of the *Venus* and command the fleet.

"Now, look-a-here, General. I'll go with these gunboats wherever you order, but I want to tell you now that I know nothing about them, and I want you to promise me now that if I lose the fleet and come in afoot, you'll not cuss me out for it."

Forrest laughed and told him to go ahead. If he couldn't hold his water dogs, run their noses into the mud, fire them, and leave for safer ground. The next day, November 1, all were in motion for Johnsonville. "Forrest's Cavalry afloat" had orders to keep within protection of the batteries on the shore. A steady rain began to fall, and the roads, naturally difficult, became worse. That night the command bivouacked near the ruins of the old railroad bridge. It rained hard during the night, and the roads grew steadily worse. The two boats got ahead of their land support and ran into three gunboats. The *Undine* escaped but Dawson was compelled to run the *Venus* ashore and abandon it. He lost with the boat the two Parrott guns and part of the supplies captured from the *Mazeppa*. The next day the *Undine* ventured too far afield and had to be run aground, fired, and abandoned.

During this skirmish with the enemy boats, a new Confederate regiment stampeded and left behind their blankets, clothes, saddles, and arms. Colonel Barteau's men appropriated all their belongings; and when the recruits returned and claimed their property, they were put to shame by the jeers of the veterans. Before the day was over, they denied ever owning any of the articles. A beef had been slaughtered but not issued when the shelling began. When one of the stampeders passed, a flash of lightning revealed it not far from camp. "There, by God," he says, "a shell has split a horse wide open." When the incident was reported to Colonel Barteau, he answered, "He must have thought that that was a wonderful shell—to split a horse open and skin him at the same time."

By nightfall, November 3, Forrest had concentrated his forces along the west bank of the Tennessee opposite Johnsonville. He ordered General Lyon, who had been an artillery officer in the regular army, to take Thrall's battery and place it opposite the south face of the landing and in easy range. Lyon moved the guns by horse to a certain point; then pushed them three hundred yards by hand. The position Forrest had selected was on a stretch of bank which fell off rapidly from the river towards the west, forming a natural rampart. Lyon sunk chambers for the guns and cut embrasures in the embankment. The men worked all night, and with so much enthusiasm that by eight o'clock next morning the battery was ready for action and completely shielded from view, although open somewhat to a plunging fire from the fort across the way. Other guns were planted above, some sunk in chambers and others kept free to move about. When daylight came, the work was not interrupted. Hickory saplings were cut and interwoven with those standing on the bank, and they served as a perfect screen to the work.

Captain Morton arrived and told the General that he was not satisfied with the positions of the guns, and that he would like to make a close reconnaissance. Forrest reluctantly gave his permission. Morton found what he considered an ideal spot directly opposite Johnsonville. He hurried back to his commander and explained in detail the advantages of the position. Forrest listened closely and asked many questions; then replied, "No, that's getting too close. They'll knock you all to pieces from the fort and the gunboats too."

"No, General, I have examined the location well. The fort is so elevated that they can't depress their guns sufficiently to affect me, and the gunboats are so much below in the river that they will fire over me, and I'll be at an angle of comparative safety."

Forrest then gave him permission to carry two guns and enough men to cut the way through the swamp. It took two hours to move the guns over a road that had to be made every step of the way. In many places the guns had to be carried over the fallen timber. Finally, by two P.M., everything was ready. Morton was to give the signal with his section. All that morning the work of the Confederates had been so secretive that the enemy never discovered their presence, and all that morning Forrest had been carefully examining the other shore with his field-glasses, a gift from Louis Napoleon after the fall of Murfreesboro. There were three gunboats, eight transports, and some eighteen barges, most of them loaded, tied up at the landing. Besides, piled high on the bank, the supplies already unloaded covered acres of ground. People were moving down towards the wharf; the decks of the gunboats were covered with the crew scrubbing the decks or washing their clothes. A few women sauntered idly down to take passage on the transports, several of which were getting up steam. No scene ever showed a greater feeling of security. Apparently they considered Old Bedford had been driven away. They did not know that he stood in the underbrush, devouring with his eyes every detail on the other bank.

Just as two gunboats, lashed together, moved away from the landing, the storm broke. Ten guns hurled ten shells above the river. Immediately steam and smoke poured from the portholes; the crew jumped into the water and swam for the landing. Women screamed and ran up the bank. One of the gunboats and the fort returned the fire. The crashing, thundering roar of fifty guns split the air; and after the third round, above all the noise, the screams of scalded men pierced to the west bank and told the gunners they had struck the boiler of one of the gunboats. The sharpshooters now joined in, hugging their rifles and squinting their eyes.

After an hour, two of the ironclads burst into flames; the one that was left to give battle now turned towards the landing, where it was deserted by its crew. The redoubt, by this time, had gotten the range of the Confederate batteries; but its shells did no damage. They broke the rammers in the hands of Morton's men and sank deep in the muddy chambers, so deep that their explosions were harmless. Forrest next gave orders to turn the artillery on the redoubt. The gunboats, wrapped in flame, floated against the transports and set them on fire. Thrall's guns were turned on two packets and their barges which were withdrawn from the rest, and they were set on fire. The cables snapped in two, and the floating fire drifted with the current, spreading ruin. By four P.M., every gunboat, transport, and barge was in flames.

The artillery was now turned upon the warehouses and the supplies piled on the ground. A few shells deftly exploded in a large mass of hay, and it was soon burning and spreading to heaps of corn and bacon. Seeing farther up the slope a large number of barrels stacked under tarpaulins, Forrest suspected their contents and ordered Brigg's section of rifled James to get their range. After a few rounds, an unmistakable blue blaze shot through the smoke into the sky, and the flaming liquid ran in streams of fire down towards the river or, as the barrels exploded, it sent its bursting streamers running against gravity. Soon the hungry graybacks were breathing deeply, as the blended odors of bacon, liquors, sugar, and coffee swept down on the western bank.

Old Bedford now turned gunner, with Bell, Buford, and Major Allison as assistants. Allison was posted behind a tree near the bank to observe the effect of his shots. When Allison reported a shot had fallen short, the General shouted with great glee—"Rickety shay! A rickety shay! I'll hit her next time. Buford, elevate the breech of that gun lower!"

When it was certain the destruction was complete, the command was withdrawn by the light of the flames. Rucker's brigade picketed the shore and supported one section that was left behind to cover the withdrawal. Captain Thrall's battery had done particularly good work. His men were mostly from White County, Arkansas, and the boys had nicknamed them the "Arkansas Rats." Riding along with them as they were leaving their position, the General called out, "Well, boys, after this fight, we will have to find a better name for you than 'The Arkansas Rats.' I am going to baptize you, right now, the 'Arkansas Braves.' "

A waggish sergeant, seeing his opportunity, called out, "General, talkin' may be very good, but somethin' to eat would sound a heap better. We've been livin' on wind for two days."

Forrest smiled and turned to a member of the staff: "Go back to my headquarters wagon, where you will find four boxes of hardtack and three hams. Have them brought right up here and issued to Captain Thrall's men."

Lincoln, Halleck, Sherman, Grant, and Thomas got wind of some movement by Forrest before it happened; but, as usual, too late to interfere. Sherman reported humorously to Grant that "Forrest seems to be scattered from East Port to Jackson, Paris, and the lower Tennessee"; General Thomas reported a capture by him of a gunboat and five transports. A provost-marshal wired that "Forrest has been in disguise alternately in Chicago, Michigan City, and Canada for two months; has fourteen thousand men, mostly from draft. On November seventh, at midnight, he will seize telegraph and rail at Chicago, release prisoners there, arm them, sack the city, shoot down all Federal soldiers, and urge concert of action with Southern sympathizers."

But on the fifth, he was located. "That devil Forrest," wrote Sherman, "was down about Johnsonville, making havoc among the gunboats and transports."

The loss to the enemy at Johnsonville was enormous. It was estimated by Forrest as high as six million dollars, as low by the Northerners as $2,200,000. At any rate the reduction of the depot was a complete success, and the interference with the river traffic sustained Forrest's contention, made to Davis before Chickamauga, that he could effectively close the rivers to the enemy, *provided he was given a free hand*. This, of course, was not granted until too late. The success here, as usual, was gained with a very small cost in men, two killed and nine wounded.

At Beauregard's orders Forrest now directed his march towards Corinth, after putting four hundred of Rucker's men across the Tennessee River, to join Hood who planned to invade Tennessee from

Florence. Before marching away, Forrest and Captain Morton returned to view the ruins. As they stood on the western bank, he turned to his young Chief of Artillery and said, "John, if they'd give you enough guns and me enough men, we could whip Old Sherman off the face of the earth!"

PART FIVE

POSTLUDE

PART FIVE

POSTLUDE

CHAPTER XXIII

Nashville

THE curtain was now about to be drawn on the last act of the war, with the scene set in the western theatre, the strategic center of Confederate hopes. Lee was holding Grant before Petersburg; Atlanta's streets were patrolled by blue men, but the Army of Tennessee, reduced to 30,599 infantry, artillery, and cavalry, was still in the field. Under Hood it had swept behind Sherman's communications and followed the river up to Florence, and there it waited for Forrest's arrival to make the last desperate play for the cause. It was a very remarkable army. Badly led except for the short weeks General Joe Johnston commanded, it never refused to move gallantly against the enemy; and now, although its confidence in its chief was none too enthusiastic, its spirits were high. It was going to fight it out on home ground.

Sherman had decided to make his march to the sea. He had retained sixty thousand of his best fighters, and with these he would sweep through Georgia for three hundred miles and destroy the largest granary of the South; then establish a new base on the sea, turn his head north and combine with Grant, when they would fall upon the Army of Northern Virginia. He had sent back Thomas to look after the Army of Tennessee, and as reënforcements for Thomas's scattered garrisons and commissary clerks he had sent Stanley and Schofield with twenty-seven thousand veterans. Wilson, one of the youngest and most capable cavalry commanders among the Northern forces, had been added to Thomas's staff as Chief of Cavalry.

Hood's prospective invasion of Tennessee was the most daring gamble of the war, and Sherman had parried with as great a gamble. If Thomas did not defeat the Army of Tennessee, Sherman's march to the sea would turn into the worst blunder of the war, for by leaving

Hood's army to his rear, he had given this Confederate an opportunity to fight an army his equal in numbers. At the moment Thomas's forces were scattered over the entire state. His only reliable body was Schofield, posted at Pulaski with twenty-seven thousand men. If Hood could cut off this detachment before it could reach Thomas at Nashville, where he was organizing, Thomas's chances of creating an army would be cut in half. The Lincoln Government, Grant, and the Northern people were fully aware of the risk involved.

Thomas's failure to concentrate would mean detailed disaster and the invasion of the Northwest. Once in Kentucky and across the Ohio Hood's presence in the borderland would give the Copperheads a rallying point and force Sherman's return. The effects of his summer campaign would then all be wiped out.

The conception of the campaign was Hood's, and its conception was brilliant. Davis neither approved nor disapproved. When Sherman did not follow his opponent, the Southern President seemed to doubt the efficacy of the movement, but he did not countermand it. He was thinking of the Georgia fields about to be laid waste and not of the gamble. By this time he had lost what influence he had retained over the people during the last six months. The personal enmity between Governor Brown and the President caused Georgia's Governor to disband the state's militia and talk of ordering the return of his soldiers operating with the armies in the field. He even made overtures to Sherman. Vance, of North Carolina, proved as great a stumbling block. The neglect the whole Southwest had felt was now at its height. Governor Magrath of South Carolina had taken a step which he hoped would lead to a Lower Southern Confederacy. He proposed that the military resources of the southeastern and Gulf states should be reorganized independently of Davis. Nothing came of it, but it very clearly showed that the disaffection of the Southern people was not because they desired to return to the Old Union but because they felt that all their sacrifice with Davis in control was useless. Davis's conscription act, with its twenty nigger clause, had probably been one of his greatest mistakes. It alienated the plain people and caused many of them to desert, saying the war "was a rich man's war but a poor man's fight." Davis forgot that he was born in a dog-run, and he forgot that the backbone of the South and its armies was the plain people. There was about him a great deal of the cotton snob's self-conscious aristocracy, and the removal of the capital to Richmond did not help matters.

There was one man in the Southern Confederacy around whom the people, especially the plain people, and the army would have rallied. If Davis had had the vision and the courage to appoint Nathan Bedford Forrest to the command at this moment, he would have revived an enthusiasm in the war. It has been the judgment of most historians that the overwhelming resources of the North in men and supplies doomed the South to failure from the beginning. But this is justification after the event, and it is not sustained by other examples in History. Frederick the Great and the little state of Prussia fought for seven years the largest countries of Europe, always against great odds, and came out victorious. And there is the defense of Thermopylae by three hundred Spartans and seven hundred Thespians against the vast hosts of Xerxes's Persians; and Hannibal's destruction of the forces of Servilius and Attilius at Cannae. These events are well known, but they are by no means exceptions to the rule. No people is conquered until its spirit is broken, and this spirit was breaking because Davis could no longer lead his people.

There is the doubt that Forrest could have led infantry as he led cavalry, but it must be considered that he always proved himself greater than his opportunity. His use of horses was merely for speedy transportation. He used them almost altogether in the last years of the war as mounted infantry. Brice's Cross-Roads had shown his ability to conduct an infantry battle and his ability to gather the fruits of a victory. He possessed most of the qualities of a great commander. He could lead men anywhere, "through a bresh fire," even. He never wasted opportunities; he could bring men to the colors when all others had failed; he could gather supplies in a barren land. His strategy was confusing to the enemy; his tactics Napoleonic, and the morale of his command, even to the end, was stiff with courage. This capacity for command would be proved within six weeks, for the confidence of the infantry in his powers would be all that would save the Army of Tennessee from annihilation. Davis and the great soldiers of the Confederacy would also understand it—too late. At Appomattox, when asked who was the greatest soldier under his command, Lee answered, "A man I have never seen, sir. His name is Forrest." And Davis, in his last flight to the West, fled because he hoped to gather an army around Forrest and Kirby-Smith and carry on the struggle.

But this was not to be, although Forrest arrived at Florence and took charge of all of Hood's cavalry, Jackson's Division, two thousand strong. He brought with him some three thousand of his own men, and together they formed a splendid veteran body of five thousand effectives. He made them a stirring speech on assuming command, and the next day he swept forward at the head of the general advance in the race to cut Schofield off at Columbia.

Schofield was slow in falling back. His cavalry was overmatched by Forrest and his information was slight, although Hatch reported Hood's advance on the nineteenth. Forrest's men swept everything before them, and they were elated. One day, after driving Wilson's men at a rapid pace, Captain Sam Barkley shouted, "These Yankees must think we eat folks." On the twenty-second, Hood's right-hand column under Stewart was at Lawrenceburg, sixteen miles west of Pulaski. The next day the two armies kept pace with each other in their race for Columbia. Storms of sleet, snow, and cold winter rains impeded the march of both forces, but Schofield was able to bring up his army in time to drive Forrest away from Columbia. Forrest then invested the town and waited for the arrival of the infantry. By the twenty-seventh, the Army of Tennessee had all been brought up, but the march over the boggy roads had so exhausted his men that Hood feared to risk an attack, although Schofield's back was to Duck River. He planned to cross over by the right flank and gave orders towards this end to Forrest late that night.

Although the river bank was heavily guarded by enemy cavalry, Forrest managed to put Jackson and Chalmers across during the twenty-eighth. Buford received such opposition that he did not effect his passage until the next morning. Once to the south of the river, Forrest drove Wilson back from Hurt's Corners and separated him from Schofield. This left the enemy without information as to Hood's movements. Schofield expected Hood to move around his flank, but he could not be sure. To be on the safe side, he ordered Stanley on the twenty-ninth to proceed to Spring Hill "to hold that place and cover the trains."

Stanley reached Spring Hill and was met by Forrest and driven into the town. Hood, crossing by pontoon, moved Cheatham's and Stewart's corps and one division of Lee's corps rapidly towards this objective. He left Lee in front of the town with his other two divisions to deceive Schofield and hold him there until he could throw the main part of his army across his line of retreat.

Hood's strategy succeeded, but his tactics failed. He brought onto the field at Spring Hill, including the cavalry, twenty-five thousand men. Stanley, with only five thouand men, the wagons, and most of the artillery, was before him and at his mercy. The Northern army was divided and open to detailed attack, but Hood went to pieces. His orders were vague and contradictory and so confusing that no concentrated attack was made. He laid the blame for the miscarriage on Cheatham, who had three divisions in position, Brown's, Cleburne's, and Bate's. The attack Cheatham ordered was to begin on the right, with Brown, and taken up successively to the left; but Brown either never received the order or refused to give it. There were other contradictory orders given to Stewart, and he and Forrest rode back to Hood's headquarters to have them explained. By that time darkness, which came at five o'clock that time of year, had settled down on the hills. In the last analysis Hood must take the blame, for when his orders were not obeyed, he should have gone to the front and personally seen to their execution. His only attempt to save the situation was to order Forrest to throw his cavalry across the road. Chalmers and Buford were both out of ammunition, and their ordnance wagons were far to the rear and behind the infantry trains. Only Jackson and his two thousand men were supplied from captures they had made. Hood said he would have the infantry furnish him, but the infantry had none to spare; so that night all of Schofield's army marched by on the turnpike towards Franklin within gunshot range and within hearing of the Confederate army. Jackson blocked the way, but his force was too feeble to do more than worry the enemy's hasty march.

Next day at Franklin, desperate at the thought of the opportunity lost before Spring Hill, Hood dashed his army to pieces against the fortifications outside the town. All of his general officers protested, but Hood would not listen. Forrest had gone with two of his division commanders and three brigadiers to the skirmish line to inspect the enemy's position. He saw it was too strong for a frontal attack. He told Hood that if he would give him one good infantry division and his cavalry he could cross the Harpeth and flank the enemy out of his position in two hours. Hood's reply was for him to prepare his cavalry for the attack.

Hood further weakened Forrest by dividing his cavalry and putting it on the two flanks. Chalmers with the strongest division was placed on the left, Jackson and Buford on the right. By four o'clock Hood had lined up Cheatham's and Stewart's corps for the slaughter; and before they advanced Forrest threw Jackson and Buford, about three thousand men, to the north of the river and engaged Wilson five thousand strong, supported by Wood's division of infantry. The cavalry battle waged for an hour, when Buford and Jackson retired to replenish their ammunition, after driving but not breaking Wilson's men. No cavalry ever fought more fiercely, but it was too weak to do more than hold Wilson, who, himself, admitted that "had his (Hood's) whole cavalry force advanced against me, it is possible that it would have succeeded in driving me back." In this case, Forrest could have fought his way to Schofield's rear, and the sickening sacrifice before Franklin might not have been in vain.

Hood was without artillery, and his men had to charge against fifty guns and some twenty-two thousand men. Never did men throw away their lives more desperately, or more heroically. In one hour and a half, five generals, Cleburne, Adams, Strahl, Granbury, and Gist, were killed; and six others were wounded, Brown, Manigault, Cockerell, Quarles, Scott, and Carter. One, General Gordon, was captured. Twelve in all. Added to these, one fifth of the army, five thousand five hundred men, lay bleeding and dying under the Northern guns. Some seven hundred and two were captured. The Army of Tennessee had shown Hood that it was not afraid of breastworks, that it was willing to fight to the bitter end with a courage that had never been matched by any army. In the night, Schofield withdrew to Nashville, less 1,222 who had been killed and wounded and 1,104 missing.

Hood followed with his skeleton army and settled down about Nashville, a mere skirmish line, to wait until Thomas chose to move out against him with the forces he was gathering there. What Hood expected to gain by this rash show of offensive can never be known. The heart of his regiments and brigades, their colonels and generals, lay under the ground in Williamson County or in the hospitals; and their skill must inevitably be missed in the crisis of another battle.

But there was a logic to Hood's mad policy. He further divided his army and sent Forrest with Buford and Jackson's divisions to Murfreesboro to attend to Rousseau, who occupied the fort with eight thousand men. Bate's division was detached to assist him. Hood should either have moved to that point with his whole army, or not at all, for if there ever was a time for Forrest to be present with the army, it was now. Late in the afternoon of December 6, Hood sent two more small brigades, Sear's and Palmer's, to reënforce him. This brought Forrest's total up to six thousand five hundred.

The next day a hostile column moved out of the town on the Salem Road. Old Bedford disposed the infantry in front and the cavalry on its flanks. He laid his plans to draw it away from the

A Group of Confederate Cavalry in the West

fortress with his infantry; then cut off its return with the cavalry and in this way surround and capture it. But, for some unknown reason, before contact had been made, Bate's Division, with the exception of Smith's brigade, broke and fled to the rear. This was the first time that men had ever broken in Forrest's presence. Flight, panic, and fear never entered his calculations, and for the moment he was stunned; then he turned and struck his spurs in "King Phillip's" sides.

An eye-witness told me that as the two of them galloped around towards the panic-stricken infantry "King Phillip" only touched the ground once in a while. He seemed to realize the importance of getting the General to the spot, and the staff was left far behind, strung out for two hundred yards. With tears streaming down his cheeks, Forrest shouted, "Rally, men, rally. For God's sake, rally!" But they broke around him as water breaks around a rock. Seeing a color-bearer fleeing with a standard, he called to him to halt; and when the man refused, he shot him and grabbed the flag; but the infantry did not gather about it. He saw an officer outstripping his men, and he called to him to halt; but his ears were closed; then in a mighty fury Forrest hurled the flag at his head. It darted through the air, stiffened its bars and stars for a moment, and fell to the ground, a limp, bullet-riddled rag. Gaus's bugle was shot from his mouth, and "King Phillip" saw a whole front of tantalizing bluecoats. He bared his lip and prepared for an individual battle. It was all Forrest could do to hold him in place, and he reared and plunged and scattered mud.

Jackson charged down on one flank; Smith held steady on the other, and at this moment Buford made an opportune attack on Murfreesboro. Rousseau recalled his men before they had time to follow up their advantage. Bate's division was sent back to the army, and another brigade took its place. This left Forrest with three small infantry brigades and the cavalry.

On the evening of the fifteenth, Hood notified Forrest to hold his forces in readiness for an emergency. A general engagement had begun at Nashville. At the moment Buford was away operating against gunboats near the Hermitage, and Jackson had just captured a train, one hundred and fifty prisoners, and two hundred thousand rations, most of which had to be destroyed. A concentration was ordered at Wilkerson's Cross-Roads. That night a staff officer brought the intelligence that the battle at Nashville had been disastrous and orders for Forrest to fall back by way of Shelbyville to Pulaski.

As his baggage train and the sick were at Triune, Forrest moved instead by way of Lillard's Mills on Duck River; and this change in his route probably saved the army from complete destruction, as it brought him in connection with it at a crucial moment. Buford was ordered to retire through La Vergne and cover the trains, and Armstrong was sent at once to Hood.

The infantry with Forrest was barefooted. It was late in December, and the heavy rains had turned the roads into deep beds of mire. But Old Bedford pushed ahead with four hundred prisoners, one hundred head of cattle, four hundred hogs, and his men. He reached the Mills and found Duck River rising rapidly. He threw about half the wagons, the prisoners, and the cattle across; then turned towards Columbia with the rest. The water had drowned the ford.

In the meantime, Chalmers's men were fighting like demons to hold back Thomas's army until Hood's shattered corps could fall back. The battle had been won by throwing Wilson's dismounted cavalry around Hood's left flank. If Forrest's whole command had been on the field, instead of Chalmers's one division, it is a question how successful this turning movement would have been, for the center and right of the Army of Tennessee held fast.

Now that the day was hopelessly lost, Chalmers, and especially Rucker, fought as only these officers knew how to fight. In the confusion Rucker ran into a squad of enemy troopers and was soon in hand-to-hand conflict with a Northern officer. The weather was so cold that the fighters could not control their horses; and Rucker, as he struck with all his might, missed aim and his sabre fell out of his hands. He closed with his enemy, wrenched his sword away from him; then, seeing he was in the midst of a regiment, turned to flee. His arm was shattered by a volley and he was thrown from his horse against a barricade of rails and knocked speechless. He was quickly carried to the rear and questioned by Hatch and Wilson. He told Hatch that "Forrest has just arrived with all the cavalry, and will give you hell tonight. Mark what I tell you." At this moment Randolph, who commanded one of Rucker's regiments, opened with an enfilading fire and threw the enemy into confusion, and Rucker with relief heard, "General Wilson has ordered everything in camp." By this time it was raining and the night was so dark a cavalryman could not see his horse's ears. Forrest was not the man to meet under any such conditions, and Rucker's ruse probably saved the army from immediate destruction.

General Stephen Lee took command of the rear with his corps, which was in fair condition, and Wilson and his nine thousand horsemen were held at bay until Cheatham's corps relieved Lee on the seventeenth. He intrenched at Rutherford's creeks to allow the trains to pass over and held his position until the eighteenth. Late that night the battleflag of Major-General Forrest reappeared among his men. His reunited cavalry was now placed in charge of the rear.

Waiting until the trains and the army had fallen behind Duck River, Forrest followed and took position behind the river, at Columbia, on the nineteenth. For miles up and down the stream he had every bridge completely destroyed, and as the river was now even with the banks, the enemy had to wait for his pontoon before he could make the effort to cross.

That night there was a meeting at the Vaught mansion to discuss whether or not Hood should hold his present line. An officer, in an effort to flatter the commander, remarked that "while God was so manifestly on our side that no man could question it, it was still very apparent that our people had not yet passed through all their sufferings." Hood replied devoutly that the remark was a just one. "He said he had been impressed with the fact at Spring Hill when the enemy was in our grasp and, notwithstanding all his efforts to strike a decisive blow, he had failed. And now again at Nashville, after the day's fighting was well nigh over, when all had gone successfully until evening, our troops had broken in confusion and fled."

In the midst of this palaver Forrest flatly brought the reality of his mind. "If we are unable to hold the state, we should at once evacuate," he said.

"But," added Hood, "let us go out of Tennessee singing hymns of praise."

Forrest let him know that there would be no army to sing hymns unless he could furnish him three thousand infantry to assist his cavalry. Hood told him he should have it. The next day Hood met General Walthall near headquarters. "General," he said, "things are in a bad condition. I have resolved to reorganize a rear guard. Forrest says he can't keep the enemy off of us any longer without a strong infantry support, but he says he can do it with three thousand infantry with you to command them. You can select any troops in the army. It is a post of great honor, but one of such great peril that I will not impose it on you unless you are willing to take it, and you had better take troops that can be relied upon, for you may have to cut your way out to get to me after the main army gets out. The army must be saved, come what may, and, if necessary, your command must be sacrificed to accomplish it."

Walthall replied, "General, I have never asked for a hard place for glory, nor a soft place for comfort, but take my chances as they come. Give me the order for the troops, and I will do my best. Being the youngest major-general in the army, I believe, my seniors may complain that the place was not offered to them, but that is a matter between you and them."

"Forrest wants you, and I want you." Just as Hood answered with these words, Forrest rode up. "Now, we will keep them back," he said.

Hood moved off to notify the various skeleton commands to form under Walthall. He rode up to the 19th Tennessee as this regiment was marching out of Columbia. "I wish to leave some infantry with General Forrest to help him until I get across the Tennessee River, and I am sure I can rely on you Tennesseans to see the work well done." Pausing a moment, he asked for a show of confidence, "The cards were fairly dealt at Nashville, boys, but they beat the game."

A private in Company E promptly answered, "Yes, General, the cards were fairly dealt, but they were mighty badly shuffled."

Walthall's division and five other fragmentary brigades—in all only one thousand, nine hundred bayonets—finally reported to Forrest for duty. Of these, three hundred were without shoes. They wrapped up their feet in rags, and Forrest told them to ride in the wagons until he needed them. His cavalry numbered about three thousand mounted men, and with this mixed force of some five thousand men it was his duty to hold Wilson's nine thousand horsemen and possibly thirty thousand infantry until Hood reached the Tennessee at Bainbridge, almost one hundred miles away.

When the news spread through the army that Old Bedford was to organize a rear guard, men rushed to headquarters and asked to join it. Desertions which daily had rolled up to the hundreds, many going over to the enemy for the love of comfort, food, and warmth, stopped now almost entirely. Seldom or never had any soldier been placed in a more trying situation, but Captain Goodman, of Chalmers's staff, wrote "that at no time in his whole career was the fortitude of General Forrest in adversity, and his power of infusing his own cheerfulness into those under his command, more strikingly exhibited than at this crisis. Defeated and broken as we were, there were not wanting many others as determined as he to do their duty to the last, and who stood out faithfully to the end; but their conversation was that of men who, though determined, were without hope, and who felt that they must gather strength even from despair; but he alone, whatever he may have felt (and he was not blind to the dangers of our position) spoke in his usual cheerful and defiant tone, and talked of meeting the enemy with as much assurance of success as he did when driving them before him a month before. Such a spirit is sympathetic, and not a man was brought in contact with him who did not feel strengthened and invigorated, as if he had heard of a reënforcement coming to our relief."

The next day Hatch shelled Columbia, but Forrest sent forward a white flag to call for a truce. Speaking with the river between them, Forrest told Hatch that only the wounded of both armies occupied the town; so the bombardment ceased. He also asked Hatch to make an exchange of some two thousand prisoners. After two hours this request was refused by Thomas; but the formalities of the refusal gave Forrest two more hours of delay. During the night Hatch put his cavalry across the river, and next morning Thomas's infantry passed over. It had been made possible by the negligence of a cavalry major. Forrest gave him a piece of his mind, closing with, "You ought to have your God-damned neck broke for letting the Yankees cross while you were stuck up in that cabin."

Six miles south of Columbia, Forrest found a strong defensive position in a gorge between two ridges, which he held until the twenty-third. That day he was driven back nine miles, but Wilson had no easy time in driving him. He would fight, and his men fought, as if the whole Confederacy depended upon his arm; then return and retreat until Wilson's advance forced him to make another stand. His temper was fierce and his nerves were raw, and if the enemy rushed ahead without support, he threw his vicious cavalry against them. As Wilson reported, "the redoubtable Forrest . . . was a leader not to be attacked by a handful of men however bold."

His artillery teams gave out. He impressed oxen and moved half his train and his guns out of danger; unhitched the teams and brought them back to those left behind, and in this relay fashion always kept his artillery and his wagons just out of reach of the enemy. During the retreat an officer from Hood's headquarters brought an order to him to send some mules to the quartermaster department. As the order was read to him, he said very quietly, "None of my mules will be sent in on that order." Next evening Major Landis came to find out why the mules had not been sent. Major Landis found out. "You go back to your quarters and don't come here again, or send anybody here about mules! The order will not be obeyed; and, moreover, if Major Ewing bothers me any further about this matter, I'll come down to his office, tie his long legs into a double bowknot around his neck, and choke him to death with his shins. It's a fool order anyway. General Hood had better send his inspectors to overhaul your wagons, rid them of all surplus baggage, tents, adjutants' desks, and everything that can be spared. Reduce the number of wagons instead of reducing the strength of the teams. Besides, I know what is before me; and if he knew the road from here to Pulaski, this order would be countermanded. I whipped the enemy and captured every wagon and ambulance in my command; have not made a requisition on the government for anything of the kind in two years, and now that they are indispensable, my teams will go as they are or not at all."

Landis did not bother him, or anybody else, after this. In fact he took over the direction of the entire retreat. He sent messengers to Hood every few hours, giving minute details about the movement of the artillery and the wagons, directing the roads that should be taken, what should be done in certain contingencies—and all this while he was engaged every minute in covering the retreat, turning to inflict blow after blow on Wilson's importunate advance. Colonel Kelly said that "when he reached Iuka, Mississippi, I heard General Hood heartily thank Forrest for the suggestions, saying to him that without his aid he should never have brought his army across the Tennessee River."

The weather was almost unendurable. It rained ice; the surface of the roads froze; snow fell, and the covering was slick as glass until the heavy wagon wheels broke through into the frigid slush beneath. In places the teams went down belly deep, and Hood's barefooted infantry had to stagger through the freezing mud up to their armpits. The jagged ice cut their frost-bitten feet and smeared the way with blood. An ox, exhausted with work, fell by the side of the road; and before the blood in his veins could congeal, the desperate men had stripped his hide from his smoking body and tied it about their feet. Stiffened fingers could barely pull the triggers, but under the stern and encouraging eye of Forrest the rear-guard held firm.

Wilson had been delayed in the beginning of the race by empty haversacks and a delayed pontoon. But now his men had plenty of rations and ammunition, and he was increasing the speed of the pursuit, for every mile he took the Confederates drew that much nearer to safety. At Pulaski, Forrest had to destroy a quantity of ammunition and several trains, but several miles out there was a fine defensive position at Anthony's Hill. He ordered Jackson to hold at Pulaski as long as he could while he made preparations to receive the enemy.

It was absolutely necessary that the rear hold a position at Anthony's Hill, for it was now only forty-two miles to Bainbridge and all of Hood's infantry had not reached the river bank. The main part of the ordnance train had been abandoned at Sugar Creek, fourteen miles south of Anthony's Hill, since all the horses had to be used to transport the pontoons. If possible the ordnance must be saved. Forrest was informed of the situation, as the progress of the army was constantly reported to him.

He knew the outcome at Anthony's Hill would mean safety or destruction, and he was very sure in his mind which it would be. The approach to the position, for two miles, was through a defile formed by two steep ridges. The ascent was sudden, and the ridges wooded. Morton's battery was hidden on the immediate summit, and in position to sweep the road and the hollow below. On the crest of the Hill Featherston's and Palmer's brigades, four hundred of Ross's Texans and four hundred of Armstrong's Mississippians, were placed in support. The rest of Jackson's division was held as cavalry on the flanks. Chalmers took post a mile and a half to the right with his own and Buford's divisions, Buford having been wounded two days before. Reynolds's and Field's brigades of infantry formed the reserve. The position was strengthened by rails and felled timber. Forrest called together the brigade and regimental officers to give them instructions. "When the infantry breaks their lines," he said, "I'll turn Ross on 'em." Colonel Field, "a wiry and heroic soldier, whose silvery voice could be heard above the battle and roar of musketry, having under him his own and Strahl's brigades, immediately replied with spirit: 'We have no such soldiers; we don't break our lines.' Forrest replied quickly, 'I don't mean that. I mean when you break the lines of the enemy, I'll throw Ross's Texans in on 'em and rout 'em.'"

He left a decoy with instructions to fire and retreat quickly up the Hill, drawing the enemy after them. Every man was in position and waiting. Old Bedford took his stand near his guns. There was not a sound. His eyes were straining under his hat. "King Phillip's" head was thrown up, his nostrils quivered, and his ears pointed. The silence almost screamed. The men lay behind their rails or along the ravines.

The enemy did not fall for the snare. They knew Old Bedford

by this time, and they were sure he would not pass up such a good defensive position. They dismounted a regiment and pushed a gun cautiously forward. Not a ragged Confederate was visible.

When the crowded blue line reached within fifty paces, Forrest broke his pose to give Morton an order. He nodded, and an explosion of canister swept the blue men to the ground. On top of it, the rebel yell, as defiant as ever, rose along the ridge. The men rose up behind it, pulled their hats down over their eyes, and jumped over their rails. The entire Northern brigade was thrown back on the infantry supports; the gun and its eight horses were captured intact; one hundred and fifty men, three hundred horses, and as many overcoats, the prize of the sally. The recall was sounded, and the victorious guard returned to their ridge.

Wilson brought up the infantry and began a turning movement, and for three hours the fight for the ridge went on. Forrest's flanks were gradually turned, but no man thought of retreat until the Old Man gave the order. He sat King Phillip, his eyes fixed immovably to the front. A courier dashed up. "General, the enemy is on our right flank." No reply. Fifteen minutes later, another courier reined in his mount. "General, the enemy is on our left flank." No reply. Still later, a third came up to report. "General, the enemy is in our rear." Forrest turned abruptly in his saddle. "Well, ain't we in thern?" Without another word he turned around and calmly surveyed the field. He had every detail of the entire line in his mind. As the courier galloped away, he mumbled under his breath, "I always carry my rear with me."

Armstrong, his couriers failing to get any response, rode up to the General and told him his men were out of ammunition. He was ordered to go back and hold his ground, which he did until the weight of the turning movement forced him to withdraw. Riding up to where Walthall and Forrest sat their horses, Armstrong spoke to Walthall; and as he spoke tears of pride and anger watered his grimy face. "General Walthall, won't you please make that damn man there on that horse see that my men are forced to retreat?"

Forrest looked at him a moment and said very tenderly that he was only gaining time for General Hood to cross Sugar Creek and that his men had done a noble part in making this possible. He then pulled out his watch and looked at it. It was four o'clock. "It is about time for us all to get out of here." He gave quick, decisive orders. The different commands fell back in perfect order, as if they were the van of a victorious army, and in a few minutes they were marching rapidly for the creek.

They reached this position, fourteen miles away, by one o'clock the next morning. Sugar Creek was a clear stream of water, with a pebbly bottom. The men bathed the mud from their clothes, built large fires, and bivouacked in the dark. That night the mules returned to carry off the abandoned ordnance train, and by dawn Wilson had caught up in a last attempt to break through and cut Hood's infantry to pieces. Fortunately a dense fog covered the land and Forrest's positions. Slowly and uncertainly the bluecoats picked their way across the creek. A whizz of lead melted the fog and struck Wilson's advance. It fell back in some confusion and recrossed the creek. Walthall's men waded the icy waters and gave it a final counter. The cavalry swung around on its flanks, and the dismounted enemy was driven back through the horseholders. The freezing Confederates came back with a great many overcoats, one hundred and fifty horses, and about one hundred prisoners.

Forrest saw Morton pulling out with his battery. "Morton, who told you to move those guns?" General Jackson, red-bearded and red-headed, was standing by. He spoke in his quiet, well-modulated tone. "I did, General." "What'd you do that fer, Jackson?" "The battery was without support, and I had it withdrawn from unnecessary danger. You were not here."

"That's always the way. I cain't never do a damn thing when there's forty orderin' around me." Jackson blushed as red as his beard, saluted, and rode off.

By one P.M. Forrest withdrew southward, and next day, December 27, his command passed safely over the Tennessee River. An infantry corps had been left to cover the passage. It quickly followed, and Wilson's "cavalry advance-guard, under the active and enterprising Spalding, reached the north bank of the river just as the bridge had been swung to the south side and the last of the rebels were disappearing in the distance."

Sergeant Hancock, of Forrest's cavalry, while riding alone on a cold day near the end of the retreat, came upon one of Hood's infantry. He was barefooted and ragged, but he still had his gun and a large piece of hog meat stuck through its bayonet. As Hancock rode up beside him, the soldier asked what command. "Forrest cavalry" was the reply.

"How I do love Forrest's cavalry," he answered quickly. "I love the very ground they walk on. If it hadn't been for them, Hood wouldn't have got out of Tennessee with a single man." As Hancock rode past him, he called out, "If you haven't plenty of rations, call around tonight and I'll divide with you."

This final salute of respect made good his words of love, love for a general who had never commanded him. Forrest had shown him at the supreme moment what his genius could do. He had shown every man, high and low, what he might have done for the cause; but it was understood too late to revive the tottering fortunes of the Confederacy, for Hood's gamble had failed and Sherman's had won, all because Hood was not equal to the execution of his daring campaign. In thirty-five days he had destroyed the Army of Tennessee. There was now no force left except Lee's army in Virginia, and this would soon give up the ghost on the sandy, piney fields around Appomattox.

CHAPTER XXIV

The Last Fight

FORREST was now made a lieutenant-general and placed in charge of all the cavalry in Mississippi, East Louisiana, and West Tennessee. His was the last body of organized men in the West. The remnants of the Army of Tennessee had been sent to North Carolina and placed under Johnston, their old leader, in an effort to stay Sherman's whirlwind march towards Lee's rear.

Forrest realized the end was near, but he threw himself into the reorganization of his department as if the war had just begun. His cavalry had been furloughed to rest and secure remounts, and they returned at the end of twenty days in large numbers. He now commanded almost ten thousand men with fat, well-fed horses. In his absence in Tennessee, Grierson had made a raid upon his dismounted men at Verona, put them to rout, and destroyed about two hundred reserve wagons, the captures from "Sookey" Smith and others. He also razed to the ground a shoe factory working five hundred hands.

With plenty of new clothes, good food, rested horses, and shebangs with cornshuck floors to sleep on, and big fires roaring, Forrest's men had a pleasant interlude of war. But while they rested, the Old Man was working like forty men to meet the different invasions he knew would soon be made into his territory. Selma was the last and largest arsenal left in the Southwest, and it was under his protection. He had all the roads clearly marked in that direction, for he had information that Wilson was preparing the greatest cavalry force the American continent had ever seen, twenty-seven thousand men, to take it. Pontoons were laid across the Cahawba, and the trees were blazed pointing the route to a quick concentration. A general notice says, "One road will have a signboard 'Tuscaloosa'; the other a signboard, 'Pleasant Ridge, Clinton, Eutaw.' The trees beside the Tuscaloosa road were blazed with an X; to Finch's Ferry with an X.

To save powder and to keep the horses in good condition, orders had been given not to race the animals and not to fire off guns just to hear the noise. One day in camp, a group of boys marked off a quarter course and in defiance of Old Bedford held a big race right in front of his headquarters. He and his staff came out and watched the race, even betting on the horses. After it was over the boys galloped by, gave three cheers for General Forrest, and rode off to meet the guard that had been sent to arrest them. The horse-racers spent the rest of the day moving heavy fence rails.

About this time a private who had made two applications for furlough without success, sent in for the third time. Forrest took the form and wrote on the back, "I told you twicest Goddamnit know." The spelling was elaborate, but the private understood the meaning.

On February 26, a member of Wilson's staff, Major Hosea, in company with General Parkhurst, met with Forrest to consider certain matters, and Hosea wrote home an account of the meeting:

"I was at the time . . . struck by what then seemed the 'aristocratic mien' of General Forrest. . . . Our present meeting was in the dim light of common tallow candles on a dark, rainy night, in the living room of a somewhat rude country residence.

"Forrest is a man fully six feet in height, rather waxen face, handsome, high full forehead, and with a profusion of light gray hair thrown back from the forehead and growing down rather to a point in the middle of the same. The lines of thought and care, in an upward curve receding, are distinctly marked and add much to the dignity of expression. The general effect is suggestive of notables of the Revolutionary times, with powdered hair as we see them in the portraits of that day; and to our unaccustomed eyes the rich gray uniform with its embroidered collar (a wreath of gold on black ground enclosing three silver stars) added much to the effect produced.

"I could not but observe the quickness of apprehension and decision displayed by Forrest in seizing the entire thought intended to be conveyed from the introductory expressions. To think quickly and concretely, and to decide likewise, seemed to be his mental habit. There was about his talk and manner a certain soldierly simplicity and engaging frankness and I was frequently lost in real admiration.

"I could not, in the dim light of tallow candles, observe the color of his eyes, but they seemed to be brown and pleasant-looking, lit up occasionally by a gleam of soldiery bravery. His expression, both pleasant and striking, is given to his physiognomy by the slightest possible elevation of the eyebrows. The latter are black with a tinge of gray, and a black moustache and chin whiskers, both cut short, add to the military bearing of the man. His face is long and cheekbones rather prominent, eyes large, though not noticeably so, and the head full above the eyes and ears. . . . His habitual expression seemed subdued and thoughtful, but when his face is lighted up by a smile, which ripples all over his features, the effect is really charming. Forrest expressed great admiration for soldierly qualities and especially for personal courage, and was evidently pleased at our recognition of the fame of his exploits at the head of his cavalry.

"His language indicates a very limited education, but *his impressive manner conceals many otherwise notable defects.* (Italics mine.) (This officer confuses the border idiom with illiteracy.) The choice of words too plainly evidences early associations, unfortunately, and one feels sometimes disappointed at errors palpable to any school boy. He invariably omits the final 'g' in the termination 'ing', and many words are inexcusably mispronounced, and he always uses the past participle in place of the past tense of such words as 'see'—as 'I seen' instead of I saw, and 'holp tote,' meaning to help carry. . . .

"In a very short time, however, these pass unnoticed. He speaks of his success with a soldierly vanity, and expresses the kindest feelings toward prisoners and wounded. I told him that I had the honor to present the compliments of my general, our cavalry Murat—Wilson— to him, in the hope of meeting him upon some future occasion. He at once accepted this as a challenge, which the friendly message might be construed to convey, and with a curl of his lip he said: 'Jist tell General Wilson that I know the nicest little place down below here in the world, and whenever he is ready, I will fight him with any number from one to ten thousand cavalry, and abide the issue. Gin'ral Wilson may pick his men, and I'll pick mine. He may take his sabers and I'll take my six-shooters. I don't want nary a saber in my command—haven't got one.' "

Wilson was a West Pointer and believed in the saber. "Well," answered Forrest, "I ain't no graduate of West Point; never rubbed my back up agin any college, but Wilson may take his sabers and I'll use my six-shooters and agree to whup the fight with any cavalry he can bring."

"At parting we shook hands all around, and just as we were leaving, the General took my hand in his own a second time, and, holding it in a cordial grasp, said in a friendly and courteous manner, 'Don't git too far away from your command when you come down into this country—some of our boys may pick you up.' "

As Major Hosea left the department, he went into the telegraph office and sent a final message to Forrest's headquarters—*Haec olim meminisse juvabit, tetigisse dextram tyranni.*

There were some seventy-five thousand available troops to make the invasion of Forrest's department, and several columns threatened him at once. He moved out on the last of March to meet Wilson and his fourteen thousand horsemen. Wilson marched quickly through Alabama in the direction of Selma. Forrest could concentrate only about six thousand six hundred men under Jackson and Chalmers. His information as to the enemy's movements was unusually accurate, and he planned to get in Wilson's front at Plantersville with Chalmers while Jackson fell upon his rear. Unfortunately his dispatches fell into Wilson's hands, and that general discovered the plan and the exact location of Forrest's brigades. By burning the pontoon over the Watauga, he cut Jackson off; then turned his overwhelming force on Roddy and Crossland, the two small brigades that were with Forrest. Old Bedford learned of the misfortune, but he hoped to get Chalmers up in time to hold Wilson in check.

In the meantime he made a stand at Bogler's Creek with fifteen hundred men and six guns. His men were soon thrown into confusion, and he and the escort were surrounded by the enemy cavalry charging with sabers drawn. He was set upon by four troopers at once. He shot one, but the others dashed down upon him with uplifted weapons. He attempted to parry with his revolver, but in the meantime he was cut and bruised over the head and shoulders. "King Phillip" dodged and pranced and bit like a two-year-old. Three other troopers rode up. He was now surrounded by six men attempting to shoot or saber him. By this time the hammer of his pistol had been hacked away, and his right arm was weak from the blows. His staff and escort could not aid him: they were as hard pressed. On either hand the road was blocked by a deep, impenetrable thicket; behind him it was choked by a two-horse wagon; to his front the six troopers. Escape looked hopeless, but no situation was ever hopeless to Bedford Forrest. He wheeled his mount towards the wagon, dug his spurs in his flanks and, lifting him with the bridle, pulled the brave animal into the air: "King Phillip" leaped the barrier in one bound and did not stop until he was thirty paces on the other side.

Forrest now fell back to Plantersville, where he was met by one of

Chalmers's brigades, Armstrong's. He had just time enough to telegraph to Taylor at Selma, when a little boy ran in and shouted, "The Yankees are coming." General Adams was with him. "Dan Adams," Forrest reported later, "was on a smart horse and got off. The big Dutchman closed on me, and had a smarter horse than mine, and he kept cutting me over the head and arms with his sword which wasn't sharp; but it made me mighty mad, and I kept dodging it, for my pistol got hitched and I couldn't get it out until he had hit me several times. When I did draw it, I dropped my reins, caught him by his hair, and fired two loads right into him." He now withdrew to the works at Selma.

"Forrest appeared," writes Taylor, "horse and rider covered with blood, and announced the enemy at his heels, and that I must move at once to escape capture. I felt anxious for him, but he said he was unhurt and would cut his way through, as most of his men had done, whom he had ordered to meet him west of the Cahawba." This was after he had made one valiant effort to man the too extensive works around Selma. He had placed Roddy on the right, the militia and citizens in the center—he had told them they had either to go in the works or in the river—and Armstrong on the left. The militia broke and his two wings were divided.

This was the last important fight of the war, and Forrest fought as if the whole world depended on his arm; but the captured dispatches doomed his plans to failure and prevented what might have been the grandest cavalry battle the American continent had ever seen; and it made certain the capture of Jefferson Davis, for it was Wilson's men who finally ran him down. It is interesting to speculate what might have happened if Davis had reached Forrest's camp in safety.

Lee surrendered to Grant and Johnston to Sherman. When this became known, great gloom settled in the camps of the last force east of the Mississippi. But General Taylor informed Forrest that he was making arrangements with General Canby to parole the soldiers in his department. On the morning the paroles were to be signed, Forrest called Major Anderson from his tent. It was day-dawn, and he had two horses saddled for a ride. Mounting, Anderson followed him into the country in complete silence, for the General's head was bent over on his chest. Coming to a cross-roads, Anderson asked, "Which road, General?"

"It makes no difference. If one of them led to hell and the other to Mexico, I wouldn't care which one I took."

He then told his inspector how bitter was the thought of surrender. He said that the idea of going to Mexico was alluring. Anderson made no effort to dissuade him, but pointed out that if he went, only a few of his men could go with him. The others must be left behind. "To these brave fellows, who have by their unflinching devotion to your fortunes made your reputation as a commander, it will be an added humiliation to be compelled to bear the bitterness of surrender without your example and inspiration."

"That settles it," Forrest replied, "I will share the fate of my men."

He then ordered Anderson to draw up a farewell address. This Anderson was prepared to do, for he had lived with him so closely that he almost knew his thoughts. Anderson sat down and wrote it out on a cracker-box near the powder magazine. Forrest read and signed it. After giving his men advice about their future conduct, he told them good-bye:

"In bidding you farewell, rest assured that you carry with you my best wishes for your future welfare and happiness. Without, in any way, referring to the merits of the cause in which we have been engaged, your courage and determination, as exhibited on many hard-fought fields, have elicited the respect and admiration of friend and foe. And I now, cheerfully and gratefully, acknowledge my indebtedness to the officers and men of my command, whose zeal, fidelity, and unflinching bravery have been the great source of my past success in arms.

"I have never, on the field of battle, sent you where I was unwilling to go myself; (How well they knew it!) nor would I now advise you to a course which I felt myself unwilling to pursue. You have been good soldiers; you can be good citizens. Obey the laws, preserve your honor, and the government to which you have surrendered can afford to be, and will be, generous.

"N. B. Forrest, Lieutenant-General."

His boys crowded around him and, with tears in their eyes, begged him to take them to Mexico. They told him they could not bear to surrender; they would follow him anywhere, even to the ends of the earth. They proposed to him to lead them to the Trans-Mississippi and there continue the struggle, "but General Forrest said no; what could not be accomplished here could never be done in the thinly settled West."

The Seventh Tennessee, one of his most faithful regiments, could not bring itself to part with "the old bullet-torn flag, whose blue cross had been triumphantly borne aloft for years at the cost of so much blood and valor. . . . On the eve of surrender, as the shadows of night fell, the men reverently gathered around the staff in front of regimental headquarters, and, cutting the silk into fragments, each soldier carried away with him a bit of the coveted treasure." It had been made from the bridal dress of a young lady of Aberdeen.

CHAPTER XXV

The Invisible Empire and its Wizard

FORREST now returned to Mississippi to take up his life again. He took as partner a Federal officer, and together they ran his large plantation in Coahoma County. One day, as he was passing through the quarters, he heard the cries of a negro woman coming from one of the cabins. He threw open the door and stalked in. Before him he saw a large negro man beating his wife to death with a club. With one blow of his foot he kicked the negro back into the room. Recovering his feet, the man grabbed an ax and turned on him. Forrest backed towards the door; then, seizing his opportunity, he charged the black, wrenched the ax from his hands and, with one blow, sank the blade deep into his head. He returned to his house, where he was followed by a group of negroes who had been soldiers. As they marched up to the porch, Forrest suddenly appeared, armed with a pistol in each hand. "Halt!" he shouted. The negroes stopped, "Order arms!" Every gun whipped in place. "Ground arms!" Down went the guns. "Now, men," he said, "get out of this yard or I will shoot the heads off every one of you." They slunk away to their work without a single protest.

Forrest sold his plantations for a good price and moved to Memphis, and in 1868 General Shackelford, of Connecticut, informed him that General Kilpatrick had insulted him in the public press. Forrest wrote at once an open letter in a Memphis paper, challenging Kilpatrick to mortal combat. He asked that all arrangements be made through General Basil Duke of Kentucky. Duke could not serve as second, as it would debar him from practicing law in that state; so he wired Dr. James Kellar in St. Louis, a mutual friend of his and Forrest's. "The doctor," as Duke wrote, "was making preparations to come to Louisville before the telegraph had ceased ticking." That same day Duke received a letter from Forrest saying that since both he and

Kilpatrick had been cavalrymen he thought they ought to fight mounted and with sabers.

To carry out this wish, Duke presented himself at the residence of Captain Bart Jenkins, of the Fourth Kentucky Cavalry, who then kept a livery stable. Captain Jenkins was a fighting man, as well as an ardent Confederate, "and I knew he would feel a profound interest in the matter at hand. When I reached the Captain's place, I was informed that he was very ill, but that I might see him. I was taken upstairs to a small room above his office, where he was lying on a lounge looking like an exceedingly sick man. In response to my inquiry regarding his condition, he respondid in a voice scarcely louder than a whisper that he had pneumonia, was so weak that he could not rise from his couch, and would not be surprised if the attack terminated fatally. After expressing due sorrow and regret and sympathy, I said that I had called to talk about the Kilpatrick affair, but, under the circumstances, could, of course, pretermit it.

" 'No, you won't,' he said, his voice perceptibly stronger; 'I want to hear about that.'

" 'Oh, well, Forrest wants to fight on horseback with sabres—'

" 'That's right,' he interrupted, and rose to a sitting position, 'That's right.'

"So I have come around here to consult you and see if I couldn't get him a good horse."

" 'You just can,' he declared in a perfectly normal tone. 'I've got the very animal you want,' and with that he got out of bed and began to put on his clothes.

" 'Don't do that, Bart,' I said, 'You've just told me that the doctor insists that you shall be very careful.'

" 'The doctor be damned,' he replied. 'Do you think I'll let a doctor interfere with important business of this kind. I want to show you my brown mare, the finest in the state, and has taken the blue ribbon at every fair in Central Kentucky. She's sixteen hands high, built just right for a man of Forrest's height, and as quick on her feet as a cat. Place the men sixty yards apart, and tell Forrest that when you give the word, he must drive in the spurs and ride straight at the other horse. She'll knock him off his feet, and Forrest can cut off Kilpatrick's head before he touches the ground. But . . . 'Y God, I must see the fight.'

"Kilpatrick, after some delay, published a statement in the Eastern papers, saying he could not afford to accept Forrest's challenge, inasmuch as a committee of Congress, appointed to investigate the alleged massacre of negroes at Fort Pillow, had declared him guilty, and he could not therefore regard him as a gentleman. General Shackel-ford . . . published a letter in response to Kilpatrick's in which he took the ground that while the report of a Congressional Com-mittee might be pertinent and valuable for many purposes, no one could consider it conclusive of a man's standing as a gentleman, and he strongly urged Kilpatrick to meet Forrest after having wantonly assailed him." But Kilpatrick's faith in the unusual powers of Congress remained unshaken, so there was no fight.

This same year Forrest was sent as a delegate to the first presidential convention after the war, when Seymour was nominated. He traveled in company with Duke and other gentlemen. The journey was un-eventful until they arrived at a small town over the line. The conductor, a former Federal captain, informed Duke that the bully of the town, so far unbeaten, had threatened to take Forrest off the train and give him a thrashing. A large crowd had formed, more out of curiosity than from any intention to take part in the proceedings. The con-ductor was worried, because he did not know just where the excite-ment might lead. He let it be known that he proposed to stand by his passenger.

Duke immediately conferred with Forrest and advised that he fol-low the conductor's suggestion and remain in his seat. Bedford re-ceived the news calmly and agreed to the part he was expected to play. When the train stopped at the depot, the bully leaped to the platform and entered the coach. He was a very powerful man, much larger than Forrest, and looked as if he were able to carry out his threat. Throwing open the door, he shouted, "Where's that damned butcher, Forrest? I want him."

"I never witnessed," writes Duke, "such an instantaneous and mar-velous transformation in one's appearance. . . . Forrest bounded from his seat, his form erect and dilated, his face the color of heated bronze, and his eyes flaming, blazing."

"I am Forrest. What do you want?"

The bully gave one look, and when Forrest charged within four feet of him, he turned and rushed out of the coach faster than he had entered it, with the man he was going to thrash close on his heels and calling to him to stop. But the bully had forgotten his threat. He dashed into and down the street "with quarterhorse speed, losing his hat as he vanished around the corner." Then the humor of the situation struck Forrest, and he burst into a great shout of laughter. In a few moments the entire crowd joined in, and many pushed forward to shake "the butcher's" hand. When the train pulled out five minutes later, Old Bedford was standing on the platform receiving the cheers and applause of the multitude and gracefully waving his thanks to his new admirers.

When he arrived in New York, he attracted so much attention that he could not move about the streets without drawing a crowd. One day it became so thick that it interfered with his progress. With great irritation he swept his mighty shoulders around and shouted. Those immediately around him turned and fled; they pushed others, and in a few minutes the streets were churning with people. For some time traffic was blocked on Fifth Avenue.

One morning later he was in his room in the hotel when a knock sounded on the door. He was still in his night-shirt; so he told his son, Willie, to see who it was. When the door was opened, a spinster, tall and angular, had squared herself in the opening. Her hair was dark and parted tightly over a high forehead; her lips and jaw were firm. She had a Bible in one hand and an umbrella in the other. She was prepared for any emergency. If religion failed her, she had a readier weapon.

Pushing Captain Willie aside, she advanced into the room. "Are you the Rebel General Forrest, and is it true that you murdered those dear colored people at Fort Pillow? Tell me, sir; I want no evasive answer."

The General rose up from his bed to his full height, his hair on end. "Yes, madam, I killed the men and women for my soldiers' dinner and ate the babies myself for breakfast."

With a scream the spinster ran out of the room, down the hallway, and into the street.

This effort on the part of the Democratic Party to reunite the South in the old political Union failed. The Black Republicans who had forced the South into secession had different ideas about reconstruction. They saw that, if the things were to be as they had been before the war, they would lose the fruits of victory; and this they did not intend to do. With the control of Congress in their hands they pushed through another kind of reconstruction, a reconstruction which aimed at complete destruction of the Southern States. Lincoln was out of the way, and Johnson, the defender of his policy, was impeached. The

Fourteenth Amendment to the Constitution virtually destroyed that document, for the clause giving the negro the vote was not the important part of the amendment. The important part lay in the clause which destroyed the power of the State Supreme Courts, for with their fall the destruction of the Old Union was assured.

The South was disarmed and helpless. With the aid of troops the servile population was used as a tool to carry out this reconstruction policy. The details are well known, and in this dark hour it looked as if the destruction of the Southern Culture would be literal, when purely by chance the means of relief appeared out of the social habits of the people.

In May, 1866, a group of boys in Pulaski, Tennessee, formed a secret order to help them while away the time. They drew up an elaborate ritual, met in secret places, and in public covered themselves and their horses with long white robes. After a few parades they noticed that the negroes took them for spirits from the other world. This gave them, because their political genius had not been destroyed, the idea which later developed into the only tactics available for suppression of the Scalawag-Carpetbag régime.

It spread rapidly over the Southern States, and General Forrest at once saw its possibilities. He went to Nashville to find his former chief of artillery. "Captain Morton had an office diagonally across from the Maxwell House. Looking from his window one day, he saw General Forrest walking impatiently around Calhoun Corner, as it was then called. Hastening down the steps to greet his former chieftain, he encountered a little negro boy, who inquired where he could find Captain Morton. He said: 'There's a man over yonder on de corner and he wants to see him, and he looks like he wants to see him mighty bad.' Captain Morton hurried across the street, and, after salutation, the General said: 'John, I hear this Ku Klux Klan is organized in Nashville, and I know you are in it. I want to join.' The young man avoided the issue and took his Commander for a ride. General Forrest persisted in his questions about the Klan and Morton kept smiling and changing the subject. On reaching a dense woods in a secluded valley outside the city, Morton suddenly turned on his former leader and said: 'General, do you say you want to join the Ku Klux?'

"General Forrest was somewhat vexed and swore a little: 'Didn't I tell you that's what I came up here for?'

"Smiling at the idea of giving orders to his erstwhile commander, Captain Morton said: 'Well, get out of the buggy.' General Forrest stepped out of the buggy, and next received the order: 'Hold up your right hand.'

"General Forrest did as he was ordered, and Captain Morton solemnly administered the preliminary oath of the order.

"As he finished taking the oath General Forrest said: 'John, that's the worst swearing that I ever did.'

"That's all I can give you now. Go to room number 10 at the Maxwell House tonight and you can get all you want. Now you know how to get in," said Captain Morton.[1]

The various leaders of the Klan realized that it must have a closer organization. A body went to Virginia to wait on General Lee and ask him to take command. He told them that his health would not permit him to serve, but he wrote a letter saying that he approved of the Klan, although his approval must be "invisible." The committee then told him that General Forrest was their next choice. "There is no man in the South who can handle so large a body of men so successfully," replied General Lee; "Will you pay my respects to the General and tell him I hope he will accept."

The meeting was held in Room Number 10 in the Maxwell House, and Lee's letter was read. In the course of the meeting a name for the Klan was discussed. Taking the word "invisible" out of Lee's note, somebody suggested the Invisible Empire; and this was adopted. The next matter was to select the commander and his title. A voice from the back of the room called out, "The Wizard of the Saddle, General Nathan Bedford Forrest." He was then elected and became the *Grand Wizard of the Invisible Empire*. His powers were supreme.

In this way was General Forrest made the last ruler of the South. Only those veterans who were honorably discharged and those who were in prison at the end of the war were eligible, something over one hundred thousand men.[2]

"It was," says Judge Albion Tourgee, a Reconstruction Judge in North Carolina, "a daring conception for a conquered people. Only a race of warlike instincts and regal pride could have conceived or executed it.

"It was a magnificent conception, and, in a sense, deserved success. It differed from all other attempts at revolution in the caution and skill required in its conduct. It was a movement made in the face of

[1] Rev. Thomas Dixon, Jr.—supported by Captain Morton.
[2] Testimony of Judge J. P. Young, Seventh Tennessee Cavalry and a member of Klan.

the enemy and an enemy of overwhelming strength. Should it succeed, it would be the most brilliant revolution ever accomplished. Should it fail—well, those who engaged in it felt that they had nothing more to lose."

It did not fail. It baffled in a few years all the efforts of the victors to destroy the Culture of the South, and it succeeded, when the fortunes of the Southern people were at their lowest, because for once it had a leader whom the people knew would not fail. It was the last brilliant example in Western Culture of what Feudalism could do.

Forrest was fitted for the command above all others, for his ways were secret, mysterious, and baffling. On the night of July 4, 1867, he gave orders for a general parade, to be conducted by the *Grand Giants* of each county. A partial record of the impression created may be gathered from the account of an eye-witness who saw the parade in Pulaski.

"On the morning of that day the citizens found the sidewalks thickly strewn with slips of paper bearing the printed words: 'The Ku Klux Klan will parade the streets tonight.'

"Soon after nightfall the streets were lined with an expectant and excited throng of people. Many came from the surrounding country. The members of the Klan in the county left their homes in the afternoon, and traveled alone or in squads of two or three, with their paraphernalia carefully concealed. If questioned, they answered that they were going to Pulaski to see the Ku Klux parade. After nightfall they assembled at designated points near the four main roads leading to the town. Here they donned their robes and disguises, and put covers of gaudy materials on their horses. A skyrocket sent up from a point in the town was the signal to mount and move. The different companies met and joined each other on the Public Square in perfect silence; the discipline was admirable. Not a word was spoken. Necessary orders were given by means of whistles. In single file, in death-like stillness, with funereal slowness, they marched and countermarched throughout the town. While the column was headed north in one street, it was going south on the other. By crossing over in opposite directions the lines were kept up in almost unbroken continuity. This marching and countermarching were kept up for about two hours, and the Klan departed as noiselessly as they came. The public was more than ever mystified.

"The efforts of the most curious to find out who were the Ku Klux failed. One gentleman from the country was confident that he could identify the riders by their horses, but, as we have said, the horses were disguised as well as the riders. Determined not to be baffled, during the halt of the column he lifted the cover of a horse that was near him and recognized his own steed and saddle on which he had ridden into town.

"Perhaps the greatest illusion produced was in regard to the numbers taking part in the parade. Reputable citizens were confident that the number was not less than three thousand. Others, whose imaginations were most easily wrought upon, were quite certain there were ten thousand. The truth is that the number of Ku Klux in the parade did not exceed four hundred."

A ghostly rider would appear from nowhere at a negro's cabin and ask for a drink of water. He would throw away the dipper and drink the bucket dry; then drawing a deep breath in "hantish" sighs would say, "That's the first good drink I've had since Shiloh." He would extend a skeleton hand, or offer his skull, to the negro—who never remained to receive the thanks due a host.

All the efforts of the Reconstruction Rulers to find out the leaders of the Klan, its hiding places, failed. Forrest was suspected and called before an investigating committee in Washington. He knew that he would be asked damaging questions; so he boldly parried. He took the initiative out of their hands by answering the questions before they made them. In that way he avoided those queries which might give his position away. For example, he knew that he was suspected as its head; so he forestalled with "It has been said that I was instrumental in getting the Klan up," a question he could truthfully answer with "No."

Almost overnight it broke the power of the Reconstruction, and in 1870, after six states had been redeemed, The Grand Wizard issued an order disbanding the Klan.

At the most tragic moment of Southern history, when all seemed lost beyond redemption, he appeared, unexpectedly, mysteriously, almost supernaturally and snatched the enjoyment of victory from the enemy's hands, from those Black Republican politicians who had set out to destroy the South and the Old Political Union. The triumph of the Ku Klux Klan was the triumph of the political genius of the South, a genius that had failed, because of its limitations, to save the Union but which, at last, had managed to save itself by following the most typical, the greatest, leader its feudalism had fashioned.

There was now nothing left for Bedford Forrest to do. He spent the short years he was to live in various occupations. He tried promoting a railroad, but the uncertain future of the Southern states disorganized the venture. He went to New York in an effort to raise enough money to carry it through, but the bankers had no money to lend him. He wrote to Mr. Farrington in Memphis that he would have to give up the house he had bought from him.

The Farringtons moved in two weeks before the Forrests moved out. The General would visit with them in the evening. When they questioned him about the war, he always answered directly. Their small son drew his chair up against the soldier's to listen, and after he had finished speaking, the boy got between his legs, put his hand on his cheeks, and asked him to tell it over again.

In these days Bedford's wife was frail but uncomplaining. There was always so much amiability in the household. When the time came to leave, he relieved her of most of the burden of packing. While everybody was busy, he would do all sorts of odd jobs, running around setting the table. He managed so well that the household moved with no apparent effort.

He leased President's Island, an island farm opposite the town of Memphis, in an effort to carry on. He spent what fortune he had left in charities to those of his soldiers who were suffering. But the unreckoned strain of the war began to tell. His mighty constitution gave way all of a sudden. Diarrhoea seized upon his intestines and gradually wore him down. During temporary relief he was to be seen on the streets of Memphis in the plain, simple clothes of a farmer, going about his business or buying a pair of red-topped boots for his grandson. One day he went to church with his wife. The sermon was about the man who built his house on sand. Afterwards he went up to the preacher and said, "I am that man." There was great rejoicing among the godly when it was learned he had come to grace.

General Morgan, his legal adviser in the lawsuits resulting from the failure of the railroad, came to see him on business. In the course of the visit he told him: "General, I am broke in health and in spirit, and have not long to live. My life has been a battle from the start. It was a fight to achieve a livelihood for those dependent upon me in my younger days, and an independence for myself when I grew up to manhood, as well as in the terrible turmoil of the Civil War. I have seen too much of violence, and I want to close my days at peace with all the world, as I am now at peace with my Maker."

At a reunion of the Seventh Tennessee Cavalry in September, 1876, he was called on to speak. "Soldiers of the Seventh Tennessee Cavalry, Ladies and Gentlemen:—I name the soldiers first, because I love them best. I am extremely pleased to meet you here today. I love the gallant men with whom I was so intimately connected during the late war. You can readily realize what must pass through a commander's mind when called upon to meet in reunion the brave spirits who through four years of war and bloodshed fought fearlessly for a cause that they thought right, and who even when they foresaw, as we all did, that the war must soon close in disaster, and that we must surrender, yet did not quail, but marched to victory in many battles, and fought as boldly and persistently in their last battles as they did in their first. Nor do I forget those many gallant spirits who sleep coldly in death upon the many bloody battlefields of the late war. I love them too, and honor their memory. I have often been called to the side, on the battle-field, of those who have been struck down, and they would put their arms around my neck, draw me down to them and kiss me, and say: 'General, I have fought my last battle, and will soon be gone. I want you to remember my wife and children and take care of them.' Comrades, I have remembered their wives and little ones, and have taken care of them, and I want every one of you to remember them too, and join with me in the labor of love. . . ."

There was no useless rhetoric in this, and the strong men before him watched the pale, thin face, and the magnificent forehead and head brought into bold relief by the wasting disease. "Soldiers, I was afraid that I could not be with you today, but I could not bear the thought of not meeting with you, and I will always try to meet with you in the future. . . ."

But this was not to be. He had stood before his men for the last time. One cold winter's day he was brought to town by raft. He lay back in an invalid's chair, wrapped in blankets and laprobes, with heated bricks at his feet, and directed the negroes who were polling the raft through the ice-blocked river. That summer he went to Hurricane Springs, near Tullahoma, with the hope the water might do him good. Major Anderson was with him, and he was shocked at the change he saw in his chief. He could see his days were numbered.

Like the General, "King Phillip" had survived the war. His spirit, like the General's, seemed broken by the long days of peace. He suffered any indignity with resignation, and there were many. One day he was hitched to a lady's buggy, which he drew through the streets of Memphis with the indifference and the lumbering gait of a family horse. As he turned a corner, he saw a short distance ahead a squad of partisan police—the ladies saw the police. All "King Phillip" noticed was a great deal of blue. In an instant up went his tail, back fell his ears, his mouth flew open. Down the street he charged, the buggy bounding after him and the women screaming. The squad scattered as of old, and "King Phillip" was left on the sidewalk, his upper lip bared and quivering with disappointment.

In the early autumn, October 29, 1877, General Nathan Bedford Forrest died at the age of fifty-six. His mother was in Texas at the time, where she had gone to nurse her refugee son, Jim Luxton. She stepped on a rusty nail as she was getting out of a buggy, and she was soon down with blood poison. In her delirium she called again and again for Bedford. He had always been near in the trying moments of her life, and she could not understand why he was absent now. Her son Jim told her that he had wired Bedford to come. He even figured out the route he would follow, and how long it would take him. In this way he was able to pacify her until she died.

CHAPTER XXVI

In a Funeral Hack

DOWN the streets of Memphis, square-backed and black, their paint blistered with the weather, a long line of iron-tired hacks and buggies rolled behind a hearse bearing the bone, the dry heart, and the tight sinew that was Forrest. The wheels turned with a slow quickness at the hubs and a steady sweep at the rims, lifting the red dust a little way from the streets to scatter it down the slick curves of the spokes, all the way to Elmwood Cemetery. Behind, no longer mounted, the gray men who rode with Forrest marched along by the thousands, following for the last time where he led. One scrawny one, his clothes strong with wood smoke and the stale sap of the Wilderness, moved on the skirt of the line. Silent and alone, he had no words for his comrades, no eyes for the procession, only a steady flow of water down the brown furrows of his cheeks.

Jefferson Davis and Governor Porter were riding in a carriage near the head of the column. Porter broke the silence of their thoughts. "History," he said, "has accorded to General Forrest the first place as a cavalry leader in the war between the states, and has named him as one of the half-dozen great soldiers of the country."

"I agree with you," answered Davis with feeling. "The trouble was that the generals commanding in the Southwest never appreciated Forrest until it was too late. Their judgment was that he was a bold and enterprising partisan raider and rider. I was misled by them, and I never knew how to measure him until I read his reports of his campaign across the Tennessee River in 1864. This induced a study of his earlier reports, and after that I was prepared to adopt what you are pleased to name as the judgment of history."

"I cannot comprehend such lack of appreciation after he fought the battle at Brice's Cross-Roads in June of 1864. That battle was not a cavalry raid nor an accident. It was the conception of a man endowed with a genius for war."

And to this second reproach Davis answered, "That campaign was not understood at Richmond. The impression made upon those in authority was that Forrest had made another successful raid, but I saw it all after it was too late."

At the grave, in this way, the full force of Bragg's vengeance was exposed—the final apostrophe to the tragedy. As the last ruler of the South was laid in the ground, and the final volley exploded through the cedars and pines, he received recognition when it was too late to be more than a wreath on the tomb.

The mourners returned to the towns and the farms, to the mansion house, and to the dogrun. Through the long winter nights, before the leaping fires, the men who rode with Forrest told over what Old Bedford did on the Streight Raid, what he said at Murfreesboro, how he looked at Brice's Cross-Roads. And as they talked, their children and, years later, their grandchildren heard only of victory, never of defeat. He became the spiritual comforter to the people of the Southwest. In a sense his whole life was a symbol of the Southern Feudalism. He emerged from the cabin, grew rich on cotton, established himself as a strong man of his Culture, and was cut down in his prime, with the virtues and vices of the Wilderness still a part of his character.

A park was set aside to his memory in Memphis, and a bronze equestrian statue raised to command it. There was some argument among his veterans as to which way it should face. One school held that it should face north, for he had never turned his back on the enemy; but the other school argued as forcibly that he had never turned his back on the South. It was finally settled, and he and his wife were reinterred beneath its base.

Fifty years later, a motor car passed the park. In the back seat was an old negress, Georgiana, a little boy's nurse. She was sitting bolt upright in the cushions in mortal fear of the speeding vehicle. As her mistress drove by the statue, she grunted:

"Humh! De Gin'ral's hoss show is gittin' poe."

"What do you mean, Georgiana? That horse can't lose weight. It's bronze."

"Well'm, I seen 'em when dey put him up dar, and I see him now —and he show is poe."

"How in the world could that happen, Georgiana?"

"I don't know'm. I regon de Gin'ral must ride him of a night."

GEN. FORREST TO HIS TROOPS.

HEADQRS. FORREST'S CAVALRY CORPS,
GAINESVILLE, ALA., May 9, 1865.

SOLDIERS:

By an agreement made between Lieut.-Gen. TAYLOR, commanding the Department of Alabama, Mississippi and East Louisiana, and Major-Gen. CANBY, commanding United States forces, the troops of this Department have been surrendered.

I do not think it proper or necessary, at this time, to refer to the causes which have reduced us to this extremity; nor is it now a matter of material consequence to us how such results were brought about. That we are BEATEN, is a self-evident fact, and any further resistance on our part would be justly regarded as the very height of folly and rashness.

The armies of Generals LEE and JOHNSTON having surrendered, you are the last of all the troops of the Confederate States Army, East of the Mississippi River, to lay down your arms.

The Cause for which you have so long and so manfully struggled, and for which you have braved dangers, endured privations and sufferings, and made so many sacrifices, is to day hopeless. The Government which we sought to establish and perpetuate, is at an end. Reason dictates and humanity demands that no more blood be shed. Fully realizing and feeling that such is the case, it is your duty and mine to lay down our arms—submit to the "powers that be"—and to aid in restoring peace and establishing law and order throughout the land.

The terms upon which you were surrendered are favorable, and should be satisfactory and acceptable to all. They manifest a spirit of magnanimity and liberality, on the part of the Federal authorities, which should be met, on our part, by a faithful compliance with all the stipulations and conditions therein expressed. As your Commander, I sincerely hope that every officer and soldier of my command will cheerfully obey the orders given, and carry out in good faith all the terms of the cartel.

Those who neglect the terms, and refuse to be paroled, may assuredly expect, when arrested, to be sent North and imprisoned.

Let those who are absent from their commands, from whatever cause, report at once to this place, or to Jackson, Miss.; or, if too remote from either, to the nearest United States post or garrison, for parole.

Civil war, such as you have just passed through, naturally engenders feelings of animosity, hatred and revenge. It is our duty to divest ourselves of all such feelings; and so far as in our power to do so, to cultivate friendly feelings towards those with whom we have so long contended, and heretofore so widely, but honestly, differed. Neighborhood feuds, personal animosities, and private differences, should be blotted out; and, when you return home, a manly, straightforward course of conduct will secure the respect even of your enemies. Whatever your responsibities may be to Government, to society, or to individuals, meet them like men.

The attempt made to establish a separate and independent Confederation has failed; but the consciousness of having done your duty faithfully, and to the end, will, in some measure, repay for the hardships you have undergone.

In bidding you farewell, rest assured that you carry with you my best wishes for your future welfare and happiness. Without, in any way, referring to the merits of the Cause in which we have been engaged, your courage and determination, as exhibited on many hard-fought fields, has elicited the respect and admiration of friend and foe. And I now, cheerfully and gratefully, acknowledge my indebtedness to the officers and men of my command whose zeal, fidelity and unflinching bravery have been the great source of my past success in arms.

I have never, on the field of battle, sent you where I was unwilling to go myself; nor would I now advise you to a course which I felt myself unwilling to pursue. You have been good soldiers; you can be good citizens. Obey the laws, preserve your honor, and the Government to which you have surrendered can afford to be, and will be, magnanimous.

N. B. FORREST, Lieut. General.

Facsimile reproduction of the only extant copy of the original, published by Stuart Wright, Winston-Salem, North Carolina, 1979.

GEN. FORREST TO HIS TROOPS

HEADQRS. FORREST'S CAVALRY CORPS,
GAINESVILLE, ALA., May 9, 1865.

SOLDIERS:

By an agreement made between Lieut. Gen. TAYLOR, commanding the Department of Alabama, Mississippi, and East Louisiana, and Major-Gen. CANBY, commanding United States forces, the troops of this department have been surrendered.

I do not think it proper or necessary at this time to refer to causes which have reduced us to this extremity; nor is it now a matter of material consequence to us how such results were brought about. That we are BEATEN is a self-evident fact, and any further resistance on our part would be justly regarded as the very height of folly and rashness.

The armies of Generals LEE and JOHNSON having surrendered, you are the last of all the troops of the Confederate States Army east of the Mississippi River to lay down your arms.

The Cause for which you have so long and so manfully struggled, and for which you have braved dangers, endured privations and sufferings, and made so many sacrifices, is to day hopeless. The government which we sought to establish and perpetuate, is at an end. Reason dictates and humanity demands that no more blood be shed. Fully realizing and feeling that such is the case, it is your duty and mine to lay down our arms—submit to the "powers that be"—and to aid in restoring peace and establishing law and order throughout the land.

The terms upon which you were surrendered are favorable, and should be satisfactory and acceptable to all. They manifest a spirit of magnanimity and liberality, on the part of the Federal authorities, which should be met, on our part, by a faithful compliance with all the stipulations and conditions therein expressed. As your Commander, I sincerely hope that every officer and soldier of my command will cheerfully obey the orders given, and carry out in good faith all the terms of the cartel.

Those who neglect the terms and refuse to be paroled, may assuredly expect, when arrested, to be sent North and imprisoned. Let those who are absent from their commands, from whatever cause, report at once to this place, or to Jackson, Miss.; or, if too remote from either, to the nearest United States post or garrison, for parole.

Civil war, such as you have just passed through, naturally engenders feelings of animosity, hatred, and revenge. It is our duty to divest ourselves of all such feelings; and as far as it is in our power to do so, to cultivate friendly feelings towards those with whom we have so long contended, and heretofore so widely, but honestly, differed. Neighborhood feuds, personal animosities, and private differences should be blotted out; and, when you return home, a manly, straightforward course of conduct will secure the respect even of your enemies. Whatever your responsibilities may be to Government, to society, or to individuals meet them like men.

The attempt made to establish a separate and independent Confederation has failed; but the consciousness of having done your duty faithfully, and to the end, will, in some measure, repay for the hardships you have undergone.

In bidding you farewell, rest assured that you carry with you my best wishes for your future welfare and happiness. Without, in any way, referring to the merits of the Cause in which we have been engaged, your courage and determination, as exhibited on many hard-fought fields, has elicited the respect and admiration of friend and foe. And I now cheerfully and gratefully acknowledge my indebtedness to the officers and men of my command whose zeal, fidelity and unflinching bravery have been the great source of my past success in arms.

I have never, on the field of battle, sent you where I was unwilling to go myself; nor would I now advise you to a course which I felt myself unwilling to pursue. You *have* been good soldiers, you *can* be good citizens. Obey the laws, preserve your honor, and the Government to which you have surrendered can afford to be, and will be, magnanimous.

N. B. FORREST, Lieut.-General

BIBLIOGRAPHICAL NOTE
AND
INDEX

BIBLIOGRAPHICAL NOTE

T HIS book has been an attempt to show General Forrest as he developed into the most typical strong man of the Agrarian South. The industrial party in the North broke its feudalism by conquest, and Forrest's part in the war is, consequently, the most dramatic and important part of his career.

For the background to this study I have gone to the newspapers of the times, private correspondence between individuals, diaries, travel gazettes, county histories, memoirs, historical magazines, and critical works on this period. Judge Samuel Cole Williams, President of the East Tennessee Historical Society, has compiled the best works on early Tennessee history, and I am particularly indebted to two of his books: *Early Travels in the Tennessee Country,* the Watauga Press, 1928; and *The Beginnings of West Tennessee,* Watauga Press, 1930. Mrs. Royall's travels in Alabama in 1817 is one of the best contemporary accounts of the manners, customs, and opinions of the times. *Flush Times in Alabama* is another excellent book. *Early Times in Middle Tennessee,* by John Carr, *A Pioneer of the West,* Nashville, Tennessee, 1857, gives a detailed account of many important people, the way they lived, and the development of the different churches. The daughters of Colonel Sam Meeks, of Columbus, Mississippi, have allowed me to see many valuable letters, three of them letters from Jefferson Davis to their grandfather, relating to the politics of Mississippi and National politics of the fifties. They, also, allowed me to use the letter from Dr. Yandell to their grandmother from which I quoted. Other sources of interest are: *The Old Road,* American Historical Magazine vol. 351; Channing, *The Jeffersonian System; Democracy in the South Before the Civil War,* G. W. Dyer; *The American Heresy,* Christopher Hollis, New York, 1930; *Life and Labor in the Old South,* Ulrich B. Phillips, Boston, 1929.

The fall of the Confederacy was due chiefly to Davis's military policy in the West, and particularly to his support of Bragg. To Mr.

Allen Tate's *Jefferson Davis, His Rise and Fall,* I am greatly indebted, for he presents the whole complex situation in a masterly way. I have related in detail Forrest's important connection with this whole problem.

The two most valuable sources for a biography of this kind are the *Records of the War of Rebellion* and *Battles and Leaders.* The Records contain the reports of battles and the correspondence, during the campaigns, both of the Northern and Southern sides. *Battles and Leaders* supplements this with the narratives of the leaders written after the war.

There are five biographies of Forrest: Jordan and Pryor's, written soon after the war and approved by Forrest who writes: "For the greater part of the statements of the narrative I am responsible." There is another, *General Forrest,* by Captain Harvey Mathes, New York, 1902. For military movements these two are the most authoritative. *Forrest,* by Captain Sheppard, The Dial Press, New York, 1931. Dr. Wyath's *General Nathan Bedford Forrest* has the greatest mass of material, anecdotal and factual, of them all. It is the richest of the source books. *Forrest's Artillery,* by Captain John Morton, Nashville. Eckenrode has a child's history of Forrest. To Jordan and Pryor, Mathes, and Dr. Wyath I acknowledge my indebtedness. Major Anderson's daughter, Mrs. Jim Ransom, of Murfreesboro, has loaned me her father's Jordan and Pryor, valuable for the notes Major Anderson added to the pages of the volume. From General Forrest's half-sister, Mrs. Mollie Fontaine, I got the account of how Bedford got the ox team out of the creek, as well as an account of her mother's death. I am also indebted to N. B. Forrest, of Atlanta, Georgia, and to Mrs. Mary Forrest Bradley, of Memphis, Tennessee. Judge J. P. Young, of Memphis, the author of *History of Seventh Tennessee Cavalry,* gave me a great deal of his time and much valuable information, several anecdotes which have not been printed before, and the details of the organization of his cavalry in Mississippi. I was allowed to see Judge Young's history of Hood's Tennessee Campaign, in manuscript form. This is, undoubtedly, the most complete and authoritative account, from both sides, of that campaign. I have had access, also, to Dr. Agnew's diary, in manuscript form, and took from it certain descriptions of the Battle of Brice's Cross-Roads, written by him the day of the battle. I have talked to all the old members of Forrest's Cavalry that I could find, and for two years I have been going over the country where his campaigns and the campaigns of the Army of Tennessee took place. I followed the Old Corn Road which Streight took on Sand Mountain, and it is very little changed by time. Brice's Cross-Roads is almost as it was in 1864.

If the reader is interested and would care to read further, I would suggest the following, by no means a complete bibliography.

Alexander, General E. P. Military *Memoirs of a Confederate*. New York. 1907.
Bigelow, Captain. *Principles of Strategy*.
Channing, Edward. *The Jeffersonian System*. New York. 1906.
Chestnut, Mary Boykin. *A Diary from Dixie*. New York. 1906.
Chinard, Gilbert. *Thomas Jefferson, An Apostle of Americanism*. Boston. 1929.
Clay Clopton, Mrs. *A Belle of the Fifties*. New York. 1904
Daniel. *A Confederate Scrap Book*.
Daves, Susan L. *Authentic History of Ku Klux Klan*. New York. 1924.
Davis, Jefferson. *The Rise and Fall of the Confederate States*. 2 vols. New York. 1881.
Dodd, William E. *The Cotton Kingdom*. (Chronicles of America Series.) New Haven. 1919.
Dodd, William E. *Lincoln or Lee*.
Duke, General Basil. *Reminiscences*. Garden City, N. Y. 1911.
Eckenrode, Hamilton James. *Jefferson Davis: President of the South*. New York. 1923.
Fiebeger, Gustave Joseph. *Campaigns and Battles*.
Fitz-Maurice, General Edward. *An Aide-de-Camp of Lee*. Boston. 1927.
Fitz-Maurice, General Edward. *Lee, the Soldier*. Boston. 1925.
Fleming, Walter Lynwood. *Ku Klux Klan*. 1904.
Force, M. F. *From Fort Henry to Corinth*. Scribners' Series. New York. 1881.
Freemantle, Lieutenant-Colonel. *Three Months in the Southern States*. London. 1863.
George, Henry. *History of 3rd, 7th, 8th, and 12th Ky. C.S.A.* Louisville. 1911.
Gordon, General J. B. *Reminiscences of the Civil War*. New York. 1903.
Grant. U. S. *Memoirs*. 2 vols. New York. 1907.
Hancock. *His Diary, A History of the Second Tennessee Cav. C.S.A.* Nashville. 1887.
Hay, Thomas Robson. *Hood's Tennessee Campaign*. New York. 1879.
Horton, R. G. *A Youth's History of the Civil War*. New York. 1866.
Hubbard, John Milton. *Notes of Private*. St. Louis. 1909.
Jones, J. B. *A Rebel War Clerk's Diary*. 2 vols. Philadelphia. 1865.
Lester, John C. *Ku Klux Klan*. New York and Washington. 1905.
Lindsley, J. B. *Military Annals of Tennessee*. Nashville. 1886.
Montgomery, Lieutenant-Colonel Frank. *Reminiscences of a Mississipian in Peace and War*. Cincinnati. 1901.
Palmer, General Joe. *His Diary* (manuscript form).
Pro Slavery Argument. Charleston. 1852.
Quintard, Bishop. *His Narrative*.
Reagan, John H. *Memoirs*. Washington. 1905.

Ridley, Bromfield L. (Staff of General Stewart.) *Battles and Sketches of the Army of Tennessee*. Mexico, Missouri. 1906.

Ropes, *The Story of the Civil War*. New York. 1894–1898.

Seitz, Don. *Braxton Bragg. General of the Confederacy*. New York. 1923.

Sherman, General W. T. *Memoirs*. New York. 1875.

Smedes, Susan Dabney. *Memorials of a Southern Planter*. New York. 1890.

Smith, Edward Conrad. *The Borderland in the Civil War*. New York. 1927.

Steele, Mathew Forney. *American Campaigns*. Washington. B. S. 1909.

Tate, Allen. *Stonewall Jackson, The Good Soldier*. New York. 1928.

Tate, Allen. *Jefferson Davis, His Rise and Fall*. New York. 1929.

Taylor, General Richard. *Destruction and Reconstruction*. New York. 1879.

Thomason, John W., Jr. *Jeb Stuart*. New York. 1930.

Upton. *Military Policy of the United States*.

U. S. Congress. *Report on Ku Klux Klan*. 1871.

Wood, Birbeck. Edmonds., J. E. *A History of the Civil War in the United States*. London. 1905.

Young, J. P. *History of the Seventh Tennessee Cavalry*. Nashville. 1905.

INDEX

Abolitionists, the, 29, 30, 31, 32
Alabama, secession of, 33
Anderson, General Robert, 39
Arkansas, secession of, 34
Atlanta campaign in North Mississippi in 1863–64, 243 ff.
Atlanta, captured by Sherman, 327

Beauregard, General P. T. G., 48 ff., 83, 85–6, 87, 88; appointed in command of whole Southwest in September, 1864, 344
Beck, Fannie, aunt of Bedford Forrest, 3, 4, 5, 18
Beersheba Springs, Tenn., 90
Bell, John, Know-Nothing Presidential candidate in 1860, 32, 33
Black Republicans, 30, 31, 32, 34
Blountsville, Ala., 160
Bolivar, Miss., 250, 253
Border States, importance attaching to political alignment and control of, in the period immediately preceding the Civil War, 31–3; effect of closing of navigation of the Mississippi River by Confederates on, 38
Bowling Green, Kentucky, military operations about, 39
Bragg, General Braxton, in command of Confederate forces in the West, 87–8, 103, 104; friction with Forrest, 104, 110–11, 114 ff., 141; his unsuccessful Kentucky campaign of 1862, 109 ff.; his mistaken estimate of Forrest's abilities, 116–17; battle of Stone River, 140; discontent with his incapacity, 144; forced to withdraw before Rosecrans's advance in Middle Tennessee in June, 1863, 183–6; arrangement and movements of his forces during the two months preceding the battle of Chickamauga, 188 ff.; evacuates Chattanooga, 198–9; the battle of Chickamauga, 206–31; loses the fruits of victory by failure to follow it up, 231–4; further friction with Forrest, 235–6, 237–9; routed at Missionary Ridge, and resigns, 248; military adviser to Davis, 272, 283, 307–8, 343

Breckinridge, General John C., 32, 33, 112, 113, 140, 144, 230
Brentwood, Tenn., capture of Federal garrison at, 145
Brice's Cross-Roads, battle of, 293 ff.
Brown, Governor, of Georgia, 87, 307, 356
Brown, John, 27
Buckner, General Simon B., 39, 48, 56, 57, 66, 67, 70 ff., 188, 201, 230
Buell, General Don Carlos, 42, 43, 47, 52–3, 86, 88, 105, 109, 110
Buford, General Abe, 270, 274, 292, 300, 302, 311, 358
Bull Run, first battle of, 38
Burnside, General Ambrose E., 188

Calhoun, John C., 29, 30
Chancellorsville, battle of, 179
Chattanooga, Tenn., threatened by Buell, 88–9; offensive against, prevented by Forrest's raid on Murfreesboro, 100–1; evacuated by Bragg, 198–9
Cherokee Indians, 8, 15
Chickamauga, the battle of, 206–31; the results of the first day, 215–18; failure of Bragg to gather the fruits of his victory, 231–4
Chickasaw Indians, 15
Civil War, causes of, to be found in economic ambitions of the industrial North rather than in slavery as an institution, 29 ff.; political events immediately preceding, 32–4; firing on Fort Sumter used by Republicans to stampede the country into war, 34; the heart of the Confederacy in the lower South and its cause to be won or lost on western battlefields, 88
Clay, Henry, 29
Colonial social conditions in Southern States, 9–10
Confederacy, its heart in the lower South, and its cause to be won or lost on Western battlefields, 88; plan in 1863 to send Lee with a great part of Army of Northern Virginia to the West, and the probable results of such action had

399

INDEX

INDEX

ANDREW NELSON LYTLE (1902–   ) contributed an essay, "The Hind Tit," to the 1930 Agrarian Symposium, *I'll Take My Stand*. He published his dramatic biography of Confederate General Nathan Bedford Forrest in 1931, which he followed with his first novel, *The Long Night* (1936), set at the time of the Civil War. Since then he has written three more novels (*At The Moon's Inn* [1941], *A Name for Evil* [1947], and *The Velvet Horn* [1957]), the novella *Alchemy* (1942), the personal chronicle *A Wake for The Living* (1975), short stories, book reviews, social and political commentary, and a group of essays on the craft of fiction. Two collections of his essays are *Southerners and Europeans* (1988) and *From Eden to Babylon* (1990). His latest book is *Kristin* (1992). As editor of *The Sewanee Review* from 1961–1972 he further influenced the direction of the South's literature. He lives today in his ancestral log house on Tennessee's Monteagle Mountain.

WALTER SULLIVAN, critic and novelist, is a member of the Faculty of English at Vanderbilt University. His novels include *Sojourn of a Stranger* and *The Long, Long Love*. He is the author of *Allen Tate: A Recollection*. His most recent work is *In Praise of Blood Sports and Other Essays*.